T0385354

The

Thomas Sowell

Reader

The

THOMAS SOWELL

Reader

BASIC
BOOKS

A Member of the Perseus Books Group
New York

Books published by Basic Books are available at special discounts for bulk purchases in the United States by corporations, institutions, and other organizations. For more information, please contact the Special Markets Department at the Perseus Books Group, 2300 Chestnut Street, Suite 200, Philadelphia, PA 19103, or call (800) 810-4145, ext. 5000, or e-mail special.markets@perseusbooks.com.

A CIP catalog record for this book is available
from the Library of Congress.

LCCN 2011908758

HC ISBN: 978-0-465-02250-2
Ebook ISBN: 978-0-465-02804-7
LSC-C
Printing 12, 2023

CONTENTS

Contents

PREFACE

Summarizing the work of a lifetime can be a challenge, even for someone who has stuck to one specialty. I found it even more challenging because of my very long lifetime and the wide-ranging fields in which I have written over the years, ranging from economic writings in academic journals to both humorous and serious newspaper columns on everything from baseball to politics to war to late-talking children— not to mention a few books on history, housing, autobiography, intellectuals and race.

Frankly, it would never have occurred to me to try to collect all these very different things within the covers of one book, had the idea not been suggested to me by John Sherer, publisher of Basic Books. I am glad he did, however. A sampling of all these items may have more things to interest the general reader than a book devoted to one subject, aimed at one audience.

In each of the various sections of the book— whether on culture, economics, politics, law, education or race— I have led off with newspaper columns before moving on to longer writings that permit more in-depth explorations. Each reader can choose from a wide spectrum of subjects to explore, and decide which to sample and which to go into more deeply. Some of the most popular of my newspaper columns have been those titled "Random Thoughts." Various unrelated statements about the passing scene from some of these columns have been collected in the "Random Thoughts" section of this book.

My hope is that this large selection of my writings will reduce the likelihood that readers will misunderstand what I have said on many controversial issues over the years. Whether the reader will agree with all my conclusions is another question entirely. But disagreements can be productive, while misunderstandings seldom are.

One reason for some misunderstandings is that my approach and my goals have been too plain and straightforward for those people who are looking for hidden agendas or other complex motives. From an early age, I have been concerned with trying to understand the social problems that abound in any society. First and foremost, this was an attempt to try to grasp some explanation of the puzzling and disturbing things going on around me. This was all for my own personal clarification, since I had neither political ambitions nor the political talents required for either elective or appointed office. But, once having achieved some sense of understanding of particular issues— a process that sometimes took years— I wanted to share that understanding with others. That is the reason for the things that appear in this book.

Thomas Sowell
The Hoover Institution
Stanford University

EDITORIAL NOTE

Identifying the books from which the material excerpted here has been taken will be done in the "Sources" section at the end of the book, for the benefit of those readers who might want to read the fuller accounts in the original. However, no similar reason applies to the numerous columns of mine reprinted from newspapers and magazines over the years, so these sources are not listed.

Thanks are due to the Yale University Press for permission to reprint my critique of John Stuart Mill's "On Liberty" from *On Classical Economics* and the first chapter of *Affirmative Action Around the World*. The autobiographical material is reprinted with the kind permission of The Free Press to excerpt the first and last chapters of *A Personal Odyssey*. Other material excerpted here from *Basic Economics, Intellectuals and Society, Migrations and Cultures, The Vision of the Anointed, Applied Economics* and *Conquests and Cultures* are all from books that are already the property of Basic Books. The chapter titled "Marx the Man" is from *Marxism: Philosophy and Economics*, which is out of print and whose copyright is mine.

Thanks are also due to my dedicated and hard-working research assistants, Na Liu and Elizabeth Costa, who have contributed so much to the original writings from which these excerpts are taken, as well as to the production of this book. I am also grateful to the Hoover Institution, which has made all our work possible.

SOCIAL ISSUES

GRASSHOPPER AND ANT

Just as the "Rocky" and "Star Wars" movies had their sequels, so should the old classic fables. Here is the sequel to a well-known fable.

Once upon a time, a grasshopper and an ant lived in a field. All summer long, the grasshopper romped and played, while the ant worked hard under the boiling sun to store up food for the winter.

When winter came, the grasshopper was hungry. One cold and rainy day, he went to ask the ant for some food.

"What are you, crazy?" the ant said. "I've been breaking my back all summer long while you ran around hopping and laughing at me for missing all the fun in life."

"Did I do that?" the grasshopper asked meekly.

"Yes! You said I was one of those old-fashioned clods who had missed the whole point of the modern self-realization philosophy."

"Gee, I'm sorry about that," the grasshopper said. "I didn't realize you were so sensitive. But surely you are not going to hold that against me at a time like this."

"Well, I don't hold a grudge— but I do have a long memory."

Just then another ant came along.

"Hi, Lefty," the first ant said.

"Hi, George."

"Lefty, do you know what this grasshopper wants me to do? He wants me to give him some of the food I worked for all summer, under the blazing sun."

"I would have thought you would already have volunteered to share with him, without being asked," Lefty said.

"What!!"

"When we have disparate shares in the bounty of nature, the least we can do is try to correct the inequity."

"Nature's bounty, my foot," George said. "I had to tote this stuff uphill and cross a stream on a log— all the while looking out for ant-eaters. Why couldn't this lazy bum gather his own food and store it?"

"Now, now, George," Lefty soothed. "Nobody uses the word 'bum' anymore. We say 'the homeless'."

"I say 'bum'. Anyone who is too lazy to put a roof over his head, who prefers to stand out in this cold rain to doing a little work—"

The grasshopper broke in: "I didn't know it was going to rain like this. The weather forecast said 'fair and warmer'."

"Fair and warmer?" George sniffed. "That's what the forecasters told Noah!"

Lefty looked pained. "I'm surprised at your callousness, George— your selfishness, your greed."

"Have you gone crazy, Lefty?"

"No. On the contrary, I have become educated."

"Sometimes that's worse, these days."

"Last summer, I followed a trail of cookie crumbs left by some students. It led to a classroom at Ivy University."

"You've been to college? No wonder you come back here with all these big words and dumb ideas."

"I disdain to answer that," Lefty said. "Anyway, it was Professor Murky's course on Social Justice. He explained how the world's benefits are unequally distributed."

"The world's benefits?" George repeated. "The world didn't carry this food uphill. The world didn't cross the water on a log. The world isn't going to be eaten by any ant-eater."

"That's the narrow way of looking at it," Lefty said.

"If you're so generous, why don't you feed this grasshopper?"

"I will," Lefty replied. Then, turning to the grasshopper, he said: "Follow me. I will take you to the government's shelter, where there will be food and a dry place to sleep."

George gasped. "You're working for the government now?"

"I'm in *public service*," Lefty said loftily. "I want to 'make a difference' in this world."

"You really have been to college," George said. "But if you're such a friend of the grasshopper, why don't you teach him how to work during the summer and save something for the winter?"

"We have no right to change his lifestyle and try to make him like us. That would be cultural imperialism."

George was too stunned to answer.

Lefty not only won the argument, he continued to expand his program of shelters for grasshoppers. As word spread, grasshoppers came from miles around. Eventually, some of the younger ants decided to adopt the grasshopper lifestyle.

As the older generation of ants passed from the scene, more and more ants joined the grasshoppers, romping and playing in the fields. Finally, all the ants and all the grasshoppers spent all their time enjoying the carefree lifestyle and lived happily ever after— all summer long. Then the winter came.

EVER WONDER WHY?

When you have seen scenes of poverty and squalor in many Third World countries, either in person or in pictures, have you ever wondered why we in America have been spared such a fate?

When you have learned of the bitter oppressions that so many people have suffered under, in despotic countries around the world, have you ever wondered why Americans have been spared?

Have scenes of government-sponsored carnage and lethal mob violence in countries like Rwanda or in the Balkans ever made you wonder why such horrifying scenes are not found on the streets of America?

Nothing is easier than to take for granted what we are used to, and to imagine that it is more or less natural, so that it requires no explanation. Instead, many Americans demand explanations of why things are not even better and express indignation that they are not.

Some people think the issue is whether the glass is half empty or half full. More fundamentally, the question is whether the glass started out empty or started out full.

Those who are constantly looking for the "root causes" of poverty, of crime, and of other national and international problems, act as if prosperity and law-abiding behavior are so natural that it is their absence which has to be explained. But a casual glance around the world today, or back through history, would dispel any notion that good things just happen naturally, much less inevitably.

The United States of America is the exception, not the rule. Once we realize that America is an exception, we might even have a sense of gratitude for having been born here, even if gratitude has become un-cool in many quarters. At the very least, we might develop some concern for seeing that whatever has made this country better off is not lost or discarded— or eroded away, bit by bit, until it is gone.

Those among us who are constantly rhapsodizing about "change" in vague and general terms seem to have no fear that a blank check for change can be a huge risk in a world where so many other countries that are different are also far worse off.

Chirping about "change" may produce a giddy sense of excitement or of personal exaltation but, as usual, the devil is in the details. Even despotic countries that have embraced sweeping changes have often found that these were changes for the worse.

The czars in Russia, the shah of Iran, the Batista regime in Cuba, were all despotic. But they look like sweethearts compared to the regimes that followed. For example, the czars never executed as many people in half a century as Stalin did in one day.

Even the best countries must make changes and the United States has made many economic, social, and political changes for the better. But that is wholly different from making "change" a mantra.

To be for or against "change" in general is childish. Everything depends on the specifics. To be for generic "change" is to say that what we have is so bad that any change is likely to be for the better.

Such a pose may make some people feel superior to others who find much that is worth preserving in our values, traditions and institutions. The status quo is never sacrosanct but its very existence proves that it is viable, as seductive theoretical alternatives may not turn out to be.

Most Americans take our values, traditions and institutions so much for granted that they find it hard to realize how much all these things are under constant attack in our schools, our colleges, and in much of the press, the movies and literature.

There is a culture war going on within the United States— and in fact, within Western civilization as a whole— which may ultimately have as much to do with our survival, or failure to survive, as the war on terrorism.

There are all sorts of financial, ideological, and psychic rewards for undermining American society and its values. Unless some of us realize the existence of this culture war, and the high stakes in it, we can lose what cost those Americans before us so much to win and preserve.

A "DUTY TO DIE"?

One of the many fashionable notions that have caught on among some of the intelligentsia is that old people have "a duty to die," rather than become a burden to others.

This is more than just an idea discussed around a seminar table. Already the government-run medical system in Britain is restricting what medications or treatments it will authorize for the elderly. Moreover, it seems almost certain that similar attempts to contain runaway costs will lead to similar policies when American medical care is taken over by the government.

Make no mistake about it, letting old people die is a lot cheaper than spending the kind of money required to keep them alive and well. If a government-run medical system is going to save any serious amount of money, it is almost certain to do so by sacrificing the elderly.

There was a time— fortunately, now long past— when some desperately poor societies had to abandon old people to their fate, because there was just not enough margin for everyone to survive. Sometimes the elderly themselves would simply go off from their family and community to face their fate alone.

But is that where we are today?

Talk about "a duty to die" made me think back to my early childhood in the South, during the Great Depression of the 1930s. One day, I was told that an older lady— a relative of ours— was going to come and stay with us for a while, and I was told how to be polite and considerate towards her.

She was called "Aunt Nance Ann," but I don't know what her official name was or what her actual biological relationship to us was. Aunt Nance Ann had no home of her own. But she moved around from relative to relative, not spending enough time in any one home to be a real burden.

At that time, we didn't have things like electricity or central heating or hot running water. But we had a roof over our heads and food on the table— and Aunt Nance Ann was welcome to both.

Poor as we were, I never heard anybody say, or even intimate, that Aunt Nance Ann had "a duty to die."

I only began to hear that kind of talk decades later, from highly educated people in an affluent age, when even most families living below the official poverty level owned a car or truck and had air-conditioning.

It is today, in an age when homes have flat-panelled TVs, and most families eat in restaurants regularly or have pizzas and other meals delivered to their homes, that the elites— rather than the masses— have begun talking about "a duty to die."

Back in the days of Aunt Nance Ann, nobody in our family had ever gone to college. Indeed, none had gone beyond elementary school. Apparently you need a lot of expensive education, sometimes including courses on ethics, before you can start talking about "a duty to die."

Many years later, while going through a divorce, I told a friend that I was considering contesting child custody. She immediately urged me not to do it. Why? Because raising a child would interfere with my career.

But my son didn't have a career. He was just a child who needed someone who understood him. I ended up with custody of my son and, although he was not a demanding child, raising him could not help impeding my career a little. But do you just abandon a child when it is inconvenient to raise him?

The lady who gave me this advice had a degree from the Harvard Law School. She had more years of education than my whole family had, back in the days of Aunt Nance Ann.

Much of what is taught in our schools and colleges today seeks to break down traditional values, and replace them with more fancy and fashionable notions, of which "a duty to die" is just one.

These efforts at changing values used to be called "values clarification," though the name has had to be changed repeatedly over the years, as more and more parents caught on to what was going on and objected. The values that supposedly needed "clarification" had been clear enough to last for generations and nobody asked the schools and colleges for this "clarification."

Nor are we better people because of it.

THE MONEY OF FOOLS

Seventeenth century philosopher Thomas Hobbes said that words are wise men's counters, but they are the money of fools.

That is as painfully true today as it was four centuries ago. Using words as vehicles to try to convey your meaning is very different from taking words so literally that the words use you and confuse you.

Take the simple phrase "rent control." If you take these words literally— as if they were money in the bank— you get a complete distortion of reality.

New York is the city with the oldest and strongest rent control laws in the nation. San Francisco is second. But if you look at cities with the highest average rents, New York is first and San Francisco is second. Obviously, "rent control" laws do not control rent.

If you check out the facts, instead of relying on words, you will discover that "gun control" laws do not control guns, the government's "stimulus" spending does not stimulate the economy and that many "compassionate" policies inflict cruel results, such as the destruction of the black family.

Do you know how many millions of people died in the war "to make the world safe for democracy"— a war that led to autocratic dynasties being replaced by totalitarian dictatorships that slaughtered far more of their own people than the dynasties had?

Warm, fuzzy words and phrases have an enormous advantage in politics. None has had such a long run of political success as "social justice."

The idea cannot be refuted because it has no specific meaning. Fighting it would be like trying to punch the fog. No wonder "social justice" has been such a political success for more than a century— and counting.

While the term has no defined meaning, it has emotionally powerful connotations. There is a strong sense that it is simply not right— that it is unjust— that some people are so much better off than others.

Justification, even as the term is used in printing and carpentry, means aligning one thing with another. But what is the standard to which we think incomes or other benefits should be aligned?

Is the person who has spent years in school goofing off, acting up or fighting— squandering the tens of thousands of dollars that the taxpayers have spent on his education— supposed to end up with his income aligned with that of the person who spent those same years studying to acquire knowledge and skills that would later be valuable to himself and to society at large?

Some advocates of "social justice" would argue that what is fundamentally unjust is that one person is born into circumstances that make that person's chances in life radically different from the chances that others have— through no fault of one and through no merit of the others.

Maybe the person who wasted educational opportunities and developed self-destructive behavior would have turned out differently if born into a different home or a different community.

That would of course be more just. But now we are no longer talking about "social" justice, unless we believe that it is all society's fault that different families and communities have different values and priorities— and that society can "solve" that "problem."

Nor can poverty or poor education explain such differences. There are individuals who were raised by parents who were both poor and poorly educated, but who pushed their children to get the education that the parents themselves never had. Many individuals and groups would not be where they are today without that.

All kinds of chance encounters— with particular people, information or circumstances— have marked turning points in many individual's lives, whether toward fulfillment or ruin.

None of these things is equal or can be made equal. If this is an injustice, it is not a "social" injustice because it is beyond the power of society.

You can talk or act as if society is both omniscient and omnipotent. But, to do so would be to let words become what Thomas Hobbes called them, "the money of fools."

BOOMERS AND BOOMERANGS

Time was when grandparents often moved in with their children and grandchildren, especially when the grandparent was a widow or widower, or just had trouble making ends meet financially. Today, it is the children and grandchildren who move in with the grandparents.

A recent Census Bureau report shows that there are three times as many households where the children and grandchildren are living in the grandparents' home as there are where the grandparents are living with their children and grandchildren. Moreover, this trend is growing.

Back in 1970, there were a little more than 2 million children under 18 who were living in their grandparents' households. By 1997, that had reached nearly 4 million. Six percent of all children under 18 live in their grandparents' households.

There was a time when any adult who had gone out into the world would be embarrassed to come back and live with his parents, much less bring his or her family too. Today, this is such a common occurrence among the baby boomers that there is a word for grown children who leave home and then come back— "boomerangs."

Perhaps the worst situation of all is when both parents have skipped out and dumped their children on grandma and grandpa. This happens about one-third of the time when grandchildren are living in their grandparents' home.

These grandparents are not rich people living on investments and annuities. Most of the grandparents are working, even if their children aren't. Moreover, they suffer more depression and other health problems than grandparents without such burdens.

Bad as this is, what is worse is to contemplate what is going to happen when the last of the responsible generation— those who feel a responsibility to look out for both their aging parents and their adult children— pass from the scene, leaving behind only the "me" generation.

This is only one of many social time bombs ticking away, while we enjoy a prospering economy. We may hope that the "me" generation will grow up when they run out of other people to dump their responsibilities on. But don't bet the rent money on it.

People don't usually grow up when there are other people who make excuses for their immaturity. In a "non-judgmental" world, who is to tell irresponsible parents to grow up?

Even when the parents are present and have their children in their own homes, they seem increasingly to be letting these children pretty much raise themselves. When a woman was complaining recently about some bratty and even dangerous behavior she sees in children, I asked, "Where are their parents?" She replied: "There are no parents today." I had to admit that she had a point.

One of the biggest excuses for lax parenting is that both parents "have to" work, in order to "make ends meet." Yet, within living memory, it was common in working-class families— black and white— for the husband to work and the wife to stay home to raise the children. Why didn't both parents have to work then, in order to make ends meet?

Were people so much richer then? On the contrary, they were much poorer. Today's families living in poverty have things that average Americans could not afford then.

People today eat in restaurants more times in a month than they used to in a year— or, in some cases, a decade. As a young man, I was uneasy when I began eating in restaurants, because I had so seldom eaten in one while growing up. As for having a car, the thought never crossed my mind.

If people in those days had lived the way we live today, of course it would have taken both parents to make ends meet. They would probably have had to put the children to work too.

People make choices and have their own priorities— and adults take responsibilities for their choices and priorities. It is a cop-out to say that they are "forced" to have two-income families just "to make ends meet."

When we have a system where children are fed in schools and other basic responsibilities are also lifted from the shoulders of their parents, why should we be surprised that the sense of parental responsibility seems to be eroding? We are not surprised when a couch potato doesn't have the kind of muscles found on someone who exercises. Our society is increasingly turning out moral couch potatoes.

IS THE FAMILY
BECOMING EXTINCT?

To the intelligentsia, the family— or "the traditional family," as they say nowadays— is just one lifestyle among many. Moreover, they periodically announce its decline, with no sign whatever of regret. Sometimes with just a touch of smugness.

The latest census data show that the traditional family— a married couple and their children— constitute just a little less than one-fourth of all households. On the other hand, such families constituted just a little more than one-fourth of all families a decade ago. Any reports of the demise of the traditional family are greatly exaggerated.

Snapshot statistics can be very misleading when you realize that people go through different stages of their lives. Even the most traditional families— including Ozzie and Harriet themselves— never permanently consisted of married couples and their children. Kids grow up and move out. People who get married do not start having children immediately. If every single person in the country got married and had children, married-couple families with children would still not constitute 100 percent of households at any given time.

With rising per-capita incomes, more individuals can afford to have their own households. These include young unmarried adults, widows and widowers, and others who often lived with relatives in earlier times. When more such households are created, traditional family households automatically become a smaller percentage of all households.

Incidentally, the growth of households containing one person— about 25 percent of all households today— is the reason why average household incomes are rising very little, even though per capita incomes have been rising very substantially. Gloom and doomers love to cite household income statistics, in order to claim that Americans' incomes are stagnating, when in fact there has been an unprecedented and sustained rise in prosperity, among women and men, blacks and whites, and virtually everybody else.

Marriage does occur later today than in the past and more people don't get married at all. But 53 percent of all households still contain married couples, with or without children currently living with them, while some of the other households contain widows and widowers whose marriages were ended only by death.

Despite attempts to equate married couples with people who are living together as "domestic partners," married couples are in fact better off than unmarried couples, by almost any standard you can think of. Married couples have higher incomes, longer lives, better health, less violence, less alcohol and less poverty. As Casey Stengel used to say, "You can look it up." One place to look it up is in the book *The Case for Marriage* by Linda Waite and Maggie Gallagher. But this is just one place among many. You don't usually hear these kinds of facts because they are not considered to be "politically correct" when the media, politicians, academia and the courts are busy trying to make all kinds of living arrangements seem equal.

The latest census report on "America's Families and Living Arrangements" contains all sorts of statistics but avoids showing the most basic statistics on the average income of married-couple families compared with "other family households" or with "non-family households." The Census Bureau apparently does not want to be politically incorrect.

If you dig through the census' numbers, however, you will discover some revealing clues. While both "unmarried partners" and "married spouses" are spread up and down the income scale, the bracket with the largest number of men who are unmarried partners is the bracket between $30,000 and $40,000. The bracket with the largest number of husbands is between $50,000 and $75,000. Among married-couple households, the bracket with the largest number of households is $75,000 and over. Among "other family groups," the bracket with the largest number of households is that under $10,000.

Women who are shacking up are four times as likely as wives to become victims of violence, and their children are 40 times as likely to be abused by live-in boy friends as by their own parents.

Despite all this, it remains dogma among those who set the ideological fashions that marriage is just another lifestyle, no better or worse than any other. Even the Census Bureau seems unwilling to publish statistical data that would go against this vision and rile up the anointed.

LIFE AT THE BOTTOM

Poverty used to mean hunger and inadequate clothing to protect you against the elements, as well as long hours of grinding labor to try to make ends meet. But today most of the people living below the official poverty line not only have enough food, they are actually slightly more likely than others to be overweight. Ordinary clothing is so plentiful that young hoodlums fight over designer clothes or fancy sneakers. As for work, there is less of that in lower income households today than among the affluent.

Most of today's poor have color TV and microwave ovens. Poverty in the old physical sense is nowhere near as widespread as it once was. Yet life at the bottom is no picnic— and is too often a nightmare.

A recently published book titled *Life at the Bottom* paints a brilliantly insightful, but very painful, picture of the underclass— its emptiness, agonies, violence and moral squalor. This book is about a British underclass neighborhood where its author, Theodore Dalrymple, works as a doctor. That may in fact make its message easier for many Americans to understand and accept.

Most of the people that Dalrymple writes about are white, so it may be possible at last to take an honest look at the causes and consequences of an underclass lifestyle, without fear of being called "racist." The people who are doing the same socially destructive and self-destructive things that are being done in underclass neighborhoods in the United States cannot claim that it is because their ancestors were enslaved or because they face racial discrimination.

Once those cop-outs are out of the way, maybe we can face reality and even talk sense about how things became such a mess and such a horror. As an emergency room physician, Theodore Dalrymple treats youngsters who have been beaten up so badly that they require medical attention— because they tried to do well in school. When that happens in American ghettos, the victims have been accused of "acting white" by trying to get an education. On the other side of the Atlantic, both the victims and the hoodlums are white.

The British underclass neighborhood in which Dalrymple works, like its American counterpart, features what he calls "the kind of ferocious young egotist to whom I would give a wide berth in the broadest daylight." He sees also "the destruction of the strong family ties that alone made emergence from poverty possible for large numbers of people."

Dalrymple's own father was born in a slum— but in a very different social setting from that of today's underclass. For one thing, his father received a real education. The textbooks from which he was taught would be considered too tough in today's era of dumbed-down education.

Dalrymple's father was given the tools to rise out of poverty, while today's underclass is not only denied those tools, but receives excuses for remaining in poverty— and ideologies blaming their plight on others, whom they are encouraged to envy and resent. The net result is an underclass generation that has trouble spelling simple words or doing elementary arithmetic, and which has no intention of developing job skills.

By having their physical needs taken care of by the welfare state, as if they were livestock, the underclass are left with "a life emptied of meaning," as Dalrymple says, since they cannot even take pride in providing their own food and shelter, as generations before them did. Worse, they are left with no sense of responsibility in a non-judgmental world.

Some educators, intellectuals, and others may imagine that they are being friends of the poor by excusing or "understanding" their self-destructive behavior and encouraging a paranoid view of the larger world around them. But the most important thing anyone can do for the poor is to help them get out of poverty, as Dalrymple's father was helped by those who taught him and held him to standards— treating him as a responsible human being, not livestock.

No summary can do justice to the vivid examples and penetrating insights in *Life at the Bottom*. It needs to be read— with the understanding that its story is also our story.

TWISTED HISTORY

One of the reasons our children do not measure up academically to children in other countries is that so much time is spent in American classrooms twisting our history for ideological purposes.

"How would you feel if you were a Native American who saw the European invaders taking away your land?" is the kind of question our children are likely to be confronted with in our schools. It is a classic example of trying to look at the past with the assumptions— and the ignorance— of the present.

One of the things we take for granted today is that it is wrong to take other people's land by force. Neither American Indians nor the European invaders believed that.

Both took other people's land by force— as did Asians, Africans, Arabs, Polynesians, and others. The Indians no doubt regretted losing so many battles. But that is wholly different from saying that they thought battles were the wrong way to settle the question of who would control the land.

Today's child cannot possibly put himself or herself in the mindset of Indians centuries ago, without infinitely more knowledge of history than our schools have ever taught.

Nor is understanding history the purpose of such questions. The purpose is to score points against Western society. In short, propaganda has replaced education as the goal of too many "educators."

Schools are not the only institutions that twist history to score ideological points. "Never Forget That They Owned Lots of Slaves" was the huge headline across the front page of the *New York Times*' book review section in its December 14, 2004 issue. Inside was an indictment of George Washington and Thomas Jefferson.

Of all the tragic facts about the history of slavery, the most astonishing to an American today is that, although slavery was a worldwide institution for thousands of years, nowhere in the world was slavery a controversial issue prior to the 18th century.

People of every race and color were enslaved— and enslaved others. White people were still being bought and sold as slaves in the Ottoman Empire, decades after American blacks were freed.

Everyone hated the idea of being a slave but few had any qualms about enslaving others. Slavery was just not an issue, not even among intellectuals, much less among political leaders, until the 18th century— and then it was an issue only in Western civilization.

Among those who turned against slavery in the 18th century were George Washington, Thomas Jefferson, Patrick Henry and other American leaders. You could research all of 18th century Africa or Asia or the Middle East without finding any comparable rejection of slavery there.

But who is singled out for scathing criticism today? American leaders of the 18th century.

Deciding that slavery was wrong was much easier than deciding what to do with millions of people from another continent, of another race, and without any historical preparation for living as free citizens in a society like that of the United States, where they were 20 percent of the total population.

It is clear from the private correspondence of Washington, Jefferson, and many others that their moral rejection of slavery was unambiguous, but the practical question of what to do now had them baffled. That would remain so for more than half a century.

In 1862, a ship carrying slaves from Africa to Cuba, in violation of a ban on the international slave trade, was captured on the high seas by the U.S. Navy. The crew were imprisoned and the captain was hanged in the United States— despite the fact that slavery itself was still legal at the time in Africa, in Cuba, and in the United States.

What does this tell us? That enslaving people was considered an abomination. But what to do with millions of people who were already enslaved was not equally clear.

That question was finally answered by a war in which one life was lost for every six people freed. Maybe that was the only answer. But don't pretend today that it was an easy answer— or that those who grappled with the dilemma in the 18th century were some special villains, when most leaders and most people around the world at that time saw nothing wrong with slavery.

Incidentally, the September 2004 issue of *National Geographic* had an article about the millions of people still enslaved around the world right now. But where was the moral indignation about that?

ANIMAL RITES

If you think there is a limit to how much childishness there is among Californians, you may want to reconsider— especially for Californians in academic communities.

Recently a mountain lion was discovered up in a tree in Palo Alto, a residential community adjacent to Stanford University. This was at about the time of day when a nearby school was getting ready to let out. There had already been an incident of a horse being found mauled by some animal on Stanford land, and some thought it might have been a mountain lion that did it.

Fearing that the mountain lion might find one of the local school children a tempting target, the police shot and killed the animal. Outrage against the police erupted up and down the San Francisco peninsula and as far away as Marin County, on the other side of the Golden Gate Bridge, more than 30 miles away.

According to the *San Francisco Chronicle*, "The police agency has been flooded with outraged calls and e-mails from people inflamed by TV news videotape of the lion lolling peacefully in a tree just before an officer shot it to death with a high-powered rifle."

Yes, the mountain lion was sitting peacefully. That is what cats do before they pounce— usually very swiftly.

Second-guessers always have easy alternatives. One protester against "the murdering of such a beautiful creature" said that it "easily could have been removed from the premises and relocated" and that the "dirty blood-thirsty bastards" who killed it should be ashamed of themselves.

The protester offered no helpful hints on how you "easily" remove a mountain lion from a tree— and certainly did not volunteer to demonstrate how to do it in person the next time the police find a mountain lion up a tree in a residential neighborhood.

Animal rights advocates said the police could have given the mountain lion "a chance" by attempting to tranquilize it while it was up in the tree, and save shooting as a last resort if it turned aggressive.

A makeshift shrine has been erected on the spot where the mountain lion died. Flowers, cards and photos have been placed around it.

This is an academic community where indignation is a way of life. Those engaged in moral exhibitionism have no time for mundane realities.

The police, of course, have to deal with mundane realities all the time. Not long before this episode, the police had tried to capture three mountain lion cubs by shooting them with tranquilizers. They missed on two out of three tries with one cub.

What if the police had shot a tranquilizer gun at the adult mountain lion in the tree and missed? Would they have had a chance to get off a second shot at a swiftly moving target before he pounced on one of the hundreds of children that were soon to be leaving school near him?

Moral exhibitionists never make allowance for the police missing, whether with tranquilizers shot at mountain lions or bullets fired at a criminal. The perpetually indignant are forever wondering why it took so many shots.

It would never occur to people with academic degrees and professorships that they are both ignorant and incompetent in vast areas of human life, much less that they should keep that in mind before they vent their emotions and wax self-righteous.

Degrees show that you have knowledge in some special area. Too often they embolden people to pontificate on a wide range of other subjects where they don't know what they are talking about. The fact that academics are overwhelmingly of the political left is perfectly consistent with their assumption that third parties— especially third parties like themselves— should be controlling the decisions of other people who have first-hand knowledge and experience.

The cops probably haven't read Chaucer and don't know what existentialism is. But they may know what danger is.

Some Palo Alto parents of small children living near where the mountain lion was killed said that the police did the right thing. There are still some pockets of sanity, even in Palo Alto.

HUMAN LIVESTOCK

An old television special featured great boxing matches of the past, including a video of a match between legendary light-heavyweight champion Archie Moore and a young Canadian fighter named Yvon Durelle. In that fight, each man was knocked down four times. Since Archie Moore was also among those serving as commentators on the program, someone asked him if he knew that this was a great boxing match while he was fighting it.

"Yes!" he replied emphatically. At the time, he had said to himself: "This is the kind of fight that any fighter would love to be in— a knockdown, drag-out— and emerge the winner."

Overcoming adversity is one of our great desires and one of our great sources of pride. But it is something that our anointed deep thinkers strive to eliminate from our lives, through everything from grade inflation to the welfare state.

The anointed want to eliminate stress, challenge, striving, and competition. They want the necessities of life to be supplied as "rights"— which is to say, at the taxpayers' expense, without anyone's being forced to work for those necessities, except of course the taxpayers.

Nothing is to be earned. "Self-esteem" is to be dispensed to school children as largess from the teacher. Adults are to have their medical care and other necessities dispensed as largess from the government. People are to be mixed and matched by race and sex and whatever else the anointed want to take into account, in order to present whatever kind of picture the anointed think should be presented.

This is a vision of human beings as livestock to be fed by the government and herded and tended by the anointed. All the things that make us human beings are to be removed from our lives and we are to live as denatured creatures controlled and directed by our betters.

Those things that help human beings be independent and self-reliant— whether automobiles, guns, the free market, or vouchers— provoke instant hostility from the anointed.

Automobiles enable you to come and go as you wish, without so much as a "by your leave" to your betters. The very idea that other people will go where they want, live where they want, how they want, and send their children to whatever schools they choose, is galling to the anointed, for it denies the very specialness that is at the heart of their picture of themselves.

Guns are completely inappropriate for the kind of sheep-like people the anointed envision or the orderly, prepackaged world in which they are to live. When you are in mortal danger, you are supposed to dial 911, so that the police can arrive on the scene some time later, identify your body, and file reports in triplicate.

The free market is a daily assault on the vision of the anointed. Just think of all those millions of people out there buying whatever they want, whenever they want, whether or not the anointed think it is good for them.

Think of those people earning whatever incomes they happen to get from producing goods or services for other people, at prices resulting from supply and demand, with the anointed cut out of the loop entirely and standing on the sidelines in helpless frustration, unable to impose their particular vision of "social justice."

The welfare state is not really about the welfare of the masses. It is about the egos of the elites.

One of the most dangerous things about the welfare state is that it breaks the connection between what people have produced and what they consume, at least in many people's minds. For the society as a whole, that connection remains as fixed as ever, but the welfare state makes it possible for individuals to think of money or goods as just arbitrary dispensations.

Thus those who have less can feel a grievance against "society" and are less inhibited about stealing or vandalizing. And the very concept of gratitude or obligation disappears— even the obligation of common decency out of respect for other people. The next time you see a bum leaving drug needles in a park where children play or urinating in the street, you are seeing your tax dollars at work and the end result of the vision of the anointed.

THE EINSTEIN SYNDROME

What have famed pianist Arthur Rubinstein, Italian dictator Benito Mussolini, India's self-taught mathematical genius Ramanujan, Nobel Prizewinning economist Gary Becker, talk show host G. Gordon Liddy and renowned physicists Richard Feynman, Edward Teller and Albert Einstein all had in common?

Aside from being remarkable people, they were all late in beginning to speak when they were children. Edward Teller, for example, did not say anything that anyone understood until he was four years old. Einstein began talking at age three but he was still not fluent when he turned nine.

While most children who are late in beginning to speak are male, there have also been some famous female late-talkers— celebrated 19th century pianist Clara Schumann and outstanding 20th century mathematician Julia Robinson, the first woman to become president of the American Mathematical Association. In addition, there have been innumerable people of exceptional ability in a number of fields who were years behind the norm for developing the ability to speak when they were children.

Parents and professionals alike have been baffled as to the reason for delayed speech in children whose precocious intellectual development was obvious, even when they were toddlers. Some of these kids can put together puzzles designed for older children or for adults. Some can use computers by themselves as early as age two, even though they remain silent while their peers are developing the ability to speak.

No one really knows for sure why this is so. These children have only begun to be studied within the past decade. My own book *The Einstein Syndrome* is one such study. More research on these children is being conducted by Professor Stephen Camarata at the Vanderbilt University medical school. He was himself late in talking.

Research on Einstein's brain has suggested to some neuroscientists that he was late in talking because of the unusual development of his brain, as revealed by an autopsy. Those portions of his brain where analytical thinking was concentrated had spread out far beyond their usual area and spilled over into adjoining areas, including the region from which speech is usually controlled. This has led some neuroscientists to suggest that his genius and his late talking could have been related.

At this point, no one knows whether this is the reason why Einstein took so long to develop the ability to speak, much less whether this is true of the other people of outstanding intellect who were also late in beginning to speak. What is known, however, is that there are a number of disabilities that are more common among people of high intellect than in the general population.

Members of the high-IQ Mensa society, for example, have a far higher than normal incidence of allergies. A sample of youngsters enrolled in the Johns Hopkins program for mathematically precocious youths— kids who can score 700 on the math SAT when they are just 12 years old— showed that more than four-fifths of them were allergic and/or myopic and/or left-handed.

This is all consistent with one region of the brain having above normal development and taking resources that leave some other region or regions with less than the usual resources for performing other functions. It is also consistent with the fact that some bright children who talk late remain impervious to all attempts of parents or professionals to get them to talk at the normal time. Yet these same kids later begin to speak on their own, sometimes after parents have finally just given up hope and stopped trying.

Noted language authority and neuroscientist Steven Pinker of M.I.T. says, "language seems to develop about as quickly as the growing brain can handle it." While this was a statement about the general development of language, it may be especially relevant to bright children who talk late. As the whole brain grows in early childhood, increasing the total resources available, the regions whose resources have been pre-empted elsewhere can now catch up and develop normally.

My research and that of Professor Camarata have turned up a number of patterns in children with the Einstein Syndrome that were similar to what biographies of Einstein himself reveal. Most children who talk late are not like those in our studies. But a remarkable number are.

Unfortunately, many of these children get misdiagnosed as retarded, autistic or as having an attention deficit disorder.

THE WRIGHT STUFF

One of the greatest inventions of the 20th century— indeed, one of the landmark inventions in the history of the human race— was the work of a couple of young men who had never gone to college and who were just bicycle mechanics in Dayton, Ohio.

That part of the United States is often referred to disdainfully as "flyover country" because it is part of America that the east coast and west coast elites fly over on their way to what they consider more important places. But they are able to fly over it only because of those mechanics in Dayton.

The Wright brothers' first airplane flight was only about 120 feet— roughly the distance from home plate to second base— and not as long as the wingspan of a 747. But it began one of the longest journeys ever taken by the human race, and that journey is not over yet, as we soar farther into space.

Man had dreamed of flying for centuries and others were hard at work on the project in various places around the world when the Wright brothers finally got their plane off the ground on December 17, 1903. It didn't matter how long or how short the flight was. What mattered was that they showed that it could be done.

Alas, Orville and Wilbur Wright are today pigeon-holed as "dead white males" whom we are supposed to ignore, if not deplore. Had either of them been a woman, or black or any of a number of other specially singled out groups, the hundredth anniversary of their flight would be a national holiday, with an orgy of parades and speeches across the length and breadth of the country.

Recently, a reporter for a well-known magazine phoned me to check on some facts about famous people who talked late and whom I had mentioned in my book, *The Einstein Syndrome*. Her editor wanted to know why there was not more "diversity" among the people I cited. Almost all of them were men, for example, and white men at that.

The vast majority of people who talk late are boys and I had no control over that. In a predominantly white society, it should not be surprising that famous men who talked late were mostly white. No doubt in China most would be Chinese.

The reporter seemed somewhat relieved when I pointed out that the distinguished mathematician Julia Robinson and famed 19th century concert pianist Clara Schumann were among the women discussed in my book. Ramanujan, a self-taught mathematical genius from India, came to my attention right after the book went into print, but the reporter seemed happy to be able to add his name to the list of famous late-talkers.

This mania for "diversity" has spread far and wide. When I looked through my nieces' high school math book, I saw many pictures of noted mathematicians but— judging by those pictures— you would never dream that anything worth noting had ever been done in mathematics by any white males.

This petty-minded falsification of history is less disturbing than the indoctrination-minded "educators" who are twisting reality to fit their vision. Those who cannot tell the difference between education and brainwashing do not belong in our schools.

History is what happened, not what we wish had happened or what a theory says should have happened. One of the reasons for the great value of history is that it allows us to check our current beliefs against hard facts from around the world and across the centuries.

But history cannot be a reality check for today's fashionable visions when history is itself shaped by those visions. When that happens, we are sealing ourselves up in a closed world of assumptions.

There is no evidence that the Wright brothers intended the airplane to ·be flown, or ridden in, only by white people. Many of the great breakthroughs in science and technology were gifts to the whole human race. Those whose efforts created these breakthroughs were exalted because of their contributions to mankind, not to their particular tribe or sex.

In trying to cheapen those people as "dead white males" we only cheapen ourselves and do nothing to promote similar achievements by people of every description. When the Wright brothers rose off the ground, we all rose off the ground.

REVISIONISTS AGAINST AMERICA

An American of Chinese ancestry got into big trouble when the private school at which he was teaching had a public discussion of the American bombing of Hiroshima. He recalled how, as someone growing up in China, he had rejoiced when he heard of the bombing, knowing that it could deliver his people from the horrors inflicted on them by the Japanese.

That of course was not the politically correct response, as he soon discovered from the backlash, hostility and ostracism that eventually culminated in his leaving the school. The anointed do not want anyone upsetting their vision. When they say "diversity," this is not what they have in mind.

Hiroshima has become one of many symbols of a countercultural hostility to America among the intelligentsia in general and the "revisionist" historians in particular. The 50th anniversary of the bombing of Hiroshima on August 6, 1945 galvanized *Newsweek* magazine into Monday-morning-quarterbacking, half a century after that Sunday.

The revisionist line is that it was unnecessary to bomb Hiroshima. We could have invaded, we could have negotiated a settlement, we could have done all sorts of things.

Newsweek magazine's estimate today is that there might have been 20,000 Americans killed in an invasion of Japan. This is quite a contrast with the estimates of the people who had the heavy responsibility of fighting the war at the time.

General Douglas MacArthur, who had been selected to command the invasion of Japan, before the atomic bomb was tested and shown to work, told Secretary of War Stimson to expect more than a million American casualties alone. British Prime Minister Winston Churchill also expected more than a million American casualties, together with half a million casualties among the British troops who were scheduled to hit the beaches with the Americans.

Anyone familiar with the history of the Japanese soldiers' bitter resistance to the death— very few were captured alive— will have no trouble understanding why such huge casualties were expected. American Marines lost more than 5,000 men taking the little island of Iwo Jima and the Japanese themselves suffered more than 100,000 deaths when Americans captured Japan's outlying island of Okinawa. That was more than were killed at Hiroshima or Nagasaki.

Newsweek's pushover scenario, which would have had Japan defeated in 90 days, would be funny if it were not so sick.

Winston Churchill's estimate to the House of Commons would have had the war with Japan ending in 1946 and the Pentagon's estimate was that Japan might even hold out until 1947.

Not only was there a Japanese army which had proven its toughness and skill on many a battlefield, there were 5,000 kamikaze planes ready for suicide attacks on Americans invading their homeland. If these planes managed to take out just 5 Americans each, they alone would have killed more troops than those in *Newsweek*'s rosy scenario.

Japan's civilian population, including children, were also being mobilized and trained in suicide attacks on enemy troops and tanks. It would have been one of the great bloodbaths of all time.

Of course Japan could have been defeated without the atomic bomb. But at what cost in lives of people killed in other ways and in larger numbers?

The other tack taken by the revisionist historians is to say that Japan was "ready to surrender" before the atomic bombs were dropped. The most obvious question is: Why didn't they do it, then? Indeed, why didn't they do it after Hiroshima was bombed, and thereby spare Nagasaki?

Whatever negotiations may have been going on behind the scenes, surrender was by no means a done deal. Even after both cities had been destroyed, it took the unprecedented intervention of the emperor himself to get the military men to agree to surrender. And even as the emperor's message was being broadcast, some military officers were killed trying to storm the studio where the broadcast originated.

The real question is not whether Japan was willing to negotiate some kind of end to the war but whether it was ready to accept the terms being offered, which involved not merely military capitulation but acceptance of American occupation of their homeland. It was this occupation, like the occupation of Germany, which turned a militaristic nation that had launched several wars in recent times into a peaceful and democratic country.

This was an historic achievement, made possible by the terms of surrender— which in turn were made possible by the two atomic bombs. On net balance, this saved not only American and British lives, but even Japanese lives— not to mention the lives of people in Asia like our Chinese American school teacher who told a bitter truth which the anointed did not want to hear.

AUTISM "CURES"?

"New Ways to Diagnose Autism Earlier" read a recent headline in the *Wall Street Journal*. There is no question that you can diagnose anything as early as you want. The real question is whether the diagnosis will turn out to be correct.

My own awareness of how easy it is to make false diagnoses of autism grew out of experiences with a group of parents of late-talking children that I formed back in 1993.

A number of those children were diagnosed as autistic. But the passing years have shown most of the diagnoses to have been false, as most of these children have not only begun talking but have developed socially.

Some parents have even said, "Now I wish he would shut up."

I did absolutely nothing to produce these results. As a layman, I refused to diagnose these children, much less suggest any treatment, even though many parents wanted such advice.

As word of my group spread, various parents would write to ask if they could bring their child to me to seek my impression or advice. I declined every time.

Yet, if I had concocted some half-baked method of diagnosing and treating these children, I could now claim a high rate of success in "curing" autism, based on case studies. Perhaps my success rate would be as high as that claimed by various programs being touted in the media.

If a child is not autistic to begin with, almost anything will "cure" him with the passage of time.

My work brought me into contact with Professor Stephen Camarata of Vanderbilt University, who has specialized in the study of late-talking children— and who is qualified to diagnose autism.

Professor Camarata has organized his own group of parents of late-talking children, which has grown to hundreds, as compared to the several dozen children in my group. Yet the kinds of children and the kinds of families are remarkably similar in the two groups, in ways spelled out in my book *The Einstein Syndrome*.

The difference is that Professor Camarata is not a layman but a dedicated professional, with decades of experience— and he too has expressed dismay at the number of false diagnoses of autism that he has encountered.

What Camarata has also encountered is something that I encountered in my smaller group— parents who have been told to allow their child to be diagnosed as autistic, in order to become eligible for government money that is available, and can be used for speech therapy or whatever other treatment the child might need.

How much this may have contributed to the soaring statistics on the number of children diagnosed as autistic is something that nobody knows— and apparently not many people are talking about it.

Another factor in the great increase in the number of children diagnosed as autistic is a growing practice of referring to children as being on "the autistic spectrum."

In other words, a child may not actually be autistic but has a number of characteristics common among autistic children. The problem with this approach is that lots of children who are not autistic have characteristics that are common among autistic children.

For example, a study of high-IQ children by Professor Ellen Winner of Boston College found these children to have "obsessive interests" and "often play alone and enjoy solitude," as well as being children who "seem to march to their own drummer" and have "prodigious memories." Many of the children in my group and in Professor Camarata's group have these characteristics.

Those who diagnose children by running down a checklist of "symptoms" can find many apparently "autistic" children or children on "the autism spectrum."

Parents need to be spared the emotional trauma of false diagnoses and children need to be spared stressful treatments that follow false diagnoses. Yet the "autism spectrum" concept provides lots of wiggle room for those who are making false diagnoses.

Real autism may not get as much money as it needs if much of that money is dissipated on children who are not in fact autistic.

But money is money to those who are running research projects— and a gullible media helps them get that money.

INSTRUCTING THE
INSTRUCTORS

No one seems to be more in need of instructions than the people who write instructions for computers and computer software. It is, of course, only an assumption that these are people. They could be aliens from outer space— and the instructions themselves suggest that this possibility should not be dismissed out of hand.

The first instruction for those who write computer instructions should be: Never start at Step Two, since whatever you say will be lost on people who do not know what Step One is.

For example, the ironically titled "Help" file on a well-known backup software begins by saying what you are to do after the "Restore" screen appears. It says nothing about how you get that screen to appear in the first place. Nor is there anything on the opening screen to offer a clue.

Instruction writers should remember that, no matter how simple or sophisticated the computer or software might be, in the end the user is going to have to push some keys on the keyboard, click a mouse or perform some other specific act, if only smashing the computer in frustration.

Too many computer instructions do not specify what act you are to perform. Instead, they *characterize* what you are to do, such as "access the backup files." If the user knew how to do that, he would not have to suffer through such instructions.

While such statements are called instructions, they could more accurately be called reminders. If you already know how to do these things, they remind you when to do it.

How the user is going to learn to perform these operations the first time is something that seems to be of little concern to the computer instruction writers. Maybe they think we will just blunder into it by guess and by golly. Often they are right. Some users have in fact learned the hard way that trial and error is sometimes faster than trying to figure out what the instructions are saying.

The first time I installed chess software in my computer, I made it a point to ignore the instructions completely. Only months later did my curiosity cause me to take a look at these instructions. If I had relied on the manual, I would still be waiting to make my opening move.

Simplifying instructions does not mean adding a lot more words. Words that specify what act you are to perform need not be any more numerous than words which characterize these same acts. Specific words are just more helpful.

As it is, computer instructions are needlessly wordy. Too often they rhapsodize about all the wonderful options and variations available for doing what you want to do. They engage in advertising puffery about the glories of the product. Since you have already bought the product, or you wouldn't have the instruction book, all of this could be eliminated.

In many cases, you would never have bought the product if you had read the instruction book beforehand and realized what an impenetrable jungle it is.

Too many computer and software producers seem to think that being condescending to the user is the same as simplifying. My backup software, for example, opens up with a screen showing a guy with a vacuous smile on his face, saying "It is now time to start a new backup job. . ." No kidding! Why do you suppose I turned on the backup software? At the end, he offers gratuitous advice on how I should number the cartridges I use.

In between, there is only the unhelpful "Help" to turn to.

Probably the main reason for instructions that do not instruct is that the writers cannot or will not put themselves in the position of the users. Instead, these writers— notice that I still will not tip my hand as to whether or not I believe they are people— seem far more interested in all the fancy features that may be used 3 percent of the time than with all the boring stuff that is used the other 97 percent of the time.

Perhaps computer companies and software companies should hire some low-tech people to try to follow the instructions written by their high-tech writers. The better manuals that could result from this process might let some users think that they really are valued customers, as they are told repeatedly by recordings while waiting to talk to someone in technical support.

APRIL FOOLS' PARTY

"This is your eyewitness news team, reporting from the big, posh April Fools' Day party at the Dewdrop Inn out at Moot Point, overlooking Dyer Straits. Everybody who is anybody is here.

"There's the karate expert Marshall Artz, timber heiress Lotta Wood, famous meteorologist Cole Winter, the British boxing sensation Battler Hastings, and the gossip columnist N. U. Endo. There's insurance magnate Justin Case, the famous efficiency expert Ben Dunn Wright, and Ivy University's dean of students, N. 'Loco' Prentiss.

"Let's talk with one of the guests. Excuse me, sir, what is your name?"

"Chester Mann."

"Are you related to that famous social justice advocate?"

"N.V. Mann? Yes."

"What kind of work do you do?"

"I run an automobile junk yard."

"What's the name of it? You might as well give it a free plug."

"Oedipus Wrecks."

"How are you enjoying the party?"

"Frankly, I am here only because my wife dragged me here."

"You don't like the party?"

"As Robinson Crusoe said, 'I don't like this atoll.'"

"As Napoleon said, 'What's your beef, Wellington?'"

"Oh, just the food, the drinks, and the people."

"Well, let me move along. Here's the famous author I. Wright, whose latest best-seller is a steamy novel about India titled *Whose Sari Now*? Incidentally, you look great in those long, flowing robes. Were you born in India?"

"No, Brooklyn."

"But I'll bet you did a lot of research in India?"

"Yes, mostly in the Punjab."

"What is it like to live in a country completely different from the Western world?"

"Actually Indians are not cut off from the Western world. For example, a friend of mine in the Punjab is obsessed with Western classical music.'"

"Likes his Beethoven and Bach, does he?"

"He's really obsessed with Haydn. He's a Haydn Sikh."

"Thank you. Let's go on to talk with some more guests. Here's the famous psychiatrist N.D. Nile, that sweet-looking actress Candy Barr and her sister Minnie who, I believe, is involved in hotels."

"Yes, I am. I have also had some hostel takeovers."

"Not everyone has been successful, of course. Over there is the well-known architect whose firm just went bankrupt— Frank Lloyd Wrong. Let's go over and see what he has to say.

"Sir, this is your eyewitness news team, checking up on how you are doing."

"Terrible! I am suffering from hardening of the arteries, curvature of the spine, cirrhosis of the liver. . ."

"Rumpole of the Bailey?"

"Absolutely."

"I understand that you are also an artist."

"Well, architecture is itself an art, as well as a science. But I also paint pictures, if that is what you mean."

"Yes, I remember a famous painting of yours showing a Rolex sitting on a half-eaten piece of watermelon."

"Yes, I called it 'Watch on the Rind.'"

"You are really on the cutting edge. Are all the people in your set like that?"

"No, actually. My uncle's wife, for example, is the most conservative person I know."

"Really?"

"Yes, I call her my status quo auntie."

"How conservative is she?"

"Once I asked her if she believed in gun control and she said: 'Yes! You've got to control those things or else the shot will go wild and miss the guy you are trying to blast!'"

"Over here is the famous weatherman, Cole Winter. He's usually pretty well informed, since he is on the same program as the news. Cole, what's the latest news?"

"A leopard was spotted in midtown Manhattan today!"

"That's not news. Leopards are spotted everywhere. Anyhow, it is time to return you to the studio. Happy April Fools' Day!"

GROWING OLD

R andom thoughts about growing old:
    Despite the problems that come with aging, I would not be a teenager again for $1,000 a day plus expenses.

I never really felt old until my younger brother retired.

This is the period of life that Disraeli referred to as "anecdotage."

Nothing is more ridiculous than discounts for senior citizens, when people in their sixties have far more wealth than people in their thirties.

These are my declining years. I decline all sorts of invitations and opportunities.

People who talk about "earlier and simpler times" are usually too young to remember those times— and how complicated they were.

An old body is like an old automobile, where the brakes need repairing today, the steering wheel next month and the transmission after that.

Looking at old photographs makes it hard for me to believe that I was ever that thin physically. And remembering some of the things I did in those days makes it hard to believe that I was ever that thin mentally.

You would think that young people, with decades of life ahead of them, would look further ahead and plan for the future more so than older people. But it is just the opposite. The young tend to be oriented to right now, while old timers think about the future of their children and grandchildren, and worry about where the country is heading in the years ahead.

They say you can't teach an old dog new tricks. But maybe the old dog already knows about tricks that only seem new to the young — and doesn't think much of those tricks.

When I was young, age forty seemed so ancient that I couldn't imagine what it would be like to be forty. Now I can barely remember what it was like to be forty.

Age gives you an excuse for not being very good at things that you were not very good at when you were young.

An old saying is that we are once a man and twice a child. The difference is that we more or less automatically have parents to look after us the first time, but whether we will have someone to show us the same love and care when we are at the other end of life is another story.

It is amazing— and appalling— how many people who are walking with the elderly try to pull them along faster than they want to go, or perhaps faster than they are able to go. What does this accomplish, except to create needless tension and stress? And how urgent is it to save a few seconds here and there?

When someone had to tell me that I was on a topless beach, I knew I was getting old.

Like so many people who are getting on in years, I am fine— so long as I remember that I am not fine.

The old are not really smarter than the young. It is just that we have already made the mistakes that the young are about to make, so we already know that these are mistakes and what the consequences are.

Some people age like fine wine and others just turn into vinegar.

Someone asked a man in his seventies at what age he started to lose interest in women. "I don't know," he said. "But when it happens, I will tell you."

I urge my fellow old-timers to write their memoirs, just so that "revisionist" historians will not be able to get away with lying about the past.

More than once, after I woke up some morning feeling like I was twenty again, I did something that ended up with me on crutches or otherwise being reminded emphatically by my body that I was definitely not twenty again.

Women may lie about their age to other people but men lie about their age to themselves.

When old-time Dodger pitching ace Don Newcombe was near the end of his career, someone asked him if he could still throw as hard as ever. "Yes, I throw the ball as hard as ever," he said. "But it just takes longer to get to the plate."

Oliver Wendell Holmes said it best: "If I could think that I had sent a spark to those who come after I should be ready to say Goodbye."

FOREIGN DOMESTICS

One of the ironies of our time is that no occupation seems less domestic than domestics. Foreign domestics are hired not only by private individuals but also by hotels across the United States and in countries overseas.

There are many layers of irony in all this.

While some people are crusading for "re-training" people for the demanding, high-tech jobs of the future, some of the most urgently needed workers are those who can do simple things reliably and conscientiously. Child care and the care of the elderly are prime examples of occupations where it is hard to get good people— and extremely important to have them.

Why is it so hard to find domestic domestics? The two principal reasons are that (1) the idea has been promoted that there is something "demeaning" about doing "menial" work and (2) the taxpayers are subsidizing this philosophy with welfare and unemployment payments. Apparently it is not considered demeaning to accept handouts, whether from the government or on street corners.

Foreigners who have not been here long enough to assimilate our more self-destructive attitudes are able to find jobs that Americans disdain. In more than 30 years in California, I have never seen a Mexican American begging on the streets, though beggars and hustlers have become a common sight and a common nuisance.

Domestic service is considered one of those "dead end" jobs that the intelligentsia and the socially sensitive deplore. Yet these jobs have not only put a roof over people's heads and food on their table, they have also been the first step out of poverty and ignorance for many people in many lands.

In centuries past, inns and eating establishments in Britain were often set up by women and men who had begun their careers as domestic servants for the well-to-do. There they learned not only the preparation of food and the care of a home, but also picked up manners, social graces, and a sense of how to manage things.

Many of the early Japanese immigrants to the United States began as domestic servants. Their conscientiousness and trustworthiness became so widely known that this reputation helped them take the next step up the economic ladder, as self-employed gardeners.

The Japanese gardener became a California institution.

He was his own boss, with a list of clients whose lawns and gardens he typically visited weekly for about an hour. Where the home had a fence or an atrium, he had to have a key, so his reputation for trustworthiness was crucial.

Many of these Japanese American gardeners did quite well for themselves, and put their children through college, so that they could go on to professional careers.

There are no dead-end jobs. There are only dead-end people.

Our current social philosophy, and the welfare state apparatus based on it, are creating more dead-end people.

No amount of re-training can help that. First of all, you cannot retrain people who have not been trained in the first place, who didn't bother to learn in school, and who have never developed a sense of responsibility.

Domestic service is more than a job. It is a window on another world. Just as nations and civilizations learn from one another, so do individuals.

People too poor to become educated, or exposed to wider cultural horizons, nevertheless learned something of another vocabulary, of cultural interests they would never have been aware of, except for working in the homes of people more fortunate and better educated than themselves.

Looking back over my own life, I can remember all sorts of books and toys brought home to me by members of my family who worked in the homes of affluent people with older children who had outgrown these things. What they also brought home to me were cultural intangibles from table manners to an interest in world affairs.

Cultural diffusion does not have to be on the scale of Europe's learning Arabic numerals or acquiring paper from China, or Japan's acquiring a whole spectrum of Western technology. Cultural diffusion can mean a foreign maid learning English in an American home, or a boy in Harlem growing up knowing that there is a much bigger world out there than Harlem.

Unfortunately, the current intellectual and social fashions destroy this whole process. In its place, they offer the poor a parasitic life in a world of ugliness and barbarism, trapped in a dark corner of ignorance and prey to demagogues who seek further to imprison them in phobias and bombastic provincialism.

Such is social progress.

CRUEL "COMPASSION"

"Compassion" has become one of a growing number of politicized words (like "access" or "diversity") whose meaning has been corrupted beyond redemption. Nowhere is there more cruel indifference to the fate of flesh-and-blood human beings than among the hawkers of compassion when they talk about babies, born and unborn.

The very phrase "unborn babies" has been driven from the language by the intelligentsia of the media and academia, who have replaced it with the bloodless and detached word "fetus." The success of this desensitization campaign may be judged by how many of us were shocked to learn from the medical movie "The Silent Scream" that what happens in an abortion is not the surgical removal of some little blob of cells but the painful dismemberment of a struggling human being, attempting in vain to flee from the fatal instruments.

Those who most loudly proclaim "the public's right to know" are nowhere to be seen when it comes to the public's right to know that. Indeed, strenuous efforts are made to prevent this movie from being shown. In politically correct Palo Alto, home of Stanford University, a mere description of the process was edited out of a newspaper column on the subject.

It is not just that the reality of abortion is a little too strong for some stomachs. Even less emotionally taxing issues like adoption reflect a very similar vision of the world in which babies are to be dealt with according to ideology and expediency.

Perhaps the most gross form of this vision is shown in laws and policies against trans-racial adoption. These laws and policies not only keep many minority children needlessly languishing in orphanages or in a series of transient foster homes when there are couples ready to adopt them; courts and bureaucracies actually drag these children in tears from the only homes they have ever known, when those homes are with non-minority families.

Shattering the lives of little two- and three-year old toddlers means nothing to the social welfare bureaucracies or to the academic and media ideologues who come up with fancy theories about the need to maintain cultural identity. Sometimes there is also a parade of speculative horrors to be feared from the adoption of minority children by white couples. Yet actual studies of children adopted across racial lines fail to turn up these horrors, and these youngsters' I.Q.s are typically higher than those of minority children raised by their own parents.

Even aside from adoptions across racial lines, there is ideological opposition to adoption, as such. A recent issue of *National Review* details media campaigns against adoption in publications ranging from the *New York Times* to *Playboy*.

To the critics, adoption is not a "solution" because it has potential problems. Children may be abused by adoptive parents, or feel second-class, or the parents may feel ambivalent, or the original mother may find herself being tracked down, decades later, by the child she put up for adoption.

Of course adoption is not a solution. Neither is anything else in life. In the real world, there are only trade-offs.

Adoption has worked out fine for all sorts of people, from President Gerald Ford to black scientist George Washington Carver, who was raised by a white couple. But of course adoptions do not always work out fine, just as things do not always turn out fine when people are raised by their biological parents.

At the heart of the opposition to adoptions, or to anything that would tend to discourage abortions, is the notion that children are expendable when they inconvenience adults. Anyone who has ever raised children knows that inconvenience is their middle name— and anyone who can look back on his own childhood honestly knows that he was at least an inconvenience, if not a real pain, to his parents on many occasions.

All that goes with the territory— that is, with a universe we did not make, having constraints we cannot escape, and offering only trade-offs, however much the intelligentsia and the politicians proclaim "solutions."

The ultra-rationalistic world of the anointed, where traditional ties and mores have been dumped into the dustbin of history, is the real goal, whether the specific issue is sex education, euthanasia or adoption.

The problem is not that some people think this way. The problem is that other people not only take them seriously, but allow them to intimidate us with their pretense of special knowledge and insight, despite a record of failed theories that goes back at least a generation, leaving a trail of social wreckage from declining educational standards to rising rates of crime, drug usage, and suicide.

Worst of all, we let them appropriate the word compassion, for use as a political lever, when so many of their actions betray their utter lack of it.

WARS OVER VALUES

Cultural wars are dirty wars, much like guerilla warfare in the jungles, with no regard for the rules of the Geneva Convention. Warfare over traditional values versus avant-garde values is raging all across the United States today, from the art galleries to the armed forces, and from the kindergarten to the Supreme Court. At issue is whose cultural values shall prevail and who shall make the decisions that reflect those values.

The categorical language of "rights" is widely used as a weapon in these cultural wars. Those who are pushing a woman's "right" to go into military combat, for example, are in effect saying that the decisions of the military commanders responsible for the lives of thousands of troops, and the decisions of the American society as to the social roles of the sexes, are all to be superseded by the visions of self-anointed and politically organized feminist advocacy groups.

The particulars of the arguments— the physical strength of the sexes, the performance of women in the military, etc.— are in one sense all beside the point. The question is not what to decide, but *who is to decide*. As elsewhere in the cultural wars, the issue is whether a vocal elite should get the power to pre-empt the decisions of others.

To the anointed, the use of words like "rights" is sufficient to put one coterie's opinions above discussion and the word "stereotypes" is enough to put the values of the society at large beneath discussion. They don't want discussion, they want power.

One of the more remarkable "rights" to emerge in recent years is the right to the taxpayers' money for anything that chooses to call itself "art"— regardless of whether the taxpayers or voters like what is produced, and regardless of whether the clear intent of this "art" is in fact to insult the values and beliefs of the public.

For people to decide what their own money is to be spent for is "censorship" in the Newspeak of the anointed.

More generally, the cultural wars are being waged to get decision-making powers transferred to elites who do not pay, either in money or in other ways. Family responsibilities, for example, have been taken over by schools, courts, social agencies, and others who pay no price if their decisions turn out disastrously for children or their parents, or for the whole society.

The basic thrust of the so-called "consumer movement" is likewise a drive for pre-empting the consumer's choice, not simply informing it. The "consumer must be protected at times from his own indiscretion and vanity," Ralph Nader said in his first article, published in *The Nation* in 1959.

It is much the same story in the economic sphere, where having an economic "plan," or perhaps even an "industrial policy" or an "energy policy" are all widely and uncritically regarded among opinion elites as good things in themselves. But government "planning" is not an alternative to chaos. It is a pre-emption of other people's plans.

Whether the sphere of activity is art, military combat, law, schools, or the economy, the issue is whether elite pre-emption shall replace both individual autonomy and democratic choice.

The courts are a major battleground in these wars over cultural values, for they are well-positioned to pre-empt the decisions of others by "interpreting" the Constitution to ban or promote whatever the judges want banned or promoted.

The bitter struggles over Supreme Court nominees in recent years have reflected this key role of the courts in imposing policies so repugnant to the public that elected representatives would not dare vote them into law.

Criminals' judge-created "rights," busing, affirmative action, and abortion, are just some of the policies pre-empted from the democratic process by judicial fiat. The issue, as Judge Robert H. Bork has said, is whether "intellectual class values" shall "continue to be enacted into law by the Supreme Court." The concern expressed by Justices O'Connor, Kennedy, and Souter as to how their ruling in the recent case of *Planned Parenthood v. Casey* would be seen by "the thoughtful part of the Nation" suggests that elite pre-emption is still in favor, even among Justices labelled "conservative."

The pre-emptive class is undoubtedly sincere. People are never more sincere than when they assume their own superiority.

Nor are they ever more ruthless. J. A. Schumpeter said that the first thing a man will do for his ideals is lie.

Disingenuous words, twisted statistics, and misleading labels are all part of the dirty war over cultural values. Cultural wars are so desperate because they are not simply about the merits or demerits of particular policies. They are about the anointed's whole conception of themselves— about whether they are in the heady role of a vanguard or in the pathetic role of pretentious and silly people, infatuated with themselves.

LOVE IS A FOUR LETTER WORD

L ove is a four-letter word but you don't hear it nearly as often as you hear some other four-letter words. It may be a sign of our times that everyone seems to be talking openly about sex but we seem to be embarrassed to talk about love.

Sex alone will not even reproduce the human race because babies cannot survive the first week of life without incredible amounts of care. That care comes from love. If the parents are too wretched to give the infant the attention he needs, then a general love of babies must lead others to set up some backup system, so that the child does not die of neglect.

The shallow people who have turned our schools into propaganda centers for the counterculture try hard to take love out of human relations. Between men and women, for example, there is just sex, if you believe the clever anointed.

But why should we believe them? Why have there been such painful laments— in letters, literature, poetry and song— for so many centuries about the breakup of love affairs? Because there are no other members of the opposite sex available? Not at all.

Sex is almost always available, if only commercially. But love is a lot harder to find. Some people do not even try after their loved one is gone. Some give up on life itself.

In short, what millions of people have done for hundreds of years gives the lie to the self-important cynics who want to reduce everything to an animal level.

Actually, many animals behave in ways which suggest that love is important to them, not only among their own species but also with human beings. Stories of dogs who have rescued or defended their owners, even at the cost of their lives, go back for centuries.

Why is love so out of fashion with the intelligentsia and others who are striving to be "with it"?

Love is one of those bonds which enable people to function and societies to flourish— without being directed from above. Love is one of the many ways we influence each other and work out our inter-related lives without the help of the anointed. Like morality, loyalty, honesty, respect, and other immaterial things, love is one of the intangibles without which the tangibles won't work.

Intellectuals are not comfortable with that. They want to be able to reduce everything to something material, predictable and— above all— controllable. Many want to be in charge of our lives, not have us to work things out among ourselves, whether through emotional ties or the interactions of the marketplace.

Another four-letter word that has fallen out of favor is "duty." It has not been banned. It has just been buried under tons of discussions of "rights." The two words used to be linked, but not any more.

In the real world, however, rights and duties are as closely tied as ever. If *A* has a right to something, then *B* has a duty to see that he gets it. Otherwise *A* has no such right.

When it is a right to freedom of speech, then it is the duty of judges to stop the government from shutting him up— or to let him sue if they do. The big problem comes when it is no longer a question of rights to be left alone but rights to things that other people have to produce. When it is a right to "decent housing," for example, that means other people have a duty to produce that housing and supply it to you— whether or not you are willing to pay what it costs.

Only because the inherent link between rights and duties is broken verbally are advocates for all sorts of sweeping new rights able to sidestep the question as to why someone else must provide individuals with what they are unwilling to provide for themselves. The claim is often made or implied that people may be willing to provide for themselves but are simply unable to do so. But, when push comes to shove, many of the intelligentsia will admit that it doesn't matter to them why someone doesn't have something that he needs. He has a "right" to it. It also doesn't matter how someone caught AIDS, he has no duty to avoid it but others have a duty to pay for it.

What is involved is not just some words but a whole vision of life. If one has the vision of the anointed who want to control other people's lives, then all those things which enable us to function independently of them and of government programs are suspect.

Four-letter words like love, duty, work, and save are hallmarks of people with a very different vision, who make their own way through life without being part of some grandiose scheme of the anointed or of government bureaucracies that administer such schemes. No wonder those words are not nearly as popular as other four-letter words.

MEANINGLESS "EQUALITY"

If one confused word can gum up social policies, the legal system, and innumerable institutions throughout society, that word is "equality." It is one of those vague pieties in which we indulge ourselves, without any serious thought as to what it means or what the actual consequences of pursuing it may be.

Anyone who questions or opposes equality is almost certain to be regarded as someone who believes in inequality— in "inferiority" and "superiority." But all of these concepts suffer from the same problem: For equality, inferiority, or superiority to have any meaning, what is being compared must first be commensurable. A symphony is not equal to an automobile. Nor is it inferior or superior. They are simply not commensurable.

Much of the emotional struggle to make women "equal" to men suffers from the same problem. So long as women have babies and men do not, the many ramifications of that difference cannot be ignored and nothing can make them commensurable. However unisex one's language may be, women are seldom very good men and men cannot be women at all.

We may regard the happiness and well-being of women as equally important as the happiness and well-being of men— and probably most people do, despite shrill cries to the contrary— but that is a statement about our value system, not about some empirical reality of women and men.

With many other groups as well, the fundamental difference between equal treatment and equal performance is repeatedly confused. In performance terms, virtually no one is equal to anyone. The same individual is not even equal to himself on different days.

Much of the moral heartburnings, social engineering, and legal entanglements of our times comes from the simple fact that statistics for different groups are different in different occupations, institutions, or income levels. It is too often assumed automatically that only different treatment before the fact can explain different results after the fact.

This dogma is so deeply imbedded that it seems almost Utopian to attempt a rational discussion of it. Yet it was wholly arbitrary to have expected performance equality in the first place— and compounded pigheadedness to want to punish someone because it didn't happen. But there is a whole class of people who believe that when the world doesn't conform to their theory, that shows that something is wrong with the world.

Let us go back to the fact that women have babies, a fact of no small importance to those of us parochial enough to be concerned about the survival of the human species. Not only do women have babies, they realize in advance that they are likely to have babies— and those who are not yet "liberated" arrange their lives with that prospect in mind.

Occupations which require continuous employment to maintain everchanging skills tend to attract fewer women than occupations you can leave to have children and return to later. You can take a few years off to see your children through the pre-school years and then return to become a good librarian, teacher, or editor, but take a few years off from computer engineering and you will return to find that you are not in Kansas anymore, Toto.

Some years ago, an economist investigated the rates of obsolescence of a wide range of occupations. A physicist lost half the value of his original knowledge in about five years, while it would take a historian more than 30 years to fall that far behind.

Although the economist did not point this out— whether through oversight or prudence— the occupations with high rates of obsolescence were often "male dominated," while the occupations that are heavily female tended to have slow rates of obsolescence.

Although differences in choices and performances are ignored or dismissed in politically correct quarters, such differences obviously affect differences in outcomes, not only as between men and women but among racial, ethnic, and other groups as well.

Since it is truly Utopian to expect to have a rational discussion of interracial differences in these times, we can look at two branches of the same race— northern Europeans and southern Europeans.

For the past few centuries, northern Europeans have been far more advanced industrially and technologically than southern Europeans— not only in Europe itself, but also when they immigrate to European-offshoot societies in the Western Hemisphere or Australia. But for a thousand years or so before that, southern Europeans were far more advanced than northern Europeans.

In short, performances vary not only from individual to individual, but also from group to group, and from one era to another. Seldom are performances equal at any given moment.

In performance terms, Japan was decidedly inferior to the West in industrial technology a century ago. No one was more painfully aware of this than the Japanese themselves. That is what spurred them on to the efforts which have enabled them to overtake the West in many fields today.

They understood that this was not a problem that could be solved by lofty talk or arbitrary presuppositions.

LITTLE THINGS

S ometimes little things give you clues about big things.

The other day, I was practicing tennis at a local playground, with the aid of a machine that fires the ball over the net to me.

A little boy, whose father was practicing on the court next to me, became fascinated with the machine.

The little fellow, about four or five years old, started walking over onto the court where I was playing— on the side where the machine was.

"No, no," I said, "that's dangerous."

The little boy kept walking onto my court, facing into the machine, which was still firing tennis balls in various directions as it turned from side to side. His father said nothing.

"That's dangerous!" I repeated, as I put down my tennis racket and started toward the other side of the net to turn off the machine.

"Michael, why don't you come on back?" the father said.

"I'm going to have to leave," I said to his father, "because this is dangerous."

"No, we'll leave," the father said. "Come on, Michael."

"No!" Michael said, still staring with fascination into the machine as it continued turning and firing tennis balls.

"Oh, Michael, come on," his father pleaded— but still without making a move to go get him.

By this time, I had reached the machine and turned it off.

Only then did Michael lose interest and leave with his father.

After this little experience with the modern middle-class parent in action (or inaction), I went home and read in the paper about a local teacher who had won a teaching award. Was this because her students had learned more than other students? Not at all.

Her greatest claim to fame was that she concentrated on giving her students "self-esteem." She didn't believe in a lot of academic demands, grading and homework. All that might have hurt the little darlings' self-esteem.

For all I know, Michael may have been one of her students.

Certainly he was far less likely to have his self-esteem hurt by his father than to have a couple of teeth knocked out by a tennis ball shot out of a machine. If he got closer and was hit in the eye, he could have lost his sight in that eye.

On that evening's television news, one of the lead stories was about students at the University of Wisconsin rushing onto a football field, breaking down the barriers and injuring several of their fellow students in the crush. A police woman on the scene said that it was impossible to physically restrain a mob of that size when they get carried away.

Of course it is impossible to control everybody. That is why people used to teach their children self-control and obedience to rules and authorities. Today, that kind of talk only gets you a condescending smile, at best.

Our award-winning teacher had a sign on her classroom wall saying, "Question Authority." Today, there is barely enough authority around to question.

This mushy abdication of responsibility to instill discipline is not peculiar to the United States. Young British soccer fans have become notorious for crossing the channel and creating riots at international soccer matches on the continent.

About 1,500 years ago, barbarians from continental Europe invaded Britain and took over. Today, British soccer fans are getting their revenge.

While many civilizations have succumbed to the onslaughts of barbarian invaders, we may be the first to succumb to the onslaughts of barbarians growing up in our midst. Every child born into this world today is as uncivilized as the cave man. If nobody gets around to civilizing him, that is the way he will grow up.

All the lofty talk about the "root causes" of crime fail to notice the obvious: People commit crimes because they are people— because they are innately selfish and do not care how their behavior affects other people, unless they have been raised to behave otherwise or unless they fear the criminal justice system.

The same people who are undermining the notion of imposing either internal or external restraints on children have also been undermining the prosecution and punishment of criminals. They have succeeded all too well on both fronts.

We will all be paying the price of that success for a long time to come.

What is amazing is not that we bought some of these modern theories that became fashionable back in the 1960s. What is staggering is that we have not reconsidered after decades of watching the consequences.

MASCOTS OF THE ANOINTED

The *New York Times* recently ran a front page story dripping with sympathy for a multiple murderer who is now very old and who, on some days, "cannot remember" why he is in prison. His victims, however, cannot remember anything on any days.

There are also photographs of him and other prisoners. One prisoner is described as having a disease that "brings mental deterioration." Another, with his legs amputated, is shown trying to catch a baseball on his knees. Yet another prisoner is shown in a wheelchair.

All sorts of heart-tugging stories are told about elderly inmates who are succumbing to various diseases and infirmities of age. There are, however, no stories at all about their victims, or their victims' widows or orphans, or how tough their lives have been.

Although the *Times* runs this as a "news" story, it is in effect a long editorial on how terrible it is to keep these prisoners locked up, years after they have ceased to be dangerous to society. This one-sided presentation includes the views of the American Civil Liberties Union and prison officials who would like to use the space taken up by these elderly prisoners. But there is not one word from a victim or from police who have had to deal with these killers.

Bias shades off into propaganda when the *Times* quotes ACLU figures that there are more than 30,000 prisoners who are 50 or older in the nation's prisons. Note that we started out with stories about people so old and infirm that they are supposedly no danger to anyone. Now we get statistics that are not about such people at all but about people "50 or older."

I don't know what would make the *New York Times* or the American Snivel Liberties Union suggest that people cease to be dangerous at 50. I am older than that and I fired a rifle and a shotgun just a few days ago. We old codgers can still pull a trigger.

One of the murderers featured in the *Times'* own story was 74 years old when he began serving his life sentence. What a shame he did not realize how harmless he was after age 50.

The propaganda game of talking about one thing and citing statistics about something else has been used in many other contexts. Stories about violence against women often begin with terrible individual tragedies and then move on to numbers about "abuse," which include such things as a husband's stomping out of the room after an argument. Statistics about serious violence against women are less than one-tenth as large as the numbers that are thrown around in the media by feminist activists. Moreover, serious violence against men is about twice as high.

In technique, as well as in bias, the *Times* story about criminals is classic liberal propaganda for one of their mascot groups. But this is not something peculiar to the *New York Times*. You can find the same kinds of stories in the *Washington Post* or the *Los Angeles Times*, or on any of the leading television networks.

Criminals are just one of the groups adopted as mascots of the media. All sorts of parasites and predators have been displayed as if they were ocelots or other exotic creatures that adorn the world of the anointed. The deeper question is: Why is it necessary for the anointed to have human mascots? And why do they choose the kind of people that they do?

Whoever is condemned by society at large— criminals, vagrants, illegal aliens, AIDS-carriers, etc.— are eligible to become mascots of the anointed, symbols of their superior wisdom and virtue. By lavishing concern on those we condemn, the anointed become morally one-up on the rest of us.

Is that important? To some it is paramount. A quarter of a century before the Gettysburg Address, Abraham Lincoln said in a speech in Springfield, Illinois, that the greatest danger to the future of the United States would come, not from foreign enemies, but from that class of people which "thirsts and burns for distinction."

These people could not find that distinction "in supporting and maintaining an edifice that has been erected by others," according to Lincoln. In other words, there is not nearly as much ego satisfaction in building up this country as in tearing it down. For example, a Stanford law student involved in the "prisoner's rights" movement said recently, "it's precisely because prisoners are viewed as the castaways of our society—

that's what draws me to them even more." She wants to know "why a person can't function in this society, what it is about this society."

Our schools and colleges are today turning out more and more people like this, who are taught to despise American society and to boost their own egos by blaming that society for sins that are common among human beings around the world. Journalism is just one of the professions being prostituted to this self-indulgence.

THE ANTI-AMERICAN
AMERICANS

Every August, there are American citizens who journey to Japan to abase themselves and their country at Hiroshima and Nagasaki. The Japanese do not go to Nanking, where they slaughtered more Chinese, in more brutal and sadistic ways, than those who were killed in both of these Japanese cities combined.

What was unique about Hiroshima and Nagasaki was the technology with which people were killed— not the number killed. More Germans were killed with older types of bombs at Dresden and more Japanese were killed in the invasion of Okinawa than died at either Hiroshima or Nagasaki.

Technological differences are not moral differences. Of all the people killed during World War II, less than one percent were killed in these two cities combined. If killing is wrong, even in wartime, then why not condemn the killing of the 99 percent, rather than single out the one percent?

The awesome power of nuclear weapons, which has hung over all our heads ever since they were invented, is certainly a reason to lament that such things are even possible. Winston Churchill spoke of the secrets of the atom as knowledge that was long "mercifully withheld from man."

But it was knowledge that our enemies were seeking, which is what prompted Albert Einstein— a pacifist— to urge President Roosevelt not to let the Nazis be the first to get it.

In addition to those merely unthinking or naive Americans who journey to Hiroshima and Nagasaki every August, there are members of the media and academia who can seldom pass up an opportunity to be morally one-up on others in general or to be anti-American in particular.

In addition, "revisionist" historians have spread the claim that the bombing of these Japanese cities was unnecessary, that Japan was ready to surrender, that an invasion would not have been so bad.

Some of the more vicious anti-Americans say that this terrible weapon would never have been used against white people. What color do they think the people were in Dresden? The first experimental nuclear bomb had not yet been tested when Dresden was obliterated and its inhabitants incinerated from the air.

Unlike those American leaders who bore the heavy responsibility of sending American troops into combat at the time, these revisionists— a much too polite word for liars— come up with rosy scenarios in which the casualties of an invasion of Japan are estimated to be a fraction of what General Douglas MacArthur or other leading military authorities of the time foresaw.

In the Pacific war, there were islands where the Japanese defenders who died fighting numbered in the thousands, while those who were taken alive barely numbered in the dozens— most of these latter being too badly wounded to either fight or commit suicide. With this kind of resistance to the death being common among the Japanese in defending their conquered lands, how could anyone expect that the defense of their own homeland would be anything other than a bloodbath for all involved?

Japanese civilians, including children, were being trained and indoctrinated to die defending Japan from invaders. The number who would have done so was undoubtedly larger than the number who died in the atomic blasts which spared them, as well as the American and British troops who would have died on the beaches and in house-to-house fighting in the cities.

Was Japan going to lose the war, even without the atomic bombs? Yes— but at what price? Would it have been possible to arrange a Japanese surrender without an invasion? Perhaps, on terms more agreeable to the Japanese. But without unconditional surrender and an occupation of Japan, how could this militaristic country have been converted into one of the most pacific nations on earth?

Without the incredible feat by which General MacArthur changed the ages-old military traditions of the Japanese, Japan could have been ready to fight again in another decade— and this time, she would in all probability have had the atomic bomb. Nor is there any reason to believe that Japan would have shown the slightest hesitation before using it or the slightest remorse afterward.

Guilt-ridden Americans might do well to read *The Rape of Nanking* or *Prisoner of the Rising Sun*. It could save them airfare to Hiroshima or Nagasaki.

"DEAD BALL" VERSUS "LIVELY BALL"?

Among baseball aficionados, it has long been accepted that there was a "dead ball era" that ended in 1920, when a livelier ball was introduced, which accounts for the dramatic increase in the number of home runs hit in the decade of the 1920s, as compared to the number of home runs hit in the two previous decades. Denials by baseball officials that the ball had been changed have been dismissed out of hand, in view of the dramatic and apparently otherwise inexplicable changes in the number of home runs hit in the 1920s and thereafter.

Proponents of this view have some formidable statistics on their side. During the first two decades of the twentieth century, only three players hit more than 20 home runs in a season and none hit as many as 30. Moreover, each of these three players hit 20 or more home runs in a season only once during those two decades. By contrast, during the single decade of the 1920s, half a dozen players hit 40 or more home runs, with Babe Ruth doing it eight times. What alternative explanation could account for this sea change? As so often happens, when there is a strong preconception shared by many people, no alternative explanation was considered, much less tested empirically.

Among the reasons for the strong belief that the ball was changed was the fact that baseball was under a cloud of distrust as a result of the fixing of the 1919 World Series by the Chicago White Sox, whom many now called the "Black Sox." At the same time, Babe Ruth had electrified the baseball world by hitting a record 29 home runs for the Boston Red Sox in 1919 and became immensely popular with the fans as a result. Here, apparently, was a golden opportunity for those who controlled major league baseball to get the public's mind off the Black Sox scandal by creating more Babe Ruths by changing to a more lively ball. A plausible theory plus some indisputable numbers often seem to add up to a proven fact. But that kind of arithmetic needs to be re-examined.

Other facts lead to a very different picture that is not only compatible with the very same numbers, but in addition stands up better under statistical scrutiny. Here is an alternative theory: Prior to Babe Ruth's spectacular emergence as a home run hitter, batting styles were quite different from what they became afterwards. Most hitters did not grasp the bat down at the end, the way Babe Ruth did, and did not swing for the fences, since that often led to striking out, which was a disgrace to be avoided. Uppercutting the ball to lift it over the fences meant flying out a lot.

It has been theorized that Ruth got away with his strange new hitting style because he began his career as a pitcher and no one bothered to "correct" his batting, since no one expected much hitting from pitchers anyway. In any event, players whose careers began after Ruth's spectacular success in hitting home runs tended to adopt his batting style, holding the bat down at the end, which produced more leverage and less control— more home runs and more strikeouts.

What would we expect to see if this alternative explanation of the changing number of home runs is the correct one? We would expect to see the leading batters of the pre-Ruth era to continue to hit relatively few home runs during the 1920s, while newer arrivals on the scene, or younger players reaching their peaks in the 1920s, would be those who supplied the big home run numbers. That is precisely what we do find.

It was not the existing sluggers who suddenly started hitting more home runs. It was the new sluggers, with new batting styles, who began hitting unprecedented numbers of home runs in the 1920s. Moreover, this did not happen immediately, but the number of batters with large home run totals increased as the decade went on, as more players tried to follow in Ruth's footsteps.

None of the leading batting stars of the years immediately before 1920— Ty Cobb, Tris Speaker, Joe Jackson, Eddie Collins— hit as many as 20 home runs in any season during the decade of the 1920s. Some of these established batting stars had big seasons in the 1920s, but that did not include big home run totals.

Eddie Collins had batting averages over .330 in five seasons during the decade of the 1920s, but he never broke into double digits in home runs. He hit four home runs in 1919, supposedly the last year of the dead ball, and three home runs in 1920, supposedly the first year of the lively ball, when Babe Ruth hit the unheard-of total of 54 home runs. Nor was Eddie Collins unique. No one else in either league hit even 20 home runs in 1920, even though they were all hitting the same ball that Babe Ruth was hitting. Seven of the eight *teams* in the American League failed to hit as many home runs in 1920 as Babe Ruth hit. So did seven of the eight teams in the National League.

As far as home runs were concerned, all that was different about 1920 was Babe Ruth. But the new-style hitters who were to follow in his wake began to make their appearance, at first on a modest scale, in 1921, when— for the first time in the twentieth century— more than one player hit 20 or more home runs in the same season. There were five others besides Babe Ruth, but none of the others hit as many as 30 home runs. None of these were the top batting stars of the pre-1920 era, who continued to show the same batting patterns they had always had.

Ty Cobb and Tris Speaker, between them, hit over .350 in seven seasons during the decade of the 1920s, but Speaker's highest home run total was 17 and Cobb never exceeded 12. Neither did Shoeless Joe Jackson, who played one year in the supposedly lively ball era, before being banned from baseball because of the Black Sox scandal. During that season, Joe Jackson batted .382, with 42 doubles, and led the league with 20 triples, but he hit just 12 home runs.

The top hitters of the past continued to hit as they always had— choked up on the bat and going for contact, rather than swinging for the fences. They struck out a lot less than the players who followed in the footsteps of Babe Ruth. Neither Cobb, Collins, Speaker, nor Jackson ever struck out 50 times in a season. Speaker, in fact, never struck out more than 25 times in a season during his entire 22-year career, though today it is common for sluggers to strike out more than a hundred times in a season.

Cobb, Speaker, and Jackson were the leading sluggers of their era, though not home run specialists. Each hit 40 or more doubles in a season several times during their careers— but they were not going for the fences. Speaker hit 50 or more doubles in a season five times and in fact still holds the major league record for the most doubles in a career. With their large numbers of doubles and triples and their high batting averages, Cobb, Speaker and

Jackson all had lifetime slugging averages higher than those of such later era sluggers as Roberto Clemente and George Brett.

If the existing top sluggers did not increase their home run totals significantly during the 1920s, how did the greatly increased home run totals happen? Those who hit 40 or more home runs during the 1920s either began their careers in that decade (Lou Gehrig, Mel Ott, Chuck Klein) or reached their peak then (Babe Ruth, Rogers Hornsby, Cy Williams). If it was the ball that was responsible for the big surge in home runs, then the old and the new batting stars alike would have seen dramatic increases in homers. But that was not what happened.

There were still some old-style batting stars among the younger players in the 1920s— George Sisler and Harry Heilmann, for example— and their records during that decade were very similar to those of the elders in whose footsteps they were following. Sisler batted over .400 twice but never hit as many as 20 home runs, despite hitting more than 40 doubles in both those seasons. Heilmann hit over .400 once and over .390 twice, and had eight seasons in which he hit 40 or more doubles, but his highest home run total in a season was 21. The 1920s was the last decade in which more than one batter hit .400, as this batting style faded away, being replaced by players swinging for the home run. In this new era, no one hit .400 during the last half of the twentieth century.

Gross numbers may suggest a change in the ball, but a finer breakdown of the statistics indicates a change in the batters. It is true, as many have pointed out, that the ball changed externally over the years, in the sense that balls used to be kept in play longer in the early years of the twentieth century, and that players could legally dirty it up more and pitchers could apply foreign substances to it in earlier years. But none of that changed suddenly in 1920, when the home run record for a season shot up from 29 to 54. Moreover, the ball changed for all players but the old and the new batting stars had very different results when it came to home runs.

What happened in 1920 was that Babe Ruth had his second full season as an outfielder and hit a stride that would typify his home run totals for the rest of the decade. What happened afterwards was that the whole style of batting changed in the generations that followed in Ruth's wake.

ECONOMICS

ONE-STAGE THINKING

When I was an undergraduate studying economics under Professor Arthur Smithies of Harvard, he asked me in class one day what policy I favored on a particular issue of the times. Since I had strong feelings on that issue, I proceeded to answer him with enthusiasm, explaining what beneficial consequences I expected from the policy I advocated.

"And then what will happen?" he asked.

The question caught me off guard. However, as I thought about it, it became clear that the situation I described would lead to other economic consequences, which I then began to consider and to spell out.

"And what will happen after that?" Professor Smithies asked.

As I analyzed how the further economic reactions to the policy would unfold, I began to realize that these reactions would lead to consequences much less desirable than those at the first stage, and I began to waver somewhat.

"And *then* what will happen?" Smithies persisted.

By now I was beginning to see that the economic reverberations of the policy I advocated were likely to be pretty disastrous— and, in fact, much worse than the initial situation that it was designed to improve.

Simple as this little exercise might seem, it went further than most economic discussions about policies on a wide range of issues. Most thinking stops at stage one. In recent years, former economic advisers to Presidents of the United States— from both political parties— have commented publicly on how little thinking ahead about economic consequences went into decisions made at the highest level.* This is not to say that there was no thinking ahead about *political* consequences. Each of the presidents they served (Richard Nixon and Bill Clinton, respectively) was so successful politically that he was re-elected by a wider margin than the vote that first put him in office.

---

* Herbert Stein and Joseph Stiglitz.

Short-run thinking is not confined to politicians but is often also found among the population at large. Nor is this peculiar to the United States or even to Western societies. When the government of Zimbabwe decreed drastic cutbacks in prices to deal with runaway inflation in June 2007, the citizens of Zimbabwe "greeted the price cuts with a euphoric— and short-lived— shopping spree," according to the *New York Times*. But, just one month later, the *Times* reported, "Zimbabwe's economy is at a halt." This was spelled out:

> Bread, sugar and cornmeal, staples of every Zimbabwean's diet, have vanished... Meat is virtually nonexistent, even for members of the middle class who have money to buy it on the black market... Hospital patients are dying for lack of basic medical supplies.[1]

That suppliers do not usually supply as much at a lower price as they do at a higher price is not a complicated economic principle, but it does require stopping to think, and especially to think beyond stage one. Price controls are essentially lies about supply and demand. In the case of Zimbabwe, the artificially low prices created the impression of an affordable abundance that was simply not there. As with other lies, political or otherwise, time may be required for the truth to come out, and it may be too late when it does. Moreover, politicians have every incentive to deny the truth when it is an unpalatable truth about something that they have advocated or supported.

UNION MYTHS

The biggest myth about labor unions is that unions are for the workers. Unions are for unions, just as corporations are for corporations and politicians are for politicians.

Nothing shows the utter cynicism of the unions and the politicians who do their bidding like the so-called "Employee Free Choice Act" that the Obama administration tried to push through Congress. Workers' free choice as to whether or not to join a union is precisely what that legislation would destroy.

Workers already have a free choice in secret-ballot elections conducted under existing laws. As more and more workers in the private sector have voted to reject having a union represent them, the unions' answer has been to take away secret-ballot elections.

Under the "Employee Free Choice Act" unions would not have to win in secret ballot elections in order to represent the workers. Instead, union representatives could simply collect signatures from the workers until they had a majority.

Why do we have secret ballots in the first place, whether in elections for unions or elections for government officials? To prevent intimidation and allow people to vote how they want to, without fear of retaliation.

This is a crucial right that unions want to take away from workers. The actions of union mobs in Wisconsin, Ohio and elsewhere give us a free home demonstration of how little they respect the rights of those who disagree with them and how much they rely on harassment and threats to get what they want.

It takes world-class chutzpa to call circumventing secret ballots the "Employee Free Choice Act." To unions, workers are just the raw material used to create union power, just as iron ore is the raw material used by U.S. Steel and bauxite is the raw material used by the Aluminum Company of America.

The most fundamental fact about labor unions is that they do not create any wealth. The are one of a growing number of institutions which specialize in siphoning off wealth created by others, whether those others are businesses or the taxpayers.

There are limits to how long unions can siphon off money from businesses, without facing serious economic repercussions.

The most famous labor union leader, the legendary John L. Lewis, head of the United Mine Workers from 1920 to 1960, secured rising wages and job benefits for the coal miners, far beyond what they could have gotten out of a free market based on supply and demand. But there is no free lunch.

An economist at the University of Chicago called John L. Lewis "the world's greatest oil salesman."

His strikes that interrupted the supply of coal, as well as the resulting wage increases that raised its price, caused many individuals and businesses to switch from using coal to using oil, leading to reduced employment of coal miners. The higher wage rates also led coal companies to replace many miners with machines.

The net result was a huge decline in employment in the coal mining industry, leaving many mining towns virtually ghost towns by the 1960s. There is no free lunch.

Similar things happened in the unionized steel industry and in the unionized automobile industry. At one time, U.S. Steel was the largest steel producer in the world and General Motors the largest automobile manufacturer. No more. Their unions were riding high in their heyday, but they too discovered that there is no free lunch, as their members lost jobs by the hundreds of thousands.

Workers have also learned that there is no free lunch, which is why they have, over the years, increasingly voted against being represented by unions in secret ballot elections.

One set of workers, however, remained largely immune to such repercussions. These are government workers represented by public sector unions.

While oil could replace coal, while U.S. Steel dropped from number one in the world to number ten, and Toyota could replace General Motors as the world's leading producer of cars, government is a monopoly. Nobody is likely to replace the federal or state bureaucracies, no matter how much money the unions drain from the taxpayers.

That is why government unions continue to thrive while private sector unions decline. Taxpayers provide their free lunch.

"AFFORDABILITY"

Many of the cant words of politics are simply evasions of reality. A prime example is the notion of making housing, college, health insurance, or other things "affordable."

Virtually anything can be made more affordable in isolation, simply by transferring resources to it from elsewhere in the economy, and having most of the costs absorbed by the U. S. Treasury.

The federal government could make a Rolls Royce affordable for every American, but we would not be a richer country as a result. We would in fact be a much poorer country, because of all the vast resources transferred from other economic activities to subsidize an extravagant luxury.

Of course it might be nice to be sitting at the wheel of a Rolls Royce, but we might be sitting there in rags and tatters, and gaunt with hunger, after having squandered enormous amounts of labor, capital, and costly materials that could have been put to better use elsewhere. That doesn't happen in a market economy because most of us take one look at the price tag on a Rolls Royce and decide that it is time for another Toyota.

The very notion of making things affordable misses the key point of a market economy. An economy exists to make trade-offs, and a market economy makes the terms of those trade-offs plain with price tags representing the relative costs of producing different things. To have politicians arbitrarily change the price tags, so that prices no longer represent the real costs, is to defeat the whole purpose.

Reality doesn't change when the government changes price tags. Talk about "bringing down health care costs" is not aimed at the costly legal environment in which medical science operates, or other sources of needless medical costs. It is aimed at price control, which hides costs rather than reducing them.

Hidden costs continue to take their toll— and it is often a higher toll than when these costs are freely transmitted through the marketplace. Less supply, poorer quality, and longer waits have been the consequences of price controls for all sorts of goods and services, in all sorts of societies, and for thousands of years of human history.

Why would anyone think that price controls on medical care would be any different, except for being more deadly in their consequences?

One of the political excuses for making things affordable is that a particular product or service is a "right." But this is only explaining one question-begging word with another.

Although it has been proclaimed that "health care is a right, not a privilege," this neat dichotomy ignores the vast territory in between, where most decisions are made as trade-offs.

If health insurance is a right and not a privilege— and not even a subject of incremental trade-offs— then the same should be even more true of food. History in fact shows all too many instances of governments trying to keep food affordable, usually with disastrous consequences.

Whether in France during the 1790s, the Soviet Union after the Bolshevik revolution, or in newly independent African nations during the past generation, governments have imposed artificially low prices on food. In each case, this led to artificially low supplies of food and artificially high levels of hunger.

People who complain about the "prohibitive" cost of housing, or of going to college, for example, fail to understand that the whole point of costs is to be prohibitive.

Why do we go through this whole rigmarole of passing around dollar bills and writing each other checks, except to force everyone to economize on the country's inherently limited resources?

What about "basic necessities"? Shouldn't they be a "right"?

The idea certainly sounds nice. But the very fact that we can seriously entertain such a notion, as if we were God on the first day of creation, instead of mortals constrained by the universe we find in place, shows the utter unreality of failing to understand that we can only make choices among alternatives actually available.

For society as a whole, nothing comes as a "right" to which we are "entitled." Even bare subsistence has to be produced— and produced at a cost of heavy toil for much of human history.

The only way anyone can have a right to something that has to be produced is to force someone else to produce it for him. The more things are provided as rights, the less the recipients have to work and the more others have to carry their load.

That does not mean more goods are available than under ordinary market production, but less. To believe otherwise is to commit the Rolls Royce fallacy on a more mundane level.

For the government to make some things more affordable is to make other things less affordable— and to destroy people's freedom to make their own trade-offs as they see fit, in the light of economic realities, rather than political visions. Trade-offs remain inescapable, whether they are made through a market or through politics. The difference is that price tags present all the trade-offs simultaneously, while political "affordability" policies arbitrarily fix on whatever is hot at the moment. That is why cities have been financing all kinds of boondoggles for years, while their bridges rusted and their roadways crumbled.

SAVING LIVES

Many highly costly laws, policies, or devices designed to safeguard the public from lethal hazards are defended on grounds that "if it saves just one human life" it is worth whatever it costs. Powerful as the moral and emotional appeal of such pronouncements may be, they cannot withstand scrutiny in a world where scarce resources have alternative uses.

One of those alternative uses is saving other human lives in other ways. Few things have saved as many lives as the simple growth of wealth. An earthquake powerful enough to kill a dozen people in California will kill hundreds of people in some less affluent country and thousands in a Third World nation. Greater wealth enables California buildings, bridges, and other structures to be built to withstand far greater stresses than similar structures can withstand in poorer countries. Those injured in an earthquake in California can be rushed far more quickly to far more elaborately equipped hospitals with larger numbers of more highly trained medical personnel. This is just one of innumerable ways in which wealth saves lives.

Natural disasters of all sorts occur in rich and poor countries alike— the United States leads the world in tornadoes, for example— but their consequences are very different. The Swiss Reinsurance Company reported that the biggest financial costs of natural disasters in 2003 were in the United States, Canada, and France. But that same year the biggest costs of natural disasters in human lives were all in Third World countries— Iran, Algeria, India, Bangladesh, and Pakistan.[1] Given the high cost of medical care and of such preventive measures against disease as water treatment plants and sewage disposal systems, Third World countries likewise suffer far more from diseases, including diseases that have been virtually wiped out in affluent countries. The net result is shorter lifespans in poorer countries.

There have been various calculations of how much of a rise in national income saves how many lives. Whatever the correct figure may be— X million dollars to save one life— anything that prevents national income from rising that much has, in effect, cost a life. If some particular safety law, policy, or device costs $5X$ million dollars, either directly or by its inhibiting effect on economic growth, then it can no longer be said to be worth it "if it saves just one human life" because it does so at the cost of 5 other human lives. There is no escaping trade-offs, so long as resources are scarce and have alternative uses.

More is involved than saving lives in alternative ways. There is also the question of how much life is being saved and at how much cost. Some might say that there is no limit on how much value should be placed on a human life. But, however noble such words may sound, in the real world no one would favor spending half the annual output of a nation to keep one person alive 30 seconds longer. Yet that would be the logical implication of a claim that a life is of infinite value. When we look beyond words to behavior, people do not behave as if they regard even their own lives as being of infinite value. For example, people take life-threatening jobs as test pilots or explosives experts when such jobs pay a high enough salary for them to feel compensated for the risk. They even risk their lives for purely recreational purposes, such as sky-diving, white-water rafting, or mountain climbing.

PICTURING THE "TRUST FUND"

They say a picture is worth a thousand words. But, in this age of spin-masters, a picture can be more deceiving than a thousand words.

In response to those economists who have been saying that the Social Security "trust fund" is a myth, *Kiplinger's* magazine sent a reporter down to Parkersburg, West Virginia, to photograph the trust fund. He came back with a picture of the securities in that trust fund, as well as a diagram of the safe in which these securities are kept and a picture of the computer that keeps track of the Social Security trust fund.

The March issue of *Kiplinger's* even gave us the latitude and longitude of Parkersburg, in case we want to go there and check it out. Yes, Virginia, there is a trust fund— or is there?

Let us think the unthinkable, that there is no Social Security trust fund. Where would the baby boomers' pensions come from? From money that will arrive in Washington after they retire.

However, since we have photographic proof that there is so a trust fund, where will the baby boomers' pensions come from? From money that will arrive in Washington after they retire. It seems that the distinction between a trust fund and no trust fund is one of those distinctions without a difference that lawyers talk about.

As a purely formal, paper transaction there is a trust fund. Money comes in from the millions of paychecks from which there has been withholding under the Federal Insurance Contributions Act— the FICA listed on paycheck stubs. The Social Security system then uses this money to buy interest-bearing securities from the Treasury Department. When cash is needed to pay retirees, some of these securities are sold to get the money to pay them their Social Security pensions.

Still looking at form, rather than substance, this system has the further political advantage that the securities held by the Social Security system are not counted as part of the national debt, because it is one government agency owing money to another. What that means is that, when the government spends more money than it receives in taxes, it spends money from FICA to cover the difference and gives the Social Security trust fund an I.O.U. that does not count as an I.O.U. in figuring the annual deficit or the accumulated national debt.

If only we could all make our debts disappear so conveniently! But we are not the government, making up our own accounting rules.

Turning from form to substance, what the government is doing is spending the Social Security money for current outlays, not only for pensions to retirees, but also for everything from Congressional junkets to nuclear missiles. What is left in the trust fund for future retirees, including the large and much-feared baby boomer generation, whose pensions are scheduled to cost trillions in the twenty-first century?

What is left is a promise to pay them. That is precisely what would be left if there were no Social Security trust fund. Treasury securities are nothing more than claims against future revenues from general taxation. Social Security can of course also draw against the continuing inflow of FICA from workers, but everybody knows that this source will be completely inadequate to pay what will be owed to the baby boomers.

The staggering amounts needed to make up the difference— greater than the costs of financing a major war— will have to come from somewhere. Either there will be huge increases in tax rates on those still working or some form of welshing on the promises made to retirees. No doubt there will be creative compromisers who will come up with some judicious blend of higher taxes and partial defaults, whether by inflation to reduce the real value of the pensions, an older retirement age or higher taxes on Social Security income, in order to take back with one hand part of what was given to retirees with the other.

No matter how it is done, it will always be possible to photograph the checks that Social Security recipients receive, thereby "proving" that there has been no default. The question is: How much comfort and reassurance that will be to a generation that knows it has been cheated out of what they were promised and paid for, even if they cannot follow the accounting sleight-of-hand by which it was done?

No, Virginia, there really is no Social Security trust fund. Politicians have already spent it, behind their smoke and mirrors.

THE ECONOMICS OF CRIME

Probably few, if any, people go through their entire lives without violating some law, but while many crimes may be committed by people in a moment of passion or a moment when temptations overcome both morality and logic, the person whose whole livelihood depends on the continuing commission of crimes is a very different phenomenon. Various studies over the years have shown that a very small percentage of the population commits a very large percentage of all crimes. Moreover, this has been true in country after country, as noted by one of the leading scholars on crime, James Q. Wilson:

> In studies both here and abroad it has been established that about 6 percent of the boys of a given age will commit half or more of all the serious crime produced by all boys of that age. Allowing for measurement errors, it is remarkable how consistent this formula is— 6 percent causes 50 percent. It is roughly true in places as different as Philadelphia; London; Racine; and Orange County, California.[1]

Very similar patterns have been found for adult criminals.[2]

Another pattern that is international is that of a concentration of violent crimes among young males. Although the absolute murder rate is far higher in Chicago than in England and Wales, the age-pattern is virtually identical. That is, the murder rate peaks in all three places in young males in their early twenties and then begins a sharp decline that continues over the rest of their lives.[3]

Criminals are not a random sample of the population at large. They are typically younger on average than the general population, disproportionately male and, at least among those caught and convicted, have lower than average IQs.[4] Nor can we assume that criminals as a whole have much higher IQs than those who are caught, since most of the serious crime committed is accounted for by those who pass through the criminal justice system, and there is not enough additional serious crime unaccounted for to indicate a large number of additional criminals. However, the career criminal cannot simply be dismissed as irrational, because there is too much evidence from too many countries that he is indeed quite rational.

It is easy enough to say that "crime does not pay," but the real question is: Does not pay whom— and compared to what? It is doubtful whether Bill Gates could have done nearly as well financially as he has by becoming a burglar or even a hit man for organized crime, but those who do pursue these criminal occupations are unlikely to have had the same alternatives available that Bill Gates had because of his particular talents and circumstances.

Given the low educational and IQ levels of many who become career criminals, crime may well be their best-paying option. Given the short time horizons of many of those who make crime their occupation— especially young people and people from lower social classes— such things as selling illegal drugs may seem lucrative in stage one, whether or not it leads to prison in stage two or perhaps never living to see stage two. Crime is one of those occupations, like sports and entertainment, in which a relatively few at the top achieve very high incomes, while most of those who enter the occupation receive very low incomes. For example, many ordinary young sellers of drugs on the street live at home with their mothers, often in public housing projects— clearly not an indication of affluence— while the lavish lifestyles of drug kingpins attract many young people into this occupation, in hopes of rising to that level.

Again, the rationality of the choices being made depends on the alternatives available. Someone with a bad record in school, and perhaps an arrest record, is likely to have very limited options in the legitimate job market. Even someone with a clean record may be prevented from earning some much-needed money by child labor laws or by minimum wage laws that set a pay scale higher than an inexperienced teenager would be worth. But crime is an occupation that is always open to everyone.

The rationality of the career criminal is demonstrated in many ways, including variations in the amount and kinds of crime committed as the costs of committing those particular crimes vary. These costs include not only the legal penalties but also the dangers faced by criminals from their potential victims. For example, burglary rates tend to be affected by the proportion of homeowners who have guns in their homes. The rate of burglary is not only much higher in Britain than in the United States— nearly twice as high— British burglars are far less likely than American burglars to "case" the premises before entering, in order to make sure that no one is home.⁵ Even if someone is at home in Britain, there is far less danger that the person at home will have a firearm, given the far more strict British gun control laws. Moreover, people convicted of burglary are treated more leniently in Britain, seldom going to jail.⁶

British and American burglars are both behaving rationally, given the respective circumstances in which they operate and consequently the different dangers which they face. While only 13 percent of burglaries in the United States occur while the home is occupied, more than 40 percent of the burglaries in Britain, the Netherlands, and Canada occur while the home is occupied.⁷ These latter three countries have much lower incidences of gun ownership than the United States, due to more severe gun control laws. After the Atlanta suburb of Kennesaw passed an ordinance requiring heads of households to keep a firearm in their homes, residential burglaries there dropped by 89 percent.⁸

Another major cost to a criminal career is the danger of incurring legal penalties, usually imprisonment. Here criminal activity in general has tended to vary over time inversely with the risk of imprisonment— which includes the risk of detection, conviction, and sentencing. In the United States, various legal reforms of the 1960s had the net effect of reducing the likelihood that anyone committing a given crime would actually spend time behind bars as a result. Crime rates skyrocketed. The murder rate, for example, was twice as high in 1974 as in 1961,⁹ and between 1960 and 1976 an average citizen's chance of becoming a victim of some major violent crime tripled.¹⁰

Data from other countries show similar trends. On a graph showing the rate of crime in Australia from 1964 to 1999 and the rate of imprisonment per 1,000 crimes committed over that same span, the two lines are virtually mirror-images of one another, with the rate of crime going up when the rate of imprisonment went down, and vice versa.¹¹ The graphs for England and Wales, New Zealand, and the United States are very similar. In the United States, the crime rate peaked in the 1980s and began falling as the rate of incarceration rose. In England and Wales, the rate of imprisonment hit bottom in the early 1990s— which is when the crime rate peaked, and then began a substantial decline as the rate of imprisonment rose. In New

Zealand, the high point in crime was reached in the early 1990s while the low point in incarceration was reached about 1985 and then began to rise again, with the crime rate falling with a lag of a few years.

Another example of the rationality of criminals is their response to the unusual American institution of the private bail bondsman, a system used by only one other country, the Philippines, which was once an American colony. In the United States, indicted criminals can pay a bail bondsman to post a bond in their behalf to guarantee their appearance in court on their trial date, so that they can stay out of jail pending trial. Typically, the charge is about ten percent of the total bail posted, all of which is returned to the bail bondsman when the client shows up for trial as scheduled.

When the client fails to show up, however, the bail bondsman forfeits the bail unless he can find the client and turn him over to the court within a short specified time. The bail bondsmen— sometimes called "bounty hunters"— are authorized to go capture those who do not show up in court. The rationality of the criminal is shown by the fact that the rate of court appearances is higher when a bail bondsman is used than when criminal defendants are released pending trial in other ways.[12] Because a bail bondsman has a vested interest in a particular individual, he is more likely than the police are to focus on capturing that particular individual, and is less likely to be inhibited in his methods of doing so. Criminals, being aware of this, are quite rational to show up for trial.

The same rationality among criminals is shown in other ways and in other countries. In pre-World War II Britain, for example, when both criminals and the police rarely carried firearms, even an accomplice to a firearms murder was subject to hanging. Therefore criminals planning a robbery together would frisk one another, to make sure no one was carrying a gun that could get all the others hanged if there was a killing and they were caught.[13] That was a very rational thing to do under the circumstances.

While the amount and nature of crimes have varied with the likelihood of punishment, this is not to say that crime rates are unaffected by cultural or other differences among countries. There are serious cultural differences which are no doubt reflected in the *absolute* levels of crime among countries, though the similarity in *trends* already noted is very striking. As one example of substantial differences between countries in the absolute levels of crime, despite similarities in trends, in the nineteenth century guns were freely available in both London and New York City, and yet the murder rate in New York was several times what it was in London.[14]

Early in the twentieth century, severe gun control laws were passed in New York State, years before such laws were imposed in England— and yet New York City continued to have several times as high a murder rate as London, as it has for two centuries. Clearly it was not such laws, or the absence of such laws, which made the difference. Eventually, Britain's gun control laws were tightened far more than those in the United States, especially after the Second World War. However, because New York's murder rate continued to be far higher than that in London, and that in the United States far higher than that in Britain, this differential was often attributed to differences in gun control laws, even though large differences in murder rates existed long before either country had gun control laws, and persisted even when the United States had gun control laws before Britain did.

While there are undoubtedly many complex factors behind the absolute crime rates in any country, the trends strongly suggest that *changes* in crime rates reflect rational reactions to changes by criminals in the costs they pay, both in punishment inflicted by the law enforcement system and the risks of being harmed by their intended victims. The asymmetrical effects of gun control laws on criminals and law-abiding citizens have been reflected in the fact that, as gun-control laws tightened in late twentieth century Britain, rates of murder and armed robbery increased,[15] which is consistent with the fact that such criminal activities became safer when there was more assurance that potential victims were unarmed.

With criminal economic activities, as with legal economic activities, behavior differs when there is free competition in a given field as compared to monopolistic control of that field. With both legal and illegal activities, there tends to be more production with competition than with monopoly. That is, the incentives and constraints tend to lead to more crime being committed when the criminals are individual independent operators than when they are part of an organized crime syndicate. For example, a small-time criminal may find it expedient to kill some local store owner for the small amount of money in the store's cash register, if only to keep the store owner from identifying him, even though this might make no sense to organized crime.

Public outrage at such a murder could result in more law enforcement activity in the area, reducing the profitability of the crime syndicate's business in illegal drugs, prostitution, and other activities by making local customers more hesitant to engage in such activities when there was an unusually large police presence in their neighborhoods. This could easily cost the crime syndicate far more money than there was in the store owner's cash register.*

Such repercussions can be largely ignored by individual criminals operating independently, since the killer of the store owner may lose little from the increased law enforcement, compared to what criminals as a whole are losing in that area. However, when the criminals in a given area are more likely to belong to a crime syndicate, their activities are restrained by organized crime leaders who have to take wider repercussions into account.

In other words, the monopolistic firm has incentives to produce less than competitive firms would have produced in the same industry, just as with legal economic activity. In this case, that means producing less crime. When there is strong organized crime control of a given neighborhood, even independent criminals operating in that neighborhood have to take into account whether some of the things that they would do otherwise might displease organized crime leaders and bring retribution.** In some cases, independent criminals may have to split their earnings with the syndicate for permission to operate, thereby reducing the rewards of crime and the incentives for being an independent career criminal.

One of the more dramatic examples of the restraining effects of a crime syndicate occurred in New York City in the 1930s, when crusading federal

---

* As with a conventional legal business, a crime syndicate will not produce beyond the point where the incremental gain in revenue is exceeded by the incremental cost. In this case, the incremental costs include the loss of revenue when there is increased law enforcement activity in response to a killing of an innocent civilian, as compared to the public's lesser concern when mobsters kill each other.
** Many years ago, I lived in a New York neighborhood where organized crime leaders lived. That neighborhood was so safe that, when my wife happened to be awake in the middle of the night while I was asleep, she did not hesitate to walk several blocks to an all-night newsstand to buy a morning paper. The fact that a newsstand was open in the middle of the night suggests that many other people in that neighborhood also felt safe going there at that time.

prosecutor Thomas E. Dewey was cracking down dramatically on organized crime, costing the crime syndicates considerable money and sending many of their members to prison. Crime boss Dutch Schultz thought that Dewey should be killed but other crime syndicate leaders decided that this would provoke too much public outrage— and consequently increased law enforcement activity that would discourage patrons of their prostitution, gambling, and other illegal activities, further reducing incomes from these enterprises. When Dutch Schultz announced that he was going to kill Dewey anyway, the syndicate had Schultz assassinated instead. They were well aware that the killing of a mobster would provoke far less public reaction than the assassination of a popular law enforcement official.

Decades later, there was a report of a desire of some crime leaders to assassinate Rudolph Giuliani when he was a federal prosecutor who sent many mobsters to prison in the 1980s. But, if so, no one repeated the mistake of Dutch Schultz. As the *New York Times* reported:

> For one thing, assassinating a prosecutor would go against decades of tradition. American Mafia leaders have generally treated their organizations as businesses primarily concerned with making money. Killing law enforcement officials, in this view, would only draw unwanted scrutiny.[16]

The same reasoning that would lead us to prefer competitive producers, when what is being produced is what people want, would lead us to prefer monopolistic producers— organized crime— when what is being produced is an activity that most people do not want. Ideally, we would prefer that no crime at all be produced but, since the ideal is seldom realized, a more realistic goal is the optimum quantity of crime. Both law enforcement and organized crime tend to reduce the total amount of crime. Even if it were possible to reduce all crime to zero by providing vastly more resources to law enforcement agencies, that would not necessarily be economically optimal. While most citizens would probably welcome more government expenditures on crime control if that in fact reduced felonies, no one would be likely to be willing to spend half the country's income— that is, reduce the standard of living in half— to prevent occasional shoplifting.

THE ECONOMICS OF
DISCRIMINATION

Bias and prejudice are attitudes. The practical question is how and to what extent such attitudes are translated into acts of discrimination. But before addressing that question, we must first be clear as to what we mean by the word "discrimination."

Policies of treating members of particular groups less favorably than similar members of other groups are usually called "discrimination" when practiced by the group with dominant political power and "reverse discrimination" or "affirmative action" when practiced *against* members of the group with dominant political power. Discrimination may also be practiced by private employers, landlords, or institutions. However, if words are to have any fixed meanings— without which discussions are fruitless— the term cannot be extended to all situations in which some groups turn out to have less favorable outcomes than others.

While biases and prejudices are conditions in people's minds, discrimination is an overt act taking place outside their minds in the real world. Nor is there necessarily a one-to-one correlation between the two, as so often assumed by those who make the fight against "racism" or "sexism" their number one priority or by those who claim that opponents of affirmative action must be assuming that prejudice and bias have been eradicated.

It is not only theoretically possible to have more discrimination where there is less bias or prejudice, and less discrimination where there is more bias and prejudice, this has in fact happened in more than one country. The degree to which subjective attitudes are translated into overt acts of discrimination depends crucially on the *costs* of doing so. Where those costs are very high, even very prejudiced or biased people may engage in little or no discrimination. The first black football player signed by the Washington Redskins in the 1960s was hired by a man reputed, among sports writers who knew him, to be deeply racist. Yet he broke a long tradition of all-white football teams in Washington by hiring a star wide receiver who was black—at a time when the Redskins' offensive game was very ineffective.

There is no inherent contradiction in a racist breaking the color line to hire blacks. Nor is there any inherent contradiction when someone who is not a racist supports racial discrimination. In each case, the respective costs they face when making their decisions must be taken into account, along with their predispositions, in any causal analysis. During the last years of the Jim Crow era in the South, there were stories of Southerners like Arkansas' Senator J. William Fulbright who voted against their consciences to continue racial segregation, because to do otherwise would be to jeopardize their political careers. Costs can matter more than personal predispositions to either racists or non-racists. In other words, the costs to decision-makers can lead to actions either more adverse or less adverse than the individual's own beliefs and feelings. In short, the costs of translating subjective attitudes, such as bias or prejudice, into overt acts of discrimination cannot be overlooked when seeking to explain why discrimination is often so much greater in some situations than in others. Different situations have different costs.

VARIATIONS IN COSTS

Where the costs of discrimination are low or non-existent for those making hiring and promotions decisions, then discrimination can become extensive, not only in terms of decisions not to hire or promote members of particular groups, but also in terms of extending such discrimination to a wider range of groups by a wider range of employers. At one time, there were said to be American railroads in which Catholics could rise only so high and others in which this was true of Protestants. In the early twentieth century, there was a time when not a single Ivy League college or university had a single Jew among its tenured faculty, despite a large number of Jewish intellectuals and scholars available.[1] This was common in both American and European universities before World War II. Nor was a black allowed in the Marine Corps, at even the lowliest rank, when World War II began. In other parts of the world as well, there has been similarly severe discrimination, sometimes even broader in its scope.

While many discussions of discrimination ignore the *cost* of discrimination to those doing the discriminating, on the most elementary economic principle that more is demanded at a lower price than at a higher price, we should expect to see the severity of discrimination vary with the cost to the discriminator. That is in fact what we find in country after country and in era after era— but only if we look at evidence.

Employment

In Poland between the two World Wars, an absolute majority of all the physicians in private practice were from the Jewish minority, which was only 10 percent of the population.[2] Yet the Polish government did not hire Jewish physicians, though many other Poles obviously became patients of Jewish physicians in the private sector, or else so many Jewish doctors could not have made a living. What was the difference between the public sector and the private sector in this regard?

In both sectors, there were both financial and medical costs to refusing to use Jewish physicians. To staff a government hospital with all-Gentile physicians, in a country where so many of the physicians were Jews, meant either having to pay more to attract a disproportionate share of the available Gentile physicians or accepting lesser-qualified physicians than some of those available from the Jewish community. In either case, financial or medical costs were entailed, if not both. However, in the case of those who made decisions within the Polish government, there was no cost at all to be paid by them. Financial costs were paid by the taxpayers and the human costs were paid by patients in government hospitals, subject to lower quality medical treatment than was available in the society at the time. Neither of these costs was a deterrent to discrimination by government officials.

In the private sector, however, both kinds of costs were paid by sick people. Concern for one's own personal health, especially in an emergency situation or when confronted with a potentially crippling or fatal disease, could easily overcome whatever anti-Jewish attitudes one might have. Given the respective incentives in the government and in the private sector, the different levels of discrimination against Jews is very much what one might expect, on the basis of the most elementary economic principles.

Poland provides examples of another phenomenon— more discrimination where there was less hostility and less discrimination where there was more hostility. Anti-Jewish feelings tended to be stronger in eastern Poland than in western Poland. Yet Jewish artisans were more prevalent in eastern Poland, just as black artisans once had better job opportunities in the American South, where racism was most rampant. In both cases, organized labor affected the cost of discrimination.

Guilds were stronger in western Poland than in eastern Poland and American labor unions were stronger in the North than in the South during the eras under discussion. To the extent that organized labor succeeds in raising pay levels above where they would be under supply and demand in a free market, they provide incentives for employers to hire fewer workers because labor is now more costly, both absolutely and relative to the cost of capital that may be substituted for labor. At the same time, wage rates raised above the level that would prevail under supply and demand attract more workers who apply for jobs that have higher pay. The net effect is that organized labor tends to create a chronic surplus of job applicants. Given that surplus, the cost to the employer of turning away qualified applicants from the "wrong" group is less than it would be if the employer had to be concerned about finding enough similarly qualified replacements for those who have been arbitrarily rejected.

Even in the absence of discrimination by guilds or unions themselves— and there was plenty of that— it would still be cheaper for employers to discriminate on their own than would be the case in a free market. Given this situation, it is not so puzzling that Jewish artisans found it easier to practice their skills in that part of Poland that was more hostile to Jews and that black American artisans found it easier to practice their skills in the Jim Crow South than in the more unionized North. Differences in costs of discrimination outweighed differences in negative predispositions.

The same pattern can be seen in employment statistics over time. Both in the American South during the Jim Crow era and in South Africa under white rule, blacks were a much higher percentage of railroad employees in the early twentieth century than they were at mid-century. In both countries, labor markets were more freely competitive in the earlier era and more controlled in the later era— and in both countries it would be hard to claim that there was less racism in the earlier era.

Not only labor unions, but also government regulation, can reduce the cost of discrimination. Where a public utility with a monopoly has its prices set by a government regulatory agency on the basis of its costs, it has little or no incentive to keep those costs down to a level that would be necessary for its survival in a competitive market. Costs of discrimination, like other costs, can simply be passed on to the customers of a regulated monopoly. When the American telephone industry was a regulated monopoly, blacks were seldom hired for even such routine jobs as telephone operators before the civil rights laws were enacted by the federal government in the 1960s and by some state governments earlier. As of 1930, for example, there were only 331 black women in the entire country working as telephone operators, out of more than 230,000 women in that occupation.[3] As late as 1950 black women were only one percent of all the women working for phone companies.

Because each local telephone company was a monopoly within its own territory, it could pass on higher costs to everyone who used telephones. Had it not discriminated, its costs would have been lower and its monopoly profits could theoretically have been higher but, because its profit rates were in fact constrained by government regulation, the phone company would never have seen that additional money anyway. Instead, its officials could indulge their racial preferences with no net loss of profits. Meanwhile, blacks were beginning to star on Broadway as early as the 1920s, in an industry with cut-throat competition, where large profits and devastating losses were both common.

The cost of refusing to hire black entertainers who could fill a theater was just too high for this industry to follow the same practices as the telephone industry. The one-to-one correspondence between racism and discrimination that is often assumed cannot explain such differences between sectors of the same economy at the same time. Even less can it explain the persistence of such differences between industries over time, when there is a complete turnover of decision-makers throughout the economy. Even after a given set of decision-makers and their individual predispositions have passed from the scene, the persistence of the same set of incentives tends to reproduce the same end results with a new set of decision-makers in the same respective industries, whatever the individual predispositions of these new decision-makers.

Given the influence of the costs of discrimination on the amount of actual discrimination, it is also possible to understand another otherwise puzzling phenomenon— the especially strong reversals of racial policies in sectors of the economy least subject to the pressures of the competitive marketplace. These include the government itself, government-regulated public utilities, and non-profit organizations, such as academic institutions, hospitals, and foundations. Colleges and universities that had never hired blacks for their faculties in pre-World War II America led the way when affirmative action in the 1960s and 1970s meant preferential hiring and promotion of black professors and preferential admissions of black students. There was also a very similar sharp reversal of hiring policies in the telephone industry, among others, at the same time. Between 1966 and 1968, not only did the hiring of blacks increase by more than 10,000 workers, blacks constituted one third of all new employees.[4] As of 2007, A.T.& T. was ranked number one in the country in promoting "diversity" or "multicultural business opportunities" among its suppliers.[5]

Sudden radical changes from especially discriminatory policies against a particular group to preferential policies toward the very same group are hard to explain by predispositions, since many of the same decision-makers were in control during the transition period. It is much easier to understand in terms of the incentives and constraints of the circumstances in which they operated. More specifically, neither discrimination nor "reverse discrimination" cost them as much as either policy would have cost decision-makers in those sectors of the economy where institutional survival depends on keeping costs within narrow limits, in order to meet competition in a free market. Once the political and social climate changed, government, government-regulated utilities, and non-profit organizations could change most quickly with the least cost to themselves.

Baseball

Because major league baseball has operated as a cartel exempted from anti-trust laws, it too had low costs of discrimination and was able to keep black players out— so long as all teams did so. But this situation changed in 1947, when the Brooklyn Dodgers hired Jackie Robinson as the first black major league ballplayer.

Because there was competition *within* the cartel among its various teams, once the color barrier was broken by just one team hiring just one black player, the cost to other teams of keeping out other black players rose sharply. The net result was that, in a matter of a relatively few years, large numbers of black players flooded into the major leagues. For a period of seven consecutive years, no white man won the National League's Most Valuable Player award. Had other teams *not* followed the lead of the Dodgers in hiring black players, all these MVP stars would have become Dodgers, giving Brooklyn a virtual monopoly of National League pennants and perhaps of world championships.

This cost was obviously much too high for the competing teams to pay for continuing racial exclusion in major league baseball. Their racial attitudes may not have changed, but the cost of translating those attitudes into discriminatory exclusions had changed drastically.

COMPETITIVE AND NON-COMPETITIVE MARKETS

The power of the free market was perhaps best demonstrated in white-ruled South Africa during the era of apartheid. Here we need not wonder about racial predispositions or about the fact that the vast majority of employers in industry, agriculture, and government were white. Yet, even in a country which became a worldwide symbol of racial oppression, white employers in competitive industries violated official government policy on a massive scale by hiring more black workers and in higher positions than the law allowed. There is no compelling evidence that these particular white employers had different racial predispositions than the white people who administered the apartheid government. What they had were very different costs of discrimination.

While government agencies and government-regulated railroads, for example, could maintain apartheid policies at virtually zero cost to themselves, it was a wholly different economic situation for people spending their own money. Home-building was a typical example:

> To build a house in Johannesburg meant either waiting for months for a white, expensive, legal building gang, or finding a black gang, perhaps with a white nominally in charge in case an official came inquiring. Most customers opted for the quicker, cheaper service.[6]

Such practices became so widespread in South Africa that the white-run apartheid government cracked down in the 1970s, fining hundreds of building construction companies.[7] Moreover, this was by no means the only industry that hired more blacks than they were allowed to by law. In the clothing industry, no blacks at all were allowed to work in certain categories of jobs, under the apartheid laws. Yet, as of 1970, blacks were an absolute majority of the workers in those job categories.[8] There were also residential areas in South Africa set aside by law for whites only— and yet there were not only many non-whites living in these areas (including black American economist Walter Williams), at least one such area had an absolute majority of non-whites. Competition in a free market simply made discrimination too expensive for many, even though violating the apartheid laws also cost money.*

The expansion of black residential areas into white residential areas has been even more common in the United States. However, this more or less continuous expansion of black ghettoes has been in contrast to the history of the original ghettoes— those of the Jews in Europe in centuries past. Jewish ghettoes in Europe in centuries past tended to become more

---

* One of the reasons for the weakening of apartheid, even before the end of white-minority rule in South Africa, was that many of the white Afrikaners, the principal supporters of apartheid, rose over the years into the ranks of business owners and now had to pay the costs of discrimination, which before had been paid by British and Jewish business owners. Faced with these costs, many Afrikaners began to lose their enthusiasm for apartheid and some even spoke out against it, despite the authoritarian and repressive South African government.

overcrowded as the Jewish population grew, though there were particular times and places where Jews were allowed to expand an existing ghetto or to set up a new ghetto to accommodate their growing populations. Here again, the difference has been in the economic costs of discrimination.

Black ghettoes have expanded through the marketplace because of the costs of excluding black renters and home buyers. This is not to say that there was no resistance by whites. Often there was organized, bitter, and even violent resistance. The key question, however, is: What was the end result? The usual end result was that black ghettoes expanded in cities across the country. Moreover, where this expansion was stopped by laws or government policies, by restrictive covenants, or by violence or the threat of violence, that reinforces the point that the costs of discrimination were too great for the expansion of black ghettoes to be stopped in the marketplace. By and large, black ghettoes continued expanding with the growth of the black population.

The boundaries of Jewish ghettoes in Europe were not determined by the marketplace but were established by the dictates of those with political power. Only when these political leaders found it expedient did these boundaries expand. That is why Jewish ghettoes tended simply to become more crowded with the passage of time and population growth. There was usually no cost to political leaders for discriminating against Jews. In particular circumstances— when there was a war on, for example, and the rulers needed the help of Jewish financiers— various proscriptions might be eased and more ghettoes allowed to be founded to relieve overcrowding. During the Thirty Years War (1618–1648), for example, new Jewish communities were permitted to be established and new occupations and markets opened up to Jews, while a synagogue was permitted to be built in Vienna for the first time in more than 200 years and a synagogue was permitted in Denmark for the first time ever.[9]

In short, costs of discrimination are not only a fact of life, they are a potent force in actual decision-making, even in countries with strong racial, ethnic, or religious predispositions. How much of a force depends on the economic incentives and constraints in particular sectors. What this means is that not only is the assumed one-to-one correlation between racism and discrimination false, but also that those who wish to reduce discrimination need to pay attention to the economic conditions which make it more expensive or less expensive for decision-makers to discriminate. Too often, however, those opposed to discrimination are also opposed to free competitive markets that make discrimination more costly. They do not think beyond stage one.

Even a given market— such as the market for housing or the labor market, for example— can have more discrimination or less discrimination according to whether its prices are determined by supply and demand or are imposed by external agencies such as government, labor unions, or a cartel. For example, when a landlord refuses to rent an apartment to people from the "wrong" group, that can mean leaving the apartment vacant longer. Clearly, that represents a loss of rent— if this is a free market. However, if there is rent control, with a surplus of applicants, then such discrimination may cost the landlord nothing.

Similar principles apply in job markets. An employer who refuses to hire qualified individuals from the "wrong" groups risks leaving his jobs unfilled longer in a free market. This means that he must either leave some work undone and some orders unfilled or else pay overtime to existing employees to get it done, losing money either way. However, in a market where wages are set artificially above the level that would exist through supply and demand, the resulting surplus of applicants can mean that discrimination costs the employer nothing. Whether these artificially higher wages are set by a labor union or by a minimum wage law does not change the principle.

In all these cases, the crucial factors in the cost of discrimination have been the presence or absence of competition and whether those making the decisions have been spending their own money or someone else's money. When one's own money is at stake, groups hostile to each other may not only fail to discriminate, they may in fact seek each other out. A landmark study of Polish immigrants and Jewish immigrants from Poland in early twentieth-century Chicago reported:

> . . . the Poles and the Jews in Chicago . . . have a profound feeling of disrespect and contempt for each other, bred by their contiguity and by historical friction in the pale; but they trade with each other on

Milwaukee Avenue and on Maxwell Street. A study of numerous cases shows that not only do many Jews open their businesses on Milwaukee Avenue and Division Street because they know that the Poles are the predominant population in these neighborhoods, but the Poles come from all over the city to trade on Maxwell Street because they know that there they can find the familiar street-stands owned by Jews.[10]

"INCOME DISTRIBUTION"

Variations in income can be viewed empirically, on the one hand, or in terms of moral judgments, on the other. Most of the contemporary intelligentsia do both. But, in order to assess the validity of the conclusions they reach, it is advisable to assess the empirical issues and the moral issues separately, rather than attempt to go back and forth between the two, with any expectation of rational coherence.

Empirical Evidence

Given the vast amounts of statistical data on income available from the Census Bureau, the Internal Revenue Service and innumerable research institutes and projects, one might imagine that the bare facts about variations in income would be fairly well known by informed people, even though they might have differing opinions as to the desirability of those particular variations. In reality, however, the most fundamental facts are in dispute, and variations in what are claimed to be facts seem to be at least as great as variations in incomes. Both the magnitude of income variations and the trends in these variations over time are seen in radically different terms by those with different visions as regards the current reality, even aside from what different people may regard as desirable for the future.

Perhaps the most fertile source of misunderstandings about incomes has been the widespread practice of confusing statistical categories with flesh-and-blood human beings. Many statements have been made in the media and in academia, claiming that the rich are gaining not only larger incomes but a growing share of all incomes, widening the income gap between people at the top and those at the bottom. Almost invariably these statements are based on confusing what has been happening over time in statistical categories with what has been happening over time with actual flesh-and-blood people.

A *New York Times* editorial, for example, declared that "the gap between rich and poor has widened in America."[1] Similar conclusions appeared in a 2007 *Newsweek* article which referred to this era as "a time when the gap is growing between the rich and the poor— and the superrich and the merely rich,"[2] a theme common in such other well-known media outlets as the *Washington Post* and innumerable television programs. "The rich have seen far greater income gains than have the poor," according to *Washington Post* columnist Eugene Robinson.[3] A writer in the *Los Angeles Times* likewise declared, "the gap between rich and poor is growing."[4] According to Professor Andrew Hacker in his book *Money*: "While all segments of the population enjoyed an increase in income, the top fifth did twenty-four times better than the bottom fifth. And measured by their shares of the aggregate, not just the bottom fifth but the three above it all ended up losing ground."[5] E.J. Dionne of the *Washington Post* described "the wealthy" as "people who have made almost all the income gains in recent years" and added that they are "undertaxed."[6]

Although such discussions have been phrased in terms of *people*, the actual empirical evidence cited has been about what has been happening over time to *statistical categories*— and that turns out to be the direct opposite of what has happened over time to flesh-and-blood human beings, most of whom *move* from one income category to another over time. In terms of statistical categories, it is indeed true that both the amount of income and the proportion of all income received by those in the top 20 percent bracket have risen over the years, widening the gap between the top and bottom quintiles.[7] But U.S. Treasury Department data, following specific individuals over time from their tax returns to the Internal Revenue Service, show that in terms of *people*, the incomes of those particular taxpayers who were in the bottom 20 percent in income in 1996 rose 91 percent by 2005, while the incomes of those particular taxpayers who were in the top 20 percent in 1996 rose by only 10 percent by 2005— and the incomes of those in the top 5 percent and top one percent actually declined.[8]

While it might seem as if both these radically different sets of statistics cannot be true at the same time, what makes them mutually compatible is that flesh-and-blood human beings *move* from one statistical category to another over time. When those taxpayers who were initially in the lowest income bracket had their incomes nearly double in a decade, that moved many of them up and out of the bottom quintile— and when those in the top one percent had their incomes cut by about one-fourth, that may well have dropped many, if not most, of them out of the top one percent. Internal Revenue Service data can follow particular individuals over time from their tax returns, which have individual Social Security numbers as identification, while data from the Census Bureau and most other sources follow what happens to statistical categories over time, even though it is not the same individuals in the same categories over the years.

Many of the same kinds of data used to claim a widening income gap between "the rich" and "the poor"— names usually given to people with different incomes, rather than different wealth, as the terms rich and poor might seem to imply— have led many in the media to likewise claim a growing income gap between the "super-rich" and the "merely rich." Under the headline "Richest Are Leaving Even the Rich Far Behind," a front-page *New York Times* article dubbed the "top 0.1 percent of income earners— the top one-thousandth" as the "hyper-rich" and declared that they "have even left behind people making hundreds of thousands of dollars a year."[9] Once again, the confusion is between what is happening to statistical categories over time and what is happening to flesh-and-blood individuals over time, as they move from one statistical category to another.

Despite the rise in the income of the top 0.1 percent of taxpayers as a statistical category, both absolutely and relative to the incomes in other categories, as flesh-and-blood human beings those individuals who were in that category initially had their incomes actually *fall* by a whopping 50 percent between 1996 and 2005.[10] It is hardly surprising when people whose incomes are cut in half drop out of the top 0.1 percent. What happens to the income of the category over time is not the same as what happens to the people who were in that category at any given point in time. But many among the intelligentsia are ready to seize upon any numbers that seem to fit their vision.[11]

It is much the same story with data on the top four hundred income earners in the country. As with other data, data on those who were among the top 400 income earners from 1992 to 2000 were *not* data on the same 400 people throughout the span of time covered. During that span, there were thousands of people in the top 400— which is to say, turnover was high. Fewer than one-fourth of all the people in that category during that span of years were in that category more than one year, and fewer than 13 percent were in that category more than two years.[12]

Behind many of those numbers and the accompanying alarmist rhetoric is a very mundane fact: Most people begin their working careers at the bottom, earning entry-level salaries. Over time, as they acquire more skills and experience, their rising productivity leads to rising pay, putting them in successively higher income brackets. These are not rare, Horatio Alger stories. These are common patterns among millions of people in the United States and in some other countries. More than three-quarters of those working Americans whose incomes were in the bottom 20 percent in 1975 were also in the *top* 40 percent of income earners at some point by 1991. Only 5 percent of those who were initially in the bottom quintile were still there in 1991, while 29 percent of those who were initially at the bottom quintile had risen to the top quintile.[13] Yet verbal virtuosity has transformed a transient cohort in a given statistical category into an enduring class called "the poor."

Just as most Americans in statistical categories identified as "the poor" are not an enduring class there, studies in Britain, Canada, New Zealand and Greece show similar patterns of transience among those in low-income brackets at a given time.[14] Just over half of all Americans earning at or near the minimum wage are from 16 to 24 years of age[15]— and of course these individuals cannot *remain* from 16 to 24 years of age indefinitely, though that age category can of course continue indefinitely, providing many intellectuals with data to fit their preconceptions.

Only by focussing on the income brackets, instead of the actual people moving between those brackets, have the intelligentsia been able to verbally create a "problem" for which a "solution" is necessary. They have created a powerful vision of "classes" with "disparities" and "inequities" in income, caused by "barriers" created by "society." But the routine rise of millions of people out of the lowest quintile over time makes a mockery of the "barriers" assumed by many, if not most, of the intelligentsia.

Far from using their intellectual skills to clarify the distinction between statistical categories and flesh-and-blood human beings, the intelligentsia have instead used their verbal virtuosity to equate the changing numerical relationship between statistical categories over time with a changing relationship between flesh-and-blood human beings ("the rich" and "the poor") over time, even though data that follow individual income-earners over time tell a diametrically opposite story from that of data which follow the statistical categories which people are moving into and out of over time.

The confusion between statistical categories and flesh-and-blood human beings is compounded when there is confusion between income and wealth. People called "rich" or "super-rich" have been given these titles by the media on the basis of income, not wealth, even though being rich means having more wealth. According to the Treasury Department: "Among those with the very highest incomes in 1996— the top 1/100 of 1 percent— only 25 percent remained in this group in 2005."[16] If these were genuinely super-rich people, it is hard to explain why three-quarters of them are no longer in that category a decade later.

A related, but somewhat different, confusion between statistical categories and human beings has led to many claims in the media and in academia that Americans' incomes have stagnated or grown only very slowly over the years. For example, over the entire period from 1967 to 2005, median real household income— that is, money income adjusted for inflation— rose by 31 percent.[17] For selected periods within that long span, real household incomes rose even less, and those selected periods have often been cited by the intelligentsia to claim that income and living standards have "stagnated."[18] Meanwhile, real per capita income rose by 122 percent over that same span, from 1967 to 2005.[19] When a more than doubling of real income per person is called "stagnation," that is one of the many feats of verbal virtuosity.

The reason for the large discrepancy between growth rate trends in household income and growth rate trends in individual income is very straightforward: The number of persons per household has been declining over the years. As early as 1966, the U.S. Bureau of the Census reported that the number of households was increasing faster than the number of people and concluded: "The main reason for the more rapid rate of household formation is the increased tendency, particularly among unrelated individuals, to maintain their own homes or apartments rather than live with relatives or move into existing households as roomers, lodgers, and so forth."[20] Increasing individual incomes made this possible. As late as 1970, 21 percent of American households contained 5 or more people. But, by 2007, only 10 percent did.[21]

Despite such obvious and mundane facts, household or family income statistics continue to be widely cited in the media and in academia— and per capita income statistics widely ignored, despite the fact that households are variable in size, while per capita income always refers to the income of one person. However, the statistics that the intelligentsia keep citing are much more consistent with their vision of America than the statistics they keep ignoring.

Just as household statistics understate the rise in the American standard of living over time, they *overstate* the degree of income inequality, since lower income households tend to have fewer people than upper income households. While there are 39 million people in households whose incomes are in the bottom 20 percent, there are 64 million people in households whose incomes are in the top 20 percent.[22] There is nothing mysterious about this either, given the number of low-income mothers living with fatherless children, and low-income lodgers in single room occupancy hotels or rooming houses, for example.

Even if every *person* in the entire country received exactly the same income, there would still be a significant "disparity" between the average incomes received by *households* containing 64 million people compared to the average incomes received by households containing 39 million people. That disparity would be even greater if only the incomes of working adults were counted, even if those working adults all had identical incomes. There are more adult heads of household working full-time and year-around in even the top *five* percent of households than in the bottom *twenty* percent of households.[23]

Many income statistics are misleading in another sense, when they leave out the income received in kind— such as food stamps and subsidized housing— which often exceeds the value of the cash income received by people in the lower-income brackets. In 2001, for example, transfers in cash or in kind accounted for more than three-quarters of the total economic resources at the disposal of people in the bottom 20 percent.[24] In other words, the standard of living of people in the bottom quintile is about three times what the income statistics would indicate. As we shall see, their personal possessions are far more consistent with this fact than with the vision of the intelligentsia.

Moral Considerations

The difference between statistical categories and actual people affects moral, as well as empirical, issues. However concerned we might be about the economic fate of flesh-and-blood human beings, that is very different from being alarmed or outraged about the fate of statistical categories. Michael Harrington's best-selling book *The Other America*, for example, dramatized income statistics, lamenting "the anguish" of the poor in America, tens of millions "maimed in body and spirit" constituting "the shame of the other America," people "caught in a vicious circle" and suffering a "warping of the will and spirit that is a consequence of being poor."[25] But investing statistical data with moral angst does nothing to establish a connection between a transient cohort in statistical categories and an enduring class conjured up through verbal virtuosity.

There was a time when such rhetoric might have made some sense in the United States, and there are other countries where it may still make sense today. But most of those Americans now living below the official poverty line have possessions once considered part of a middle class standard of living, just a generation or so ago. As of 2001, three-quarters of Americans with incomes below the official poverty level had air-conditioning (which only one-third of Americans had in 1971), 97 percent had color television (which fewer than half of Americans had in 1971), 73 percent owned a microwave oven (which fewer than one percent of Americans had in 1971) and 98 percent of "the poor" had either a videocassette recorder or a DVD player (which no one had in 1971). In addition, 72 percent of "the poor" owned a motor vehicle.[26] None of this has done much to change the rhetoric of the intelligentsia, however much it may reflect changes in the standard of living of Americans in the lower income brackets.

Typical of the mindset of many intellectuals was a book by Andrew Hacker which referred to the trillions of dollars that become "the personal income of Americans" each year, and said: "Just how this money is apportioned will be the subject of this book."[27] But this money is not *apportioned* at all. It becomes income through an entirely different process.

The very phrase "income distribution" is tendentious. It starts the economic story in the middle, with a body of income or wealth existing *somehow*, leaving only the question as to how that income or wealth is to be distributed or "apportioned" as Professor Hacker puts it. In the real world, the situation is quite different. In a market economy, most people receive income as a result of what they produce, supplying other people with some goods or services that those people want, even if that service is only labor. Each recipient of these goods and services pays according to the value which that particular recipient puts on what is received, choosing among alternative suppliers to find the best combination of price and quality— both as judged by the individual who is paying.

This mundane, utilitarian process is quite different from the vision of "income distribution" projected by those among the intelligentsia who invest that vision with moral angst. If there really were some pre-existing body of income or wealth, produced *somehow*— manna from heaven, as it were— then there would of course be a moral question as to how large a share each member of society should receive. But wealth is *produced*. It does not just exist *somehow*. Where millions of individuals are paid according to how much what they produce is valued subjectively by millions of other individuals, it is not at all clear on what basis third parties could say that some goods or services are over-valued or under-valued, that cooking should be valued more or carpentry should be valued less, for example, much less that not working at all is not rewarded enough compared to working.

Nor is there anything mysterious in the fact that at least a thousand times as many people would pay to hear Pavarotti sing as would pay to hear the average person sing.

Where people are paid for what they produce, one person's output can easily be worth a thousand times as much as another person's output to those who are the recipients of that output— if only because thousands more people are interested in receiving some products or services than are interested in receiving other products and services— or even the same product or service from someone else. For example, when Tiger Woods left the golf tournament circuit for several months because of an injury, television audiences for the final round of major tournaments declined by varying amounts, ranging up to 61 percent.[28] That can translate into millions of dollars' worth of advertising revenue, based on the number of television viewers.

The fact that one person's productivity may be a thousand times as valuable as another's does not mean that one person's *merit* is a thousand times as great as another's. Productivity and merit are very different things, though the two things are often confused with one another. An individual's productivity is affected by innumerable factors besides the efforts of that individual— being born with a great voice being an obvious example. Being raised in a particular home with a particular set of values and behavior patterns, living in a particular geographic or social environment, merely being born with a normal brain, rather than a brain damaged during the birth process, can make enormous differences in what a given person is capable of producing.

Moreover, third parties are in no position to second-guess the felt value of someone's productivity to someone else, and it is hard even to conceive how someone's merit could be judged accurately by another human being who "never walked in his shoes." An individual raised in terrible home conditions or terrible social conditions may be laudable for having become an average, decent citizen with average work skills as a shoe repairer, while someone raised from birth with every advantage that money and social position can confer may be no more laudable for becoming an eminent brain surgeon. But that is wholly different from saying that repairing shoes is just as valuable to others as being able to repair maladies of the brain.

To say that merit may be the same is not to say that productivity is the same. Nor can we logically or morally ignore the discrepancy in the relative urgency of those who want their shoes repaired versus those in need of brain surgery. In other words, it is not a question of simply weighing the interest of one income recipient versus the interest of another income recipient, while ignoring the vastly larger number of other people whose well-being depends on what these individuals produce.

If one prefers an economy in which income is divorced from productivity, then the case for that kind of economy needs to be made explicitly. But that is wholly different from making such a large and fundamental change on the basis of verbal virtuosity in depicting the issue as being simply that of one set of "income distribution" statistics today versus an alternative set of "income distribution" statistics tomorrow.

As for the moral question, whether any given set of human beings can be held responsible for disparities in other people's productivity— and consequent earnings— depends on how much control any given set of human beings has maintained, or can possibly maintain, over the innumerable factors which have led to existing differences in productivity. Since *no* human being has control over the past, and many deeply ingrained cultural differences are a legacy of the past, limitations on what can be done in the present are limitations on what can be regarded as moral failings by society. Still less can statistical differences between groups be automatically attributed to "barriers" created by society. Barriers exist in the real world, just as cancer exists. But acknowledging that does not mean that all deaths— or even most deaths— can be automatically attributed to cancer or that most economic differences can be automatically attributed to "barriers," however fashionable this latter non sequitur may be in some quarters.

Within the constraints of circumstances, there are things which can be done to make opportunities more widely available, or to help those whose handicaps are too severe to expect them to utilize whatever opportunities are already available. In fact, much has already been done and is still being done in a country like the United States, which leads the world in philanthropy, not only in terms of money but also in terms of individuals donating their time to philanthropic endeavors. But only by assuming that everything that has not been done could have been done, disregarding costs and risks, can individuals or societies be blamed because the real world does not match some vision of an ideal society. Nor can the discrepancy between the real and the vision of the ideal be automatically blamed on the existing reality, as if visionaries cannot possibly be mistaken.

MINIMUM WAGE LAWS

Minimum wage laws make it illegal to pay less than the government-specified price for labor. By the simplest and most basic economics, a price artificially raised tends to cause more to be supplied and less to be demanded than when prices are left to be determined by supply and demand in a free market. The result is a surplus, whether the price that is set artificially high is that of farm produce or labor.

Making it illegal to pay less than a given amount does not make a worker's productivity worth that amount— and, if it is not, that worker is unlikely to be employed. Yet minimum wage laws are almost always discussed politically in terms of the benefits they confer on workers receiving those wages. Unfortunately, the real minimum wage is always zero, regardless of the laws, and that is the wage that many workers receive in the wake of the creation or escalation of a government-mandated minimum wage, because they either lose their jobs or fail to find jobs when they enter the labor force. The logic is plain and an examination of the empirical evidence from various countries around the world tends to back up that logic, as we shall see.

Unemployment

Because the government does not hire surplus labor the way it buys surplus agricultural output, a labor surplus takes the form of unemployment, which tends to be higher under minimum wage laws than in a free market.

Unemployed workers are not surplus in the sense of being useless or in the sense that there is no work around that needs doing. Most of these workers are perfectly capable of producing goods and services, even if not to the same extent as more skilled or more experienced workers. The unemployed are made idle by wage rates artificially set above the level of their productivity. Those who are idled in their youth are of course delayed in acquiring the job skills and experience which could make them more productive— and therefore higher earners— later on. That is, they not only lose the low pay that they could have earned in an entry-level job, they lose the higher pay that they could have moved on to and begun earning after gaining experience in entry-level jobs. Younger workers are disproportionately represented among people with low rates of pay. Only about two percent of American workers over the age of 24 earn the minimum wage.[1]

Although most modern industrial societies have minimum wage laws, not all do. Switzerland and Hong Kong have been among the exceptions— and both have had very low unemployment rates. In 2003, *The Economist* magazine reported: "Switzerland's unemployment neared a five-year high of 3.9% in February."[2] Back in 1991, when Hong Kong was still a British colony, its unemployment rate was below 2 percent.[3] Although Hong Kong still did not have a minimum wage law at the end of the twentieth century, in 1997 new amendments to its labor law under China's rule mandated many new benefits for workers, to be paid for by their employers.[4] This imposed increase in labor costs was followed, predictably, by a higher unemployment rate that reached 7.3 percent in 2002[5]— not high by European standards but a multiple of what it had been for years. In 2003, Hong Kong's unemployment rate hit a new high— 8.3 percent.[6]

Higher costs for a given quantity and quality of labor tend to produce less employment, just as higher prices for other things tend to produce fewer sales. Moreover, higher costs in the form of mandated benefits have the same economic effect as higher costs in the form of minimum wage laws. The explicit minimum wage rate understates the labor costs imposed by European governments, which also mandate various employer contributions to pension plans and health benefits, among other things. Europe's unemployment rates shot up when such government-mandated benefits to be paid for by employers grew sharply during the 1980s and 1990s.[7] In Germany, such benefits accounted for half of the average labor cost per hour. By comparison, such benefits accounted for less than one-fourth the average labor costs per hour in Japan and the United States. Average hourly compensation of manufacturing employees in the European Union countries in general is higher than in the United States or Japan.[8] So is unemployment.

Comparisons of Canada with the United States show similar patterns. Over a five-year period, Canadian provinces had minimum wage rates that were a higher percentage of output per capita than in American states, and unemployment rates were correspondingly higher in Canada, as was the average duration of unemployment, while the Canadian rate of job creation lagged behind that in the United States. Over this five-year period, three Canadian provinces had unemployment rates in excess of 10 percent, with a high of 16.9 percent in Newfoundland, but none of the 50 American states averaged unemployment rates in double digits over that same five-year period.[9]

A belated recognition of the connection between minimum wage laws and unemployment by government officials has caused some countries to allow their real minimum wage levels to be eroded by inflation, avoiding the political risks of trying to repeal these laws explicitly,* when so many voters think of such laws as being beneficial to workers. These laws are in fact beneficial to those workers who continue to be employed— those who are on the inside looking out, but at the expense of the unemployed who are on the outside looking in.

Labor unions also benefit from minimum wage laws, and are among the strongest proponents of such laws, even though their own members typically make much more than the minimum wage rate. There is a reason for this. Just as most goods and services can be produced with either much labor and little capital or vice versa, so can most things be produced using varying proportions of low-skilled labor and high-skilled labor, depending on their relative costs. Thus experienced unionized workers are competing for employment against younger, inexperienced, and less skilled workers, whose pay is likely to be at or near the minimum wage. The higher the minimum wage goes, the more the unskilled and inexperienced workers are likely to be displaced by more experienced and higher skilled unionized workers. Just as businesses seek to have government impose tariffs on imported goods that compete with their products, so labor unions use minimum wage laws as tariffs to force up the price of non-union labor that competes with their members for jobs.

Among two million Americans earning no more than the minimum wage in the early twenty-first century, just over half were from 16 to 24 years of age— and 62 percent of them worked part time.[10] Yet political campaigns to increase the minimum wage often talk in terms of providing "a living wage" sufficient to support a family of four— such families as most

* In the United States, the minimum wage remained unchanged during the entire two terms of the Reagan administration in the 1980s. This meant that it declined in real terms, adjusted for inflation. See Bradley R. Schiller, *The Economics of Poverty and Discrimination*, tenth edition, pp. 108–109.

minimum wage workers do not have and would be ill-advised to have before they reach the point where they can feed and clothe their children. The average family income of a minimum wage worker is more than $44,000 a year— far more than can be earned by someone working at minimum wages. But 42 percent of minimum-wage workers live with parents or some other relative. Only 15 percent of minimum-wage workers are supporting themselves and a dependent,[11] the kind of person envisioned by those who advocate a "living wage."

Nevertheless, a number of American cities have passed "living wage" laws, which are essentially local minimum wage laws specifying a higher wage rate than the national minimum wage law. Their effects have been similar to the effects of national minimum wage laws in the United States and other countries— that is, the poorest people have been the ones who have most often lost jobs.[12]

The huge financial, political, emotional, and ideological investment of various groups in issues revolving around minimum wage laws means that dispassionate analysis is not always the norm. Moreover, the statistical complexities of separating out the effects of minimum wage rates on employment from all the other ever-changing variables which also affect employment mean that honest differences of opinion are possible. However, when all is said and done, most empirical studies indicate that minimum wage laws reduce employment in general, and especially the employment of younger, less skilled, and minority workers.[13]

A majority of professional economists surveyed in Britain, Germany, Canada, Switzerland, and the United States agreed that minimum wage laws increase unemployment among low-skilled workers. Economists in France and Austria did not. However, the majority among Canadian economists was 85 percent and among American economists was 90 percent.[14] Dozens of studies of the effects of minimum wages in the United States and dozens more studies of the effects of minimum wages in various countries in Europe, Latin America, the Caribbean, Indonesia, Canada, Australia, and New Zealand were reviewed in 2006 by two economists at the National Bureau of Economic Research. They concluded that, despite the various approaches and methods used in these studies, this literature as a whole was one "largely solidifying the conventional view that minimum wages reduce employment among low-skilled workers."[15]

Those officially responsible for administering minimum wage laws, such as the U. S. Department of Labor and various local agencies, prefer to claim that these laws do not create unemployment. So do labor unions, which have a vested interest in such laws as protection for their own members' jobs. In South Africa, for example, *The Economist* reported:

> The main union body, the Congress of South African Trade Unions (Cosatu) says joblessness has nothing to do with labour laws. The problem, it says, is that businesses are not trying hard enough to create jobs.[16]

In Britain, the Low Pay Commission, which sets the minimum wage, has likewise resisted the idea that the wages it set were responsible for an unemployment rate of 17.3 percent among workers under the age of 25, at a time when the overall unemployment rate was 7.6 percent.[17]

Even though most studies show that unemployment tends to increase as minimum wages are imposed or increased, those few studies that seem to indicate otherwise have been hailed in some quarters as having "refuted" this "myth."[18] However, one common problem with some research on the employment effects of minimum wage laws is that surveys of employers before and after a minimum wage increase can survey only those particular businesses which survived in both periods. Given the high rates of business failures in many industries, the results for the surviving businesses may be completely different from the results for the industry as a whole.* Using such

---

* Imagine that an industry consists of ten firms, each hiring 1,000 workers before a minimum wage increase, for an industry total of 10,000 employees. If three of these firms go out of business between the first and the second surveys, and only one new firm enters the industry, then only the seven firms that were in existence both "before" and "after" can be surveyed and their results reported. With fewer firms, employment per firm may increase, even if employment in the industry as a whole decreases. If, for example, the seven surviving firms and the new firm all hire 1,100 employees each, this means that the industry as a whole will have 8,800 employees— fewer than before the minimum wage increase— and yet a study of the seven surviving firms would show a 10 percent *increase* in employment in the firms surveyed, rather than the 12 percent *decrease* for the industry as a whole. Since minimum wages can cause unemployment by (1) reducing employment among all the firms, (2) by pushing marginal firms into bankruptcy, or (3) discouraging the entry of replacement firms, reports based on surveying only survivors can create as false a conclusion as interviewing people who have played Russian roulette.

research methods, you could interview people who have played Russian roulette and "prove" from their experiences that it is a harmless activity, since those for whom it was not harmless are unlikely to be around to be interviewed. Thus you would have "refuted" the "myth" that Russian roulette is dangerous.

Even an activist organization that has been promoting "living wage" laws, the Association of Community Organizations for Reform Now (ACORN), sought to get its own employees exempted from minimum wage laws. Its argument: "The more that Acorn must pay each individual outreach worker— either because of minimum wage or overtime requirements— the fewer outreach workers it will be able to hire."[19]

It would be comforting to believe that the government can simply decree higher pay for low-wage workers, without having to worry about unfortunate repercussions, but the preponderance of evidence indicates that labor is not exempt from the basic economic principle that artificially high prices cause surpluses. In the case of surplus human beings, that can be a special tragedy when they are already from low-income, unskilled, or minority backgrounds and urgently need to get on the job ladder, if they are ever to move up the ladder by acquiring experience and skills.

Conceivably, the income benefits to those low-wage workers who keep their jobs could outweigh the losses to those who lose their jobs, producing a net benefit to low-income individuals and families as a whole— at least in the short run, ignoring the long-run consequences of a failure of many low-skilled people to acquire job experience and skills, which could be a larger economic loss in the long run than the loss of pay in an entry-level job. But to say that there might conceivably be benefits to low-income people does not mean that this will in fact happen. A study of the effects of minimum wages in Brazil explored this possibility:

> The purpose of this study is to examine whether the minimum wage in Brazil has beneficial effects on the distribution of family incomes, in particular raising incomes of low-income families. While such distributional effects are the most common rationale for minimum wages, economic theory makes no prediction that they will occur. Minimum wages are predicted to reduce employment, and research for both Brazil and the United States tends to confirm this prediction. But all this implies

is that minimum wages will harm some workers while benefiting others. The distributional effects depend on the magnitudes of the gains and losses, and where they occur in the income distribution— a purely empirical question. Research for the United States finds no gains to low-income families from minimum wage increases, and if anything increases in poverty. . . . Overall, then, we do not regard the evidence as lending support to the view that minimum wages in Brazil have beneficial distributional effects from the perspective of low-income families.[20]

Unemployment varies not only in its quantity as of a given time, it varies also in how long workers remain unemployed. Like the unemployment rate, the *duration* of unemployment varies considerably from country to country. Countries which drive up labor costs with either high minimum wages or generous employee benefits imposed on employers by law, or both, tend to have longer-lasting unemployment, as well as higher rates of unemployment. In Germany, for example, there is no minimum wage law but government-imposed mandates on employers, job security laws, and strong labor unions artificially raise labor costs anyway. Unemployment in Germany lasts 12 months or longer for more than half the unemployed, while in the United States only about 10 percent of the unemployed stay unemployed that long.[21]

Differential Impact

Because people differ in many ways, those who are unemployed are not likely to be a random sample of the labor force. In country after country around the world, those whose employment prospects are reduced most by minimum wage laws are those who are younger, less experienced or less skilled. This pattern has been found in New Zealand, France, Canada, the Netherlands, and the United States, for example.[22] It should not be surprising that those whose productivity falls furthest short of the minimum wage would be the ones most likely to be unable to find a job.

In early twenty-first century France, the national unemployment rate was 10 percent but, among workers under the age of twenty five, the unemployment rate was more than 20 percent.[23] In Belgium, the unemployment rate for workers under the age of twenty five was 22 percent and in Italy 27 percent.[24] During the global downturn in 2009, the unemployment rate for workers under the age of 25 was 21 percent in the European Union countries as a whole, with more than 25 percent in Italy and Ireland, and more than 40 percent in Spain.[25] In Australia, the *lowest* unemployment rate for workers under the age of 25, during the entire period from 1978 to 2002, never fell below 10 percent, while the *highest* unemployment rate for the population in general barely reached 10 percent once during that same period.[26] Australia has an unusually high minimum wage, relatively speaking, since its minimum wage level is nearly 60 percent of that country's median wage rate,[27] while the minimum wage in the United States is just over one-third of the American median wage rate.

Some countries in Europe set lower minimum wage rates for teenagers than for adults, and New Zealand simply exempted teenagers from the coverage of its minimum wage law until 1994. This was tacit recognition of the fact that those workers less in demand were likely to be hardest hit by unemployment created by minimum wage laws.

Another group disproportionately affected by minimum wage laws are members of unpopular racial or ethnic minority groups. Indeed, minimum wage laws were once advocated explicitly because of the likelihood that such laws would reduce or eliminate the competition of particular minorities, whether they were Japanese in Canada during the 1920s or blacks in the United States and South Africa during the same era.[28] Such expressions of overt racial discrimination were both legal and socially accepted in all three countries at that time.

Again, it is necessary to note how price is a factor even in racial discrimination. That is, surplus labor resulting from minimum wage laws makes it cheaper to discriminate against minority workers than it would be in a free market, where there is no chronic excess supply of labor. Passing up qualified minority workers in a free market means having to hire more other workers to take the jobs they were denied, and that in turn usually means either having to raise the pay to attract the additional workers or lowering the job qualifications at the existing pay level— both of which amount to the same thing economically, higher labor costs for getting a given amount of work done.

The history of black workers in the United States illustrates the point. From the late nineteenth century on through the middle of the twentieth century, the labor force participation rate of American blacks was slightly higher than that of American whites. In other words, blacks were just as employable at the wages they received as whites were at their very different wages. The minimum wage law changed that. Before federal minimum wage laws were instituted in the 1930s, the black unemployment rate was slightly *lower* than the white unemployment rate in 1930.[29] But then followed the Davis-Bacon Act of 1931, the National Industrial Recovery Act of 1933 and the Fair Labor Standards Act of 1938— all of which imposed government-mandated minimum wages, either on a particular sector or more broadly.

The National Labor Relations Act of 1935, which promoted unionization, also tended to price black workers out of jobs, in addition to union rules that kept blacks from jobs by barring them from union membership. The National Industrial Recovery Act raised wage rates in the Southern textile industry by 70 percent in just five months and its impact nationwide was estimated to have cost blacks half a million jobs. While this Act was later declared unconstitutional by the Supreme Court, the Fair Labor Standards Act of 1938 was upheld by the High Court and became the major force establishing a national minimum wage. The inflation of the 1940s largely nullified the effect of the Fair Labor Standards Act, until it was amended in 1950 to raise minimum wages to a level that would have some actual effect on current wages. By 1954, black unemployment rates were double those of whites and have continued to be at that level or higher. Those particularly hard hit by the resulting unemployment have been black teenage males.

Even though 1949— the year before a series of minimum wage escalations began— was a recession year, black teenage male unemployment that year was lower than it was to be at any time during the later boom years of the 1960s. The wide gap between the unemployment rates of black and white teenagers dates from the escalation of the minimum wage and the spread of its coverage in the 1950s.[30] The usual explanations of high unemployment among black teenagers— inexperience, less education, lack of skills, racism— cannot explain their rising unemployment, since all these things were worse during the earlier period when black teenage unemployment was much lower. Taking the more normal year of 1948 as a basis for comparison, black male teenage unemployment then was less than half of what it would be at any time during the decade of the 1960s and less than one-third of what it would be in the 1970s. Unemployment among 16 and 17-year-old black males was no higher than among white males of the same age in 1948.[31] It was only after a series of minimum wage escalations began that black male teenage unemployment not only skyrocketed but became more than double the unemployment rates among white male teenagers. In the early twenty-first century, the unemployment rate for black teenagers exceeded 30 percent. After the American economy turned down in the wake of the housing and financial crises, unemployment among black teenagers reached 40 percent.[32]

THE ROLE OF ECONOMICS

Among the questions often raised about the history of economic analysis are: (1) Is economics scientific or is it just a set of opinions and ideological biases? and (2) Do economic ideas reflect surrounding circumstances and events and change with those circumstances and events?

Scientific Analysis

There is no question that economists as individuals have their own respective preferences and biases, as do all individuals, including mathematicians and physicists. But the reason mathematics and physics are not considered to be mere subjective opinions and biased notions is that there are accepted *procedures* for testing and proving beliefs in these disciplines. It is precisely because individual scientists are likely to have biases that scientists in general seek to create and agree upon scientific methods and procedures that are unbiased, so that individual biases may be deterred or exposed.

In economics, the preferences of Keynesian economists for government intervention and of University of Chicago economists for relying on markets instead of government, may well have influenced their initial reactions to the analysis and data of the Phillips Curve, for example. But the fact that they shared a common set of analytical and empirical procedures in their professional work enabled them to reach common conclusions as more data came in over time, undermining the Phillips Curve.

Controversies have raged in science, but what makes a particular field scientific is not automatic unanimity on particular issues but a commonly accepted set of procedures for resolving differences about issues when there are sufficient data available. Einstein's theory of relativity was not initially accepted by most physicists, nor did Einstein want it accepted without some empirical tests. When the behavior of light during an eclipse of the sun provided a test of his theory, the unexpected results convinced other scientists that he was right. A leading historian of science, Thomas Kuhn, has argued that what distinguishes science from other fields is that mutually contradictory theories cannot co-exist indefinitely in science but that one or the other must prevail and the others disappear when enough of the right data become available.[1]

Thus the phlogiston theory of combustion gave way to the oxygen theory of combustion and the Ptolemaic theory of astronomy gave way to the Copernican theory. The history of ideologies, however, is quite different from the history of science. Mutually contradictory ideologies can co-exist for centuries, with no resolution of their differences in sight or perhaps even conceivable.*

What scientists share is not simply agreement on various conclusions but, more fundamentally, agreement about the ways of testing and verifying conclusions, beginning with a careful and strict definition of the terms being used. The crucial importance of definitions in economics has been demonstrated, for example, by the fallacies that result when popular discussions of economic policies use a loose term like "wages" to refer to such different things as wage rates per unit of time, aggregate earnings of workers, and labor costs per unit of output.** A prosperous country with higher wage rates per unit of time may have lower labor costs per unit of output than a Third World country where workers are not paid nearly as much.

Mathematical presentations of arguments, whether in science or economics, not only make these arguments more compact and their complexities easier to follow than a longer verbal presentation would be, but can also make their implications clearer and their flaws harder to hide. For example, when preparing a landmark 1931 scholarly article on economics, one later reprinted for decades thereafter, Professor Jacob Viner of the University of Chicago instructed a draftsman on how he wanted certain

---

* This theme is explored in my book *A Conflict of Visions*.
** During the Great Depression of the 1930s successive American administrations of both political parties sought to maintain high wage rates per unit of time as a way of maintaining labor's "purchasing power"— which depends on the aggregate earnings of workers. But, among economists, both Keynesian and non-Keynesian, it was understood that the number of workers employed was affected by the wage rate per unit of time, so that higher wage rates could mean fewer people employed— and those earning no income reduce purchasing power. A common fallacy in popular discussions of international trade is that countries with high "wages"— that is, wage rates per unit of time— cannot compete with countries that have low "wages," on the assumption that the high-wage countries will have higher production costs.

complex cost curves constructed. The draftsman replied that one of the set of curves with which Professor Viner wanted to illustrate the analysis in his article was impossible to draw with all the characteristics that Viner had specified. As Professor Viner later recognized, he had asked for something that was "technically impossible and economically inappropriate," because some of the assumptions in his analysis were incompatible with some of his other assumptions.[2] That flaw became apparent in a mathematical presentation of the argument, whereas mutually incompatible assumptions can co-exist indefinitely in an imprecise verbal presentation.

Systematic analysis of carefully defined terms and the systematic testing of theories against empirical evidence are all part of a scientific study of any subject. Clearly economics has advanced in this direction in the centuries since its beginnings.

However, economics is scientific only in the sense of having some of the procedures of science. But the inability to conduct controlled experiments prevents its theories from having the precision and repeatability often associated with science. On the other hand, there are other fields with a recognized scientific basis which also do not permit controlled experiments, astronomy being one and meteorology being another. Moreover, there are different degrees of precision among these fields. In astronomy, for example, the time when eclipses will occur can be predicted to the second, even centuries ahead of time, while meteorologists have a high error rate when forecasting the weather a week ahead.

Although no one questions the scientific principles of physics on which weather forecasting is based, the uncertainty as to how the numerous combinations of factors will come together at a particular place on a particular day makes *forecasting* a particular event that day much more hazardous than *predicting* how those factors will interact *if* they come together.

Presumably, if a meteorologist knew in advance just when a warm and moisture-laden air mass moving up from the Gulf of Mexico would encounter a cold and dry air mass moving down from Canada, that meteorologist would be able to predict rain or snow in St. Louis to a certainty, since that would be nothing more than the application of the principles of physics to these particular circumstances. It is not those principles which are uncertain but all the variables whose behavior will determine which of those principles will apply at a particular place at a particular time. What is scientifically known is that the collision of cold dry air and warm moist air does not produce sunny and calm days. What is unknown is whether these particular air masses will arrive in St. Louis at the same time or pass over it in succession— or miss it completely. That is where statistical probabilities are calculated as to whether they will continue moving at their present speeds and without changing direction.

In principle, economics is much like meteorology. There is no example in recorded history in which a government increased the money supply ten-fold in one year without prices going up. Nor does anyone expect that there ever will be. The effects of price controls in creating shortages, black markets, product quality decline, and a reduction in auxiliary services, have likewise been remarkably similar, whether in the Roman Empire under Diocletian, in Paris during the French Revolution or in the New York housing market under rent control today. Nor has there been any fundamental difference whether the price being controlled was that of housing, food, or medical care.

Controversies among economists make news, but that does not mean that there are no established principles in this field, any more than controversies among scientists mean that there is no such thing as established principles of chemistry or physics. In both cases, these controversies seldom involve predicting what *would* happen under given circumstances but forecasting what *will* in fact happen in circumstances that cannot be completely foreseen. In short, these controversies usually do not involve disagreement about fundamental principles of the field but about how all the trends and conditions will come together to determine which of those principles will apply or predominate in a particular set of circumstances.

Among the many objections made against economics have been claims that it is "simplistic," or that it assumes too much self-interested and materialistic rationality, or that the assumptions behind its analyses and predictions are not a true depiction of the real world.

Implicit in the term "simplistic" is that a particular explanation is not just simple but *too* simple. That only raises the question: Too simple for what? If the facts consistently turn out the way the explanation predicts, then it has obviously not been too simple for its purpose— especially if the facts do *not* turn out the way a more complicated or more plausible-sounding explanation predicts. In short, whether or not any given explanation is too simple is an empirical question that cannot be decided in advance by how plausible, complex, or nuanced an explanation seems on the face of it, but can only be determined after examining hard evidence on how well its predictions turn out.*

A related attempt to determine the validity of a theory by how plausible it looks, rather than how well it performs when put to the test, is the criticism that economic analysis depicts people as thinking or acting in a way that most people do not think or act. But economics is ultimately about systemic *results*, not personal *intentions*.

Economists on opposite ends of the ideological spectrum have understood this. Karl Marx said that capitalists lower their prices when technological advances lower their costs of production, not because they *want* to but because market competition forces them to.[3] Adam Smith likewise said that the benefits of a competitive market economy are "no part" of capitalists' intentions.[4] As Marx's collaborator Engels said, "what each individual wills is obstructed by everyone else, and what emerges is something that no one willed."[5] It is "what emerges" that economics tries to predict and its success or failure is measured by that, not by how plausible its analysis looks at the outset.

Personal bias is another fundamental question that has long been raised about economics and its claim to scientific status. J.A. Schumpeter, whose massive *History of Economic Analysis*, published in 1954, remains unequalled for its combination of breadth and depth, dealt with the much-discussed question of the effect of personal bias on economic analysis. He found ideological bias common among economists, ranging from Adam Smith to Karl Marx— but what he also concluded was how little effect these biases

---

* There was consternation among wine connoisseurs when economist Orley Ashenfelter said that he could predict the prices of particular wines using data on the weather during the season in which its grapes were grown, without either tasting the wine or paying any attention to the opinions of experts who had tasted it. But his methods turned out to predict prices more accurately than the opinions of experts who had tasted the wine.

had on these economists' analytical work, which can be separated out from their ideological comments or advocacies.

In a scholarly journal article as well, Schumpeter singled out Adam Smith in particular: "In Adam Smith's case the interesting thing is not indeed the absence but the harmlessness of ideological bias."[6] Smith's unrelievedly negative picture of businessmen was, to Schumpeter, an ideological bias deriving from Smith's background in a family which "did *not* belong to the business class" and his intellectual immersion in the work of "similarly conditioned" intellectuals. But "all this ideology, however strongly held, really did not much harm to his scientific achievement" in producing "sound factual and analytic teaching."[7]

Similarly with Karl Marx, whose ideological vision of social processes was formed before he began to study economics, but "as his analytic work matured, Marx not only elaborated many pieces of scientific analysis that were neutral to that vision but also some that did not agree with it well," even though Marx continued to use "vituperative phraseology that does not affect the scientific elements in an argument."[8] Ironically, Marx's view of businessmen was not quite as totally negative as that of Adam Smith.*

According to Schumpeter, "*in itself* scientific performance does not require us to divest ourselves of our value judgments or to renounce the calling of an advocate of some particular interest." More bluntly, he said, "advocacy does not imply lying,"[9] though sometimes ideologies "crystallize" into "creeds" that are "impervious to argument."[10] But among the hallmarks of a scientific field are "rules of procedure" which can "crush out ideologically conditioned error" from an analysis.[11] Moreover, having "something to formulate, to defend, to attack" provides an impetus for factual and analytical work, even if ideology sometimes interferes with it.

---

* In *Capital*, Marx said, "I paint the capitalist and the landlord in no sense *couleur de rose*. But here individuals are dealt with only in so far as they are the personifications of economic categories. . . My stand-point. . .can less than any other make the individual responsible for relations whose creature he socially remains, however much he may subjectively raise himself above them." Contrary to many others on the left, Marx did not see capitalists as controlling the economy but just the opposite: "Free competition brings out the inherent laws of capitalist production, in the shape of external coercive laws having power over every individual capitalist." Karl Marx, *Capital*, Vol. I, pp. 15, 297.

Therefore "though we proceed slowly because of our ideologies, we might not proceed at all without them."[12]

Events and Ideas

Does economics influence events and do events influence economics? The short answer to both questions is "yes" but the only meaningful question is— to what extent and in what particular ways? John Maynard Keynes' answer to the first question was this:

> . . .the ideas of economists and political philosophers, both when they are right and when they are wrong, are more powerful than is commonly understood. Indeed the world is ruled by little else. Practical men, who believe themselves to be quite exempt from any intellectual influences, are usually the slaves of some defunct economist. Madmen in authority, who hear voices in the air, are distilling their frenzy from some academic scribbler of a few years back. I am sure that the power of vested interests is vastly exaggerated compared with the gradual encroachment of ideas.[13]

In other words, it was not by direct influence over those who hold power at a particular point in time that economists influence the course of events, according to Keynes. It was by generating certain general beliefs and attitudes which provide the context within which opinion-makers think and politicians act. In that sense, the mercantilists are still an influence on beliefs and attitudes in the world today, centuries after they were refuted decisively within the economics profession by Adam Smith.

The question whether economics is shaped by events is more controversial. At one time, it was widely believed that ideas are shaped by surrounding circumstances and events, and that economic ideas were no exception. No doubt something in the real world starts people thinking about economic ideas, as is no doubt true of ideas in other fields, including science and mathematics. Trigonometry has been thought to have been given an impetus by a need to re-survey land in Egypt after recurring floods along the Nile wiped out boundaries between different people's properties in ancient times.

That is one kind of influence. A more immediate and direct influence has been assumed by those who believed that the Great Depression of the 1930s spawned Keynesian economics. But even if the Great Depression inspired

Keynes' thinking and the widespread acceptance of that thinking among economists around the world, how typical was that of the way that economics has evolved historically, much less how ideas in other fields have evolved historically?

Were more things falling down, or was their falling creating more social problems, when Newton developed his theory of gravity? Certainly there were not more free markets when Adam Smith wrote *The Wealth of Nations*, which advocated freer markets precisely because of his dissatisfaction with the effects of various kinds of government intervention that were pervasive at the time.* The great shift within nineteenth century economics from a theory of price determined by production costs to a theory of price determined by consumer demand was not in response to changes in either production costs or consumer demand. It was simply the unpredictable emergence of a new intellectual insight as a way of resolving ambiguities and inconsistencies in existing economic theory. As for depressions, there had been depressions before the 1930s without producing a Keynes.

Nobel Prize-winning economist George Stigler pointed out that momentous events in the real world may have no intellectual consequences: "A war may ravage a continent or destroy a generation without posing new theoretical questions," he said.[14] The tragic reality is that wars have spread ruination and devastation across continents many times over the centuries, so that there need be no new issue to confront intellectually, even in the midst of an overwhelming catastrophe.

Whatever its origins or its ability to influence or be influenced by external events, economics is ultimately a study of an enduring part of the human condition. Its value depends on its contribution to our understanding of a particular set of conditions involving the allocation of scarce resources which have alternative uses. Unfortunately, little of the knowledge and understanding within the economics profession has reached the average citizen and voter, leaving politicians free to do things that would never be tolerated if most people understood economics as well as Alfred Marshall understood it a century ago or David Ricardo two centuries ago.

---

* No one writes a 900-page book to say how happy he is with the way things are going.

POLITICAL ISSUES

IVAN AND BORIS— AND US

There is an old Russian fable, with different versions in other countries, about two poor peasants, Ivan and Boris. The only difference between them was that Boris had a goat and Ivan didn't. One day, Ivan came upon a strange-looking lamp and, when he rubbed it, a genie appeared. She told him that she could grant him just one wish, but it could be anything in the world.

Ivan said, "I want Boris' goat to die."

Variations on this story in other countries suggest that this tells us something about human beings, not just Russians.

It may tell us something painful about many Americans today, when so many people are preoccupied with the pay of corporate CEOs. It is not that the corporate CEOs' pay affects them so much. If every oil company executive in America agreed to work for nothing, that would not be enough to lower the price of a gallon of gasoline by a dime. If every General Motors executive agreed to work for nothing, that would not lower the price of a Cadillac or a Chevrolet by one percent.

Too many people are like Ivan, who wanted Boris' goat to die.

It is not even that the average corporate CEO makes as much money as any number of professional athletes and entertainers. The average pay of a CEO of a corporation big enough to be included in the Standard & Poor's index is less than one-third of what Alex Rodriguez makes, about one-tenth of what Tiger Woods makes and less than one-thirtieth of what Oprah Winfrey makes.

But when has anyone ever accused athletes or entertainers of "greed"?

It is not the general public that singles out corporate CEOs for so much attention. Politicians and the media have focused on business leaders, and the public has been led along, like sheep.

The logic is simple: Demonize those whose place or power you plan to usurp.

Politicians who want the power to micro-manage business and the economy know that demonizing those who currently run businesses is the opening salvo in the battle to take over their roles.

There is no way that politicians can take over the roles of Alex Rodriguez, Tiger Woods or Oprah Winfrey. So they can make any amount of money they want and it doesn't matter politically.

Those who want more power have known for centuries that giving the people somebody to hate and fear is the key.

In 18th century France, promoting hatred of the aristocracy was the key to Robespierre's acquiring more dictatorial power than the aristocracy had ever had, and using that power to create a bigger bloodbath than anything under the old regime.

In the 20th century, it was both the czars and the capitalists in Russia who were made the targets of public hatred by the Communists on their road to power. That power created more havoc in the lives of more people than czars and capitalists ever had combined.

As in other countries and other times, today it is not just a question of which elites win out in a tug of war in America. It is the people at large who have the most at stake.

We have just seen one of the biggest free home demonstrations of what happens in an economy when politicians tell businesses what decisions to make.

For years, using the powers of the Community Reinvestment Act and other regulatory powers, along with threats of legal action if the loan approval rates varied from the population profile, politicians have pressured banks and other lending institutions into lending to people they would not lend to otherwise.

Yet, when all this blows up in our faces and the economy turns down, what is the answer? To have more economic decisions made by politicians, because they choose to say that "deregulation" is the cause of our problems.

Regardless of how much suffocating regulation may have been responsible for an economic debacle, politicians have learned that they can get away with it if they call it "deregulation."

No matter what happens, for politicians it is "heads I win and tails you lose." If we keep listening to the politicians and their media allies, we are all going to keep losing, big time. Keeping our attention focused on CEO pay— Boris' goat— is all part of this game. We are all goats if we fall for it.

RONALD REAGAN
(1911–2004)

There are many ways to judge a President or anyone else. One old-fashioned way is by results. A more popular way in recent years has been by how well someone fits the preconceptions of the intelligentsia or the media.

By the first test, Ronald Reagan was the most successful President of the United States in the 20th century. By the second test, he was a complete failure.

Time and time again President Reagan went against what the smug smarties inside the beltway and on the TV tube said. And time and again he got results.

It started even before Ronald Reagan was elected. When the Republicans nominated Governor Reagan in 1980, according to the late *Washington Post* editor Meg Greenfield, "people I knew in the Carter White House were ecstatic." They considered Reagan "not nearly smart enough"— as liberals measure smart.

The fact that Ronald Reagan beat President Jimmy Carter by a landslide did not cause any re-evaluation of his intelligence. It was luck or malaise or something else, liberals thought.

Now the media line was that this cowboy from California would be taught a lesson when he got to Washington and had to play in the big leagues against the savvy guys on Capitol Hill.

The new President succeeded in putting through Congress big changes that were called "the Reagan revolution." And he did it without ever having his party in control of both houses of Congress. But these results caused no re-evaluation of Ronald Reagan.

One of his first acts as President was to end price controls on petroleum. The *New York Times* condescendingly dismissed Reagan's reliance on the free market and repeated widespread predictions of "declining domestic oil production" and skyrocketing gasoline prices.

The price of gasoline fell by more than 60 cents a gallon. More luck, apparently.

Where the new President would really get his comeuppance, the smart money said, was in foreign affairs, where a former governor had no experience. Not only were President Reagan's ideas about foreign policy considered naive and dangerously reckless, he would be going up against the wily Soviet rulers who were old hands at this stuff.

When Ronald Reagan referred to the Soviet Union as an "evil empire," there were howls of disapproval in the media. When he proposed meeting a Soviet nuclear buildup in Eastern Europe with an American nuclear buildup in Western Europe, there were alarms that he was going to get us into a war.

The result? President Reagan's policies not only did not get us into a war, they put an end to the Cold War that had been going on for decades.

Meanwhile, Soviet Premier Mikhail Gorbachev, who was the media's idea of a brilliant and sophisticated man, had a whole Communist empire collapse under him when his policies were put into effect. Eastern Europe broke free and Gorbachev woke up one morning to find that the Soviet Union that he was head of no longer existed— and that he was now a nobody in the new Russian state.

But that was just bad luck, apparently.

For decades it had been considered the height of political wisdom to accept as given that the Soviet bloc was here to stay— and its expansion was so inevitable that it would be foolhardy to try to stop it.

The Soviet bloc had in fact expanded through seven consecutive administrations of both Republicans and Democrats. The first territory the Communists ever lost was Grenada, when Ronald Reagan sent in American troops.

But, once again, results carried no weight with the intelligentsia and the media.

Reagan was considered to be completely out of touch when he said that Communism was "another sad, bizarre chapter in human history whose last pages even now are being written." But how many "smart" people saw the end of the Soviet Union coming?

Ronald Reagan left this country— and the world— a far better place than he found it. And he smiled while he did it. That's greatness— if you judge by results.

THE "COMPASSION"
RACKET

Our hearts automatically go out to the people of Florida, who are being battered by a series of hurricanes in rapid succession. But we have brains as well as hearts— and the time is long overdue to start using them.

Hurricanes come through Florida every year about this time. And, every year, politicians get to parade their compassion by showering the taxpayers' money on the places that have been struck.

What would happen if they didn't?

First of all, not as many people would build homes in the path of a well-known disaster that comes around like clockwork virtually every year. Those who did would buy insurance that covers the costs of the risks they choose to take.

That insurance would not be cheap— which would provide yet another reason for people to locate out of harm's way. The net result would be fewer lives lost and less property damage. Is it not more compassionate to seek this result, even if it would deprive politicians of television time?

In ABC reporter John Stossel's witty and insightful book *Give Me A Break*, he discusses how he built a beach house with only "a hundred feet of sand" between him and the ocean. It gave him a great view— and a great chance of disaster.

His father warned him of the danger but an architect pointed out that the government would pick up the tab if anything happened to his house. A few years later, storm-driven ocean waves came in and flooded the ground floor of Stossel's home. The government paid to have it restored.

Still later, the waves came in again, and this time took out the whole house. The government paid again. Fortunately for the taxpayers, Stossel then decided that enough was enough.

In politics, throwing the taxpayers' money at disasters is supposed to show your compassion. But robbing Peter to pay Paul is not compassion. It is politics.

The crucial fact is that a society does not have one dime more money to devote to the resources available to help victims of natural disasters by sending that money through government agencies. All that it does is change the incentives in such a way as to subsidize risky behavior.

The same money can just as well come through insurance companies. Even if most insurance companies are unwilling to insure people living in particularly vulnerable areas, or living in homes that are inadequate to withstand hurricane-force winds, there are always insurers who specialize in high risks— and who charge correspondingly higher premiums.

Lloyds of London, for example, has already been moving into the market for insurance for homes costing half a million dollars or more and located along coastal waters, whether in Florida or the Hamptons or elsewhere. If rich people want to put their mansions at risk, there is no reason why they shouldn't pay the costs, instead of forcing the taxpayers to pay those costs.

What about "the poor"? As in so many other cases, the poor are the human shields behind which big-government advocates advance. If you are seriously concerned about the poor themselves, you can always subsidize them and avoid subsidizing others by having means tests.

Means tests are anathema to the political left because that puts an end to their game of hiding behind the poor. Compassion is a laudable feeling but it can also be a political racket. As with so many government programs that people have come to rely on, phasing out state and federal disaster relief programs would not be easy. In an election year, it is impossible.

Fortunately, there are years in between elections, in which it is at least theoretically possible to talk sense. Whether the risks are hurricanes, earthquakes, floods or forest fires, people who have gotten themselves out on a limb by taking risks in the expectation that the government will bail them out can be gradually weaned away from that expectation by phasing out disaster relief.

The alternative is to keep on forcing taxpayers to be patsies forever, while politicians bask in the glow of the compassion racket by throwing the taxpayers' money hither and yon, while the media applaud the courage of those who rebuild in the path of known disasters.

SPOILED BRAT POLITICS

An editorial in a recent issue of the *National Geographic*'s *Traveler* magazine complained that kayakers in Maine found "residential development" near national parks and urged its readers to use their "influence" to prevent such things.

"You are the stakeholders in our national parks," it said.

Really? What stake do kayakers and others of like mind have that is not also a stake held by people who build the vacation homes whose presence offends the kayak set? Homeowners are just as much citizens and taxpayers as kayakers are, and they are even entitled to equal treatment under the 14th Amendment.

The essence of bigotry is denying others the same rights you claim for yourself. Green bigots are a classic example.

The idea that government is supposed to make your desires override the desires of other citizens has spread from the green bigots to other groups who claim privileges in the name of rights.

In California, a group of golfers in wheelchairs are suing a hotel chain for not providing them with special carts that will enable them to navigate the local hotel's golf course more comfortably and play the game better.

According to a newspaper account, the kinds of carts the golfers in wheelchairs want "have rotating seats so a golfer can swing and strike a ball from the tee, the fairway and on the green without getting out of the vehicle." If golfers want this kind of cart, there is nothing to stop them from buying one— except that they would rather have other people be forced to pay for it.

One of the golfers in this lawsuit has been confined to a wheelchair as a result of a diving accident and another as a result of a gunshot wound. Apparently the hotel had nothing to do with either event.

There was a time when people would have said that the hotel is not responsible for these golfers being in wheelchairs and therefore it has no obligation to spend additional money for special carts in order to help their scores on the links. But that was before the Americans with Disabilities Act, under which the hotel is being sued.

If the government wanted to do something for the disabled or the handicapped, it could have spent its own tax money to do so. Instead, it passed the Americans with Disabilities Act, which created a right to sue private institutions, in order to force them to spend their money to solve the problems of individuals with special problems or special desires, whether serious or frivolous.

It was a lawyer's full-employment act, creating another legally recognized victim group, empowered to claim special privileges, at other people's expense, in the name of equal rights.

Nor could such legislation make the usual claim that it was coming to the defense of the poor and the downtrodden. Golf courses are not the natural habitat of the poor and the downtrodden.

One of the plaintiffs in the golf-course lawsuit has been the managing partner in a large law firm. He says, "I just want the same opportunity as everyone else" to "get out and play 18 holes with my friends and colleagues."

Equal opportunity does not mean equal results, despite how many laws and policies proceed as if it does, or how much fashionable rhetoric equates the two.

An example of that rhetoric was the title of a recent *New York Times* column: "A Ticket to Bias." That column recalled bitterly the experience of a woman in a wheelchair who bought a $300 ticket to a rock concert but was unable to see when other people around her stood up. This was equated with "bias" on the part of those who ran the arena.

The woman in the wheelchair declared, "true equality remains a dream out of reach." Apparently only equality of results is "true" equality.

A recent publication of the American Historical Association shows this same confusion when it says that doors "are largely closed" to people who want to become historians if they didn't graduate from a top-tier college. In other words, unequal results proves bias that closed doors, according to this rhetoric.

Confusion between equal opportunity and equal results is a dangerous confusion behind many kinds of spoiled brat politics.

THE LEFT'S VOCABULARY

A recent angry e-mail from a reader said that certain issues should not be determined by "the dictates of the market." With a mere turn of a phrase, he had turned reality upside down.

Decisions by people free to make their mutual accommodations with other free people were called "dictates" while having third parties tell all of them what they could and couldn't do was not.

Verbal coups have long been a specialty of the left. Totalitarian countries on the left have called themselves "people's democracies" and used the egalitarian greeting "comrade"— even though some comrades had the arbitrary power of life and death over other comrades.

In democratic countries, where public opinion matters, the left has used its verbal talents to change the whole meaning of words and to substitute new words, so that issues would be debated in terms of their redefined vocabulary, instead of the real substance of the issues.

Words which have acquired connotations from the actual experiences of millions of human beings over generations, or even centuries, have been replaced by new words that wipe out those connotations and substitute more fashionable notions of the left.

The word "swamp," for example, has been all but erased from the language. Swamps were messy, sometimes smelly, places where mosquitoes bred and sometimes snakes lurked. The left has replaced the word "swamp" with "wetlands," a word spoken in pious tones usually reserved for sacred things.

The point of this verbal sleight-of-hand is to impose the left's notions of how other people can use their own land. Restrictive laws about "wetlands" have imposed huge costs on farmers and other owners of land that happened to have a certain amount of water on it.

Another word that the left has virtually banished from the language is "bum." Centuries of experience with idlers who refused to work and who hung around on the streets making a nuisance— and sometimes a menace— of themselves were erased from our memories as the left verbally transformed those same people into a sacred icon, "the homeless."

As with swamps, what was once messy and smelly was now turned into something we had a duty to protect. It was now our duty to support people who refused to support themselves.

Crimes committed by bums are covered up by the media, by verbally transforming "the homeless" into "transients" or "drifters" whenever they commit crimes. Thus "the homeless" are the only group you never hear of committing any crimes.

More to the point, third parties' notions are imposed by the power of the government to raise our taxes to support people who are raising hell on our streets and in parks where it has often become too dangerous for our children to play.

The left has a whole vocabulary devoted to depicting people who do not meet standards as people who have been denied "access." Whether it is academic standards, job qualifications or credit requirements, those who do not measure up are said to have been deprived of "opportunity," "rights" or "social justice."

The word games of the left— from the mantra of "diversity" to the pieties of "compassion"— are not just games. They are ways of imposing power by evading issues of substance through the use of seductive rhetoric.

"Rights," for example, have become an all-purpose term used for evading both facts and logic by saying that people have a "right" to whatever the left wants to give them by taking from others.

For centuries, rights were exemptions from government power, as in the Bill of Rights. Now the left has redefined rights as things that can be demanded from the taxpayers, or from private employers or others, on behalf of people who accept no mutual obligations, even for common decency.

At one time, educators tried to teach students to carefully define words and systematically analyze arguments. They said, "We are here to teach you how to think, not what to think."

Today, they are teaching students what to think— political correctness. Instead of knowledge, students are given "self-esteem," so that they can vent their ignorance with confidence.

UNFUNDED MANDATES

Nothing so epitomizes contemporary liberalism as unfunded mandates, in which the federal government establishes programs and forces the states to pay for them. The very need to weigh benefits against costs— the essence of economics— is evaded by this irresponsible exercise of arrogance. It is like impulse buying and charging it to somebody else's credit card.

The great hysteria in the media about the wonderful programs that will be lost if unfunded mandates are stopped misses the whole point. If these programs are as wonderful as they are said to be, then they should be paid for. Nothing is easier than to make a verbal case for almost anything, but are you willing to put your money where your mouth is?

If you are not even willing to put the taxpayers' money where your mouth is, there is something wrong somewhere.

The number of things that are beneficial vastly exceeds what any nation can afford. That is why both individuals and organizations must weigh trade-offs all the time. Unfunded mandates, hidden taxes, and a whole range of environmental restrictions, are all ways of making costly decisions without having to weigh those costs against the benefits.

It is government by magic words, whether those words are "safety," "minimum wages," or "clean air."

Can anybody be against "safety"? Not verbally and not politically. But, in real life, do we go around in suits of armor?

Do we refuse to drive or ride in cars? Of course not. We weigh the risks against the benefits.

Only in grandiloquent political rhetoric do we claim that safety must be achieved at all costs. We can do it there only because those costs are to be paid by somebody else. When even the big spenders in Washington are not willing to pay from the federal treasury, then we have lost all sense of trade-offs. We have become like small children who want everything— and cry if we don't get it.

What is the minimum wage law but an unfunded mandate imposed on private organizations? If everyone deserves "a living wage" or "a decent standard of living," then why don't those who think that way supply these things? If it is "society's" responsibility to see that no one falls below some economic level, then why don't we raise the taxes and pay for that level?

Why is someone who runs a print shop or a bakery more responsible for other people's economic level than someone who works in a thousand other occupations? TV pundits and editorial office saints often make more money than the great majority of businessmen. Why single out employers to dump this responsibility on?

We all want clean air and water, don't we? The only problem is that there has never been any such thing. No water and no air has ever been 100 percent pure, at least not since Adam and Eve made the wrong decision back in the garden. There are different levels of impurities with different levels of consequences.

No one wants to breathe air full of sulphur or drink water with sewage in it, so it makes sense to remove some impurities— but not every trace of everything that every hysterical crusader can think of.

There are wells being shut down by the government because they have traces of chemicals more minute than you can find in a bottle of soda or a can of beer.

Any one of us could make the air in his own home cleaner by installing all sorts of costly filters and we could eliminate many impurities in water by drinking only water that we distilled ourselves. But we don't do that, do we? We think it is too costly, whether in money or in time.

Only when we are putting costs on other people do we go hog wild like that. Making us pay is one way to make us think.

Environmental agencies have been having a field day putting restrictions on how other people can use their own property. These restrictions may cut the value of the property in half or even reduce it to zero. There is never a lack of pretty words to justify this.

But what if those agencies had to compensate the owner for the losses they have imposed on him?

If the restrictions' benefits to "society" outweigh the losses to the owner, then it makes sense to pay the money and everybody ends up better off. But when you confiscate property by the back door, you can just say some lofty words and keep going. You don't have to weigh anything against anything.

In reality, many of the things being financed by unfunded mandates or imposed on businesses and property owners are not for the benefit of "society." They are for the benefit of the careers or the egos of those who promote programs. That is why things that cannot be justified have to be financed under the table.

REFLECTIONS ON TERM LIMITS

The Reflecting Pool between the Washington Monument and the Lincoln Memorial may be the only thing in Washington that is reflecting. Preoccupation with the never-ending task of political fund-raising, fighting daily brushfires, and trying to put the right spin on the crisis du jour leaves very little time for the nation's political leaders to step back and contemplate deeper and enduring questions amid the swirl of events and rhetoric.

Reflection is not a luxury but a prime necessity. Anyone who has ever done anything as mundane as looking for a house knows how much time and thought goes into weighing one place against another and both against the bank account, not to mention the conflicting demands of getting to work, getting the children in a good school and many other considerations.

Imagine if in one year you had to decide— and vote on— complex environmental issues, foreign policy around the world, racial issues at home, military defense, judicial appointments, and regulating public utilities, pharmaceutical drugs, the stock market and the safety of mines, airports, food and vaccines. Even if we arbitrarily assume that none of these things is any more complicated than buying a house, how many people could handle all the problems of buying a house ten times in one year?

Worse yet, these national and international issues are not the sole— or even the main— business of those in Congress or the White House. Their main business is getting re-elected. That is also the main business of those who work for them, even though theoretically these staffers and appointees work for the country and certainly are paid by the taxpayers.

One of the strongest cases for term limits is that a one-term rule would free up a major block of time, and eliminate a major conflict-of-interest, among elected officials and their staffs, by eliminating their overwhelming preoccupation with getting re-elected. Those advocates of term limits who wish merely to restrict the number of terms forfeit much of this advantage for, if three terms are allowed for a Congressman, then in two-thirds of those terms the Congressman and his staff will still be preoccupied with re-election.

If the fear is that two years is too short a time for a member of the House of Representatives to get the lay of the land and become an effective legislator, then instead of allowing three two-year terms, one six-year term could be established. The point is to get people focussed on national concerns, not their own re-election.

Those who fear that we would lose the great "expertise" that members of Congress develop after years of dealing with certain issues fail to see that much of that expertise is in the arts of packaging, log-rolling, creative accounting and other forms of deception. Those who dominate the national political scene— and often the local scene, as well— are experts only in the law and in political machinations.

Genuine experts in particular fields seldom have either the incentive or the political talents to get elected to public office.

A leading surgeon, engineer, corporate executive, scientist or financial consultant earns far more than the salary of any public official in Washington. What incentive is there for someone like this to sacrifice his family's present well-being and future security, unless he is so driven by the desire for power that any sacrifice seems worth it?

Anyone with such a craving for power is the last person to trust with power.

One of the greatest economic moves we could make would be to pay every member of Congress a million dollars a year, but with no perks and no pension. Paying this salary to each member of Congress for the entire 21st century would cost less than running the Department of Agriculture for one year.

This would pay for itself many times over because many government agencies and programs could be eliminated by a Congress not concerned with raising campaign money from special interests that benefit from bureaucracies ostensibly set up to serve the public.

With such a salary, people who are at the top of many fields could afford to spend one term in Washington performing a civic duty without sacrificing their families— and without any prospect that this could be a career from which they could retire with a pension.

The absence of perks would emphasize that they were not little tin gods but simply citizens temporarily serving in government. They could also bring some real expertise to Washington, expertise in something besides politics.

THE SURVIVAL OF THE LEFT

Biologists explain how organisms adapt to their physical environment, but ideologues also adapt to their social environment. The most fundamental fact about the ideas of the political left is that they do not work. Therefore we should not be surprised to find the left concentrated in institutions where ideas do not have to work in order to survive.

The academic world is the natural habitat of half-baked ideas, except for those fields in which there are decisive tests, such as science, mathematics, engineering, medicine— and athletics. In all these fields, in their differing ways, there comes a time when you must either put up or shut up. It should not be surprising that all of these fields are notable exceptions to the complete domination of the left on campuses across the country.

In the humanities, for example, the test of deconstructionism is not whether it can produce any tangible results but whether it remains in vogue. So long as it does, professors skilled in its verbal sleight-of-hand can expect to continue to receive six-figure salaries.

You might think that the collapse of communism throughout Eastern Europe would be considered a decisive failure for Marxism, but academic Marxists in America are utterly undaunted. Their paychecks and their tenure are unaffected. Their theories continue to flourish in the classrooms and their journals continue to litter the library shelves.

Socialism in general has a record of failure so blatant that only an intellectual could ignore or evade it. Even countries that were once more prosperous than their neighbors have found themselves much poorer than their neighbors after just one generation of socialistic policies. Whether these neighboring countries were Ghana and the Ivory Coast or Burma and Thailand, it has been the same story around the world.

Nor is economic failure the worst of it. The millions slaughtered by Stalin, Mao and Pol Pot for political reasons are an even grimmer reality.

People who live and work in a world where there is a business bottom line, an athletic scoreboard, a military battlefield or life-and-death surgery may find it hard to fully appreciate the difference between that kind of world and one in which the only decisive test is whether your colleagues like what you are saying.

Academia is only one of the places where wholly subjective criteria rule—and where leftists predominate. Endowed institutions such as foundations and museums likewise often face no test other than what like-minded people find "exciting" and what enables those who run these institutions to get the heady feeling that they are "making a difference." The same is true of cultural institutions supported involuntarily by the taxpayers, such as the Smithsonian or the National Endowments for the Arts and the Humanities.

Taxpayer-supported "public" radio and television are similarly insulated from reality and similarly dominated by the left, not only in the United States but in other countries as well. All the nostrums of the left that have brought hunger to millions in countries which used to have surplus food to export, all the pretty words and ugly realities that have caused millions more to flee the lands of their birth, these nostrums live on in public television—much like old classic movies with familiar lines that the audience of aficionados can recite along with the characters on the screen.

These endowed and insulated institutions, often full of contempt for the values of American society and Western civilization, are not the only bastions of the left counter-culture. So are Hollywood and Broadway. Although show biz faces the financial need to get an audience, the truth of what they portray is hardly crucial. If they can make it punchy and sexy, then those who complain about historical inaccuracies and ideological bias can be dismissed as irrelevant pedants.

Why are leftists able to crowd out other kinds of people from these places? Because those who are willing to subject themselves to the test of reality, whether as a businessman in the marketplace or as a surgeon in an operating room, have many other places in which to work and live. They do not need special sheltered niches in which to hide and to cherish their precious notions.

Darwinian adaptation to environment applies not only to nature but also to society. Just as you don't find eagles living in the ocean or fish living on mountain tops, so you don't find leftists concentrated where their ideas have to stand the test of performance.

POLITICS IN ONE LESSON

Henry Hazlitt wrote a book called *Economics in One Lesson*. Charles Murray's book, *What It Means to be a Libertarian*, could have been titled *Politics in One Lesson*. Unlike *The Bell Curve*, which Murray co-authored, this book has no footnotes, only a couple of very simple diagrams, and is a slender volume written in an easy, essay style.

Seldom has so much substance and wisdom been packed into so few words, demonstrating in the process that the case against the welfare state and the regulatory state is very straightforward. Those who oppose Murray's conclusions will undoubtedly consider them "simplistic," since elaborate and even convoluted arguments are considered signs of sophistication, rather than desperate expedients to try to salvage a position contrary to plain facts and plain logic.

Murray begins by running through the main functions of government that he would reduce or eliminate. He would eliminate entirely all government regulation of products and services, leaving tort law to deal with "harms caused by defective products in normal use." Indeed, the requirement that product liability be restricted to harms caused "in normal use" would itself be a revolutionary rollback in existing tort law, in which the consumer's own dangerous behavior does not prevent the manufacturer from being held liable for the bad consequences.

Among the federal cabinet-level departments to be destroyed entirely, in this libertarian vision, are the Departments of Agriculture, Commerce, Energy, Transportation and Housing and Urban Development. Among the programs to be ended would be Social Security, Medicare, Medicaid, anti-trust actions, welfare, aerospace exploration and all regulation of terms and conditions of employment, including civil rights laws.

You might think that such a sweeping agenda would require a huge book to justify the slaughter of so many sacred cows. But, in fact, the political justifications for these huge governmental activities are remarkably vulnerable, as Murray demonstrates by puncturing them with a few well-placed thrusts.

146

For all his uncompromising libertarianism, Murray rejects the atomistic vision of some libertarian intellectuals, as he also rejects the popular "me generation" attitudes of self-fulfillment that "gave short shrift to parenting and neighboring." Indeed, one of his strongest objections to the welfare state is that it turned over to government bureaucracies "a large portion of the responsibility for feeding the hungry, succoring the sick, comforting the sad, nurturing the children, tending the elderly, and chastising the sinners."

In short, many of the things that liberals say should be done by "society" Murray agrees should be done in society— but not by government. Murray wants humanitarian acts done at the individual level and in ways that do not induce dependency or deprive people of personal responsibility by writing federal blank checks to subsidize anti-social and self-destructive behavior.

One of the major contributions of this book is exposing the fallacy of government agencies that use statistical "before and after" comparisons to claim success in their activities. Often the benefits claimed are part of a trend that began long before the program in question began and the slope of the trend line was not visibly changed afterwards.

Thus the steepest drop in poverty occurred during the 1950s, before the "war on poverty" began. Yet all further continuation of this trend is automatically credited to government social programs that began in the 1960s. It is much the same story when one plots the trend of increasing black representation in the professions. Murray finds that "the steepest slope of the trendline occurs in the early 1960s, before even the original Civil Rights Act of 1964."

It is much the same story with statistical trends after legislation on health, education, safety, and labor. The decades-long downward trend in automobile fatality rates leveled off after the 55 MPH speed limit was imposed and test scores actually declined after massive federal spending on education.

Murray freely admits that his proposals— which would cut government by more than half— are not at all politically feasible today or perhaps even within his lifetime. But of course the whole point of writing such a book is to begin the process of changing people's minds. Most of the New Deal would have been politically impossible just five years before Franklin D. Roosevelt was elected.

THE PATTERN OF
THE ANOINTED

They went to work with unsurpassable efficiency. Full employment,
a maximum of resulting output, and general well-being ought to
have been the consequence. It is true that instead we find misery,
shame and, at the end of it all, a stream of blood. But that was a
chance coincidence.

—*Joseph A. Schumpeter*[1]

What is intellectually interesting about visions are their assumptions and their reasoning, but what is socially crucial is the extent to which they are resistant to evidence. All social theories being imperfect, the harm done by their imperfections depends not only on how far they differ from reality, but also on how readily they adjust to evidence, to come back into line with the facts. One theory may be more plausible, or even more sound, than another, but if it is also more dogmatic, then that can make it far more dangerous than a theory that is not initially as close to the truth but which is more capable of adjusting to feedback from the real world. The prevailing vision of our time— the vision of the anointed— has shown an extraordinary ability to defy evidence.

Characteristic patterns have developed among the anointed for dealing with the repeated failures of policies based on their vision. Other patterns have developed for seizing upon statistics in such a way as to buttress the assumptions of the vision, even when the same set of statistics contain numbers that contradict the vision. Finally, there is the phenomenon of honored prophets among the anointed, who continue to be honored as their predictions fail by vast margins, time and again.

PATTERNS OF FAILURE

A very distinct pattern has emerged repeatedly when policies favored by the anointed turn out to fail. This pattern typically has four stages:

STAGE 1. THE "CRISIS": Some situation exists, whose negative aspects the anointed propose to eliminate. Such a situation is routinely characterized as a "crisis," even though all human situations have negative aspects, and even though evidence is seldom asked or given to show how the situation at hand is either uniquely bad or threatening to get worse. Sometimes the situation described as a "crisis" has in fact already been getting better for years.

STAGE 2. THE "SOLUTION": Policies to end the "crisis" are advocated by the anointed, who say that these policies will lead to beneficial result A. Critics say that these policies will lead to detrimental result Z. The anointed dismiss these latter claims as absurd and "simplistic," if not dishonest.

STAGE 3. THE RESULTS: The policies are instituted and lead to detrimental result Z.

STAGE 4. THE RESPONSE: Those who attribute detrimental result Z to the policies instituted are dismissed as "simplistic" for ignoring the "complexities" involved, as "many factors" went into determining the outcome. The burden of proof is put on the critics to demonstrate to a certainty that these policies alone were the only possible cause of the worsening that occurred. No burden of proof whatever is put on those who had so confidently predicted improvement. Indeed, it is often asserted that things would have been even worse, were it not for the wonderful programs that mitigated the inevitable damage from other factors.

Examples of this pattern are all too abundant. Three will be considered here. The first and most general involves the set of social welfare policies called "the war on poverty" during the administration of President Lyndon

B. Johnson, but continuing under other labels since then. Next is the policy of introducing "sex education" into the public schools, as a means of reducing teenage pregnancy and venereal diseases. The third example will be policies designed to reduce crime by adopting a less punitive approach, being more concerned with preventive social policies beforehand and rehabilitation afterwards, as well as showing more concern with the legal rights of defendants in criminal cases.

The "War on Poverty"

Governmental policies designed to alleviate the privations of the poor go back much further than President Johnson's "war on poverty," and of course reach far beyond the boundaries of the United States. What was different about this particular set of social programs, first proposed to Congress during the Kennedy administration and later enacted into law during the Johnson administration, was that their stated purpose was a reduction of *dependency*, not simply the provision of more material goods to the poor. This was the recurring theme of the "war on poverty," from the time President Kennedy introduced this legislation in 1962 until President Johnson saw it passed and signed it into law in 1964.

John F. Kennedy stated the purpose of the "war on poverty" to be "to help our less fortunate citizens to help themselves."[2] He said: "We must find ways of returning far more of our dependent people to independence."[3] The whole point of currently increased federal spending on this effort was "to strengthen and broaden the rehabilitative and preventive services" offered to "persons who are dependent or who would otherwise become dependent," so that long-run savings in government spending were expected from a subsequent decline in dependency. As President Kennedy put it:

> Public welfare, in short, must be more than a salvage operation, picking up the debris from the wreckage of human lives. Its emphasis must be directed increasingly toward prevention and rehabilitation— on reducing not only the long-range cost in budgetary terms but the long-range cost in human terms as well.[4]

The same theme of increased short-run spending for long-run savings, as a result of reduced dependency, was a theme repeated in a *New York Times* editorial:

> President Kennedy's welfare message to Congress yesterday stems from a recognition that no lasting solution to the problem can be bought with a relief check. Financial help to the needy must be supplemented by a vastly expanded range of professional and community services. Their aim: to keep men, women and children from having to rely on public assistance by making them useful, creative citizens. The President does not pretend it will be cheap to provide the needed build-up in staff, facilities and rehabilitation allowances. The initial cost will actually be greater than the mere continuation of handouts. The dividends will come in the restoration of individual dignity and in the long-run reduction of the need for government help.[5]

The *Congressional Quarterly* of the same date (February 2, 1962) likewise reported: "The President stressed that the welfare program should be directed toward the prevention of dependence and the rehabilitation of current relief recipients."[6]

The same theme carried over into the Johnson administration, where the antipoverty program was sold as a way to "break the cycle of poverty" and to make "taxpayers out of taxeaters."[7] "Give a hand, not a handout" was the slogan of the "war on poverty." In keeping with that theme, President Johnson said in August 1964, when the legislation was finally passed: "The days of the dole in our country are numbered."[8] This initial thrust of the war on poverty programs must be clearly recognized at the outset, for one of many responses to the failures of government programs has been to redefine their goals after the fact, to make the programs look "successful."

A subsidiary theme of the "war on poverty" was that social programs were a way of heading off urban violence. Lyndon Johnson spoke of "conditions that breed despair and violence." He said:

> All of us know what those conditions are: ignorance, discrimination, slums, poverty, disease, not enough jobs.[9]

The same theme was echoed in the celebrated 1968 Kerner Commission report on ghetto riots, which proclaimed that pervasive discrimination and segregation were "the source of the deepest bitterness and lie at the center of the problem of racial disorder."[10] The riots of 1967 were attributed to "the failure of all levels of government— Federal and state as well as local— to come to grips with the problems of our cities." In keeping with this theme that bad social conditions and official neglect lead to despair, which in turn leads to violence, civil rights leaders and other minority spokesmen began regularly predicting "a long hot summer" of violence if their demands for more government programs were not met.[11] Such predictions became a staple of political discourse and have remained so over the years. Government agencies seeking to expand their budgets and extend their powers likewise encouraged the belief that social programs reduced the incidence of riots and other violence, while a reduction of such programs would escalate civil disorder.[12]

A diametrically opposite set of beliefs and predictions came from critics of the "war on poverty" proposals. Senator Barry Goldwater predicted that these programs would "encourage poverty" by encouraging "more and more people to move into the ranks of those being taken care of by the government."[13] Nor did he expect expanded social programs to lead to a more harmonious society, for he saw their underlying philosophy as an "attempt to divide Americans" along class lines, to "pigeon-hole people and make hyphenated Americans."[14] As these programs got underway, the mayors of Los Angeles, San Francisco, and Detroit blamed the "war on poverty" for "fostering class struggle" through its support of community activists, radical intellectuals, and others with a vested interest in disaffection and turmoil.[15] The assumption that initial increases in government spending on social programs would lead to reduced spending in later years, as dependency declined, was likewise disputed by opponents like columnist Henry Hazlitt, who said, "we can expect the price tag to increase geometrically as the years go on."[16]

From an analytical standpoint, the issues were virtually ideal for testing: Two conflicting sets of belief led logically to opposite conclusions, stated in terms that could be tested empirically. Almost never, however, were such empirical tests made. The views expressed in the vision of the anointed became axiomatic. A re-examination of that vision, as it applied to the "war on poverty," shows that it went through the four stages already described:

STAGE 1: THE "CRISIS": Given that the purpose of the "war on poverty" was to reduce dependency, the question is: How much dependency was there at the time and was it increasing or decreasing before the new policies were instituted? In short, what was the "crisis" for which the anointed were proposing a "solution"?

As of the time the "war on poverty" programs began, the number of people who lived below the official poverty line had been declining continuously since 1960, and was only about half of what it had been in 1950.[17] On the more fundamental issue of *dependency*, the situation was even more clearly improving. The proportion of people whose earnings put them below the poverty level *without counting government benefits* declined by about one third from 1950 to 1965.[18] In short, dependency on government transfers as a means of warding off poverty was declining when the "war on poverty" began.

STAGE 2: THE "SOLUTION": The Economic Opportunity Act was passed in 1964, creating the Office of Economic Opportunity, the "war on poverty" agency. As an historian of poverty programs put it, "Congress was quick to buy a program that might help welfare wither away."[19] The Council of Economic Advisers declared, "conquest of poverty is well within our power."

STAGE 3: THE RESULTS: The percentage of people dependent upon the federal government to keep above the poverty line *increased*. Although the number of such dependent people had been declining for more than a decade before the "war on poverty" programs began, this downward trend now reversed itself and began rising within a few years after that program got underway.[20]

Official poverty continued its decline for some time, as massive federal outlays lifted many people above the official poverty line, but not out of dependency— the original goal. Eventually, however, even official poverty began to rise, so that a larger number of people were in poverty in 1992 than had been in poverty in 1964, when the "war on poverty" began.[21] Although the Office of Economic Opportunity itself was modestly funded, by government standards, it was a spearhead, a catalyst, and to some extent a coordinator of anti-poverty programs in other agencies as well. The massive expansion of anti-poverty social programs continued even after the Office of Economic Opportunity was disbanded in 1974 and its programs were reassigned to other agencies. Over-all federal spending on programs for the poor escalated as eligibility rules for welfare and Social Security were loosened, the size of benefits was increased, and unemployment insurance was made more available to more people, and for longer periods of time.[22]

Despite initial claims that various government services would lead to reduced federal outlays on welfare programs as more people became self-sufficient, the very opposite happened. The number of people receiving public assistance more than doubled from 1960 to 1977.[23] The dollar value of public housing rose nearly five-fold in a decade and the amount spent on food stamps rose more than ten-fold. All government-provided in-kind benefits increased about eight-fold from 1965 to 1969 and more than 20-fold by 1974.[24] Federal spending on such social welfare programs not only rose in dollar terms and in real terms, but also a percentage of the nation's Gross National Product, going from 8 percent of GNP in 1960 to 16 percent by 1974.[25]

As for urban ghetto riots, they raged across the country during this era.[26] Later, they declined sharply after the beginning of the Nixon administration, which opposed the whole "war on poverty" approach and eventually abolished the Office of Economic Opportunity, which had been the spearhead of this program. Still later, during the eight years of the Reagan presidency— supposedly the nadir of neglect— major urban riots became virtually extinct. The fact that the actual course of events followed a pattern diametrically the opposite of what was assumed and proclaimed by those with the vision of the anointed made not the slightest dent in the policies they advocated or in the assumptions behind those policies. In this respect as in others, the vision of the anointed had achieved a sacrosanct status, hermetically sealed off from the contaminating influence of facts.

STAGE 4: THE RESPONSE: The failure of the "war on poverty" to achieve its goal of reducing dependency— and in fact an *increasing* dependency as these policies went into effect— brought no acknowledgement of failure. In the many retrospective evaluations of these programs in later years and decades, most of their political and media proponents resolutely ignored the original goal of reducing dependency. The goal was instead redefined as reducing poverty by transferring resources. As former Johnson White House aide Hodding Carter III put it, "millions of people were lifted out of poverty during the period, or had their plight considerably alleviated, by government programs and public expenditures."[27] A member of President Johnson's Cabinet suggested yet another criterion of success: "Ask the 11 million students who have received loans for their college education whether the Higher Education Act failed." Similar questions were suggested for those who used a wide range of other government programs.[28] In short, the test for whether a program was good for the country as a whole was whether those who personally benefitted from it found it beneficial. Yet a third line of defense of failed policies has been to claim moral merit for their good intentions. Hodding Carter III was only one of many to use this defense when he wrote of the "war on poverty" as "a clear, steady trend away from the majority's long and shameful disregard of the other, hidden America of hard-core hopelessness."[29]

Related to the moral redemption of the uncaring masses was the excitement and inspiration of the elite. At a twentieth anniversary commemoration of the Johnson administration's social programs, another former aide to President Johnson referred to "the vision that excited and inspired the nation."[30] Mrs. Johnson spoke of the "sense of caring" and the "exhilaration" of her husband's efforts.[31] Finally, it was asserted that things would have been even worse, were it not for these programs. "The question is not what the bottom line is today— with poverty up— but where would we be if we didn't have these programs in place?" said Professor Sheldon Danziger, Director of the University of Wisconsin's Institute for Research on Poverty. "I think we'd have poverty rates over 25 percent."[32] Even though poverty and dependency were going down for years before the "war on poverty" began, Professor Danziger chose to assert that poverty rates would have gone up. There is no possible reply to these heads-I-win-and-tails-you-lose assertions, except to note that they would justify any policy on any subject anywhere, regardless of its empirically observed consequences.

In short, no matter what happens, the vision of the anointed always succeeds, if not by the original criteria, then by criteria extemporized later—and if not by empirical criteria, then by criteria sufficiently subjective to escape even the possibility of refutation. Evidence becomes irrelevant.

Sex Education

Among the many crusades which gathered new steam during the 1960s was the crusade to spread sex education into the public schools and through other channels. Among the first acts of the Office of Economic Opportunity in 1964 was making a grant to a Planned Parenthood unit in Texas. From a total expenditure of less than half a million dollars in fiscal year 1965, O.E.O. expanded its financing of sex education more than five-fold by fiscal year 1966.[33] Not only did the federal government begin in the late 1960s to greatly expand its own expenditures on sex education— often known as "family planning" or by other euphemisms— but it also began to mandate that states promote such programs as well. The number of patients served by "family planning" clinics increased approximately five-fold between 1968 and 1978.[34] As early as 1968, the National Education Association in its *NEA Journal* was saying that a federally funded project in a Washington school "demonstrated the need for sex education as an integral part of school curriculum beginning in the early grades." Some of the pregnant girls counseled "reported feeling that if they had studied human sexuality with understanding teachers during elementary school, they would not have become pregnant."[35] Sex education and "family planning" clinics— so-called despite their being established to prevent having babies— not only grew rapidly but also changed in the clientele they served. As a study of this era put it:

Family planning services grew phenomenally from the mid-60s to the mid-70s. In 1964, the federal government made its first family planning grant, which served only married women. By 1970, Congress had passed the first national family planning and population legislation. Federal expenditures grew from $16 million to close to $200 million. In 1969, there were less than a quarter of a million teenagers using family planning clinics; by 1976 this had swollen to 1.2 million.[36]

According to the Alan Guttmacher Institute, a leading research and advocacy organization promoting sex education, the federal government's support of "family planning services" rose from less than $14 million in 1968 to $279 million a decade later[37]— nearly a twenty-fold increase. By the early 1980s, nearly two-thirds of the money received by "family planning" agencies came from the federal government.[38] What was the purpose of all this activity? "Sex education is considered one of the primary tools to help adolescents avoid unwanted pregnancy," according to a typical comment of the period.[39] Once more, we have the four-stage pattern:

STAGE 1: THE "CRISIS": In 1968, it was claimed that "contraception education and counseling is now urgently needed to help prevent pregnancy and illegitimacy in high school girls."[40] The head of Planned Parenthood testified before a Congressional subcommittee in 1966 as to the need for sex education "to assist our young people in reducing the incidence of out-of-wedlock births and early marriage necessitated by pregnancy."[41] The incidence of venereal disease among young people was cited by the head of the New York City Board of Education as showing the need for "a crash educational program." An article in the *American School Board Journal* in 1969 depicted sex education as a way of combatting "illegitimacy and venereal disease."[42] *PTA Magazine* likewise urged sex education to combat "the spiraling rate of venereal diseases, the pregnancies before marriage, the emotionally disastrous results of irresponsible sexual behavior."[43]

Similar statements abounded from a variety of sources. But what was in fact the situation when this kind of "crisis" mentality was being used to push

for more sex education in the schools? Fertility rates among teenage girls
had been *declining* for more than a decade since 1957.[44] Venereal disease was
also *declining*. The rate of infection for gonorrhea, for example, declined
every year from 1950 through 1959, and the rate of syphilis infection was,
by 1960, less than half of what it had been in 1950.[45] This was the "crisis"
which federal aid was to solve.

> STAGE 2: THE "SOLUTION": Massive federal aid to sex
> education programs in the schools, and to "family planning"
> clinics, was advocated to combat teenage pregnancy and
> venereal disease. After sex education, according to a "Professor
> of Family Life," a boy "will find decreased need for casual,
> irresponsible and self-centered experimentation with sex."[46]
> Critics opposed such actions on various grounds, including a
> belief that sex education would lead to more sexual activity,
> rather than less, and to more teenage pregnancy as well. Such
> views were dismissed in the media and in politics, as well as by
> the advocates of sex education. The *New York Times* editorially
> rejected "emotions and unexamined tradition" in this area[47] and
> its education editor declared: "To fear that sex education will
> become synonymous with greater sexual permissiveness is to
> misunderstand the fundamental purpose of the entire
> enterprise."[48] As in many other cases, *intentions* were the
> touchstone of the vision of the anointed.
>
> STAGE 3: THE RESULTS: As early as 1968, nearly half of all schools
> in the country— public and private, religious and secular—
> had sex education, and it was rapidly growing.[49] As sex
> education programs spread widely through the American
> educational system during the 1970s, the pregnancy rate
> among 15 to 19 year old females rose from approximately 68
> per thousand in 1970 to approximately 96 per thousand by
> 1980.[50] Among unmarried girls in the 15 to 17 year old
> bracket, birth rates rose 29 percent between 1970 and 1984,[51]
> despite a massive increase in abortions, which more than

doubled during the same period. Among girls under 15, the number of abortions surpassed the number of live births by 1974.[52] The reason was not hard to find: According to the Alan Guttmacher Institute, the percentage of unmarried teenage girls who had engaged in sex was higher at every age from 15 though 19 by 1976 than it was just five years earlier.[53] The rate of teenage gonorrhea tripled between 1956 and 1975.[54] Sargent Shriver, former head of the Office of Economic Opportunity, which led the early charge for more sex education and "family planning" clinics, testified candidly to a Congressional Committee in 1978: "Just as venereal disease has skyrocketed 350% in the last 15 years when we have had more clinics, more pills, and more sex education than ever in history, teen-age pregnancy has risen."[55] Such candor was, however, the exception rather than the rule among those who had pushed for sex education and birth control ("family planning") clinics.

STAGE 4: THE RESPONSE: Sex education advocates continue to treat as axiomatic the need for more sex education to combat teenage pregnancy and venereal disease. As late as 1980, and in spite of mounting evidence, the Alan Guttmacher Institute proclaimed: "Teenage pregnancy can, through better education and preventive services, be, if not altogether avoided, at least reduced, and through better maternity, abortion and social services, be reduced in its personal impact on the teenager who does get pregnant." Opposition to sex education continued to be dismissed as a "simplistic view" in *The American Biology Teacher* journal.[56] Congressman James H. Scheuer of New York found that the alarming statistics on rising teenage pregnancy only "highlights the need for strong leadership by the Federal Government in solving this problem."[57] The very possibility that "strong" federal "leadership" might have worsened the situation was not even mentioned. To the Alan Guttmacher Institute as well, an "almost quadrupling" of venereal disease between 1960 and 1972[58] only showed that more "broadly based national programs channeled through the public school system are needed and are long overdue."[59]

Opposition to sex education has been depicted as "a threat to a democratic society."[60] When confronted with the evidence that pregnancy and abortions increased during the 1970s, sex education advocates often deny that sex education was widespread during that decade, by restricting the term "sex education" to *compulsory* sex education, which tended to be mandated later.

Although sex education programs have been sold to the public, to Congress, and to education officials as ways of reducing such tangible social ills as teenage pregnancy and venereal disease, many of the leaders of this movement have long had a more expansive agenda. As a Congressional committee report noted gingerly:

> The primary objective of Federal efforts in family life and sex education has been to reduce unwanted pregnancy rates among teenagers, while the primary goal of most sex educators appears to be encouragement of healthy attitudes about sex and sexuality.[61]

In short, however politically useful public concern about teenage pregnancy and venereal disease might be in obtaining government money and access to a captive audience in the public schools, the real goal was to change students' *attitudes*— put bluntly, to brainwash them with the vision of the anointed, in order to supplant the values they had been taught at home. In the words of an article in *The Journal of School Health*, sex education presents "an exciting opportunity to develop new norms."[62] Only in the light of this agenda does it make sense that so-called "sex education" should be advocated to take place throughout the school years— from kindergarten to college— when it could not possibly take that much time to teach basic biological or medical information about sex. What takes that long is a constant indoctrination in new attitudes.[63] An example of such indoctrination may be useful:

A popular sex instructional program for junior high school students, aged 13 and 14, shows film strips of four naked couples, two homosexual and two heterosexual, performing a variety of sexually explicit acts, and teachers are warned with a cautionary note from the sex educators not to show the material to parents or friends: "Many of the materials of this program shown to people outside the context of the program itself can evoke misunderstanding and difficulties."[64]

Parents who learned of this program and protested were quickly labeled "fundamentalists" and "right-wing extremists," even though they were in fact affluent Episcopalians in Connecticut.[65] Here is an almost textbook example of the vision of the anointed, pre-empting the decisions of parents as to when and how their own children shall be introduced to sex— and dismissing out of hand those with different views. Nor was this episode peculiar to this particular school. Similar things have happened all over the country.[66] Parents are denigrated both in discussions of public policy and in the materials given to students in the schools.[67] A typical comment from "experts" is that "sex and sexuality have become far too complex and technical to leave to the typical parent, who is either uninformed or too bashful to share useful sexual information with his child."[68]

This utter certainty of being right, even to the point of circumventing parents, is completely consistent with the vision, however inconsistent it is with decades of empirical evidence on the actual consequences of "healthy attitudes about sex" as promoted by "experts." The key point about the sex education crusade, from the standpoint of understanding the vision of the anointed, is that evidence proved to be as irrelevant here as on other issues.

Criminal Justice

Like so many negative social trends, soaring crime rates began in the 1960s, amid glowing optimism about how much better things could be if the traditional beliefs of the many were replaced by the special new insights of the few. In the case of criminal justice, however, the policy changes did not originate so much in legislation as in judicial and administrative rulings and policies. But the *zeitgeist* alone did not initiate the changing policies, which depended on specific people doing specific things. Among the key people whose words and actions set the tone for the changes in the criminal justice system in the 1960s were the Chief Justice of the U. S. Supreme Court, the

Attorney General of the United States, and the Chief Judge of the Circuit Court of Appeals for the District of Columbia, then as now regarded as de facto the second highest court in the land. By name they were, respectively, Earl Warren, Ramsey Clark, and David L. Bazelon. What was the problem or "crisis" they were attempting to "solve"?

> STAGE 1:THE "CRISIS": Although Chief Judge Bazelon said in 1960 that "we desperately need all the help we can get from modern behavioral scientists"[69] in dealing with the criminal law, the cold facts suggest no such desperation or crisis. Since the most reliable long-term crime data are on murder, what was the murder rate at that point? The number of murders committed in the United States in 1960 was less than in 1950, 1940, or 1930— even though the population was growing over those decades and murders in the two new states of Hawaii and Alaska were counted in the national statistics for the first time in 1960.[70] The murder *rate*, in proportion to population, was in 1960 just under half of what it had been in 1934.[71]

As Judge Bazelon saw the criminal justice system in 1960, the problem was not with "the so-called criminal population"[72] but with society, whose "need to punish" was a "primitive urge" that was "highly irrational"[73]— indeed, a "deep childish fear that with any reduction of punishment, multitudes would run amuck."[74] It was this "vindictiveness," this "irrationality" of "notions and practices regarding punishment"[75] that had to be corrected. The criminal "is like us, only somewhat weaker," according to Judge Bazelon, and "needs help if he is going to bring out the good in himself and restrain the bad."[76] Society is indeed guilty of "creating this special class of human beings," by its "social failure" for which "the criminal serves as a scapegoat."[77] Punishment is itself a "dehumanizing process" and a "social branding" which only promotes more crime.[78] Since criminals "have a special problem and need special help," Judge Bazelon argued for "psychiatric treatment" with "new, more sophisticated techniques" and asked:

Would it really be the end of the world if all jails were turned into hospitals or rehabilitation centers?[79]

Chief Judge Bazelon's views were not the isolated opinions of one man but expressed a widespread vision among the anointed, many of whom lionized him for such statements.[80] The same therapeutic vision was still apparent more than a quarter of a century later, when Supreme Court Justice William J. Brennan referred to "the etiology of crime," for which he called upon "psychiatrists and psychologists," as well as "experts in the behavioral sciences," for help.[81] Brennan's long-time colleague on the Supreme Court, Justice William O. Douglas, likewise took the therapeutic approach:

> Rehabilitation of criminals has seldom been attempted. Killing them or locking them up is the tried-and-true ancient method. Why not turn our faces toward rehabilitation?[82]

The therapeutic vision also permeated the writings and speeches of President Lyndon Johnson's Attorney General Ramsey Clark:

> Rehabilitation must be the goal of modern corrections. Every other consideration must be subordinated to it. To rehabilitate is to give health, freedom from drugs and alcohol, to provide education, vocational training, understanding and the ability to contribute to society.
>
> Rehabilitation means the purpose of law is justice— and that as a generous people we wish to give every individual his chance for fulfillment. The theory of rehabilitation is based on the belief that healthy, rational people will not injure others, that they will understand that the individual and his society are best served by conduct that does not inflict injury, and that a just society has the ability to provide health and purpose and opportunity for all its citizens. Rehabilitated, an individual will not have the capacity— cannot bring himself— to injure another or take or destroy property.[83]

With Attorney General Clark, as with Chief Judge Bazelon and others, the problem was with the benighted public and its outdated attitudes. Society imposes long prison sentences "because we are angry," according to Clark, but "this will not reduce crime." He said: "If it is the public safety we are concerned about, the question is how persons convicted of crimes can be rehabilitated, not how long they should be locked up."[84] Again, it is necessary to emphasize that these were not the isolated opinions of one man. Ramsey Clark's book, *Crime in America* was widely praised among the opinion elites. *New York Times* columnist Tom Wicker, for example, called Clark "an awesomely knowledgeable professional" and praised his "generosity and understanding" as well as his "courage and persistence and eloquence."[85] The *Saturday Review* called *Crime in America* one of "the best books written on violence in America."[86] Similar praise appeared in *Time* magazine,[87] in *The New Republic*,[88] and, as far away as London, the *Times Literary Supplement* said in its review of *Crime in America* that no one has "done more to state the problem and light the way to improvement than Ramsey Clark."[89] More importantly, the Attorney General, Chief Judge Bazelon, and justices of the Supreme Court were not simply people whose words received a large and favorable public notice from opinion-making elites. They were people in a position to act.

>   STAGE 2: THE "SOLUTION": A series of landmark Supreme Court
>   decisions in the 1960s changed the course of criminal justice in
>   the United States. *Mapp v. Ohio* (1961), *Escobedo v. Illinois*
>   (1964), and *Miranda v. Arizona* (1966) successively expanded
>   the rights of criminals in the custody of the police by making
>   their convictions invalid if the procedures specified by the
>   courts were not followed in detail by the police. *Gideon v.
>   Wainwright* (1963) required states to provide free attorneys to
>   criminal defendants, subject to the threat that their convictions
>   would be overturned, even if guilt was unquestioned, when
>   such attorneys were not provided. In California, even when
>   state-appointed attorneys were supplied, if these attorneys'
>   defense strategies were second-guessed by appellate judges and
>   considered inadequate, convictions could be overturned on
>   grounds of denial of the constitutional right to counsel.[90]

Although the U. S. Supreme Court began this judicial revolution in criminal law in the 1960s, even earlier Chief Judge Bazelon had expanded the scope of the "insanity" defense in the landmark case of *Durham v. United States* (1954) and he continued to lead the D. C. Circuit Court of Appeals toward more expansive views of criminals' rights. In addition, courts across the land involved themselves more and more in the administration of prisons, prescribing better living conditions and imposing on the prison system a duty to provide prisoners with access to law books, in order to prepare appeals of their convictions. Moreover, sentences were less often imposed and tended to be of shorter duration.[91]

In short, the vision of the anointed triumphed in the criminal justice system. The assumptions underlying its actions were the same as elsewhere. Sweeping presumptions about the irrationality and mean-spiritedness of the public were made without either evidence or a sense of need for evidence. Conversely, the validity and applicability of the beliefs of "experts" were taken as axiomatic. Judge Bazelon, for example, referred to the insanity defense as "merely one way of welcoming the psychiatrist into the courtroom."[92] Whatever the merits or demerits of this approach, it fulfilled the essential requirements for the vision of the anointed: It established that the anointed and the benighted were on vastly different moral and intellectual planes, and it justified taking decisions out of the hands of those who passed the existing laws in response to the voting public and put these decisions in the hands of judges responsive to those with "expertise." Moreover, it put the burden of proof on others. As Judge Bazelon put it, "in the absence of decisive empirical data,"[93] he was prepared to experiment. There was no suggestion of what empirical data should be used to test the success of that experiment, either absolutely or relative to the approach discarded with such disdain.

Although judges took the lead in this revolution in criminal justice, they were seconded by those in politics and in the media who shared the prevailing vision. President Lyndon Johnson saw social programs as the real way to fight crime. As quoted in the *New York Times*:

> "I don't know why some people sit idly by and are willing to take the more expensive route— the delinquency route, the jail route, the penitentiary route," he asserted.
> "It takes more of our money to take care of a convict in a penitentiary than it does to prepare a boy to be a good, taxpaying citizen who can read and write," he said. . .[94]

Similar views were expressed by 1968 Democratic vice presidential candidate Edmund Muskie. Responding to the law and order issues raised by his opponents in the election campaign, Senator Muskie responded:

> But you can't have law and order based on ignorance. . . You've got to build it by education, enlightenment and opportunity. That's the way to make a society safe.[95]

These views did not pass unchallenged, though the legal changes became "the law of the land," largely by judicial rather than legislative process. On the Supreme Court itself, there were bitter dissents from the continued expansions— or creations— of criminals' "rights." The *Miranda* decision of 1966, which climaxed the judicial revolution in the criminal law, led to this scene in the Supreme Court:

> Justice Harlan, his face flushed and his voice occasionally faltering with emotion, denounced the decision as "dangerous experimentation" at a time of a "high crime rate that is a matter of growing concern."
> He said it was a "new doctrine" without substantial precedent, reflecting a balance in favor of the accused.
> Justice White said:
> "In some unknown number of cases the Court's rule will return a killer, a rapist or other criminal to the streets and to the environment which produced him, to repeat his crime whenever it pleases him.
> "As a consequence, there will not be a gain, but a loss, in human dignity."[96]

Such dissents were brushed aside and outcries from the public and from law enforcement officials were dismissed. At a 1965 judicial conference, where a former police commissioner of New York City complained about the trend of the Supreme Court's decisions on criminal law, his concerns were immediately met with sarcastic ridicule by a law professor who asked, "I wonder what rights we'd have left if we always yielded to the police hysteria." Justice William J. Brennan and Chief Justice Earl Warren who, according to a *New York Times* account, sat "stony-faced" during the police commissioner's statements then "frequently roared with laughter" as the law professor poured scorn and derision on those statements, which were characterized as "simplistic, narrow-minded and politically expedient."[97] The benighted were simply not to be taken seriously by the anointed.

Had anyone been seriously interested in testing the opposing theories of crime empirically, those theories were ideally suited for such testing, since each theory led to conclusions which were not only logically consistent with its own premises but which were virtually inescapable, given their respective premises. Moreover, these conclusions were clearly distinguishable empirically and data were readily available.

In the prevailing vision of the anointed, emphasis on punishment was mistaken when what was needed were therapeutic alternatives to punishment, social programs to get at the "root causes" of crime, and more rights for those accused and convicted of crimes, so as to establish that the law was fair and worthy of respect, which respect would then be an ingredient in more law-abiding behavior by those otherwise alienated from society. By contrast, the traditional view would lead one to expect a rising crime rate after the changes of the 1960s. If punishment deters, as the traditionalists believed, then the reduction in imprisonment that occurred in the 1960s would tend to produce more crime. But if imprisonment itself exacerbated the crime problem, as Judge Bazelon, Ramsey Clark, and numerous others with the vision of the anointed claimed, then this reduction in imprisonment would tend to reduce crime. Similarly, if social programs for the poor, for minorities, and for the mentally disturbed were needed to get at the "root causes" of crime, as the anointed claimed, then the vast and unprecedented expansion of such programs during the 1960s should have reduced the crime rate. The logical implications of each vision were quite clear. All that was needed was empirical evidence.

STAGE 3:THE RESULTS: Crime rates skyrocketed. Murder rates suddenly shot up until the murder rate in 1974 was more than twice as high as in 1961.[98] Between 1960 and 1976, a citizen's chances of becoming a victim of a major violent crime tripled.[99] The number of policemen murdered also tripled during the decade of the 1960s.[100] Young criminals, who had been especially favored by the new solicitude, became especially violent. The arrest rate of juveniles for murder more than tripled between 1965 and 1990, even allowing for changes in population size.[101]

As in other areas, such evidence has made little or no difference in the vision of the anointed, except to spur them on to new feats of ingenuity in interpretation.

> STAGE 4:THE RESPONSE: Since neither criminal law changes nor any other social changes are likely to produce truly instantaneous effects, there was a brief period during which no change in the crime rate was discernible— and this momentary lull provided occasions for expressions of much disdain toward those who had predicted that the new criminal justice practices would lead to higher crime rates. Just two months after the *Miranda* decision in 1966, the *New York Times* declared that "the gloomy predictions of its critics have been happily unrealized."[102] However, once the crime rates had clearly begun to rise in the wake of this and many other judicial changes designed to reduce them, the tactics of the proponents of those innovations shifted. Among the early responses to soaring crime rates, in the wake of policies designed to reduce them, were denials that crimes were in fact more frequent. Increased reporting of crime or better collection of statistics was held responsible for the upsurge in the official statistics.[103] However, as James Q. Wilson put it, "by 1970, enough members of the liberal audience had had their typewriters stolen to make it difficult to deny the existence of a crime wave."[104] Moreover, even in the absence of accumulating personal experience, it was difficult to believe that soaring murder statistics reflected simply better record keeping, since it had always been hard to ignore a dead body.

An alternative to denying rising crime rates was to make it socially unacceptable to talk about it, by equating discussions of "law and order" with racism, since it was well known that crime rates were higher among blacks. "Law and order" was "an inflammatory statement," according to the well-known psychiatrist Karl Menninger. "What it really means, I'm afraid, is that we should all go out and find the niggers and beat them up."[105] This was only one of many expressions of the prevailing vision by Dr. Menninger, whose book, *The Crime of Punishment* was widely hailed as it blamed "society" for crime, treated criminals as more wronged than wronging, and urged a substitution of psychiatric treatment for punishment. Another remarkable attempt to evade the bitter implications of the data on the reversal of the crime rate decline after the criminal justice system was transformed in the 1960s was made in another highly touted book, *Criminal Violence, Criminal Justice* by Charles E. Silberman, who wrote:

> For all the talk about the decline in punishment and the hobbling effect of the Warren Court, moreover, what data are available indicate that contemporary criminal courts prosecute, convict, and incarcerate a larger proportion of those arrested for a felony today than did the courts of the 1920s.[106]

What was not explained was why the 1920s were selected as a base period for determining the effect of the Warren Court, which began in 1953 and whose landmark criminal law decisions were made in the 1960s. If this desperate expedient of choosing an irrelevant base period suggests that Silberman's conclusions could not have been supported if his before-and-after comparison had been based on the actual dates of the actual decisions, or even on the date of the beginning of the Warren Court, a look at a few readily available facts confirms that suspicion. First of all, the likelihood that someone who committed a serious crime would be arrested fell until it was only one-fifth as high by 1979 as it had been in 1962.[107] As for going to prison, an earlier trend toward rising imprisonment rates was ended in the late 1950s and early 1960s, and imprisonment rates remained low as crime rates rose during the 1960s.[108]

In short, contrary to what Silberman suggests, criminals were no longer being apprehended, convicted, and incarcerated as they were before the Warren Court remade the criminal law. Moreover, the consequences were precisely what anyone without the vision of the anointed would have expected: When Earl Warren became Chief Justice in 1953, the homicide rate in the United States was 4.8 per 100,000 population— lower than it had been in four decades.[109] But a sharp rise in homicides began in the

1960s, more than doubling from 1963 to 1973,[110] and by 1991 the rate for murder and deliberate manslaughter alone was 9.8 per 100,000[111]— even omitting other forms of homicide which had been counted in earlier statistics. Whatever the weight of before-and-after statistics, in so far as they are cited at all, the "before" year selected can change the conclusion completely. Silberman's selection of the 1920s as his base of comparison suggests a desperate evasion of the obvious. Once again, it must be noted that Charles E. Silberman's views were not simply the opinions of one man, as the widespread praise of his book in the elite media demonstrated.[112]

The general public and law enforcement officials who did not share the elite vision continued to complain, but while their concerns found some response in the political arena, the anointed were unmoved. Chief Justice Earl Warren brushed aside those whose "self-righteous indignation" about rising crime rates was based on "oversimplification." According to the Chief Justice, "all of us must assume a share of the responsibility," for he attributed the rising crime rates to the fact that "for decades we have swept under the rug" the slum conditions which breed crime.[113] He ignored the fact that crime rates had been *declining* during all those decades when it should have been rising, according to his theory. Nor is there any reason to believe that Warren ever reconsidered that theory as crime rates continued to soar, for he said in his memoirs:

> A sizable proportion of the American people, too, groping for a reason for so much criminal activity in our disturbed society but overlooking the root causes of crime— such as the degradation of slum life in the ghetto, ignorance, poverty, the drug traffic, unemployment, and organized crime (often made possible by the corruption of law enforcement officials)— joined in placing the blame on the courts and particularly on the Supreme Court.[114]

No attempt was made to show how any of these other factors had worsened so dramatically during the 1960s as to explain the complete turnaround in the historically declining murder rate, for example, or why none of the supposed benefits of the new criminal justice reforms materialized. The relationship between theory and evidence was simply not discussed. The vision was axiomatic.

"ON LIBERTY"
RECONSIDERED

A mong the many writings of John Stuart Mill, the one most likely to have been read by people living today is *On Liberty*, and the ideas expressed in it taken as most characteristic of Mill's philosophy. Yet this small and plainly written work is often profoundly misunderstood.

Although *On Liberty* has become a symbol invoked against the intrusions of government into people's personal lives or its stifling of ideas, Mill was unmistakably clear that intrusive government was *not* the object of his concern in this particular essay. He asserted, "the era of pains and penalties for political discussion has, in our own country, passed away."[1] Even a government press prosecution the year before *On Liberty* was published "has not" in Mill's words, "induced me to alter a single word of the text."[2] Various other government restrictions Mill dismissed as "but rags and remnants of persecution."[3] The government was not what Mill feared nor what *On Liberty* was meant to warn against. It was the social "tyranny of the majority"[4] and "the despotism of Custom"[5] that he opposed in *On Liberty*. He said:

> In England, from the peculiar circumstances of our political history, though the yoke of opinion is perhaps heavier, that of law is lighter, than in most other countries of Europe; and there is considerable jealousy of direct interference, by the legislative or the executive power, with private conduct; not so much from any just regard for the independence of the individual as from the still subsisting habit of looking on the government as representing an opposite interest to the public.[6]

What then is the subject of *On Liberty*? Mill says in the first paragraph of that essay that its subject is "the nature and limits of the power which can be legitimately exercised by society over the individual"[7]— society, not government. Mill declared:

> Like other tyrannies, the tyranny of the majority was at first, and is still vulgarly, held in dread, chiefly as operating through the acts of the public authorities. But reflecting persons perceived that when society itself is the tyrant— society collectively, over the separate individuals who

compose it— its means of tyrannizing are not restricted to acts which it may do by the hands of its political functionaries. Society can and does execute its own mandate: and if it issues wrong mandates instead of right, it practices a social tyranny more formidable than many kinds of political oppression.[8]

While society's disapproval is "not usually upheld by such extreme penalties" as government may have at its disposal, there are "fewer means of escape," with social disapproval "penetrating more deeply into the details of life, and enslaving the soul itself."[9] Mill says in *On Liberty*: "Our merely social intolerance kills no one, roots out no opinions, but induces men to disguise them, or to abstain from any active effort for their diffusion."[10] Admitting that some rules of conduct must be imposed, both by law and by public opinion, Mill nevertheless thought that "the sole end for which mankind is warranted, individually or collectively, in interfering with the liberty of any of their number, is self-protection."[11] *On Liberty* argued that individuals should be free to do as they like "without detriment to their estimation" in the eyes of others.[12] This was, however, an asymmetrical principle, as Mill applied it. To say that people should be free to do as they like "without detriment to their estimation" in the eyes of others is to say that others have no right to express their own opinions or even to quietly shun those whose conduct they disapprove.

This central principle elaborated in *On Liberty* is asymmetrical in yet another way. It becomes clear, especially in the later parts of *On Liberty*, that Mill's special concern is with the effects of public opinion and customs on the intellectual elite. "Customs are made for customary circumstances and customary characters,"[13] he says. Exceptional people should be exempt from the influence of mass public opinion— but mass public opinion should not be exempt from the influence of the intellectual elite. On the contrary, one of the arguments for the exemption of the elite from the social influence of the masses is that this will enable the elite to develop in ways that can then enable them to exert social influence over the masses:

> There is always need of persons not only to discover new truths, and point out when what were once truths are true no longer, but to commence new practices, and set the examples of more enlightened conduct, and better taste and sense in human life. It is true that this

benefit is not capable of being rendered by everybody alike: there are but few persons, in comparison with the whole of mankind, whose experiments, if adopted by others, would be likely to be any improvement on established practice. But these few are the salt of the earth; without them, human life would become a stagnant pool.[14]

Thus *On Liberty*, which seems at first to be an argument for being non-judgmental towards individuals in general, turns out to be an argument for a *one-way* non-judgmental attitude toward special individuals who are to apply social influence on others that others are to refrain from applying to them.

Throughout Mill's writings over his lifetime, special intellectual elites were depicted as the salvation of society in general and of the masses in particular. Great things could be achieved, Mill said in one of his early writings, "if the superior spirits would but join with each other" for social betterment.[15] He called upon the universities to "send forth into society a succession of minds, not the creatures of their age, but capable of being its improvers and regenerators."[16]

According to *On Liberty*, democracy can rise above mediocrity, only where "the sovereign Many have let themselves be guided (which in their best times they always have done) by the counsels and influence of a more highly gifted and instructed One or Few."[17] *On Liberty* is an argument for the differential treatment of an intellectual elite, cast in the language of greater freedom for all. In this and in Mill's other writings, it is these elites— "the best and wisest,"[18] the "thinking minds,"[19] "the most cultivated intellects in the country,"[20] "those who have been in advance of society in thought and feeling"[21]— that he looked to for the progress of society. What Mill called "the general progress of the human mind" was in reality the special progress of special minds who were to lead others. Even when they lacked the power or influence to carry out this role, the intellectual elite had the duty of "keeping alive the sacred fire in a few minds when we are unable to do more," as Mill wrote to a friend.[22]

In short, the excogitated conclusions of the intellectual elite were more or less automatically assumed to be superior to the life experiences of millions, as distilled into social values and customs. The role of the masses was to be taught by their betters and the role of their betters was to be taught by the best. Mill wrote to Harriet Taylor that they must write in order to provide material from which "thinkers, when there are any after us, may nourish themselves & then dilute for other people."[23] As for the masses, Harriet Taylor wrote to Mill that "for the great mass of peoples I think wisdom would be to make the utmost of sensation while they are young enough & then die."[24]

MARX THE MAN

After a century of myths and counter-myths, of deification and demonizing, it is hard to realize that behind all the portraits and caricatures to be seen on printed pages and on banners, there really was a flesh-and-blood human being named Karl Marx. He was born in the little German town of Trier in the Rhineland in 1818, in a three-story townhouse in a fashionable part of town. A baron lived nearby,[1] and his four-year-old daughter was destined to become Karl Marx's wife. The people who signed as witnesses on Karl Marx's birth certificate were prominent citizens. The Marxes, like their neighbors and friends, had servants, property, education, and local prominence. Unlike most of their neighbors and friends, however, both Heinrich Marx and his wife Henrietta were descended from a long line of rabbis. Indeed, the town's chief rabbi was his brother, but they were brothers estranged from each other, since Heinrich Marx had abandoned the faith of his fathers.[2] Karl Marx was baptized a Lutheran, and throughout his life he spoke of Jews in the third person— and seldom complimentarily.

Marx was the third child born in his family, the second to survive, and the oldest boy. Younger brothers and sisters were born annually for the next four years, and then two more at two-year intervals.[3] The father was a prosperous lawyer, who also owned vineyards, as well as houses whose rents supplemented his income. He was a man of wide culture and political liberalism. His son idolized him, and in later years spoke of him often to his own children, though they had never seen him— his death having occurred decades before. Marx's mother was Dutch and spoke German with a heavy Dutch accent. She was a devoted housewife, not a woman of learning, and though her son loved her in childhood, they were soon estranged in his early adulthood. When she died, many years later, Marx expressed not the slightest sorrow.[4]

YOUTH

Karl Marx grew up a brilliant, spoiled child, who bullied his younger sisters and taunted his schoolmates with sarcastic witticisms— in addition to entertaining both with imaginative stories. He had a swarthy complexion that in later years earned him the nickname "The Moor"— a name used far more often in his inner circle (including his children) than was his real name. His neighbor, Baron von Westphalen, took a great interest in Marx as a youth, and the learned baron would often take long walks with him discussing Homer, Shakespeare, Voltaire, or other great writers in any of a number of languages that the baron spoke.[5]

As a young man, Karl Marx attended the University of Bonn for one year. There he was an enthusiastic student, but also an enthusiastic drinker, and took part in rowdiness and at least one duel.[6] His father transferred him to the University of Berlin, a larger and more serious institution. But the self-indulgent, bohemian and spendthrift habits that Marx had exhibited at Bonn continued at Berlin, where he was sued several times for non-payment of debts.[7] His father's letters show growing recriminations directed not only at his son's prodigious capacity to waste money— a talent he never lost throughout his life— but also at a more disturbing personal characteristic, egomania.[8] One of Marx's many poems of this period says:

> *Then I will wander godlike and victorious*
> *Through the ruins of the world*
> *And, giving my words an active force,*
> *I will feel equal to the creator.*[9]

The themes of destruction, corruption, and savagery run through Marx's poems of this era,[10] two of which were published in a small literary magazine of the time under the title "Savage Songs."[11] There was nothing political about these writings. Marx had not yet turned his attention in that direction. He was simply, as one biographer said, "a man with a peculiar faculty for relishing disaster."[12] A contemporary description of Marx as a student depicts the same demonic personality— again, not yet in a political context:

> *But who advances here full of impetuosity?*
> *It is a dark form from Trier, an unleashed monster,*
> *With self-assured step he hammers the ground with his heels*

And raises his arms in all fury to heaven
As though he wished to seize the celestial vault and lower it to earth.
In rage he continually deals with his redoubtable fist,
As if a thousand devils were gripping his hair.[13]

In short, Marx's angry apocalyptic visions existed before he discovered capitalism as the focus of such visions.

Marx entered the University of Berlin a few years after the death of its most famous professor— G.W.F. Hegel, whose posthumous influence was even greater than during his lifetime.[14] Marx began to associate with a group called the Young Hegelians, who were preoccupied with philosophy in general and religion in particular— or rather, with atheism, for they were radical critics of Christianity. Marx's formal studies languished; he took only two courses in his last three years at the University of Berlin.[15] Marx became a "bohemian student, who merely regarded the university as his camping ground"[16] and he was largely self-taught.[17] The death of his father in 1838, and his long engagement to Jenny von Westphalen eventually made it necessary that he prepare to bring his studies to a close. Although he had studied at the University of Berlin, he applied for a doctorate at the University of Jena— an easier institution, noted as a diploma mill.[18] His doctoral dissertation was on two ancient materialist philosophers, Democritus and Epicurus.

EARLY CAREER

Searching aimlessly for a career, Marx drifted into journalism and became editor of *Rheinische Zeitung*, a liberal newspaper, reflecting Marx's own political views at that time, as well as that of the Rhineland middle class in general. Under the Prussian repression of that era, liberalism was an embattled and endangered creed, and Marx made the newspaper more controversial and more widely read than before.

His running of the paper was characterized by a contemporary as "a dictatorship of Marx"[19]— as so many groups with which he was affiliated would be throughout his lifetime. Another contemporary described him as "domineering, impetuous, passionate, full of boundless self-confidence."[20] Marx engaged in a running battle of wits with the government's censors,[21] and— ironically— tried to restrain some of the more radical of the newspaper's writers.[22] Among these was another young man from an affluent background named Moses Hess, a communist who eventually converted still another such offspring of wealth to communism— Friedrich Engels.[23] Marx, however, purged Hess from the newspaper for his "smuggling into the newspaper of communist and socialist dogmas disguised as theatrical criticism."[24] Only after Marx finally resigned as editor, to spare the paper from being banned, did he begin the studies that would eventually lead him to communism.

During the same period in the early 1840s Marx had a decisive break with his family. Now that his father was dead, and the estate had to suffice for eight people to live on, Frau Marx was not inclined to continue indefinitely sending money to her eldest son, now fully grown and holding a doctoral degree. Marx had continued his already long-standing practice of running up bills that he could not pay, and was outraged that his mother cut off his remaining small allowance. As he put it in a letter to a friend: "Although they are quite rich, my family has placed difficulties in my way which have temporarily placed me in an embarrassing situation."[25] Such temporary embarrassments were to become a permanent feature of Marx's life over the next four decades. Nevertheless, he eventually persuaded the aristocratic von Westphalens to let him marry their daughter— now 29 years old— who had waited faithfully for him for seven years.

It was not a marriage whose prospects were viewed with favor by either family. There was a church wedding in 1843, but most of her family and all of his family stayed away. However, the bride's mother paid for the honeymoon and in addition turned over to the couple a small legacy which she had received. This legacy was held in the form of coins in a strong box— which Marx and his bride then left open in their hotel rooms, inviting any visitors to take whatever they might need. It was empty before they returned to her home,[26] where they lived with her mother for several months.

In October 1843, Marx and his wife— now pregnant— moved to Paris, where he was hired to contribute to a publishing venture— a bilingual journal for German and French readers. Only one issue ever appeared. Marx and the editor quarreled and broke up, leaving Marx without funds in a foreign land.

A collection was hastily taken up by friends in Cologne, and the couple was rescued— as they would be again and again throughout their lives. Here in Paris Marx began the studies that led him to communism. He also began to meet other radical figures of the time— including the radical poet Heinrich Heine, Russian anarchist Mikhail Bakunin, and the French radical writer Pierre Joseph Proudhon. Heine, though at first a great friend of the Marxes, was eventually alienated by Karl Marx's arrogance and dogmatism.[27] In later years, Heine described the Paris radicals— including Marx— as a "crowd of godless, self-appointed gods."[28] Among these radicals was a young German whom Marx had met briefly before— Friedrich Engels.

COLLABORATION WITH ENGELS

Engels, two years younger than Marx, came from an even wealthier family, which owned half-interest in a factory in Germany and half-interest in another factory in England.[29] His father had never been as indulgent as Marx's father, and Engels never attended a university, but he was well read and by middle age could read and write nearly two dozen languages.[30] Engels was sent away at seventeen to get on-the-job training in the family business in Bremen. Here he was "not overworked"— he was, after all, an owner's son— and was known to have beer, cigars, poems, and correspondence with him, and to take a leisurely lunch and a nap afterwards in a hammock.[31] He also found time to study Hegel. Engels eventually became a member of the Young Hegelians, and in 1842 had his first brief meeting with the editor of the *Rheinische Zeitung*, Karl Marx. Their first meeting was cool, for Marx viewed Engels at that point as just another member of the radical group whose literary contributions to the paper were causing him trouble with the censors.

From 1842 to 1844, Engels lived in Manchester, England, working in the family business there and observing the conditions of the working people in this industrial town— observations which led to his first book, *The Conditions of the Working Class in England in 1844*. When he passed through Paris on his way back to the Rhineland in 1844, he again met Marx— and this time, many days of discussion found them "in complete agreement on questions of theory"[32]— as they continued to be for the remaining decades of their lives. At this juncture, Engels was not only further advanced than Marx on the road to communism, but was also much better versed in economics. Although their first joint publication— *The Holy Family*— appeared a year later, there was at that point no suggestion of a continuing collaboration between them. The forward to *The Holy Family* promised future writings from the pair— "each for himself, of course."[33] But in reality later events brought them together again in England, in a permanent alliance in which their ideas and words were so intermingled that it would be rash to say conclusively, a hundred years later, what was Marx's and what was Engels'. Even Marx's daughter, after his death, mistakenly published a collection of her father's newspaper articles that later turned out all to have been written by Engels.[34]

The most famous of their explicitly collaborative writings was of course *The Communist Manifesto*. Its genesis typified the pattern of Marxian political intrigue. A radical organization in London called the League of the Just was in process of reorganization to become the Communist League, and it involved several people in the drawing up of its credo. One of these submitted his draft to Engels who confessed to Marx that "*just between ourselves* I played a hellish trick on Mosi"[35]— substituting the Marxian program for the draft entrusted to him. Engels realized the enormity of his betrayal, for he cautioned Marx to utter secrecy, "otherwise we shall be deposed and there will be a murderous scandal."[36] Thus Marx and Engels made themselves the voices of communism. Engels wrote up a document in question-and-answer format, but then decided that he did not like it. He turned his work over to Marx to re-do in some other format, and suggested the title, *The Communist Manifesto*. Slowly the document evolved, written mostly in the style of Marx, though reproducing some ideas from Engels' earlier draft. It was published in February 1848 as *The Manifesto of the Communist Party*, with no authors listed, as though it were the work of some major organization, rather than of a relative handful of radical refugees.

The members of the Communist League were overwhelmingly intellectuals and professionals, with a very few skilled craftsmen. Their average age was under thirty.[37] It had the same kind of social composition that would in later years characterize the so-called International Working Mens

Association, and many other radical groups in which the youthful offspring of privilege called themselves the proletariat. When Engels was elected as delegate to the Communist League in 1847, in order to conceal what was in fact an unopposed election, in Engels' own words, "a working man was proposed for appearances' sake, but those who proposed him voted for me."[38]

Ironically, the year 1848 was a year of revolutions, but revolutions which differed from that described in *The Communist Manifesto*. The bourgeoisie and the proletariat were in revolutionary alliance against the autocratic European governments on the continent. During the upheavals that swept across Europe, Marx and Engels returned to Germany— Marx to edit a newspaper, the *Neue Rheinische Zeitung*, in his familiar dictatorial style.[39] Engels worked at first as his chief assistant, until he had to flee an order for his arrest for inciting to violence. Engels made his way through France to Switzerland, enjoying along the way "the sweetest grapes and loveliest of girls."[40] This continued Engels' long-lasting pattern of womanizing,[41] which included the wife of a fellow communist whose seduction he revealed to another communist "when in my cups."[42] He was particularly fond of French women, reporting to Marx in 1846 "some delicious encounters with *grissettes*"[43] and later observing:

> If I had an income of 5,000 fr. I would do nothing but work and amuse myself with women until I went to pieces. If there were no Frenchwomen, life wouldn't be worth living.[44]

In 1849, Engels returned to Germany, where the revolution was being suppressed, and took part in armed fighting against the government forces. An expulsion order was issued against Marx, who had to liquidate the newspaper with ruinous financial losses.[45] By the latter half of 1849 Marx and Engels had separately made their ways to England, where they were destined to spend the rest of their lives.

EXILES

The dream of returning to the continent in triumph, after revolutions there, continued to fascinate Marx and Engels. One scholar has counted more than forty anticipations of impending revolution in their letters and writings over the next thirty years— none of which materialized.[46] But as early as 1850, Marx and Engels had to begin making some preparations for a livelihood in England. Marx was then thirty-two, Engels thirty, and neither of them had ever been self-supporting. They had lived off allowances and gifts from their families (including Marx's wife's family), off small inheritances from relatives, the sale of belongings, borrowings, credit defaults, emergency collections among friends and colleagues, and a few scattered and meager earnings from their writings. Now most of these sources had dried up.

Both Marx and Engels were estranged from their families, who were as disappointed at their prolonged dependency as they were repelled by their doctrines. Still, as late as 1849, Marx's much-despised mother advanced him enough money from his future inheritance to enable him to live comfortably for years— though in fact it was all gone within one year, much of it spent to buy arms for abortive uprisings and to finance Marx's newspaper.[47] Engels' pious father, described by the younger Engels as "bigoted and despotic,"[48] nevertheless supported him financially.[49] At age thirty, Engels accepted his father's offer to work in the family business in Manchester.[50] This became the source of Engels' livelihood— and much of Marx's. The young Engels called it "forced labor"— a painfully ironic term in view of what that phrase was to come to mean in twentieth-century Communist societies. Engels complained, for example, that "I've now got to be at the office no later than 10 in the morning."[51]

The firm, in which Engels' father had half-interest, employed about 800 workers. Though Engels began on a modest level in the management, his position and his pay rose over the years until he was able to retire at age fifty with substantial funds for himself and at the same time provide a very generous annuity that relieved Marx of financial worry for the rest of his life. But before reaching that point, the financial position of Marx and his growing family was often dire and occasionally desperate.

In 1850 the Marx family moved into the slums of London, where they spent most of the next twenty years. During this time, it was often difficult for Marx to come up with the money to pay the rent, buy groceries or pay his bills. The family often dodged creditors, were evicted for non-payment of rent, on some occasions had to live on bread and potatoes, frequently pawned their meager belongings, and had three children die amid the squalor— including one for whom there was no money for a burial until a gift was received for that purpose. Yet, despite the very real and very painful poverty in which Marx often found himself, his known sources of income were sufficient for a lower middle class family standard of living at that time, and was about three times the income of an unskilled worker.[52] A contemporary German exile with a similar income to Marx's boasted of eating "luscious beef-steak" regularly.[53]

Marx's only regular earnings were as a foreign correspondent for the *New York Tribune*, but Engels supplemented this even in the early years before his own finances were solid; and other gifts and inheritances added materially to Marx's resources. The problem was Marx's chronic inability to manage money, and especially his and his wife's tendency to splurge when large sums came in. Moreover, Marx spent at least £100 on a futile lawsuit against an obscure slanderer named Vogt— enough to support a family for months in those times[54]— and wasted still more money and time on a long-forgotten book of rebuttal called *Herr Vogt*, for which he was sued in court to collect the unpaid costs of publication.[55] In 1864, Marx received a number of inheritances that added up to ten times what he had been living on annually[56]— and yet he was still debt-ridden in 1868 when Engels came to his rescue by paying off Marx's debts and then giving him an annuity.

Ironically, Marx's most important research and writing were done during these years of travail and heartbreak, and he produced little during the last dozen or so years of his life when he led a prosperous bourgeois existence. During the 1850s he buried himself in the reading room of the British Museum during the day, studying economics. Until late at night and into the wee hours of the morning he scribbled the voluminous manuscripts that represented several abortive attempts to write the book that eventually emerged as *Capital*. Engels wrote little during this period, when he was working as a capitalist in Manchester and underwriting Marx's efforts in the communist cause of overthrowing capitalism.

Physical ills dogged Marx increasingly with the passing years. His irregular sleeping habits, alcohol consumption, and lack of personal cleanliness or exercise may well have contributed to these, as his improvidence made his family prey to hunger, disease, and the deaths of three children in infancy and early childhood. But he blamed these tragedies— like most of his troubles— on other people. The death of his infant son he blamed on "bourgeois misery," which he apparently considered also the cause of the boils that covered his body, for he promised to make the bourgeoisie pay for them via his revolutionary writings.[57] Marx repeatedly denounced creditors who insisted on collecting what he owed them.[58] He even lost his temper at his wife for her bouts of tears in the midst of mounting tragedies.[59]

Even during the long years of poverty, the Marx household had a maid, Helene DeMuth, better known by her nickname of Lenchen. She had been a servant of the elder Baroness von Westphalen, who in 1845 sent her as a present to her daughter, who was unprepared to take care of children or a household. Though the Marxes were seldom in a position to pay her, "dear, faithful Lenchen" remained in their service to their dying days— and then went to work for Engels. In her youth she passed up suitors and other opportunities for jobs to stay and serve the Marxes. In 1851, during the most desperate period of the Marx family, when Marx's wife was pregnant, Lenchen soon became pregnant too. Only a few friends knew of the child's birth, he was sent away to be raised by a working class family, and there was no father's name on the birth certificate. Marx's wife was told that Engels— a bachelor— was the father, but long after the deaths of Marx and his wife, it came out that in fact the father was Karl Marx. Engels confirmed it on his death bed to Marx's tearful daughter.[60] In his life he had taken the blame for Marx, in order to save his friend's marriage, but in death Engels was apparently not prepared to take the blame forever.

The child himself, Freddy DeMuth, grew up with no relationship with Marx, and never visited his mother as long as the Marxes were alive. Only after their deaths, when Helene DeMuth became Engels' housekeeper, did the boy begin visiting his mother— entering and leaving by the back door. He was sacrificed first to Marx's convenience, then to Marx's image. His mother apparently loved him; when she died, she left everything to him.[61]

Marx's human relationships in general were self-centered, if not exploitative. When his wife gave birth to a child who died immediately, Marx briefly mentioned his own reactions in a letter to Engels, so totally ignoring the effect on his wife that Engels' reply reminded him that "you don't say how *she* is."[62] In 1851, at the age of thirty-three, Marx "wrote to my mother, threatening to draw bills on her and, in the event of non-payment, going to Prussia and letting myself be locked up."[63] When his mother refused to be blackmailed this way, Marx complained of her "insolent" reply.[64] After his mother later died in 1863, Marx's letter to Engels was a model of brevity wasting no sentiment on "the old woman" and focusing entirely on getting his inheritance immediately.[65] Nor was this the only occasion when death in the family was seen in purely economic terms. Earlier, in 1852, he referred to some "good news"— the illness of "my wife's indestructible uncle"— and added: "If that dog dies now I'll be out of trouble" financially.[66]

Because Marx wanted German socialist Ferdinand Lassalle to "find me some literary business in Germany" to supplement "my diminished income and increased expenditure,"[67] he cultivated him with flattery to his face and contempt behind his back. Marx referred to Lassalle's book on Hegel as an "exhibition of enormous erudition" when writing to Lassalle and as a "silly concoction" when writing to Engels.[68] Marx added that Lassalle was a "Jewish nigger,"[69] based on Marx's analysis of his appearance:

> It is now perfectly clear to me that, as testified also by his cranial formation and hair growth, he is descended from the negroes who joined Moses's exodus from Egypt (unless his paternal mother or grandmother was crossed with a nigger). Well, this combination of Jewish and Germanic stock with the negroid basic substance is bound to yield a strange product. The fellow's importunity is also nigger-like.[70]

Engels likewise seized upon Lassalle's ancestry, called him "a true Jew"[71] and "From firtht to latht the thtupid Yid."[72]

Crude and repulsive as Marx's and Engels' racial remarks to each other often were, there is no need to make them still worse by putting them in the same category as twentieth-century racism that has justified genocide.[73] Marx's much criticized essay, "On the Jewish Question,"[74] for example, contains clear statements of his distaste for what he considered to be Jewish cultural or social traits, but in the end it was a defense of Jews' right to full political equality, written as a reply to a contemporary who had claimed that Jews should be required to give up their religion before receiving equal civil status. Marx hoped that the characteristics he disliked in Jews would fade away with the disappearance of capitalism, thus leading to "abolishing the essence of Jewry"[75]— but hardly in the sense of Hitler and the Nazis. Similarly, despite his anti-Negro stereotypes, during the American Civil War he conducted propaganda for the North and for the emancipation of slaves.[76] Perhaps more indicative, he agreed to the marriage of his eldest daughter to a man known to have some Negro ancestry, after discouraging other suitors.[77] Likewise, Engels in 1851 expressed to a friend his hope that "the present persecution of Jews in Germany will spread no further."[78] Marx and Engels were, in short, inconsistent and privately crude, but hardly racial fanatics.

THE FIRST INTERNATIONAL

Along with *The Communist Manifesto* and *Capital*, the other milestone in Marx's career was his leadership of the First International— The International Working Mens Association. Marx's legendary fame today makes it difficult to realize that he was an obscure figure with no substantial following in the early 1860s, that his writings were largely ignored,[79] and that even a man as knowledgeable as John Stuart Mill could live for twenty years in the same city, writing on the same topics, in utter ignorance that someone named Karl Marx even existed.[80] The International Working Mens Association rescued him from that obscurity. As in the earlier case of the Communist League, Marx appeared on the scene just as an existing organization was in process of reorganizing, and seized the opportunity to maneuver his way to control. Initially, Marx was only one of a number of people on a committee charged with drafting a statement of purpose for the International in 1864. He had taken no active part in the organization before,[81] was only belatedly brought into the discussions and was mentioned last on the list of participants.[82] Yet Marx was able to get the group bogged down in interminable discussions, as a prelude to his *coup*. As he described it in a letter to Engels:

> In order to gain time I proposed that before we "edited" the preamble we should "discuss" the rules. This was done. It was an hour after midnight before the first of the 40 rules were agreed to. Cremer said (*and this was*

what I was aiming for): We have nothing to show the committee, which meets on October 25. We must postpone the meeting to November 1. But the sub-committee can get together on October 27 and attempt to reach a definite conclusion. This was agreed to, and the "documents" were "sent back" for my opinion.[83]

From here on, it was Marx's show. On a "pretext" (Marx's own word), "I altered the whole preamble, threw out the *declaration des principes* and finally replaced the 40 rules with ten."[84] He then maneuvered some Marxists into key positions in the new organization,[85] and by 1867 was writing to Engels of "this powerful machinery *in our hands*" and of his own influence "from behind the scenes."[86] The membership of the International was, however, never predominantly Marxist, and conflicting currents were always at work. Engels only *hoped* that the *next* International would become communist and "openly proclaim our principles."[87] Eventually, the commanding figure of the Russian revolutionary anarchist Mikhail Bakunin rose to challenge Marx for control of the International. Their struggle for control ultimately destroyed the organization. Marx managed to get Bakunin expelled and had the headquarters of the International transferred to the United States, where it would be safe from other European revolutionary challenges— even though he knew that would also mean its demise as well. It was a rule-or-ruin tactic that would appear again and again in later communist infiltrations of non-communist organizations.

TWILIGHT YEARS

In the decade that remained of his life after the destruction of the International, Marx published little. His financial worries were largely behind him, but illnesses plagued him and his wife. The completion of *Capital* was delayed not only by illness, but also by Marx's side excursions into other subjects— notably the history of Russia, which required him to learn the Russian language. Even Engels did not know that Marx had let the manuscripts of Volumes II and III of *Capital* sit untouched for years while he dallied with other matters.[88] When Engels discovered this after Marx's death, he said that "If I had been aware of this, I would not have let him rest day or night until everything had been finished and printed."[89] Engels had been vainly urging Marx since 1845 to finish the projected book on economics.[90] As it was, much of the last two decades of Engels' life were taken up trying to decipher and assemble the manuscripts for the remaining two volumes of *Capital*. Realizing the monumental task that this involved, and his own advancing age, Engels initiated the young Karl Kautsky into the mysteries of Marx's handwriting, enabling Kautsky to eventually assemble the remaining manuscripts into *Theories of Surplus Value*, a separate three-volume work originally intended by Marx as the final volume of *Capital*. Thus a work begun in the middle of the nineteenth century was not completely published until the end of the first decade of the twentieth century.

Marx once observed that all his earnings from *Capital* would not pay for the cigars he smoked while writing it. It took four years to sell one thousand copies.[91] And though translations began to appear with the passing years, Marx remained in his lifetime a little known figure outside the ranks of revolutionaries. His greatest notoriety came as a defender of the bloody activities of the Paris Commune of 1871. His book on the subject, *The Civil War in France*, sold far more copies than *The Communist Manifesto*.[92] Marx relished this public notoriety, though it also included death threats.

The Marx family, even after being relieved from dire poverty, had many rocky roads to travel. Marx's wife, a beauty in her youth, found herself with a pock-marked face as result of illness— in her words "looking more like a kind of rhinoceros which has escaped from a zoo than a member of the Caucasian race."[93] She remained a nervous wreck and irritable with her children as a result of decades of strain, for which her pampered upbringing had not prepared her. While her mother's servant, Helene DeMuth, had been a godsend to a young wife unable to take care of children, money, or a household, Lenchen's handling of these responsibilities may also have retarded or prevented Jenny Marx from maturing. Her immaturity was still evident long after she ceased to be young. At age fifty, she realized a lifetime ambition by giving a ball, complete with uniformed servants and hired musicians.[94] Even as a middle-aged woman and the wife of a revolutionary, she had visiting cards printed up identifying herself as "Baroness von Westphalen."[95] Nor where these the only vanities in which she and Marx indulged. They continued to give their daughters piano lessons, music and dancing lessons, even when this sometimes meant not paying the rent.[96]

Keeping up appearances was a major item in the Marxes' budget throughout their lives. During his worst years of financial desperation, Marx strove mightily and with pained embarrassment to prevent visitors from discovering his poverty (though Engels pointed out how futile and pointless this was[97])— even when this required his wife to "take everything that was not actually screwed down to the pawn shop"[98] to pay for entertaining them. During one of his worst financial crises Marx contemplated "the most extreme reduction of expenditure," which might include requiring him to "move into purely proletarian accommodation," and "get rid of the maids."[99]

The three Marx daughters all became involved with men unable to support them— two through marriage and one in a common-law relationship. All received money at one time or other from Engels— the eldest to pay overdue rent,[100] the middle daughter repeatedly for a variety of reasons,[101] and the youngest in a large inheritance which she did not live long to enjoy.[102]

Marx's relationships with his children and grandchildren, however, show his most happy and human side. He was a gentle and indulgent father, who amused his children with his own original fairy tales and picnicked and played with them with great relish.[103] The deaths of those who perished in childhood severely affected him for years afterwards.[104] Marx wrote in a letter:

> Bacon says that really important men have so many contacts with nature and the world, and have so much to interest them, that they easily get over their loss. I am not one of these important men. My child's death has shattered my heart and brain, and I feel the loss as keenly as on the first day.[105]

ASSESSMENTS

Marx with his children was a very different man from the Marx described by his adult contemporaries. When his father questioned whether his heart was as good as his head,[106] he raised a question that many others would continue to raise about Marx throughout his life. A fellow revolutionary said of Marx: "If his heart had matched his intellect, and if he possessed as much love as hate, I

would have gone though fire for him," but "*a most dangerous personal ambition
has eaten away all the good in him*" (emphasis in the original).[107] Still another
radical contemporary, Proudhon, wrote to Marx, "for God's sake, after we have
abolished all the dogmatisms *a priori*, let us not of all things attempt in our turn
to instill another kind of dogma into the people." He said:

> Let us have decent and sincere polemics. Let us give the world an
> example of learned and farsighted tolerance. But simply because we are
> at the head of the movement, let us not make ourselves the leader of a
> new intolerance, let us not pose as the apostle of a new religion— even
> though this religion be the religion of logic, the religion of reason.[108]

Carl Schurz, while still a youthful revolutionary in Germany (before his
later fame as a liberal in the United States), met Marx and formed an
opinion of him that accords with the impressions of many others:

> I have never seen a man whose bearing was so provoking and
> intolerable. To no opinion, which differed from his, he accorded the
> honor of even a condescending consideration. Everyone who
> contradicted him he treated with abject contempt; every argument that
> he did not like he answered either with biting scorn at the unfathomable
> ignorance that had prompted it, or with opprobrious aspersions upon the
> motives of him who had advanced it.[109]

Marx liked to glare at anyone who challenged his conclusions and say "I
will annihilate you!" The radicals and revolutionaries whom Marx successively
alienated over a period of forty years reads like a *Who's Who* of the nineteenth-
century political left. Even the patient and long-suffering Engels came close
to a break with Marx, whose curt and clumsy remarks on the death of Engels'
common-law wife in 1863 wounded his friend. Engels wrote:

> All my friends, including philistine acquaintances, have shown me
> more sympathy and friendship on this occasion, which inevitably
> affected me quite closely, than I had a right to expect. You found the
> moment suitable for a demonstration of the superiority of your cool
> manner of thinking. So be it![110]

Marx's apology brought forgiveness[111] and the historic partnership
continued.

The younger Marx of the 1840s presented a more humane vision in his
writings, and has become something of a refuge for modern radicals

disillusioned with the more blatantly severe later Marx, who seemed to presage Lenin and Stalin. Lighthearted humor also brightened some of these earlier writings[112] in a way seldom seen again in the later works of Marx and Engels. Yet it would be a mistake to ignore the authoritarian and terroristic elements that were as present in these earlier writings as in the later ones— and in Engels as well as Marx. Engels' first draft for *The Communist Manifesto* included compulsory labor,[113] a deliberate undermining of the family by ending the dependence "of the wife upon the husband and of the children upon the parents,"[114] and the erection of "common dwellings for communities of citizens" to replace family homes. Marx's *Neue Rheinische Zeitung* declared on its last day of publication: *"When our turn comes, we shall not disguise our terrorism."*[115]

A current vogue, aptly characterized as "Engels-baiting"[116] makes it especially important to assess Engels' role in Marxism. Engels was much more than Marx's friend and benefactor. He was one of the very few people with whom Marx had intellectual interchange, and by far the most important. For most of his life, Marx, as an obscure autodidact, was utterly cut off from participation in the world of universities, learned journals, scholarly conferences, and other institutionalized intellectual exchange. Nor did he have any intellectual interaction, by correspondence or in person, with the leading minds of his time— Mill, Darwin, Tolstoy, Menger, or Dostoevski, for example. Marx's relationship with contemporary radical intellectuals was one of tutelage or hostility. His correspondence consisted overwhelmingly of gossip, intrigue, and passing remarks on current events and contemporary personalities. Only with Engels were serious intellectual matters discussed with even occasional regularity.

Engels' early economic writing provided the basic conception that Marx systematized and elaborated in the massive volumes of *Capital*. Finally, Engels' piecing together and editing of the many manuscripts for the posthumous volumes of Marx's magnum opus was a monumental work of dedication and self-sacrifice, stretching over more than a decade.

Engels was not only a far clearer writer than Marx, but often more subtly and accurately conveyed Marx's theories— especially of history— for he did not so readily indulge in Marx's penchant for epigrams at the expense of accuracy. Engels' letters on the Marxian theory of history are a major contribution to understanding what Marx actually did in his historical writings, as distinguished from how Marx tried to encapsulate his practice in clichés that continue to obscure more than they reveal.

There is no way to know what Engels would have accomplished in the decades he devoted, first to earning a living for both himself and Marx, and then to completing Marx's unfinished work. But what he actually accomplished was both impressive and indicative. His *Socialism: Utopian and Scientific* remains the best summary of the system of thought that bears the name of Marx. How much of Marxism originated in fact with Engels is a question that may never be answered. Engels was clearly a precursor of Marxian crisis theory in economics, as Marx himself indicated.[117] Engels' letters to Marx also presage the content and title of Marx's *Eighteenth Brumaire*.[118] But the collaborative writings of Marx and Engels and their unrecorded conversations over a period of forty years preclude any definitive disentangling of their respective contributions to Marxism.

In 1883, at the graveside of Marx, Engels painted an idealized picture that provided the stuff of which legends are made. He began: "On the 14th day of March, at a quarter to three in the afternoon, the greatest living thinker ceased to think." According to Engels, "Marx discovered the law of development of human history," and also "the special law of motion governing the present-day capitalist mode of production."[119] Innumerable slanders Marx "brushed aside as though it were cobweb," and "though he may have had many opponents he had hardly one personal enemy."[120] This was at best a highly sanitized picture of a man who personalized every quarrel and whose letters to Engels were full of spiteful gossip and petty intrigues. Finally, Engels' funeral oration ended with these words: "His name will endure through the ages, and so also will his work!"[121] Marx's name has indeed become infinitely better known than when he died in relative obscurity in London a hundred years ago. How much of what has happened in the twentieth century is "his work"— and in what sense— is a much larger and more complex question. For Marx the man, he perhaps wrote his own best epitaph when he said: "Nothing that is human is foreign to me."[122] Others made him an abstraction and an icon.

LEGAL ISSUES

PENNY-WISE ON CRIME

For more than 200 years, the political left has been coming up with reasons why criminals should not be punished as much, or at all. The latest gambit in Missouri is providing judges with the costs of incarcerating the criminals they sentence.

According to the *New York Times*, "a three-year prison sentence would run more than $37,000 while probation would cost $6,770." For a more serious crime, where a 5-year imprisonment would cost more than $50,000, it would cost less than $9,000 for what is described as "five years of intensive probation."

This is only the latest in a long line of "alternatives to incarceration" schemes that are constantly being pushed by all sorts of clever people, not only in Missouri but across the United States and across the Atlantic, especially in Britain.

The most obvious question that is being resolutely ignored in these scientific-sounding calculations is: What is the cost of turning criminals loose? Phrases like "intensive probation" may create the illusion that criminals at large are somehow under control of the authorities but illusions are especially dangerous when it comes to crime.

Another question that ought to be obvious is: Why are we counting only the cost to the government of putting a criminal behind bars, but not the cost to the public of turning him loose?

Some may say that it is not possible to quantify the costs of the dangers and anxieties of the public when more criminals are walking the streets. That is certainty true, if you mean the full costs. But we can quantify the money costs— and just the money costs to the public vastly exceed the costs to the government of locking up criminals.

In Britain, where the "alternatives to incarceration" vogue has led to only 7 percent of convicted criminals being put behind bars, the annual cost of the prison system has been estimated at just under two billion pounds sterling. Meanwhile, the annual financial cost alone of crimes committed against the public has been an estimated sixty billion pounds sterling.

In the United States, the cost of incarcerating a criminal has been estimated as being $10,000 a year less than the cost of turning him loose.

In all these calculations we are leaving out the costs of violence, intimidation and the fears that people have for the safety of themselves and their children, not to mention the sense of helplessness and outrage when the society refuses to pay as much attention to innocent victims as they lavish on the criminals who victimize them.

These are all important costs. But it is unnecessary to take them into account, when just the money costs of turning criminals loose is enough to show what reckless nonsense is being preached to us by arrogant elites in the media, in academia and elsewhere.

Deception of the public by advocates of leniency to criminals has been institutionalized in legal practices that create the illusion of far more punishment being meted out than is actually the case. "Concurrent sentences" are one of the most blatant of these frauds.

When a criminal has been convicted of multiple crimes, having him serve his sentences for these crimes "concurrently" means that he actually serves no more time for five crimes than he would serve for whichever of those crimes has the longest sentence. In other words, the other four crimes are "on the house."

Sentences in general overstate how long the criminal will actually spend behind bars. Probation, furloughs, parole and time off for good behavior lead the list of reasons for turning a criminal loose before he serves the sentence that was announced to the public when he was convicted.

Even "life imprisonment without the possibility of parole"— often offered as a substitute for execution for first degree murder— can be misleading. There is no such thing as life imprisonment without the possibility of a liberal governor being elected, and then commuting or pardoning the murderer later on. And, of course, the murderer can commit murder again behind bars.

With all the things that liberals are willing to spend vast sums of money on, it is a little much to have them become penny-wise when it comes to keeping criminals off the streets.

JUSTICE FOR LITTLE ANGELO

Little Angelo finally got justice, though he died too young to even know what justice meant. Angelo Marinda lived only eight months and it took more than twice that long to convict his father of his murder.

Tragically, the policies and the mindset among the authorities responsible for the well-being of children— the practices and notions that put this baby at risk— are still in place and more such tragedies are just waiting to happen. Little Angelo came to the authorities' attention only 12 days after he was born, when he turned up at a hospital with broken bones.

How would a baby less than two weeks old have broken bones? And what do you do about it?

Many of us would say that you get that baby away from whoever broke his bones and never let them near him again. But that is not what the "experts" say. Experts always have "solutions." How else are they going to be experts?

The fashionable solution is called "family reunification services." The severity of little Angelo's injuries would have made it legally possible to simply take him away and put him up for adoption by one of the many couples who are hoping to adopt a baby.

But no. Through the magic of "family reunification services" parents are supposed to be changed so that they will no longer be abusive.

A social worker told the court two years ago that the San Mateo County Children and Family Services Agency "will be recommending reunification services, as the parents are receptive to receiving services." The fact that little Angelo's sister had already had to be removed from that same home did not seem to dampen this optimism.

At the heart of all this is the pretense to knowledge that we simply do not have and may never have. There are all sorts of lofty phrases about teaching "parenting skills" or "anger management" or other pious hopes. And children's lives are being risked on such unsubstantiated notions.

Little Angelo himself apparently knew better. After months in a foster home, he was allowed back for a visit with his parents and "had a look of fear in his eyes" when he saw them.

But "expertise" brushes aside what non-experts believe— and little Angelo was not an expert, at least not in the eyes of the social workers who were in charge of his fate. The fact that he had returned from a previous visit with bruises did not make a dent on the experts.

Social workers thought it would be nice if little Angelo could have a two-day unsupervised visit with his parents at Christmas. It was a visit from which he would not return alive.

Now, more than 16 months after the baby's death, Angelo's father has been convicted of having literally shaken him to death.

Incidentally, there were experts who testified on the father's behalf at the trial, one of whom gave testimony that contradicted what he himself had written in a book. This expert had never seen little Angelo, dead or alive.

The time is long overdue for us to stop pretending to know things that nobody knows— not even people with impressive letters in front of their names or behind their names. Whether these experts are simply cynical guns for hire or really believe their own theories and rhetoric is beside the point. Unsubstantiated theories are no foundation for risking the lives of the helpless.

How anyone could break the bones of a newborn baby is something that people may speculate about. But to claim to know how to turn such parents into decent human beings is reckless. And to risk a baby's life on such speculation is criminal.

It is too bad that only one man will go to jail for this crime. There ought to be room in a cell somewhere for the social workers and their bosses who made this murder possible in the face of blatant evidence about the dangers that an infant could see, even if the responsible adults refused to see.

The pretense of knowledge allows judges, social workers, and others to "do something" by sending people to "training" in "parenting skills" and other psychobabble with no track record of success. And it allows children like little Angelo to be killed.

LOVE THOSE KILLERS!

Most of us were horrified to learn that Andrea Yates had killed five of her own children by drowning them— one at a time — in a bathtub. But that may be because we are not among the morally anointed. Big time celebrities like Rosie O'Donnell and Today Show hostess Katie Couric apparently see things differently.

"I felt such overwhelming empathy for her of what it must have been like for her to do that," said Rosie O'Donnell. "When you've been on the edge you can understand what it's like to go over."

Katie Couric on the Today Show seemed likewise to think the big issue was Mrs. Yates' psyche. She said: "Mrs. Yates, after you drowned your five children, how did that make you feel?"

The Today Show put on the screen information showing where to send donations to the legal defense fund for Andrea Yates. In Houston, the local chapter of the National Organization for Women formed something called "The Andrea Yates Support Coalition" and is planning to raise money for her defense.

This has apparently become a so-called woman's issue because the claim is being made that Mrs. Yates suffered from postpartum depression and that either that or the drugs she had to take caused her to kill her children. But of course the reason we hold trials is to find out which claims by either side can stand up in court.

The judge has slapped a gag order on the attorneys in this case, in order to prevent pre-trial publicity from biasing the jury. But, in reality, that just means that the public will hear only Andrea Yates' side of the story before the trial. We will of course never hear the children's side of the story.

Unfortunately, the vogue of leaping to the defense of killers is not limited to women or even to the United States. Just this summer, two teenage boys who had sadistically murdered a two-year-old toddler in Britain when they were ten years old were released from prison— and given new identities, so that they would not suffer any bad consequences from members of the public who were not as much in tune with current non-judgmental fashions.

What other people might suffer from these young killers in the course of another half century or more of their lives did not seem to raise nearly as much concern. Shrinks said that they were no danger to others— which is what shrinks said about some of the American teenagers who later killed their schoolmates in shooting sprees.

At a cost of about $2 million to the British taxpayers, the young British killers and their families have been set up in three-bedroom homes. They have even been given spending money, with which one of the parents has bought a car.

Even before being released from "imprisonment"— in facilities without bars but with TV and other amenities, including karate lessons and spending money for Christmas— the young killers were allowed out on supervised furlough to see sports events and even visit shopping malls. It was at a shopping mall that they had lured the little toddler away and then tortured him to death.

The foreman of the jury that convicted them recalls seeing the terrible pictures of the little toddler's body and then catching the eye of one of the young killers— who smirked in the courtroom. However, the politically correct line in Britain, as in the United States, is that expressed by a "penal reform" advocate, who said: "If children do something wrong, they should be dealt with through the care system and not the criminal justice system."

Meanwhile, the liberal media in England has vilified the mother of the murdered child, who has protested these boys' early release and the posh life provided for them and their families. The media "compared her unfavourably with more forgiving mothers," according to *The Guardian* newspaper. Apparently all mothers should be non-judgmental about their babies' sadistic young killers.

Back in the 1960s, it was considered eccentric, at least, when Norman Mailer took up the cause of a convicted murderer and managed to get him released from behind bars. It was no doubt considered somewhat more than eccentric by a man that the ex-con killed after being released. But today, what was once considered eccentric is par for the course in certain elite circles.

Outcries of outrage from the public only confirm the anointed in their own smug sense of being special— nobler and wiser than the common herd. What a price to pay so that some people can feel more non-judgmental than thou or simply affirm within their own little coterie that they are one of Us instead of one of Them.

LAW ON TRIAL

Law itself is on trial in an Albany courtroom where four New York City policemen are accused of murder in the shooting death of Amadou Diallo, an African immigrant. For a shockingly large number of people, the fact that the cops are white and the man who was shot was black is all they need to know in order to take sides.

And taking sides is the issue for them, not finding the truth or dispensing justice. This approach has already been tried extensively throughout the South during the Jim Crow era. It took decades of struggle and sacrifice— including the sacrifice of lives— to break down that system of double-standard "justice." Now it has come back into fashion again, with a new color scheme.

The tragic facts of the Diallo shooting are pretty plain. Even before the police arrived on the scene, Amadou Diallo was— for whatever reason— stationed in a doorway at night and periodically looking both ways up and down the street. Another resident of the area, coming home from work, was struck by what this resident says seemed to him at the time to be "suspicious" behavior. The prosecuting attorney immediately objected to this word and the judge immediately ordered it stricken from the record.

When a police car with four cops inside rolled by later, after midnight, they too considered Diallo's behavior suspicious. When they stopped the car and got out, Diallo fled back inside the building. There, in a dimly lit hallway, he reached inside his jacket and pulled out a black object and held it out toward the cops. One of the policemen yelled "Gun!" By a horrible coincidence, another policeman toppled backwards off the steps onto the sidewalk, as if he had been shot, and his fellow officers opened fire on Diallo.

The driver of the car rushed toward the fallen officer and asked where he had been hit. But he had not been hit. He had just lost his balance and fallen back off the steps. Nor did Diallo have a gun. He had taken out his wallet and held it out toward the police. It was a tragedy of errors.

Enter the race hustlers, the politically correct media and politicians in an election year. Al Sharpton, who first gained fame by making wild accusations against policemen in the Tawana Brawley hoax, has of course jumped in with both feet and mobs of supporters. Hillary Clinton has called it "murder"— and she is a lawyer who should know better, especially with a trial going on.

Even in the courtroom, the atmosphere of intimidation has continued, unchecked by the judge who considered it offensive when a witness said that he found Diallo's actions suspicious.

Witnesses who have anything to say that might support the policemen's testimony have had wholly unnecessary identifying information publicized and read into the record. The witness who said that his suspicions caused him to pay attention to Diallo as he walked home after parking his truck not only had his address, but his apartment number as well, identified by the prosecutor in open court.

Supposedly this was to show that he lived in the rear and could not have seen what happened after he got home. But the witness had never claimed to have seen anything from his apartment. What this uncalled-for statement did was put the witness on notice in the courtroom that local neighborhood hotheads now knew where to find him and his family. It was a shot across his bow, a warning not only to him, but to any other witness who might say anything that would support what the policemen had said.

Do we wonder why witnesses don't come forward?

A nurse who heard the shots while attending a patient across the street was asked for the name of her patient, even though the patient was not a witness and never claimed to have seen or heard anything. When that was objected to, she was then asked whether the patient was male or female and how old. This was unconscionable in the atmosphere of hostility and lawlessness that has been whipped up over this shooting.

As someone who taught pistol shooting in the Marine Corps, I was not the least bit surprised by the number of shots fired— or by the fact that most of them missed. Nobody counts his own shots, much less other people's shots, in a life-and-death situation. This is not an arcade game, where lights go off to tell you whether you hit the target. You shoot until it looks safe to stop.

A lot of lights ought to go off about this trial and the way both witnesses and justice itself are being threatened, inside and outside the courtroom.

ABORTED KNOWLEDGE

A certain professor who teaches students who aspire to become speech pathologists begins by showing them the development of the various organs involved in speech. When he shows his class an ultrasound picture of the development of the palate in an unborn baby, it is not uncommon for one or two women in his class to have tears in their eyes, or to say to him afterward that they have had an abortion and were very much affected by seeing what an unborn baby looks like.

For too long we have been led to believe that an abortion is the removal of some unformed material, something like having an appendix operation. The very expression "unborn baby" has almost disappeared from the language, being replaced by the more bloodless and antiseptic term "fetus."

Many vocal advocates who declare themselves "pro-choice" do not want women to have the choice of knowing just what they are choosing before having an abortion. Ferocious opposition has stopped the showing of pictures of an abortion in process— even in schools or colleges that show movies of naked adults performing various sex acts. Still photographs of aborted fetuses have been banned as well.

The particularly grisly procedure know as "partial-birth abortion" cannot even be referred to in much of the media, where it is called a "late-term abortion"— another bloodless term and one that shifts the focus from what happens to when it happens.

What happens in a partial-birth abortion is that a baby who has developed too far to die naturally when removed from his mother's body is deliberately killed by having his brains sucked out. When this is done, the baby is not completely out of his mother's body because, if he were, the doctor would be charged with murder. There is no medical reason for this procedure, which has been condemned by the American Medical Association. There is only a legal reason— to keep the doctor and the mother out of jail.

All this is smoothly covered over in the media by calling such actions a "late-term abortion" and refusing to specify what happens. Such patterns of determined evasions and obfuscations show that "pro-choice" in practice often really means pro-abortion. Knowledge is the first thing being aborted.

Philosophical questions about when life begins may preoccupy some people on both sides of the abortion controversy. But the raw physical facts of what happens in various kinds of abortion have turned many others, including physicians, from being pro-abortion to being anti-abortion. One doctor who had performed many abortions never performed another one after seeing an ultrasound movie of the baby's reactions.

With most other medical procedures, "informed consent" is the watchword. But, when the issue is abortion, great efforts are made to keep "choice" from becoming too informed.

Politically and legally, the abortion issue is too complex for any easy resolution. We have gone through a quarter of a century of bitter controversy precisely because the Supreme Court went for an easy resolution back in 1973 with the *Roe v. Wade* decision.

Before then, various states had made differing efforts to wrestle with and balance the weighty concerns on both sides of the abortion issue. But Supreme Court Justice Harry Blackmun rushed in where angels fear to tread, with a one-size-fits-all decision, washed down with the blatant lie that this was based on the Constitution.

Far from settling things, *Roe v. Wade* has led to polarization and escalating strife all across the country, including bombings and assassinations. It has corrupted the media, academia and other sources that are supposed to inform us, but which have instead become partisan organs of political correctness.

However this highly-charged issue is ultimately resolved— and there is no resolution on the horizon today— surely honesty must be part of that resolution. Political catch-phrases like "a woman's right to do what she wants with her own body" cannot be applied to situations where a baby is killed at the very moment when he ceases to be part of his mother's body.

One of the few signs of hope for some ultimate resolution is that most people on both sides of this controversy are not happy about abortions. The women who shed tears at the very sight of an unborn baby may not be politically committed to either side of this issue, but their feelings may be part of what is needed to bring opposing sides together.

GUN CONTROL MYTHS

Professor Joyce Lee Malcolm of Bentley College deserves some sort of special prize for taking on the thankless task of talking sense on a subject where nonsense is deeply entrenched and fiercely dogmatic. In her recently published book, *Guns and Violence*, Professor Malcolm examines the history of firearms, gun control laws and violent crime in England. What makes this more than an exercise in history is its relevance to current controversies over gun control in America.

Gun control zealots love to make highly selective international comparisons of gun ownership and murder rates. But Joyce Lee Malcolm points out some of the pitfalls in that approach. For example, the murder rate in New York City has been more than five times that of London for two centuries— and during most of that time neither city had any gun control laws.

In 1911, New York state instituted one of the most severe gun control laws in the United States, while serious gun control laws did not begin in England until nearly a decade later. But New York City still continued to have far higher murder rates than London.

If we are serious about the role of guns and gun control as factors in differing rates of violence between countries, then we need to do what history professor Joyce Lee Malcolm does— examine the history of guns and violence. In England, as she points out, over the centuries "violent crime continued to decline markedly at the very time that guns were becoming increasingly available."

England's Bill of Rights in 1688 was quite unambiguous that the right of a private individual to be armed was an individual right, independently of any collective right of militias. Guns were as freely available to Englishmen as to Americans, on into the early 20th century.

Nor was gun control in England a response to any firearms murder crisis. Over a period of three years near the end of the 19th century, "there were only 59 fatalities from handguns in a population of nearly 30 million people," according to Professor Malcolm. "Of these, 19 were accidents, 35 were suicides and only 3 were homicides— an average of one a year."

The rise of the interventionist state in early 20th century England included efforts to restrict ownership of guns. After the First World War, gun control laws began restricting the possession of firearms. Then, after the Second World War, these restrictions grew more severe, eventually disarming the civilian population of England— or at least the law-abiding part of it.

It was during this period of severe restrictions on owning firearms that crime rates in general, and the murder rate in particular, began to rise in England. "As the number of legal firearms have dwindled, the numbers of armed crimes have risen," Professor Malcolm points out.

In 1954, there were only a dozen armed robberies in London but, by the 1990s, there were more than a hundred times as many. In England, as in the United States, drastic crackdowns on gun ownership by law-abiding citizens were accompanied by ever greater leniency to criminals. In both countries, this turned out to be a formula for disaster.

While England has not yet reached the American level of murders, it has already surpassed the United States in rates of robbery and burglary. Moreover, in recent years the murder rate in England has been going up under still more severe gun control laws, while the murder rate in the United States has been going down as more and more states have allowed private citizens to carry concealed weapons— and have begun locking up more criminals.

In both countries, facts have no effect whatever on the dogmas of gun control zealots. The fact that most guns used to murder people in England were not legally purchased has no effect on their faith in gun control laws there, any more than faith in such laws here is affected by the fact that the gun used by the recent Beltway snipers was not purchased legally either.

In England as in America, sensational gun crimes have been seized upon and used politically to promote crackdowns on gun ownership by law-abiding citizens, while doing nothing about criminals. American zealots for the Brady Bill say nothing about the fact that the man who shot James Brady and tried to assassinate President Reagan has been out walking the streets on furlough.

GUN CONTROL MYTHS: PART II

Talking facts to gun control zealots is only likely to make them angry. But the rest of us need to know what the facts are. More than that, we need to know that much of what the gun controllers claim as facts will not stand up under scrutiny.

The grand dogma of the gun controllers is that places with severe restrictions on the ownership of firearms have lower rates of murder and other gun crimes. How do they prove this? Simple. They make comparisons of places where this is true and ignore all comparisons of places where the opposite is true.

Gun control zealots compare the United States and England to show that murder rates are lower where restrictions on ownership of firearms are more severe. But you could just as easily compare Switzerland and Germany, the Swiss having lower murder rates than the Germans, even though gun ownership is three times higher in Switzerland. Other countries with high rates of gun ownership and low murder rates include Israel, New Zealand, and Finland.

Within the United States, rural areas have higher rates of gun ownership and lower rates of murder, whites have higher rates of gun ownership than blacks and much lower murder rates. For the country as a whole, hand gun ownership doubled in the late 20th century, while the murder rate went down. But such facts are not mentioned by gun control zealots or by the liberal media.

Another dogma among gun control supporters is that having a gun in the home for self-defense is futile and is only likely to increase the chances of your getting hurt or killed. Your best bet is to offer no resistance to an intruder, according to this dogma.

Actual research tells just the opposite story. People who have not resisted have gotten hurt twice as often as people who resisted with a firearm. Those who resisted without a firearm of course got hurt the most often.

Such facts are simply ignored by gun control zealots. They prefer to cite a study published some years ago in the *New England Journal of Medicine* and demolished by a number of scholars since then. According to this discredited study, people with guns in their homes were more likely to be murdered.

How did they arrive at this conclusion? By taking people who were murdered in their homes, finding out how many had guns in the house, and then comparing them with people who were not murdered in their homes.

Using similar reasoning, you might be able to show that people who hire bodyguards are more likely to get killed than people who don't. Obviously, people who hire bodyguards already feel at risk, but does that mean that the bodyguards are the reason for the risk?

Similarly illogical reasoning has been used by counting how many intruders were killed by homeowners with guns and comparing that with the number of family members killed with those guns. But this is a nonsense comparison because most people who keep guns in their homes do not do so in hopes of killing intruders.

Most uses of guns in self-defense— whether in the home or elsewhere— do not involve actually pulling the trigger. When the intended victim turns out to have a gun in his hand, the attacker usually has enough brains to back off. But the lives saved this way do not get counted.

People killed at home by family members are highly atypical. The great majority of these victims have had to call the police to their homes before, because of domestic violence, and just over half have had the cops out several times. These are not just ordinary people who happened to lose their temper when a gun was at hand.

Neither are most "children" who are killed by guns just toddlers who happened to find a loaded weapon lying around. More of those "children" are members of teenage criminal gangs who kill each other deliberately.

Some small children do in fact get accidentally killed by guns in the home— but fewer than drown in bathtubs. Is anyone for banning bathtubs? Moreover, the number of fatal gun accidents fell, over the years, while the number of guns was increasing by tens of millions. None of this supports the assumption that more guns mean more fatal accidents.

Most of the gun controllers' arguments are a house of cards. No wonder they don't want any hard facts coming near them.

POWER TO THE PARASITES

It may be a landmark in the history of American business— and of American society— if Dow Corning's filing for bankruptcy is the beginning of the end for this corporation. Lawsuits for huge damages against the company for its silicone breast implants are behind this latest development.

It is not that these implants have been proven to cause medical problems. Rather, it has been unnecessary to prove anything in order to get cases put before juries who are free to hand out other people's money in whatever amounts strike their fancy, in response to whatever appeals the plaintiff's lawyers make.

Scientific study after scientific study has failed to turn up evidence to substantiate the claims made by those suing Dow Corning over breast implants. Meanwhile, back in the courts, judges and juries are handing out multimillion dollar awards in damages.

The fate of one corporation is not a major national issue but what it implies about our whole system of justice has grim implications for the future of this country. As a critic said, more than half a century ago, "Law has lost its soul and become jungle." That is even more true today.

The media have a heavy responsibility in all this. Their willingness to serve as a megaphone for all sorts of politically correct groups and movements has sent them off and running like a pack of hounds after any business accused of anything by the radical feminists, the environmentalists, or other favorites of the anointed.

The very idea that the burden of proof is on the party who makes a legal charge has gone out the window as far as whole categories of charges are concerned. This is nowhere more true than in so-called "women's issues" but it is also true in racial issues, environmental issues and other crusades pushed by strident activists.

More than individual injustices are involved. A whole class of parasites has been created and sanctified, ranging from the panhandlers in the streets to the lawyers in the suites. You can believe that Dow Corning will not be the last of their prey.

All over this country, doctors, local governments, corporations, universities, and many others are being targeted for lawsuits by attorneys on the prowl wherever there is money to be had. Anyone with a "deep pocket" is fair game. And many of these deep pockets are nothing more than a lot of much shallower pockets of taxpayers and stockholders.

Two centuries ago, British statesman Edmund Burke warned of the dangers to any society that promotes the idea that some of its citizens are the natural prey of others. Yet that is not only what the litigation explosion is all about. It is what all the political talk of "the rich" is all about.

This is the age of the complaining classes, whether they are lawyers, community activists, radical feminists, race hustlers, or other squeaking wheels looking for oil.

No society ever thrived because it had a large and growing class of parasites living off those who produce. On the contrary, the growth of a large parasitic class marked the decline and fall of the Roman Empire and the collapse of Spain from the heights of its golden age.

Despite Karl Marx's use of the term "proletariat" to describe the working class, the Roman proletariat was not so much a working class as an underclass supported by government handouts. But the parasites in ancient Rome also included a large and growing bureaucracy. The Byzantine Empire and later the Ottoman Empire likewise developed over the centuries bureaucracies so suffocating and corrupt as to bring their eras of glory to an end.

More than a thousand years after the collapse of Rome, Spain used the wealth it extracted from its vast empire to support growing numbers of Spaniards in idleness. Not only were vagabonds begging everywhere, there were also large numbers of educated parasites with no skills to use to add to the country's output but with big ideas about how its wealth ought to be spent.

No small part of our social problems today come from miseducated degree-holders who have nothing to contribute to the wealth of the society but who are full of demands and indignation— and resentment of those who are producing.

A study of the decline of great societies concluded that "disappearances of empires due to catastrophes have been extremely rare in history." Rather, they slowly but steadily corrode and crumble from within. There is usually "a growing amount of wealth pumped by the State from the economy," while "extravagances of fashion and license" develop among the people. Does this sound uncomfortably similar to what we see around us today?

MEDICAL LAWSUITS

When a friend told me recently that he was going to undergo a painful medical procedure to see if he has cancer, it reminded me of a time years ago when I faced a similar prospect. The testing procedure in my case would have been both painful and with some risk of infection.

Fortunately, it was a two-part procedure. The first part was uncomfortable but not painful or with any great risk of infection. After a young doctor had put me through that part, an older specialist took over and examined the results—and he decided not to proceed with the second part of the test.

When my wife asked me if that meant that I did not have cancer, my answer was, "No."

"What it means," I said, "was that the doctor weighed the alternatives and decided that, since the chance that I had cancer was sufficiently small, and the danger of infection from the test itself was sufficiently large, the best choice was not to go any further."

My wife seemed not completely put at ease by that, so I added: "Like anybody else, this doctor can be wrong. But, if it turns out that I do have cancer and die, I don't want anybody to sue that man. Nobody is infallible and no patient has a right to infallibility."

Since this was many years ago, apparently the doctor's choice was the right one. But how many doctors feel free to make such choices in today's legal climate, where frivolous lawsuits and junk science can lead to multimillion-dollar awards or settlements?

After so many megabucks awards grew out of claims that babies born with cerebral palsy could have been spared if only the doctor had delivered them by Caesarean section, C-section births rose sharply. But it did not reduce cerebral palsy.

While the C-section births may not protect babies from cerebral palsy, they protect doctors from being ruined financially by glib lawyers and gullible juries. Those lawyers who claim that their big-bucks awards don't add much to the cost of medical care are counting only the sums of money they collect.

But needless operations and needless tests are not free, either financially or otherwise.

Today, I cannot help wondering whether my friend is going to be put through a painful procedure for his sake or because the doctor dares not fail to do this test, for fear of a lawsuit somewhere down the road. This is one of the hidden costs of frivolous lawsuits and runaway damage awards, quite aside from the sums of money pocketed by lawyers.

When I was growing up, it would never have occurred to me that Dr. Chaney, our family physician, was doing anything other than giving it his best shot for the sake of our health.

It probably never occurred to Dr. Chaney that we might sue him. For one thing, he knew we didn't have enough money to hire a lawyer, so that was out of the question in the first place.

Trust between doctor and patient is not a small thing. Sometimes it can be the difference between life and death. Our laws recognize the enormous importance of that relationship by exempting doctors from having to testify to what a patient has told them, even if it is a murder case.

To go to these lengths to protect the doctor-patient relationship— and then blithely throw it away with easy access to frivolous lawsuits makes no sense. Neither does creating a massive medical bureaucracy to pay for treatments and medication, where that means that patients can go only to those doctors preselected for them by some insurance company or the government.

One of my favorite doctors retired early and spent some time explaining to me why he was doing so. The growing red tape was bad enough but the deterioration of the doctor-patient relationship soured him even more.

Earlier in his career, patients came to him because someone had recommended him and they came with a wholly different attitude from that of someone who had been assigned to him by an insurance company. He now found much more of a distrustful, if not adversarial, attitude that didn't do him any good or the patient any good.

That may be the biggest cost of our current bureaucratic and legal environment.

PASSING IN REVIEW

It was a classic line from the *New York Times*: "How America raises the children of inner cities may be the ultimate test of the country's political and economic arrangements."

Apparently, if it sounds lofty and poetic, who cares if it makes any sense?

America does not raise children. It has never raised children. And it is never going to raise children. No amount of verbal collectivization will ever change that reality.

Perhaps it is too much to expect realism from an essay in the Book Review section of the *New York Times*, but it is gross irresponsibility to review books about youth crime in the ghetto by making all of America responsible. Personal responsibility may be anathema to the *New York Times*, but it is what is desperately needed to deal with the ugly violence that threatens the residents of black communities across the country.

Not trusting its readers to get the blame-America message the first time, the *Times* essay repeats it endlessly. The "alarming rise in violence" is due to "American values." The hoodlums and thugs "aspire to embrace all the trappings of mainstream America." It is due to his "American upbringing" that a ghetto drug dealer went wrong. It was "essentially American dreams" that ghetto criminals were pursuing, in order "to compensate for the hurt of growing up poor, jobless and outcast."

Haven't got it yet? The essay closes by recommending reading about the "very American dreams" that lead ghetto youths into crime.

Most black youths do not grow up to be criminals. Apparently they must grow up in some foreign country and then immigrate here later. Most non-ghetto youths likewise do not grow up to be criminals. They must all be foreigners too.

More is involved here than a little irresponsible rhetoric. The steady drumbeat of blame-society, hate-America talk is all too typical of the mindset that has led to the destruction of both moral values and law enforcement over the past 30 years. No one has done more of that than the

New York Times, though many others have added their voices to the chorus— including people in high places who should have known better.

Like Attorney General Janet Reno in the Clinton administration, Lyndon Johnson's Attorney General back in the 1960s, Ramsey Clark, was convinced that the way to deal with criminal activity was to deal with the social "root causes" of crime. So was the Chief Judge of the D. C. Circuit Court of Appeals, David L. Bazelon. So was Supreme Court Chief Justice Earl Warren.

According to Warren, the reason for rising crime rates was that "for decades we have swept under the rug" the slum conditions that breed crime. Yet during those decades, the crime rate was going down— not up, as Warren's "root causes" theory would suggest. When Earl Warren became Chief Justice in 1953, the homicide rate in the United States was 4.8 per 100,000 population, the lowest it had been in four decades.

Non-white males had a *declining* murder rate during decades of "neglect" in "our disturbed society," as Warren called it. It was only after the Warren Court's judicial revolution in the criminal justice system that murder rates shot up— and kept on rising. By 1991, the rate for murder and deliberate manslaughter was 9.8 per 100,000, more than twice as high as when Warren joined the Supreme Court, even though the new statistics did not count all the homicides that were counted in the earlier statistics.

Maybe there was some plausible excuse for talking about "root causes" and "our disturbed society" as causes of crime 30 years ago. But we now have 30 years of experience to the contrary. During that time there have been all sorts of expensive social programs, reduced law enforcement— and intellectuals making excuses for criminals.

The soaring crime rates that followed the liberal nostrums of the 1960s have produced no change of mind. Liberals are often wrong but never in doubt. They are still blaming social conditions, "society," America.

It will never occur to them to blame themselves.

Does anyone seriously believe that excuse-making and counterproductive policies on crime are a favor to black communities? It is now so widely known and so well documented that black people are the main victims of black criminals that there is no room for honest misunderstanding on this subject.

Is the well-being of black people less important than scoring ideological points or denouncing America?

Those who respond to concerns about crime in the streets by talking about "crime in the suites" may score a verbal point, but urban residents in general and black inner-city residents in particular are not huddled in their apartments at night behind doubly locked doors for fear of being sold junk bonds.

ARE COPS RACIST?

In much of the liberal media, large-scale confrontations between police and people who are breaking the law are usually reported in one of two ways. Either the police used "excessive force" or they "let the situation get out of hand."

Any force sufficient to prevent the situation from getting out of hand will be called "excessive." And if the police arrive in large enough numbers to squelch disorder without the need for using any force at all, then sending in so many cops will be called "over-reacting." After all, with so little resistance to the police, why were so many cops necessary? Such is the mindset of the media.

Add the volatile factor of race and the media will have a field day. If an incident involves a white cop and a black criminal, you don't need to know the specific facts to know how liberals in the media will react. You can predict the words and the music.

Heather Mac Donald of the Manhattan Institute does have the facts, however, in her new book, *Are Cops Racist?* Unfortunately, those who most need to read this book are the least likely to do so. They have made up their minds and don't want to be confused by facts.

For the rest of us, this is a very enlightening and very readable little book. Ms. Mac Donald first tackles the issue of "racial profiling" by the police and shows what shoddy and even silly statistical methods were used to gin up hysteria. Then she moves on to police shootings and other law-enforcement issues.

Suppose I were to tell you that, despite the fact that blacks are just 11 percent of the American population, more than half the men fined for misconduct while playing professional basketball are black— and concluded that this shows the NBA to be racist. What would your reaction be?

"Wait a minute!" you might say. "More than half the players in the NBA are black. So that 11 percent statistic is irrelevant."

That is exactly what is wrong with "racial profiling" statistics. It is based on blacks as a percentage of the population, rather than blacks as a percentage of the people who do the kinds of things that cause police to stop people and question them.

A professor of statistics who pointed this out was— all too predictably— denounced as a "racist." Other statisticians kept quiet for fear of being smeared the same way. We have now reached the dangerous point where ignorance can silence knowledge and where facts get squelched by beliefs.

Heather Mac Donald also goes into facts involving police shootings, especially when the cops are white and the suspect is black. Here again, an education awaits those who are willing to be educated.

People in the media are forever expressing surprise at how many bullets were fired in some of these police shootings. As someone who once taught pistol shooting in the Marine Corps, I am not the least bit surprised.

What surprises me is how many people whose ignorance of shooting is obvious do not let their ignorance stand in the way of reaching sweeping conclusions about situations that they have never faced. To some, it is just a question of taking sides. If it is a white cop and a black suspect, then that is all they feel a need to know.

The greatest contribution of this book is in making painfully clear the actual consequences of cop-bashing in the media and in politics. The police respond to incentives, like everyone else.

If carrying out their duties in the way that gets the job done best is going to bring down on their heads a chorus of media outrage that can threaten their whole careers, many cops tend to back off. And who pays the price of their backing off? Mainly those blacks who are victims of the criminals in their midst.

Drug dealers and other violent criminals have been the beneficiaries of reduced police activity and of liberal judges throwing out their convictions because of "racial profiling." These criminals go back to the black community— not the affluent, suburban and often gated communities where journalists, judges, and politicians live.

The subtitle of *Are Cops Racist?* is: "How the War Against the Police Harms Black Americans."

THE MEANING OF LAW

E llie Nesler is the mother of a sexually abused child who shot dead the man who was in court to face charges of being the guilty party.

Strong feelings have been aroused on both sides of this issue.

There are people collecting money to defend Nesler and others who are denouncing the "vigilante" actions of people who take the law into their own hands.

We all understand why people should not take the law into their own hands. A civilized society would not be possible if everyone did that. Unfortunately, many of those who condemn this woman have been strangely silent for decades, as all sorts of other people have taken the law into their own hands for all sorts of other reasons.

For no one should taking the law into their own hands be more inexcusable than for judges, who not only know better but who have sworn to uphold the law. Yet judges at all levels, up to and including the Supreme Court, have been applauded for deciding cases on the basis of fashionable social theories, rather than the written law.

Indeed, one of the reasons for the bitter frustration of people like Ellie Nesler is that courts have become a plaything of the anointed, rather than an instrument for upholding the laws of the land. The man she killed had already been convicted of sexual molestation before and had been let off with wrist-slap "punishment."

Judges have made it increasingly difficult for American society to protect itself from anyone or anything, by creating new "rights" out of thin air and by leaning over backward for the benefit of those with anti-social behavior.

In short, judges have taken the law into their own hands, instead of carrying out the laws duly passed by democratically elected representatives, reflecting the concerns of a self-governing people. The pretense that judges do this to uphold the Constitution is wearing so thin that growing numbers of people now see this as the fraud that it is.

For more than a century and a half after the Constitution was written, the greatest legal minds in the history of the Supreme Court failed to discover these new criminal "rights" discovered by intellectual lightweights and ideological zealots on the High Court during the past 30 years.

Such judges have taken the law into their own hands— and that is ultimately why Ms. Nesler took the law into her own hands, to defend her child when the law refuses to defend him. Many of those who condemn her are all too willing to let judges play fast and loose with the law, provided they end up with "politically correct" decisions.

When people ask for Supreme Court justices with "compassion" or with "sensitivity," what are they asking for, except people who will lean the way they want justices to lean?

An even-handed application of rules is a demanding job and a heavy responsibility. Even an umpire cannot have "compassion" or "sensitivity." He can either call them honestly as he sees them or prostitute his profession by leaning toward pitchers or batters or base runners.

When courts of law become courts of political correctness, those who suffer are not just those who lose particular cases. The whole society loses. Law exists for a reason— and that reason is not so that judges can indulge their own egos or flatter themselves that their squeamishness is a higher morality.

American society today is polarized over the issue of abortion, not simply because people have different opinions on the subject— which they always have— but because Justice Harry Blackmun imposed his own social opinion under the dishonest pretense of discovering a constitutional "right" that no one else had ever found in the Constitution.

He took the law into his own hands— and was roundly applauded by many of the same people who now condemn the anguished mother of a traumatized child.

This same spirit of playing fast and loose with the law, in order to impose a social agenda or "make a statement" has spread downward from the Supreme Court to other appellate courts and into the trial courts.

Nothing has been more deeply embedded, for centuries, in the Anglo-American legal traditions than the notion that the accused is innocent until proven guilty. Yet there are both civil rights and antitrust cases where only a few flimsy statistics are enough to force the accused to try to prove his innocence.

This perversion of the law is not only accepted but applauded because it reaches politically correct conclusions.

Radical feminists are in fact working hard to extend this presumption of guilt to those accused of sexual harassment.

If we are going to condemn people who take the law into their own hands, let us start with those who are sworn to uphold the law, who cold-bloodedly decide to twist that law to their own purposes, not with an overwrought mother whose child has been victimized because the law was lax.

FREEDOM VERSUS DEMOCRACY

The only time I have left a court room with more respect for the law than I had going in was in a court in Hong Kong, when it was under British colonial rule.

The case involved a Chinese laborer accused of theft, an accusation with considerable circumstantial evidence behind it. This case was presided over by a crusty old British judge, of upper-class demeanor and wearing the traditional white wig. He kept both lawyers on a short leash and let the witnesses know too that he had no tolerance for nonsense.

It would be hard to find two individuals more different in background and status than the Chinese laborer on trial and the British judge in charge of the case. Yet race and class were not destiny, despite the current dogmas of our intelligentsia. What was clear from the outset was that the judge was determined to see that this man got a fair trial— no more and no less. In the end, the laborer was acquitted.

One need only look around the world today, much less back through the pages of history, to see how rare and precious something as basic as a fair trial has been. Whether or how long such trials will exist in Hong Kong under the Communists is another question, and a very painful one.

Meanwhile, too many Western journalists continue to play the game of moral equivalence: There was no democracy in Hong Kong under the British, they say, and there is no democracy there now. Some hark back to the evils of 19th century imperialism that led to Britain's acquiring Hong Kong in the first place. There seems to be much less interest in 20th century totalitarianism in China that sent so many refugees fleeing to Hong Kong, among other places.

Democracy and freedom are too often confounded. Britain itself did not have anything close to democracy until the Reform Act of 1832. But it had freedom long before that.

The fundamentals of freedom— limited government, separation of powers, an independent judiciary, free speech, jury trials— existed in Britain for many generations before the franchise was extended to most males. The whole spirit, and many of the phrases, of the Constitution of the United States derive from British law and government.

Just as freedom can exist without democracy, so democracy can crush freedom. During the Reconstruction era after the Civil War, blacks in the South had many rights that they lost when the occupying Union army was withdrawn and democratically elected state governments took over, ushering in the Jim Crow era.

Today, the confusion between freedom and democracy leads far too many Americans, including those in high places, to seek to spread democracy around the world— in complete disregard of the circumstances of the particular countries. In some respects, we may be more dangerous to our friends than to our enemies, when we pressure them to set up at least the trappings of democracy.

Both freedom and democracy have prerequisites. When those prerequisites do not exist, democracy especially can be a house of cards.

Whether in Eastern Europe and the Balkans between the two World Wars or in Africa in the postwar era, many newly created democratic governments collapsed into authoritarianism or worse. It is much easier to imitate the outward institutional forms of Western democracy than to synthesize the centuries of traditions that make those institutions work.

Our insistence on at least a charade of democracy is dangerous in another way— to ourselves. Relations among nations, especially among the great powers, are not matters of personal friendship or international social work. Their primary goal is, or should be, the safety of the American people in a world that has always been dangerous, long before the Cold War came and went.

We cannot go around the world acting like a common scold, however good that makes us feel or however well it plays politically at home. Nuclear proliferation is far more important than "human rights" pronouncements— and how much cooperation we get in trying to deal with dangerous threats like this may depend on how much political capital we have squandered by insulting other countries whose help we need.

The British were very wise to have given Hong Kong freedom. But they may also have been wise in not attempting to experiment with democracy, where the traditions needed for it simply did not exist.

JUDICIAL ACTIVISM AND JUDICIAL RESTRAINT

While there are many controversies over particular aspects of the law, the most fundamental controversy has long been over who should control the law and who should change the law. American intellectuals, since at least the middle of the twentieth century, have overwhelmingly favored expansion of the role of judges beyond that of applying laws created by others to themselves remaking the law to "fit the times"— which is to say, making the law fit the prevailing vision of the times, the vision of the anointed intellectuals.

Where the Constitution of the United States is a barrier to this expanded role of judges, then judges have been urged to "interpret" the Constitution as a set of values to be applied as judges choose, or updated as they think appropriate, rather than as a set of specific instructions to be followed. That is what "judicial activism" means, though verbal virtuosity has managed to confuse that meaning with other meanings.

Judicial Activism

Those who advocate a greatly expanded latitude for judges to "interpret" laws to suit the presumed necessities or spirit of the times, rather than being bound by what the words meant when the laws were enacted, seem implicitly to assume that activist judges will bend the law in the direction preferred by such advocates— in effect, promote the vision of the anointed. But judicial activism is a blank check for going in any direction on any issue, depending on the predilections of particular judges.

While Chief Justice Earl Warren used expansive interpretations of the law to outlaw racial segregation in public schools in 1954, almost exactly a century earlier Chief Justice Roger Taney had used expansive interpretations of the law to say in the *Dred Scott* case that a black man "had no rights which the white man was bound to respect."[1] It was the dissenters in that case who insisted on following the laws as written and the legal precedents, showing that free blacks had exercised legally recognized rights in parts of the country even before the Constitution was adopted, as well as thereafter.[2]

Intellectuals of the Progressive era and later may well have correctly read the tendencies of their times for judicial activism to move the law in the direction of these intellectuals' goals and values. But that is neither inherent nor inevitable. If the principle of free-wheeling judicial law-making becomes established and accepted across the ideological spectrum, then swings of the ideological pendulum over time can unleash a judicial war of each against all, in which the fundamental concept of law itself is undermined, along with the willingness of the people to be bound by the arbitrary dictates of judges. In the meantime, the sophistry of "results"-oriented judges can make a mockery of the very concept of law, including the Constitution of the United States.

A classic case of judicial sophistry for the sake of desired social "results" was the 1942 case of *Wickard v. Filburn*, which established a precedent and a rationale that extended far beyond the issues in that particular case. Under the Agricultural Adjustment Act of 1938, the federal government had the power to control the production and distribution of many agricultural products. That power derived from the authority of Congress to regulate interstate commerce, as provided by the Constitution. Yet the law was applied to a farmer in Ohio who grew what the Supreme Court itself characterized as "a small acreage of winter wheat,"[3] for his own consumption and that of his farm animals. This farmer planted about 12 acres more than the Department of Agriculture permitted but he challenged the federal government's authority to tell him what to grow on his own farm, when that produce did not enter interstate commerce or even intrastate commerce.

The Supreme Court ruled that the federal authority extended to "production not intended in any part for commerce but wholly for consumption on the farm."[4] The reasoning of the High Court was:

> One of the primary purposes of the Act in question was to increase the market price of wheat, and to that end to limit the volume thereof that could affect the market. It can hardly be denied that a factor of such volume and variability as home-consumed wheat would have a substantial influence on price and market conditions. This may arise because being in marketable condition such wheat overhangs the market

and, if induced by rising prices, tends to flow into the market and check price increases. But if we assume that it is never marketed, it supplies a need of the man who grew it which would otherwise be reflected by purchases in the open market. Home-grown wheat in this sense competes with wheat in commerce.[5]

Thus wheat which did not enter any commerce at all was ruled to be subject to federal control under the interstate commerce clause of the Constitution. Under such expansive stretching of the law, virtually anything could be called "interstate commerce," which in fact became a magic phrase justifying virtually any expansion of federal power over the years, contrary to the Tenth Amendment's limitation on federal authority. In 1995, there was consternation in some quarters when the Supreme Court voted 5 to 4 in *U.S. v. Lopez* that carrying a gun near a school was not "interstate commerce," so that Congress had no authority to ban it, though all the states had that authority and most in fact did ban it. What made the vote close and the result surprising was that it rejected the long-standing practice of courts stretching the phrase "interstate commerce" to cover— and rubber stamp— virtually anything that Congress chose to regulate.

Some judicial activists not only make rulings that stretch the law but even go directly counter to it. A classic example of this was the 1979 case of *United Steelworkers of America v. Weber*. Section 703(a) of the Civil Rights Act of 1964 made it illegal for an employer "to discriminate against any individual with respect to his compensation, terms, conditions, or privileges of employment, because of such individual's race" or various other characteristics. Section 703(d) more specifically forbade such discrimination in "any program established to provide apprenticeship or other training." Nevertheless, a white employee, Brian F. Weber, was denied admission to a training program where places were awarded on the basis of seniority, even though black employees with less seniority were admitted, because racially separate seniority lists were used and racial quotas were established.

That this was counter to the plain meaning of the Act was not explicitly denied in the U.S. Supreme Court opinion written by Justice William J. Brennan. But Justice Brennan rejected "a literal interpretation" of the Civil Rights Act, preferring instead to seek the "spirit" of the Act in Congress' "primary concern" for "the plight of the Negro in our economy."[6] Because that presumed purpose was not to protect whites from racial discrimination, the Act was deemed not to protect Brian F. Weber, who lost the case. The emergence of this decision from the clear language of the Act to the contrary was likened to the great escapes of Houdini, in the dissenting opinion of Justice William H. Rehnquist.[7]

In all three of these examples— *Dred Scott, Wickard v. Filburn* and *Weber*— the decisions reflected the "results" preferred rather than the written law. They are classic concrete examples of judicial activism. Unfortunately, the meaning of the phrase has been obfuscated in recent years and so requires some closer scrutiny.

"Judicial activism" is an idiomatic expression whose meaning cannot be determined by the separate meanings of its words, any more than the meaning of the exclamation "Hot dog!" can be determined by referring to a separate definition of "hot" and "dog." Nevertheless, in recent times, some have attempted to redefine judicial activism by how *active* a judge has been in declaring laws or government actions unconstitutional. However, the Constitution itself is a limitation on the powers of Congress, as well as on the powers of the other branches of government. Judges have been considered duty-bound to invalidate legislation that goes counter to the Constitution, ever since the landmark case of *Marbury v. Madison* in 1803, so how often they perform that duty is not solely in their hands, but depends also on how often others do things that exceed the powers granted them by the Constitution. The real issue regarding judicial activism is over whether the *basis* of a judge's decisions is the law created by others, including the Constitution, or whether judges base their decisions on their own particular conception of "the needs of the times" or of "social justice" or of other considerations beyond the written law or the legal precedents.

There is another idiomatic expression used for the practice of a judge who confines his role to following the written law— "judicial restraint" or following the "original intent" of law. Here again, the meaning of these terms cannot be understood simply from the separate meaning of each word. Judicial restraint means making judicial rulings based on laws created by others, rather than being based on the judge's own assessment of what would be best for either the parties in the case at hand or for society at large.

Justice Oliver Wendell Holmes exemplified this legal philosophy when he said that his role as a judge "is to see that the game is played according to the rules whether I like them or not."[8] He also said: "The criterion of constitutionality is not whether we believe the law to be for the public good."[9] But, since the judge who believes in judicial restraint makes the existing law the paramount consideration in deciding cases, that often means that such a judge must be *active* in striking down new laws which violate the restrictions of the Constitution, which is "the supreme law of the land."

In short, activity is *not* what distinguishes the judicial activist from the practitioner of judicial restraint, since these are just idiomatic expressions for different philosophies of carrying out a judge's function. Judges who base their decisions on the kinds of social, economic, or other considerations of the sort urged by Roscoe Pound or Louis Brandeis are judicial activists in the sense that has stirred controversy, whether they declare many laws or few laws unconstitutional.

Although Justice William O. Douglas was a classic judicial activist in the sense of paying only the most token attention to the Constitution in making rulings based on his own policy preferences— the most famous example being basing his ruling in *Griswold v. Connecticut* on "emanations" from the "penumbras" of the Constitution— he nevertheless deferred to legislators who passed liberal social legislation, using language dear to the heart of advocates of judicial restraint, saying that the court should not be a "super-legislature" but leave social policy to Congress and state legislators.[10] But when the existing law represented social policy that he disapproved, Justice Douglas did not hesitate to intervene and declare it unconstitutional— as he did in *Griswold v. Connecticut*— even if he had nothing more on which to base his ruling than "emanations" that he somehow discerned coming from the "penumbras" of the Constitution,[11] which not even the greatest legal minds, on or off the court, had ever discerned before.

The high tide of judicial activism was the Warren Court of the 1950s and 1960s, when Chief Justice Earl Warren and a like-minded majority on the Supreme Court decided to remake social policy in both civil and criminal areas, almost invariably to the applause of the intelligentsia in the media and in academia. However, as justices with a more judicially restrained view of their role later went on the court, beginning with the Warren Burger Court in 1969, many among the intelligentsia sought to turn the previous complaints about judicial activism against the new judges, by measuring how *active* these judges were in declaring laws unconstitutional or in amending the precedents established by judicial activists such as those of the Warren Court era.

Liberal journalist Michael Kinsley accused Antonin Scalia of judicial activism when Scalia wrote an opinion as a Circuit Court of Appeals judge which, in Kinsley's words, over-ruled "a major piece of legislation passed by large majorities in both houses of Congress and signed with a flourish by a popular president"[12]— as if these were things that make a law Constitutional. Linda Greenhouse of the *New York Times* called the decision that carrying a gun near a school was not interstate commerce an exercise of "raw power" by the Supreme Court because in *U.S. v. Lopez* it "invalidated a law that two houses of Congress and the President of the United States approved"[13]— as if other laws over-ruled by the Supreme Court as unconstitutional, ever since *Marbury v. Madison* in 1803, were not also duly passed laws.

Under the title, "Dissing Congress," a *Michigan Law Review* article said that "the Court in *Lopez* had taken an important step in developing its new version of judicial activism, under which Congress was accorded less respect for its handiwork."[14] Senator Herb Kohl likewise denounced the *Lopez* decision as "a piece of judicial activism that ignores children's safety for the sake of legal nit-picking." However, the *Washington Post* took a more measured view in its editorial on the case:

> One would never guess from the senator's comment, for example, that most states already prohibit the carrying of weapons in schools. In fact, Alfonso Lopez, the San Antonio teenager whose conviction was reversed in this case, was initially arrested on state charges that were dropped only when the federal government took over the prosecution. Clearly, the invalidation of this statute does not leave the nation's children vulnerable at their desks. And it may cause federal legislators to think twice about rushing into every problem area without even considering "nit-picking" questions of federalism.[15]

Senator Kohl was by no means the only law-maker to argue in "results"-oriented terms, rather than in terms of Constitutional limitations on federal power. Senator Arlen Specter said, "I think that crime is a national problem" and "Guns and drugs are the principal instrumentalities of crime." But liberal law professor Laurence Tribe saw beyond "results"-oriented criteria in this case, as reported in the *Chicago Sun-Times*:

> "Congress has pushed the outer edge of the envelope rather carelessly," said Harvard Law School professor Laurence H. Tribe, who noted that lawmakers did not present findings of a link between interstate commerce and the dangers of guns on school grounds. He said the ruling revealed that "this court takes structural limits (to Congress' power) more seriously than people had thought. . . which liberals and pragmatists find dismaying."[16]

The new definition of judicial activism included not only failing to defer to Congress but also the overturning of judicial precedents. In Linda Greenhouse's words, the *Lopez* case "was the first time in 60 years that the Court had invalidated a Federal law on the ground that Congress had exceeded its Constitutional authority to regulate interstate commerce."[17] But judges take an oath to uphold the Constitution, not an oath to uphold precedents. Otherwise, *Dred Scott* and *Plessy v. Ferguson* would have been set in concrete forever.

The *Lopez* case was by no means the only one that caused many among the intelligentsia to denounce the later Supreme Court for "judicial activism" on the basis of its having declared some law or policy unconstitutional. Professor Cass Sunstein of the University of Chicago lamented in 2001: "We are now in the midst of a remarkable period of right-wing judicial activism." This has produced, among other things, he said, an "undemocratic judiciary"[18]— when in fact an appellate court with the power to overrule laws passed by elected officials is inherently undemocratic, so that Professor Sunstein's complaint would apply to the Constitution of the United States itself, rather than to those who carry out their function under that Constitution.

Yet Sunstein complained again in 2003 that "the Rehnquist Court has struck down at least 26 acts of Congress since 1995," and is thereby "guilty of *illegitimate activism*" for— among other things— having "struck down a number of affirmative action programs" as well as striking down "federal legislation as beyond congressional power under the Commerce Clause." According to Professor Sunstein, the Supreme Court has "forbidden

Congress from legislating on the basis of its own views" of what the Fourteenth Amendment means.[19] But if Congress can determine the extent of its own powers under the Fourteenth Amendment, or any other provision of the Constitution, then the Constitution becomes meaningless as a limit on Congressional power or on government power in general.

In a similar vein, an article in the *New Republic* titled "Hyperactive: How the Right Learned to Love Judicial Activism" claimed that conservative judges "have turned themselves into the mirror image of the judicial activists whom they have spent their careers attacking."[20] Using this new redefinition of judicial activism, a *New York Times* writer charged Chief Justice John Roberts with sometimes supporting "judicial action, even if it meant trampling on Congress and the states."[21] A later *New York Times* editorial declared "a willingness to strike down Congressional laws" to be "the most common objective criteria"[22] of judicial activism. This redefinition sidesteps the whole crucial question whether the laws over-ruled were in fact consistent or inconsistent with the Constitution of the United States. But this key issue is repeatedly left out of claims that the Supreme Court is "activist" when it fails to uphold legislation or particular precedents.

The new definition of judicial activism lends itself to a purely numerical basis for deciding who is and who is not a judicial activist— Professor Sunstein, for example, basing his charges on how many "federal laws per year" the Supreme Court has declared unconstitutional.[23] That notion has spread from the intelligentsia into politics. Thus Senator Patrick Leahy used this new definition of judicial activism when he asserted, "The two most activist judges we have right now are Justice Thomas and Justice Scalia, who have struck down and thus written laws of their own in place of congressional laws more than anybody else on the current Supreme Court."[24] Since these are the two justices most identified with judicial restraint, it was a verbal coup to turn the tables and label them conservative activists. Blurring the line between judicial activism and judicial restraint not only defuses criticism of liberal activist judges but enables points to be scored by invoking moral equivalence against judicially restrained judges who can also be called "activist" by simply redefining the term.

Genuine judicial activism, like many other social phenomena, may be more readily understood by examining the incentives and constraints facing those involved. One constraint on judges' actions that has clearly weakened over the years is the disapproval of peers, whether in the judiciary or among legal scholars in the law schools. Judicial activism for litigants or causes favored by the prevailing vision of the intellectuals can expect acceptance, at a minimum, and in many cases celebration or lionizing of activist judges. In short, incentives favor judicial activism.

Judges, like intellectuals, usually become famous among the general public only when they step out beyond the bounds of their professional competence to become philosopher-kings deciding social, economic or political issues. Not even Chief Justice Earl Warren's admirers tried to portray him as a great legal scholar.[25] Both he and Chief Justice Roger Taney a century earlier became famous for making sweeping pronouncements about society on a sociological, rather than a legal, basis for their landmark rulings. With pronouncements going beyond the range of their expertise or competence being virtually a prerequisite for popular prominence, it is hardly surprising that so many judges, like so many intellectuals, have said so many things that make no sense.

Judicial Restraint and "Original Intent"

"Judicial restraint" has sometimes been summed up in another idiomatic expression— namely, following the "original intent" of the law. Many among the intelligentsia have seized upon the word "intent" to claim that it is difficult or impossible to discern exactly what those who wrote the Constitution, or legislation for that matter, actually intended, especially after the passing of many years. Thus Professor Jack Rakove of Stanford University said: "Establishing the intention behind any action is a tricky business" and "The task grows geometrically more complex when we try to ascribe intent to groups of people— especially men who were acting two centuries ago, who left us incomplete records of their motives and concerns, and who reached their decisions through a process that fused principled debate with hard-driven bargains."[26]

The key word in all of this— and the key fallacy in this common line of reasoning— is the word "behind." Practitioners of judicial restraint are seeking to understand and apply the written law as it stands— as instructions for both judges and the citizenry— *not* discover the motivations, beliefs, hopes or fears that might have been *behind* the writing of the law. Judicial restraint means undertaking an inherently less complicated task. Even the simplest law, such as a 65 miles an hour speed limit, can be expanded into a complex question of unanswerable dimensions if looked at in terms of the attitudes, values, etc., *behind* the intentions of those who created that law, rather than being looked at as an explicit instruction, readily understood.

Looking at laws in terms of the subjective intentions of those who wrote them is not only a more complicated approach, it is an approach that seeks or claims to discern the value judgments or the "spirit" behind the laws— which gives judges far greater latitude for interpretation, and thus far more opportunities to adjust the laws to meet "the needs of the time," "social justice," or whatever other synonym for the individual predilections of particular judges. But critics of judicial restraint project such difficulties onto others who are *not* looking *behind* laws, but undertaking a far more straightforward task of reading laws as explicit instructions, rather than as general statements of values.

As Justice Antonin Scalia put it, "despite frequent statements to the contrary, we do not really look for subjective legislative intent." What he is seeking is "the original meaning of the text," adding: "Often— indeed, I dare say usually— that is easy to discern and simple to apply."[27] Nor is Justice Scalia unique in this. From William Blackstone in eighteenth century England to Oliver Wendell Holmes and Robert Bork in twentieth century America, those seeking to stick to the original meaning of laws have made it very clear that they were *not* talking about events taking place within the inner recesses of the minds of those who write laws. For one thing, the votes which provide the political, legal and moral authority of laws are votes on what is publicly set before those who vote. In other words, *nobody voted on what was in the back of somebody else's mind.* Moreover, nobody can obey or disobey what is in the back of somebody else's mind.

It was the publicly known meaning of the words of the laws, "to be understood in their usual and most known signification" as of the time they were used, according to Blackstone,[28] that determines how a judge should interpret them. For Holmes as well, legal interpretation of what the law-maker said did not mean trying to "get into his mind."[29] Holmes said: "We do not inquire what the legislature meant; we ask only what the statute means."[30] In a letter to British jurist Sir Frederick Pollock, Holmes said "we don't care a damn for the meaning of the writer."[31] The judge's job, according to Holmes, is to "read English intelligently— and a consideration of consequences comes into play, if at all, only when the meaning of the words used is open to reasonable doubt."[32] Judge Robert H. Bork has likewise argued that judges should render decisions "according to the historical Constitution."[33]

Despite such plain statements by advocates and practitioners of judicial restraint over a long span of years, much verbal virtuosity has been deployed by others to expand the task to unachievable dimensions by turning the question into one of discerning subjective motives, beliefs, hopes and fears *behind* the creation of the law. Professor Rakove, for example, said that at the time of the Constitutional Convention in 1787, James Madison "approached the Convention in the grip of a great intellectual passion,"[34] that he had "fear" of certain policies regarding property and religion,[35] and that he "privately described" Constitutional amendments in a particular way.[36]

Similarly, Professor Ronald Dworkin has argued at considerable length against original intent on grounds that the "mental events" in the minds of legislators or writers of the Constitution are difficult or impossible to discern,[37] that "it seems even plainer that we have no fixed concept of a group intention," nor any way of deciding "which aspects of individual mental states are relevant to a group intention."[38] Justice William J. Brennan likewise spoke of the "sparse or ambiguous evidence of the original intention" of the framers of the Constitution.[39] In a similar vein, others point out that "public statements often do not reflect actual intentions."[40]

Such attempts to change the question from the plain *meaning* of a law to an esoteric quest for discovering what was *behind* the creation of the law are often used by those who espouse judicial interpretations that go beyond what the law explicitly says— and sometimes even directly counter to the written law, as Justice William J. Brennan did in the *Weber* case. Professor Ronald Dworkin defended the *Weber* decision on grounds that "the question of how Title VII should be interpreted cannot be answered simply by staring at the words Congress used."[41] The verbal virtuosity of referring to simply "staring" at words— apparently as the only alternative to adventurous reinterpretations— contrasts sharply with Holmes' statement about simply reading English intelligently.

To Dworkin, the significance of the *Weber* decision was that it was "another step in the Court's efforts to develop a new conception of what equality requires in the search for racial justice."[42] Why judges are to preempt such decisions and rule on the basis of their own new conceptions of social issues, under the guise of interpreting the law, while going directly counter to what the law says, was a question not raised, much less answered.

Saying that it is hard or impossible to discern what was meant by a law has often been a prelude to making decisions that ignore even the plainest meanings— as in the *Weber* case— in order to impose notions currently in vogue in elite circles as the law of the land. Dworkin and others have openly advocated as much, which makes their tactical agnosticism about "intent" a red herring. For those who do not intend to follow the original meaning of laws, the ease or difficulty of discovering that meaning is irrelevant, except as a distracting talking point.

The Constitution was a very plainly written document, and when it used phrases like "an establishment of religion," for example, it referred to something well known to people who had already lived under an established church, the Church of England. The prohibition against an establishment of religion had nothing to do with a "wall of separation" between church and state, which appears nowhere in the Constitution, but was a phrase from Thomas Jefferson, who was not even in the country when the Constitution was written. There was nothing esoteric about the phrase "an establishment of religion." For more than a hundred years after the Constitution was written, it never meant that it was illegal to display religious symbols on government property, however much some people in later times might wish that this was what it meant, and however much some modern judges might be willing to accommodate that wish.

Similarly with phrases like "due process" or "freedom of speech," which had a long history in British law before those same phrases were placed in the Constitution of the United States by people who had only recently ceased to be British subjects. They were not coining new phrases for new or esoteric concepts whose meanings judges would have to divine *de novo*.

Judicial restraint involves not only upholding Constitutional provisions and the provisions of legislation that are within the authority of Congress or the states, it also involves a reluctance to over-rule prior court decisions. Without such a reluctance, laws could become so changeable with the changing personnel of courts that citizens would find it difficult to plan economic or other endeavors that take time to come to fruition, for it would be impossible to predict what the turnover of judges and their changing of laws would be in the meantime.

Needless to say, this reluctance to overturn prior court decisions cannot be absolute, but must be a matter of cautious judgment. If some legal scholar today should publish an article or book showing convincingly that *Marbury v. Madison* was wrongly decided in 1803, no court today would be likely to over-rule that decision, on which two centuries of precedents have been built and under which all sorts of endeavors and commitments have been undertaken during those centuries, relying on the legal system that evolved in the wake of *Marbury v. Madison*.

Yet, ironically, many of the same intellectuals who heartily supported the Warren Court's overturning of long-standing precedents during the 1950s and 1960s also bitterly condemned later and more conservative courts which cut back on some of the precedents established by liberal justices, especially in decisions during the Warren Court era. Thus, under the headline "The High Court Loses Restraint," a *New York Times* editorial reacted to the *Lopez* decision by saying: "In deciding that Congress lacks the power to outlaw gun possession within 1,000 feet of a school, the Supreme Court has taken an unfortunate historical turn and needlessly questioned previously settled law."[43] Citing Justice Stephen Breyer, the *Times* emphasized "the value of judicial restraint," defined by them as "deferring to Congress when Congress showed a rational basis for finding an interstate commercial impact in its law." But to *defer* to those whose powers the Constitution specifically limited would be to make a mockery of those limitations. If Congress itself is to decide how far its powers extend, what purpose can there be in Constitutional limitations on the power of Congress or of the federal government?

Inconsistent as such reactions from the intelligentsia have been, when viewed as commentary on jurisprudence, these reactions are perfectly consistent when viewed as part of a "results"-oriented role for courts, since the intelligentsia clearly preferred the social results of the Warren Court's decisions to the social results of many decisions of later courts. But court decisions based on the social results preferred by judges, rather than on the law as written, have a number of adverse effects on law as a fundamental framework within which members of society can plan their own actions. The most obvious effect is that no one can predict what social results judges will turn out to prefer in the future, leaving even the most clearly written laws surrounded by a fog of uncertainty that invites increased litigation.

The opposite of the results-oriented judge is the judge who will rule in favor of litigants that the judge may personally despise, if the law is on that side in that case. Justice Oliver Wendell Holmes, for example, voted in favor of Benjamin Gitlow in the 1925 case of *Gitlow v. New York*— and then said afterwards, in a letter to Harold Laski, that he had just voted for "the right of an ass to drool about proletarian dictatorship."[44] Likewise, Holmes dissented in *Abrams v. United States* in favor of appellants whose views he characterized in his judicial opinion itself as "a creed that I believe to be the creed of ignorance and immaturity."[45] As he told Laski, "I loathed most of the things in favor of which I decided."[46] Conversely, he could rule against litigants he personally viewed favorably. In another letter to Laski, Holmes said that he had to "write a decision against a very thorough and really well expressed argument by two colored men— one bery black— that even in intonations was better than, I should say, the majority of white discourses that we hear."[47] Holmes was not taking sides or seeking "results," but applying the law.

RACE AND
ETHNICITY

OLDER BUDWEISER

B ack in the days of the Habsburg Empire, there was a town in Bohemia called Budweis. The people in that town were called Budweisers and the town had a brewery which produced beer with the same name— but different from the American Budweiser.

Like many communities in Bohemia during that era, Budweis had people of both Czech and German ancestries, speaking different languages, though many were also bilingual. They got along pretty well and most people there thought of themselves as Budweisers, rather than as Czechs or Germans. But that would later change— for the worse—not only in Budweis, but throughout Bohemia.

The mayor of Budweis spoke both Czech and German but refused to be classified as a member of either group. His point was that we are all Budweisers.

As with virtually all groups in virtually all countries and in virtually all eras, there were differences between the Germans and the Czechs in Budweis. Germans were more educated, more prosperous, and more prominent in business and the professions.

The German language at that point had a much wider and richer literature, the Slavic languages having acquired written versions centuries later than the languages of Western Europe. Educated Bohemians of whatever ethnicity were usually educated in German.

Those Czechs who wished to rise into the upper echelons, whether in business, the military, or the professions, had to master the German language and culture, in order to fit in with those already at the higher levels.

People on both sides learned to live with this situation and Czechs were welcomed into the German cultural enclaves in Bohemia when they mastered that culture. In Budweis, they could all be Budweisers.

As in so many other countries and in so many other times, the rise of a newly educated intellectual class in the 19th century polarized the society with ethnic identity politics. All over Bohemia, the new Czech intelligentsia urged Czechs to think of themselves as Czechs, not Bohemians or Budweisers or anything else that would transcend their ethnic identity.

Demands were made that street signs in Prague, which had been in both Czech and German before, now be exclusively in Czech. Quotas were demanded for a certain percentage of Czech music to be played by the Budweiser orchestra.

If such demands seem petty, their consequences were not small. People of German ancestry resisted ethnic classifications but the Czech intelligentsia insisted and Czech politicians went along with the trend on many issues, large and small.

Eventually, Germans as well began in self-defense to think of themselves as Germans, rather than as Bohemians or Budweisers, and to defend their interests as Germans. This ethnic polarization in the 19th century was a fateful step whose full consequences have not yet ended completely, even in the 21st century.

A crucial turning point was the creation of the new nation of Czechoslovakia when the Habsburg Empire was broken up after the First World War. Czech leaders declared the new nation's mission to include a correction of "social injustice" so as to "put right the historic wrongs of the seventeenth century."

What were those wrongs? Czech nobles who revolted against the Habsburg Empire back in the 17th century were defeated and had their lands confiscated and turned over to Germans. Presumably no one from the 17th century was still alive when Czechoslovakia was created in the 20th century, but Czech nationalists kept the grievance alive— as ethnic identity ideologues have done in countries around the world.

Government policies designed to undo history with preferential treatment for Czechs polarized the existing generation of Germans and Czechs. Bitter German reactions led eventually to demands that the part of the country where they lived be united with neighboring Germany. From this came the Munich crisis of 1938 that dismembered Czechoslovakia on the eve of World War II.

When the Nazis conquered the whole country, the Germans now lorded it over the Czechs. After the war, the Czech reaction led to mass expulsions of Germans under brutal conditions that cost many lives. Today refugees in Germany are still demanding restitution.

If only the grievances of past centuries had been left in the past! If only they had all remained Budweisers or Bohemians.

"DIVERSITY" IN INDIA

If facts carried some weight with those who are politically correct, the recent outbreak of savage and lethal violence in India's state of Gujarat might cause some reassessments of both India and "diversity."

This is only the latest round in a cycle of violence and revenge between the Hindus and the Muslims in that country. The death toll has reached 489 people in a few days. That includes the Hindu activists who were firebombed while on a train returning from the site of a razed mosque, where they planned to build a Hindu temple, and many Muslims then slaughtered by Indian mobs in retaliation.

These mobs have burned Muslim women and children alive in their homes. Nor is such savagery new in India or limited to clashes between Hindus and Muslims. At other times and places, it has been one caste against another, locals versus outsiders, or the storm trooper organization Shiv Sena against anybody who gets in their way. In some places, thugs resentful of Western influence attack shops that sell Valentine cards.

None of this fits the pious picture of peaceful and spiritual India that so captivates many Americans. India has served as one of the foreign Edens to which those Americans turn, in order to show their disdain for the United States.

At one time, the Soviet Union played that role, then China, then Cuba, and for some, India. What happens in the real India doesn't matter. It is the symbolic India of their dreams to which they impute all the virtues they declare to be lacking in the USA.

It is not India's fault that we have some fatuous Americans who want to put Indians up on a pedestal, in order to score points against their fellow Americans. But we need to be aware of the truth as well.

Those who are constantly gushing about the supposed benefits of "diversity" never want to put their beliefs to the test of looking at the facts about countries where people are divided by language, culture, religion, and in other ways, such as caste in India. Such countries are all too often riddled with strife and violence.

India is one of the most diverse nations on earth. No more than one-third of its people speak any given language and the population is divided innumerable ways by caste, ethnicity, religion and numerous localisms. Lethal riots have marked its history from the beginning.

When India gained its independence in 1947, the number of Hindus and Muslims who killed each other in one year exceeded the total number of blacks lynched in the entire history of the United States. Yet we are told that we should be like those gentle people, as if India were a nation of Gandhis. In reality, Gandhi was assassinated for trying to stop internecine strife in India.

If there is no need to impute wholly unrealistic sainthood to India, there is also no need to single it out for demonization. Many other countries with the much-touted "diversity" have likewise been racked by internal slaughters and atrocities.

Only about 20 miles away from India, the island nation of Sri Lanka has suffered more deaths among its majority and minority populations, as a result of internal strife and civil war, than the much larger United States suffered during the Vietnam War. Other such "diverse" countries as Rwanda and those in the Balkans have a similar catalogue of horrors.

"Diversity" is not just a matter of demographics. It is also a matter of "identity" and identity politics. Sri Lanka was one of the most peaceful nations on earth before demagogues began hyping identity and demanding group preferences and quotas back in the 1950s.

Demographically, the United States has always been diverse, having received immigrants from all over the world. However, until recent times, it was understood by all that they came here to become Americans— not to remain foreign. By the second generation, most were speaking English, and by the third generation they were speaking only English.

Today, however, our citizen-of-the-world types are doing all they can to keep foreigners foreign and domestic minorities riled up over grievances, past and present, real and imaginary. Above all, they want group identity and group preferences and quotas.

In short, they want all the things that have brought on the kinds of disasters from which India and other such "diverse" countries have suffered grievously.

THE SLAVERY CARD

One of the many sad signs of our times is that people are not only playing the race card, they are playing the slavery card, which is supposedly the biggest trump of all. At the so-called "million man march" in Washington, poet Maya Angelou rang all the changes on slavery, at a rally billed as forward-looking and as being about black independence rather than white guilt. Meanwhile, best-selling author Dinesh D'Souza was being denounced in the media for having said that slavery was not a racist institution.

First of all, anyone familiar with the history of slavery around the world knows that its origins go back thousands of years and that slaves and slaveowners were very often of the same race. Those who are ignorant of all this, or who think of slavery in the United States as if it were the only slavery, go ballistic when anyone tells them that this institution was not based on race.

Blacks were not enslaved because they were black, but because they were available at the time. Whites enslaved other whites in Europe for centuries before the first black slave was brought to the Western Hemisphere.

Only late in history were human beings even capable of crossing an ocean to get millions of other human beings of a different race. In the thousands of years before that, not only did Europeans enslave other Europeans, Asians enslaved other Asians, Africans enslaved other Africans, and the native peoples of the Western Hemisphere enslaved other native peoples of the Western Hemisphere.

D'Souza was right. Slavery was not about race. The fact that his critics are ignorant of history is their problem.

What was peculiar about the American situation was not just that slaves and slaveowners were of different races, but that slavery contradicted the whole philosophy of freedom on which the society was founded. If all men were created equal, as the Declaration of Independence said, then blacks had to be depicted as less than men.

While the antebellum South produced a huge volume of apologetic literature trying to justify slavery on racist grounds, no such justification was considered necessary in vast reaches of the world and over vast expanses of time. In most parts of the world, people saw nothing wrong with slavery.

Strange as that seems to us today, a hundred years ago only Western civilization saw anything wrong with slavery. And two hundred years ago, only a minority in the West thought it was wrong.

Africans, Arabs, Asians and others not only maintained slavery long after it was abolished throughout the Western Hemisphere, they resisted all attempts of the West to stamp out slavery in their lands during the age of imperialism. Only the fact that the West had greater firepower and more economic and political clout enabled them to impose the abolition of slavery, as they imposed other Western ideas, on the non-Western world.

Those who talk about slavery as if it were just the enslavement of blacks by whites ignore not only how widespread this institution was and how far back in history it went, they also ignore how recently slavery continued to exist outside of Western civilization.

While slavery was destroyed in the West during the nineteenth century, the struggle to end slavery elsewhere continued well into the twentieth century— and pockets of slavery still exist to this moment in Africa. But there is scarcely a peep about it from black "leaders" in America who thunder about slavery in the past.

If slavery were the real issue, then slavery among flesh-and-blood human beings alive today would arouse far more outcry than past slavery among people who are long dead. The difference is that past slavery can be cashed in for political benefits today, while slavery in North Africa only distracts from these political goals. Worse yet, talking about slavery in Africa would undermine the whole picture of unique white guilt requiring unending reparations.

While the Western world was just as guilty as other civilizations when it came to enslaving people for thousands of years, it was unique only in finally deciding that the whole institution was immoral and should be ended. But this conclusion was by no means universal even in the Western world, however obvious it may seem to us today.

Thousands of free blacks owned slaves in the antebellum South. And, years after the Emancipation Proclamation in the United States, whites as well as blacks were still being bought and sold as slaves in North Africa and the Middle East.

Anyone who wants reparations based on history will have to gerrymander history very carefully. Otherwise, practically everybody would owe reparations to practically everybody else.

"MINORITIES"

Years ago, when I was running a research project in Washington, a memorandum came down from on high, telling us that there was money available to hire "minority" professionals for the summer, without having to take it out of the regular project budget.

"Wonderful!" I said. "There's a Jewish lady up at Princeton who wants to come down here and help me out, but I don't have any money to pay her."

This idea was shot down immediately.

"Jews are not a minority," I was told. "And Jews from Princeton are definitely not a minority."

It did no good to point out that Jews are only 3 percent of the population, and so must be a minority. Nor did it do any good to say that Jews were defined as an ethnic minority in the research project itself. The powers that be turned a deaf ear to all such arguments.

In a sense, they were right. The word "minority" had already become one of many politically corrupted words. It no longer meant a statistically smaller part of the population. It meant people you feel sorry for.

After all their achievements, nobody felt sorry for Jews any more. Therefore they were not a "minority."

Nobody feels sorry for Asian Americans any more, after so many success stories. Therefore, they are increasingly excluded from "minority" status in programs and policies at some colleges and universities.

A few years ago, a memorandum from the U.S. Air Force Academy gave lower cut-off scores for "minority" applicants being recruited but Asian Americans had to meet the same standards as whites. Few institutions are so impolitic as to put such policies in writing or so unfortunate as to have them leak out. But there is growing evidence that this practice extends well beyond the Air Force Academy.

When Berkeley used verbal test score cut-offs to eliminate applicants in 1984 and 1986, "minority" students were exempted— but Asian American students were not. Many Asians were wiped out by the verbal cut-off scores because their strong suit tends to be math.

At Harvard, the test scores of Asian American applicants were virtually the same as those of white applicants, but the Asian Americans actually admitted had test scores substantially higher than those of whites who were admitted. In terms of test scores, Asians had to be better to get in.

It is not just Asians and Jews who lose their "minority" status because of outstanding performance. Some financial aid programs have also passed over those blacks who score above a certain level, in favor of those blacks who did poorly, who "really need" help. They want people they can feel sorry for.

Academic smoothies are never at a loss to explain away whatever they do. At M.I.T., for example, the director of admissions has responded to criticisms of large test score disparities among people admitted from different racial and sex backgrounds by downgrading the importance of test scores. Differences in test scores have only a modest correlation with later academic performance, he said.

This familiar argument is clever but phony. The average M.I.T. student scores in the top one percent in math. Just where in that top one percent probably doesn't matter a lot, as the director of admissions says. But it does matter that he is in the top one percent.

By the same token, the difference of a few million dollars between one Rockefeller and another probably doesn't matter that much. But that doesn't mean that it makes no difference how much money you have.

It makes a very real difference that 90 percent of the white M.I.T. students score higher in math than the average black M.I.T. student. A substantially higher percentage of the black students fail to finish M.I.T., and those who do graduate have substantially lower grade-point averages.

The tragedy is that this waste— more than one-fourth of the black students don't graduate at M.I.T.— is completely unnecessary.

The average black student at M.I.T. is well above the national average on math tests. He is just not in the stratospheric level of other M.I.T. students. At most colleges, universities, or technical institutes, these same black students would be on the dean's list.

In short, black students with every prospect of success are artificially turned into failures by being mismatched with their college. This is not peculiar to M.I.T. It is a nationwide phenomenon among elite schools, who are more interested in having a good-looking body count from every group than they are in the price that has to be paid.

Everyone pays a very high price for this academic fad. Disadvantaged minority students pay the highest price of all. Asians may be lucky that they are not considered a "minority."

RACE, ROMANCE
AND REALITY

During one of the ghetto riots of the 1960s, my brother was out in the streets asking the rioters: "Where are you going to shop after you burn down this man's store?"

Although a riot is not the best place for a Socratic dialogue, my brother somehow returned home safely. Today, more than 30 years later, no one has yet answered his question. Reality, however, has answered it decisively and painfully: Low income and minority neighborhoods across the country are sadly lacking in stores— and the stores they have charge higher prices for substandard goods, sold in dirtier surroundings by less polite clerks and owners.

The title of a study by the New York City Department of Consumer Affairs— *The Poor Pay More for Less*— summed it up. Some residents of low-income areas have to go far from where they live to shop in more upscale neighborhoods and pay for a ride back home with their groceries. An organization for the elderly in some upper Manhattan, low-income neighborhoods has arranged for bus trips to New Jersey for them to do their shopping.

It was not like this when I grew up in Harlem in the 1940s. It was less than half a block to a drugstore, no more than half a block to a grocery store and there was a supermarket across the street from that store. You didn't have to go two blocks to find a butcher shop or a stationery store or an optician. There was a dentist across the street.

I can't remember any of these people being rude to me when I was a kid. There were too many alternatives around for that. There was not enough difference in prices to make it worth spending a nickel to ride a subway to another neighborhood for shopping.

People who live in low-income and minority neighborhoods today are still paying the price for the riots of the past, as well as numerous other counterproductive social trends that began in the 1960s. The same romanticism that turned mob violence and looting into an uprising of the oppressed still insists on seeing the problems of these neighborhoods in similar terms.

When black economist Walter Williams wrote an article explaining the higher costs behind higher prices in ghetto stores, a quarter of a century ago, he was denounced as "a white racist" by people who obviously had never seen him. The politically acceptable reasons for higher prices were racism and exploitation. But it was hard for an economist to reconcile exploitation with stores closing down and leaving neighborhoods where they were supposedly making big bucks off the locals.

The armies of community activists and other professional protesters spawned by the Great Society programs of the 1960s are fierce in their indignation at the lack of stores in ghetto neighborhoods. Among the many things they blame are never community activists and the romantic vision of victimhood and resentment that they spawn.

My first glimpse of that vision came at Cornell University back in the late '60s, as I passed a group of black students in the hall near my office. They had just come from a class on ghetto economic problems, taught by the local radical guru.

"How are we going to get *those Jews* out of Harlem?" one of the students bitterly asked.

They seemed unreceptive to my question as to whom they planned to replace them with. Nor was it an easy question. It hasn't really been answered to this day.

What is an even tougher question to deal with is: How do you explain why black communities across the country were seldom served by black grocers or other storekeepers? The stark choices seemed to be to "blame the victim" or to blame "society" or some other group.

In reality, there is nothing at all unusual about situations where the businesses in a given community are run predominantly by people who are not part of that community. It was common for generations for the entrepreneurial Chinese to be the predominant businessmen in communities of Malays, Indonesians, Vietnamese and others in Southeast Asia. So were the Jews among the Slavs in Eastern Europe, the Lebanese among the people of Sierra Leone, and other similar groups in countries around the world.

There are far too many interwoven historical, cultural, and economic strands to try to disentangle to explain why any given group at any given juncture is where it is. What we can do is to save the romantic hogwash. Its price is too high, much like the price of groceries in the ghetto.

DOG-IN-THE-MANGER POLITICS

A plastic surgeon of Chinese ancestry in Sydney, Australia, may not sound like an average individual, but the moral of his story is all too common in countries around the world. Born in Malaysia, this plastic surgeon was in one of many high-level positions occupied by the Chinese minority and coveted by the Malay majority. Moreover, under the country's affirmative action policies, he understood that his days as a plastic surgeon were numbered.

He took it all without bitterness, offering to stay on to treat disfigured children and others until a Malay plastic surgeon was available to replace him. But he missed the point. They wanted him out of there, whether or not there was a Malay to replace him and whether or not disfigured people had anyone else to turn to.

The surgeon relocated to Australia, where he was apparently doing quite well by the time I encountered him. The real victims of the Malaysian government's policies were still in Malaysia.

This dog-in-the-manger approach is by no means peculiar to Malaysia. Envy of others' success and embarrassment at being visibly unable to match their performance have been political driving forces behind many programs of preferences and quotas.

When Romania acquired additional territory from the defeated Central Powers after the First World War, it also acquired universities which were culturally either German or Hungarian. One of their top priorities was to get rid of the Germans and the Hungarians on the faculties and transform the universities into Romanian bastions.

At that point, roughly three-quarters of all Romanians were still illiterate, so replacing these foreign professors with Romanians of comparable caliber was very unlikely. But replacement was not the issue: Getting rid of those who were better qualified was the issue.

Despite all the zeal expended in converting German and Hungarian universities in the new provinces of Bukovina and Transylvania into

Romanian universities, there was no urgency at all about creating a university in the province of Bessarabia, where none existed. Moreover, when Hungarian students living in Romania began going to Hungary to attend universities there, the Romanian government forbad them to do so.

What is involved is not just envy. It is the threat to one's ego that is crucial in promoting dog-in-the-manger policies. When Nigeria became an independent nation, back in the 1960s, many of the educated, skilled, business and professional people in northern Nigeria were from tribes in southern Nigeria.

One of the top priorities of northern Nigerian politicians was to get rid of such people. The hope was to replace them eventually with northern Nigerians. But, in the meantime, the northern Nigerians wanted them out of there, even if they had to hire Europeans to replace them or suffer a deterioration of the services being performed by the southern Nigerians.

Having Europeans in these occupations was far less of a threat to the ego than having fellow Africans so dramatically outperforming the locals.

Such attitudes are not unknown in the United States, whether or not ethnic or racial differences are involved. The same dog-in-the-manger can be found when the issue is class. Liberals have never ceased denouncing Ronald Reagan's "tax cuts for the rich" in the early 1980s, despite the actual results, including a record-breaking period of economic expansion.

After the tax *rate* was cut on the highest income brackets (and on others), not only did the total tax *receipts* rise but the percentage of those receipts paid by "the rich" also rose. Why then were the liberals unhappy? Because those in the upper brackets paid these vastly greater taxes out of rising incomes, while retaining a higher percentage of those incomes for themselves.

The dog-in-the-manger principle requires that the rich be made worse off. Any policy that fails to do that has failed politically, regardless of what economic benefits it may bring to the society as a whole.

While such attitudes are sufficiently widespread around the world that they cannot be attributed to a particular culture, neither are they inevitable. Very often, the key ingredient in the rise of explosive resentments is the rise of an intelligentsia preoccupied with invidious comparisons rather than general well-being.

Ironically, all too often the rich themselves have been the patrons of such intellectuals, whether at the universities, the foundations or other institutions supported by their donations.

"FRIENDS" OF BLACKS

Who was it who said, "if the Negro cannot stand on his own legs, let him fall"?

Ronald Reagan? Newt Gingrich? Charles Murray?

Not even close. It was Frederick Douglass!

This was part of a speech in which Douglass also said: "Everybody has asked the question. . . 'What shall we do with the Negro?' I have had but one answer from the beginning. Do nothing with us! Your doing with us has already played the mischief with us. Do nothing with us!"

Frederick Douglass had achieved a deeper understanding in the 19th century than any of the black "leaders" of today. Those whites who feel a need to do something with blacks and for blacks have been some of the most dangerous "friends" of blacks.

Academia is the home of many such "friends," which is why there are not only double standards of admissions to colleges but also in some places double standards in grading. The late David Riesman called it "affirmative grading."

A professor at one of California's state universities where black students are allowed to graduate on the basis of easier standards put it bluntly: "We are just lying to these black students when we give them degrees." That lie is particularly deadly when the degree is a medical degree, authorizing someone to treat sick people or perform surgery on children.

For years, Dr. Patrick Chavis was held up as a shining example of the success of affirmative action, for he was admitted to medical school as a result of minority preferences and went back to the black community to practice medicine. In fact, he was publicly praised by the Lawyers Committee for Civil Rights— just two weeks before his license was suspended, after his patients died under conditions that brought the matter to the attention of the Medical Board of California.

An administrative law judge referred to Chavis' "inability to perform some of the most basic duties required of a physician." A year later, after a fuller investigation, his license was revoked.

Those who had for years been using Chavis as a shining example of the success of affirmative action suddenly changed tactics and claimed that an isolated example of failure proved nothing. Sadly, Chavis was not an isolated example.

When a professor at the Harvard Medical School declared publicly, back in the 1970s, that black students were being allowed to graduate from that institution without meeting the same standards as others, he was denounced as a "racist" for saying that it was cruel to "allow trusting patients to pay for our irresponsibility"— trusting black patients, in many cases.

Why do supposedly responsible people create such dangerous double standards? Some imagine that they are being friends to blacks by lowering the standards for them. Some don't think that blacks have what it takes to meet real standards, and that colleges and universities will lose their "diversity"— and perhaps federal money with it— if they don't lower the standards, in order to get an acceptable racial body count.

My own experience as a teacher was that black students would meet higher standards if you refused to lower the standards for them. This was not the royal road to popularity, either with the students themselves or with the "friends" of blacks on the faculty and in the administration. But, when the dust finally settled, the students met the standards.

We have gotten so used to abysmal performances from black students, beginning in failing ghetto schools, that it is hard for some to believe that black students once did a lot better than they do today, at least in places and times with good schools. As far back as the First World War, black soldiers from New York, Pennsylvania, Illinois, and Ohio scored higher on mental tests than white soldiers from Georgia, Arkansas, Kentucky, and Mississippi.

During the 1940s, black students in Harlem schools had test scores very similar to those of white working class students on the lower east side of New York. Sometimes the Harlem scores were a little higher or a little lower, but they were never miles behind, the way they are today in many ghetto schools.

If blacks could do better back when their opportunities were worse, why can't today's ghetto students do better? Perhaps blacks have too many "friends" today.

GIVING BUSINESS
THE BUSINESS

Television characters like J. R. Ewing in "Dallas" may have portrayed businessmen as Machiavellian devils but, in some respects at least, businessmen seem much more likely to be patsies than predators.

For years now, the Capital Research Center in Washington has been documenting how corporate America has been bankrolling all sorts of left-leaning groups, whose programs attack or undermine the free market in general and big corporations in particular. When developers subsidize environmental extremists, and employers contribute money to groups seeking to have government deny those employers the right to hire whatever individuals can do the job best, then something very strange is going on.

An even stranger, and perhaps more dangerous, development has been the hiring of so-called "diversity consultants" by big-name corporations all across the country.

These "diversity consultants" will come in to harangue your employees with the latest trendy notions on race and ethnicity. Or they will arrange weekend retreats where they can browbeat the staff and management. They put out brochures, videotapes, newsletters, or anything else that will send out The Word and bring in the money.

These professional intimidators don't come cheap. The more skilled or brazen of them charge thousands of dollars per day— and many will not work by the day, but insist on a long-term contract.

What are their skills? What are their credentials? What benefits can they promise?

Their skills are considerable. They have been known to reduce some employees to tears with their badgering, sneers and insinuations, just as they have been known to reduce some college students to tears when they take their act onto the campus.

They are great at laying on guilt trips or getting personal in a nasty way. Often they treat adults like children— or like guinea pigs.

Sometimes they ask the employees to line up and those who are religious to step to the right, those who believe that they are not racists to step forward, and so on. Above all, the "diversity" types do not discuss on the same plane with others. They lay down the social dogma from on high.

Credentials? Merely asking such a question is like asking to be accused of "insensitivity," if not racism. There are no formal credentials required to be known as a "diversity consultant." Effrontery and gall are pretty much the essentials. They are the secular versions of Elmer Gantry.

What benefits do they promise to employers? Usually nothing tangible that you can see any time soon. That would be "simplistic"— and not very profitable to the consultants.

The relationship between employees of different racial and ethnic backgrounds is supposed to be a great mystery, whose unraveling will require much time and much "re-education."

Black and white employees who were watching the same TV programs at home the previous night, and perhaps eating the same junk food at the mall during lunchtime, are taught to think of each other as exotic creatures from different worlds— unable to understand each other, except with the painful and expensive help of "diversity consultants."

How did businesses— or the country— manage to keep from coming apart all those years before these secular messiahs arrived on the scene? More important, why doesn't someone demand that they put up or shut up?

Have businesses— or colleges— that go in for this kind of bombast had happier relations among the various racial, ethnic or other groups afterwards? Or is it always "too early to see results yet"? In academia, the results seem to be that colleges which go in for this kind of brainwashing have more intergroup strife than before and more than colleges where no such programs exist.

Businesses that persist in subjecting their employees to this kind of indignity may see lawsuits for stress before they see any tangible benefits. As one who deplores the litigation explosion, I nevertheless think a few multimillion dollar damage awards would be a very healthy thing, to help restore sanity and common decency where these qualities are currently taking a back seat to being on the side of the politically correct angels.

Both the patterns of corporate philanthropy to their political enemies and the susceptibility of corporate management to such unproven nostrums as "diversity consultants" may suggest a death-wish to the more psychologically inclined.

A more rationalistic explanation might be that it is all for the sake of public relations, even if the top corporate executives themselves think it is bunk.

Whatever the explanation, it is bad business in the long run, not only for business itself but for this country.

STEREOTYPES VERSUS
THE MARKET

There is much loose talk about "stereotypes" these days. Often, it makes me think back to an episode many years ago.

Back during the Korean war, a young Marine named Albert Greuner graduated from the photography school at Pensacola Naval Air Station and was ordered to report for duty as a photographer at the photo lab at Camp Lejeune, North Carolina. Yet, when he arrived at Camp Lejeune, he discovered that his orders had been changed. He was now told to report instead to the supply depot, where he was assigned to handle photographic supplies.

Baffled and disappointed by the sudden change, Greuner told me his story— and was further taken aback when I burst out laughing. In reality, I was part of the reason for his misfortune.

Some months earlier, the photo lab received its first group of graduates from the photography school at the Pensacola Naval Air Station. By and large, we were better photographers than those they had. However, we were also young draftees with attitudes wholly different from those of career Marines.

We saw the Marine Corps as just an unwelcome interlude in our lives, and we were less than awed by our superiors or by their rules or orders. We hung out together and became known— not always affectionately— as "the Pensacola gang."

When the captain in charge of the photo lab had had about as much of us as he could stand, he cleaned out the lot of us, breaking up the Pensacola gang and scattering us individually to various other places around the base. When he later received word that another photographer from Pensacola had been assigned to his lab, the captain had him transferred, sight unseen.

It so happened that Greuner was a different sort of fellow, and would probably have gotten along very well in the photo lab. But he never got the chance— because of the behavior of his predecessors.

Today, that would be called "stereotyping" and the captain would be criticized for not judging Greuner as an individual. However, whatever the merits of that argument in this particular case, no one goes around judging everyone as an individual, however popular such cant may be.

When you are walking down a dark street at night and see a shadowy figure in an alley up ahead, do you judge him as an individual— or do you cross the street and pass on the opposite side? Judging him as an individual could cost you your life. It may turn out that he is just a kindly neighbor out walking his dog, but you discover that only after the fact.

The high cost of knowledge is often overlooked when discussing social policies, and especially social policies in the emotionally charged area of race and ethnicity. In real life, decisions are based on imperfect knowledge, simply because there is no other kind.

Recently a black, middle class professional wrote of his resentment when he was asked to pay for his meal in advance in an Asian-owned restaurant— especially after he noted that a white couple that came in was not asked to do the same. Was this arbitrary racism or self-protection based on experience in this neighborhood? That was the key question he did not ask— nor do most journalistic stories or even scholarly studies.

The same man also expressed resentment at the looks of aversion he received from fellow-blacks in another establishment, because he was wearing his hair in dreadlocks. Clearly this was not a question of racism, but of repugnance toward the kind of people who "make a statement" with that kind of hairstyle.

Apparently, neither blacks, whites, nor Asians judge each person as an individual. Probably no one else in the world does either, though the intelligentsia may talk that way.

Fortunately, the marketplace puts a price on incorrect generalizations, as it does on all sorts of other incorrect assumptions behind economic decisions. Even the most racist owner of a professional basketball team could not refuse to hire blacks, unless he were willing to face bankruptcy— and thereby cease to be a basketball owner.

Theoretically, racists could simply absorb the losses created by their own discrimination. Empirically, it is very hard to find people who are willing to lose hard cash, in order to discriminate.

Racists may prefer their own group to others, but they prefer themselves most of all.

That is why discrimination has always been most prevalent where it costs discriminators the least— in government employment, in regulated utilities, or in non-profit organizations. That was true throughout the pre-civil rights era, just as reverse discrimination is generally strongest in such organizations today.

This is not an American pattern but a world-wide pattern. Yet those who wish to fight against discrimination often try to move employment decisions and other decisions out of the marketplace and into the hands of people who pay no price— politicians, bureaucrats, and judges.

RECYCLED "RACISM"

One of the things that happens when you get old is that what seems like news to others can look like a re-run of something you have already seen before. It is like watching an old movie for the fifth or sixth time.

A headline in the September 14, 2005 issue of the *New York Times* says: "Blacks Hit Hardest By Costlier Mortgages." Thirteen years earlier, virtually the identical story appeared in the *Wall Street Journal* under the title, "Federal Reserve Details Pervasive Racial Gap in Mortgage Lending."

Both stories were based on statistical studies by the Federal Reserve showing that blacks and whites have different experiences when applying for mortgage loans— and both stories imply that racial discrimination is the reason.

The earlier study showed that blacks were turned down for mortgage loans a higher percentage of the time than whites were and the later story shows that blacks resorted to high-priced "subprime" loans more often than whites when they financed the purchase of a home.

Both amount to the same thing— less credit being extended to blacks on the same terms as credit extended to whites.

Both studies also say that this is true even when black and white loan applicants have the same income. The first time around, back in 1992, this seemed like a pretty good case for those who blamed the differences on racial discrimination.

However, both research and old age tend to produce skepticism about things that look plausible on the surface. Just scratching the surface a little often makes a plausible case collapse like a house of cards.

For example, neither study took credit histories into account. People with lower credit ratings tend to get turned down for loans more often than people with higher credit ratings, or else they have to go where loans have higher interest rates. This is not rocket science. It is Economics 1.

Blacks in the earlier study turned out to have poor credit histories more often than whites. But the more recent news story did not even look into that.

Anyone who has ever taken out a mortgage loan knows that the lenders not only want to know what your current income is, they also want to know what your net worth is. Census data show that blacks with the same income as whites average less net worth.

That is not rocket science either. Not many blacks have affluent parents or rich uncles from whom they could inherit wealth.

The earlier study showed that whites were turned down for mortgage loans more frequently than Asian Americans and the more recent study shows that Asian Americans are less likely than whites to take out high-cost "subprime" loans to buy a house.

Does that mean that whites were being discriminated against? Or are statistics taken seriously only when they back up some preconception that is politically correct?

These are what could be called "Aha!" statistics. If you start out with a preconception and find numbers that fit that preconception, you say, "Aha!" But when the numbers don't fit any preconception— when no one believes that banks are discriminating against whites and in favor of Asian Americans— then there is no "Aha!"

Both this year's study and the one years ago provoked an outburst of accusations of racism from people who are in the business of making such accusations. Moreover, where there is a "problem" proclaimed in the media there will almost invariably be a "solution" proposed in politics.

Often the solution is worse than the problem.

The older study showed that most blacks and most whites who applied for mortgage loans got them— 72 percent of blacks and 89 percent of whites. So it is not as if most blacks can't get loans.

Apparently the gap has narrowed since then, for the *New York Times* reports that lenders have developed "high-cost subprime mortgages for people who would have been simply rejected outright in the past on the basis of poor credit or insufficient income."

Of course, the government can always step in and put a stop to these high-cost loans, which will probably mean that people with lower credit ratings can't buy a home at all.

GEOGRAPHY VERSUS EQUALITY

O ne of the seemingly invincible notions of our times is that great disparities in income and wealth are strange, suspicious and probably sinister. However, there are large differences in productivity behind income and wealth differences, whether among nations or among individuals. Many of these national differences in productivity are due to geography, rather than to human beings.

In the early twentieth century, the average income in the Balkans was only about one-fourth of the average income in Western European nations. Much of this was a result of geography.

Western Europe had produced an industrial revolution, based not only on technology but also on the presence of iron ore and coal deposits, the key ingredients in the production of iron and steel— which in turn were key ingredients of industrial production. Not only were such deposits lacking in the Balkans, there was no economically feasible way to ship them there. There were no such networks of navigable waterways in the Balkans as in Western Europe, and mountain ranges blocked off much of the region from overland shipments.

Not only have material things suffered from geographical handicaps, so have the people themselves. Isolated peoples have usually been backward peoples, whether they were isolated by mountains, jungles, or other geographical handicaps, such as living on tiny islands scattered across a vast and empty sea.

Put differently, the size of a people's cultural universe influences how far they can develop, technologically and culturally. When British settlers crossed the Atlantic and confronted the Iroquois in North America, they did not confront each other simply as the British versus the Iroquois. They confronted each other as people with very different cultural universes of very different sizes.

The British were able to cross the Atlantic in the first place only because of cultural advances that they had borrowed from other peoples in Europe, Asia and the Middle East. The British steered their ships with rudders invented in China. They were able to navigate with instruments based on trigonometry, invented in Egypt. Their calculations were done with numbers invented in India. Much of what they knew about the world in general was acquired by reading material written in letters invented by the Romans.

The Iroquois had no similar cultural universe. They could not draw upon the cultures of the Aztecs or the Incas, for none of these three groups knew of each other's existence, much less the existence of other cultures on the other side of the oceans that surrounded and insulated them all.

One reason for the greater cultural isolation in the Western Hemisphere was that North and South America contained no horses, oxen or other animals capable of carrying heavy loads for long distances. This limited how much trading could go on and how great a distance it would pay to move products by the costly use of human porters. In turn, that meant limiting the range of cultural contacts in general.

Indian canoes could travel for considerable distances on water but there was little or no economic incentive to build larger vessels, capable of longer trips, since there were severe limits on how much cargo could be moved when the vessels landed.

Just the fact that the vast Eurasian land mass spreads from east to west, while the continents of the Western Hemisphere spread from north to south, also limited the size of the cultural universe differently in the two regions of the world. At a time when most of the human race was engaged in agriculture or in animal hunting or animal husbandry, knowledge of specific crops and particular animals was far more widely applicable when spread from east to west than when spread from north to south.

Knowledge of rice cultivation, for example, could spread all the way across Asia and into Europe because much of Asia and Europe are in similar latitudes, with similar climates. But bananas could not spread from Central America to Canada, because north-south movement involves bigger changes in climate.

Similarly, many tropical animals do not exist in colder climates, so knowledge of how to hunt or domesticate animals cannot be transferred as far from north to south as it can from east to west.

All this is not a matter of praise or blame, or even of genes. Human beings may discriminate against particular groups, but geography discriminates more powerfully against whole peoples, nations and civilizations.

ASSUMPTIONS BEHIND AFFIRMATIVE ACTION

With affirmative action suddenly coming under political attack from many directions, and with even liberals backing away from it, we need to question not only its underlying assumptions but also what some of the alternatives are.

At the heart of the affirmative action approach is the notion that statistical disparities show discrimination. No dogma has taken a deeper hold with less evidence— or in the face of more massive evidence to the contrary.

A recent story in the *Wall Street Journal* revealed that more than four-fifths of all the doughnut shops in California are owned by Cambodians. That is about the same proportion as blacks among basketball stars. Clearly, neither of these disparities is due to discrimination against whites.

Nor are such disparities new or peculiar to the United States. In medieval Europe, most of the inhabitants of the towns in Poland and Hungary were neither Poles nor Hungarians. In nineteenth-century Bombay, most of the shipbuilders were Parsees, a minority in Bombay and less than one percent of the population of India.

In twentieth-century Australia, most of the fishermen in the port of Freemantle came from two villages in Italy. In southern Brazil, whole industries were owned by people of German ancestry and such crops as tomatoes and tea have been grown predominantly by people of Japanese ancestry.

Page after page— if not book after book— could be filled with similar statistical disparities from around the world and down through history. Such disparities have been the rule, not the exception. Yet our courts have turned reality upside down and treated what happens all over this planet as an anomaly and what is seldom found anywhere— proportional representation— as a norm.

Why are such disparities so common? Because all kinds of work require particular skills, particular experience, particular locations and particular orientations. And none of these things is randomly distributed.

Local demagogues who thunder against the fact that Koreans run so many stores in black ghettoes merely betray their ignorance when they act as if this were something strange or unusual. For most of the merchants in an area to be of a different race or ethnicity from their customers has been common for centuries in Southeast Asia, Eastern Europe, West Africa, the Caribbean, Fiji, the Ottoman Empire and numerous other places.

When German and Jewish merchants moved into Eastern Europe in the Middle Ages, they brought with them much more experience in that occupation than that possessed by local Eastern European merchants, who were often wiped out by the new competition. Even when the competition takes place between people who are racially and ethnically identical, all kinds of historical, geographical and other circumstances can make one set of these people far more effective in some activities than the others.

Mountain people have often lagged behind those on the plains below, whether highland Scots versus lowland Scots or the Sinhalese in the highlands of Sri Lanka versus the Sinhalese on the plains. The Slavs living along the Adriatic coast in ports like Dubrovnik were for centuries far more advanced than Slavs living in the interior, just as coastal peoples have tended to be more advanced than peoples of the interior hinterlands in Africa or Asia.

Some disparities of course have their roots in discrimination. But the fatal mistake is to infer discrimination whenever the statistical disparities exceed what can be accounted for by random chance. Human beings are not random. They have very pronounced and complex cultural patterns.

These patterns are not unchanging. But changing them for the better requires first acknowledging that "human capital" is crucial to economic advancement. Those who make careers out of attributing disparities to the wickedness of other people are an obstacle to the development of more human capital among the poor.

There was a time, as late as the mid-nineteenth century, when Japan lagged far behind the Western industrial nations because it was lacking in the kind of human capital needed in a modern economy. Importing Western technology was not enough, for the Japanese lacked the knowledge and experience required to operate it effectively.

Japanese workmen damaged or ruined machinery when they tried to use it. Fabrics were also ruined when the Japanese tried to dye them without understanding chemistry. Whole factories were badly designed and had to be reconstructed at great cost.

What saved the Japanese was that they recognized their own backwardness— and worked for generations to overcome it. They did not have cultural relativists to tell them that all cultures are equally valid or political activists to tell them that their troubles were all somebody else's fault. Nor were there guilt-ridden outsiders offering them largess.

Affirmative action has been one of the great distractions from the real task of self-development. When it and the mindset that it represents passes from the scene, poorer minorities can become the biggest beneficiaries, if their attention and efforts turn toward improving themselves. Unfortunately, a whole industry of civil rights activists, politicians and miscellaneous hustlers has every vested interest in promoting victimhood, resentment and paranoia instead.

THE MULTICULTURALISM
CULT

The world has been multicultural for centuries before this word was coined. Moreover, it has been multicultural in a very real and practical way, directly the opposite of the way being urged by today's "multiculturalism" cult.

The very paper on which these words are written was invented in China, as was the art of printing. The letters come from ancient Rome and the numbers from India, via the Arabs. All this is being written by a man whose ancestors came from Africa, while listening to music by a Russian composer.

Even leaders of nations are not necessarily from those nations themselves. Napoleon was not French, Stalin was not Russian and Hitler was not German.

Crops have been as multicultural as people. Much of the world's rubber comes from Malaysia, but the Malaysian rubber trees themselves came from seeds brought from Brazil. The cocoa grown in Nigeria and the potatoes grown in Ireland likewise both originated in the Western Hemisphere before Columbus arrived.

A list of all the crops, technology and ideas that have spread from one people or one nation to another would be a list of most of the crops, technology or ideas in the world. The reason why all these things spread was, quite simply, that some things were considered better than others— and people wanted the best they could get.

This is completely the contrary to the philosophy of the "multiculturalism" cult, where things are not better or worse, but just different. Yet people around the world do not simply "celebrate diversity," they pick and choose which of their own cultural features they want to keep and which they want to dump in favor of something better from somebody else.

When Europeans first discovered paper and printing from China, they did not "celebrate diversity," they stopped giving themselves writers' cramp from copying scrolls and started letting the printing presses do the work. When American Indians saw horses for the first time after Europeans brought them here, they did not "celebrate diversity," they started riding off to hunt instead of walking.

Everything from automobiles to antibiotics has spread around the world because people wanted the best they could get, not the inefficient ways that the multiculturalist cult calls "living in harmony with nature." Too often, before modern medicine was accepted, that meant dying young instead of living to a healthy old age. People preferred to live, even if it wasn't "in harmony with nature."

The issue is not what I say or what the multiculturalists say. The issue is what millions of human beings actually do when they have a choice. Around the world, they treat cultural features as things that help them cope with life, not museum pieces to oooh and aaah over.

When they find their own ways of doing some things better, they keep them. When they find someone else's ways of doing other things better, they use them and drop what they used before. What they do not do is what the multiculturalists do— say that it is all just a matter of "perceptions," that nothing is better or worse than anything else.

Multiculturalism is one of those affectations that people can indulge in when they are enjoying all the fruits of modern technology and can grandly disdain the processes that produced them.

None of this would be anything more than another of the many foibles of the human race, except that the cult of multiculturalism has become the new religion of our schools and colleges, contributing to the mushing of America. It has become part of the unexamined assumptions underlying public policy and even decisions in courts of law.

Who would be surprised that people from different cultural backgrounds are "represented" differently in different jobs, colleges, or income levels, except for the unspoken assumption that these different cultures are equally effective for all things?

Yet you need only turn on the television set and watch professional basketball to realize that one segment of the population plays the game a lot better than others. If you watch the commercials that sponsor these events, you are often watching ads for beer companies that were almost invariably established by people of German ancestry.

274 The Thomas Sowell Reader

Since Germans have been brewing beer since the days of the Roman Empire, should we be surprised that they excel as much in this as blacks excel in basketball? Any standard based on quality will have "over-representation" and "under-representation" of different groups, however much such "disparate impact" may shock the editorial writers and provoke judges to rush in where angels fear to tread.

LIFE IS CULTURALLY BIASED

The vitriolic controversy developing around *The Bell Curve* by Richard Herrnstein and Charles Murray has raised again questions about mental tests and their meaning.

One of the charges made is that the tests are themselves unfair. But, long before the present controversy, someone replied to similar charges by pointing out: "The tests are not unfair. *Life* is unfair— and tests measure the results."

The same could be said of the charge that tests are "culturally biased." *Life* is culturally biased. We live twice as long as people in some of the poorer parts of the world, not because we are more deserving, individually smarter or otherwise more meritorious, but simply because we had the dumb luck to be born into a culture which produces cures and preventions for deadly diseases that have ravaged the human race for centuries.

The cultural features which advance medical science have by no means been universal. Indeed, they have been fairly recent, as history is measured, even in the civilizations where they now exist. Any test which tests for those kinds of features must be culturally biased— indeed, *should* be culturally biased.

There may well have been individuals born into ignorant and primitive backwaters of the world who had brain cells fully as well-functioning as those of Pasteur, Salk or other medical pioneers, but who never developed the same capabilities and never left a trace of their existence to benefit the rest of mankind. If tested by our culturally biased tests, those individuals would undoubtedly have scored low— and should have, if our purpose was the practical one of picking people actually able to do the kinds of things that needed doing in medical science.

What would have happened under other cultural circumstances is a cosmic question— a question for God, perhaps, but not for intellectuals who act as if they are God.

As limited human beings, we must make our choices among the alternatives actually available. A culture-free society has never been one of those alternatives.

Any test designed to predict future performances in any field or in any society is trying to predict what will happen in a given cultural context. There is nothing inherently sinister about this.

These are the conditions we face— or should face.

Few things are discussed as unintelligently as intelligence. Seldom do those who talk— or shout— about this subject bother to define their terms. Is "intelligence" the abstract potentiality that exists at the moment of conception? The developed capabilities with which the same individual faces the world two decades later?

In between, all sorts of things have happened— and happened differently for different individuals and groups. An alcoholic or drug-addicted mother begins damaging her child even before birth. Her irresponsibility, brutality or stupidity is almost certain to do more damage to the child in the years that follow.

What good would it do us to know that child's innate potential at the moment of conception? It certainly would not enable us to predict what is likely to happen now that he is what he is.

Suppose that we had such a miraculous test and discovered that we started out with an Einstein and ended up with an idiot. Would that mean that the test was unfair because it showed that he was an idiot? Or would it mean that life itself was tragically unfair— not only to him, but to the whole society that now has to contend with him as he is?

Maybe such a test would have some social value as a means of shocking us into a realization of what enormities result from subsidizing teenage pregnancy, for example. Yes, it would be hard on all concerned, including the public, to deny welfare to the teenager. But would it be worse than what happens because we cannot bring ourselves to deny it?

Such questions could at least be asked if we had the kind of miraculous test hoped for by some. But there is no sign that we are even close to developing such a test.

The much-vexed question of heredity versus environment, and of possible intergroup differences in inherited potential, are better able to produce heated controversies than enlightened reasoning. Does anyone seriously doubt that heredity plays some role in some differences? Or that it is seldom the whole story?

The Bell Curve itself says: "It should be no surprise to see (as one does every day) blacks functioning at high levels in every intellectually challenging field." But that did not stop the shouts of those who are in the business of shouting. Anyone who actually reads the book— which may not include all of its critics— will discover that race is not even considered in the first 12 chapters. That is hardly what the book is about, though that is what the noise is about.

My own view as a former teacher is that most American students, of whatever background, are operating so far below their capacity that the limits of that capacity is an academic question.

BOOKER T. WASHINGTON
AFTER ONE HUNDRED
YEARS

"**I** felt a good deal as I suppose a man feels when he is on his way to the gallows," Booker T. Washington wrote of his state of mind when he was on his way to make the historic speech at the Atlanta Exposition of 1895 that would mark the turning point in his life— and in the life of race relations in America. Looking back on that event a hundred years later gives us not only a clearer picture of how race relations have evolved but also a radically different picture of one of the key figures in that evolution— a figure far more often caricatured than understood.

There was good reason for Booker T. Washington to be apprehensive. For a black man to be invited to address the distinguished audience at the Exposition was itself controversial. The South was a tinderbox of raw emotions over racial issues and more than a hundred blacks a year were being lynched. Voting rights, the right to serve in public office or on juries, and even basic personal security against violence, were rights that Southern blacks once enjoyed during the U.S. Army's occupation of the South for two decades after the Civil War, but these and other rights were now eroding throughout the South after that army had long since gone home and had been disbanded.

The restoration of home rule in the South meant the restoration of white majority rule— the rule of an embittered people who had lost a devastating war and then seen their slaves freed and placed on an equal legal plane with themselves, in some cases serving as public officials ruling over them with the backing of the bayonets of the Union army. In the angry backlash that followed, blacks were increasingly barred from public office and from the ballot box, and laws were being passed segregating the races in public transportation and other public accommodations. The right to a fair trial became a mockery for blacks and the shadow of the Ku Klux Klan and other white terrorist night riders fell over black communities across the South. It was in this atmosphere that Washington rose to address the dignitaries and common folk of both races at the Atlanta Exposition.

What could Washington say to this audience of white Southerners— many of whom, he knew, had come only to see him make a fool of himself— and at the same time be true to the blacks in the audience who were full of pride that someone of their race was for the first time being given the honor of addressing an audience including such dignitaries as the governor of Georgia?

"By one sentence," Washington said later, " I could have blasted, in a large degree, the success of the Exposition." More than that, one careless remark could have blasted any hopes of racial peace and progress.

It is hard to judge anyone's performance without knowing what cards he was dealt before deciding how well he played them. Not only on this occasion, but throughout his career, Booker T. Washington was dealt one of the toughest hands of any black leader in American history.

The central theme of his talk was given in one sentence: "There is no defence or security for any of us except in the development of the highest intelligence of all." He disarmed his audience by waving aside issues which were already lost causes for his generation, such as racial integration. "In all things that are purely social we can be as separate as the fingers, yet one as the hand in all things essential to mutual progress." But neither here nor anywhere else did he renounce equal rights under the law: "It is important and right that all privileges of the law be ours, but it is vastly more important that we be prepared for the exercise of these privileges," he said in Atlanta.

By linking rights and responsibilities, Washington was able to address both the blacks and the whites in the audience on common ground. And by linking the fates of the two races, he was able to enlist the support of some whites by arguing that blacks would either help lift up the South or help to drag it down.

In the context of the times, the speech was a masterpiece. It was reprinted in newspapers across the country and praised by blacks and whites alike, Northerners and Southerners. The governor of Georgia came over to shake Washington's hand after the speech and Grover Cleveland wrote to him about the "enthusiasm" with which he had read it. Overnight Booker T. Washington was recognized as a leader of his people— indeed, *the* leader of his people, the successor to Frederick Douglass who had died just a few months earlier.

The historic differences that would later arise between Washington and the more militant W.E.B. Du Bois were differences of emphasis and priorities, not differences of fundamental principles. Du Bois was in fact among those who sent messages of congratulation to Washington on his Atlanta Exposition speech.

As one of the founders and long-time pillars of the National Association for the Advancement of Colored People, Du Bois concentrated on the restoration and advancement of political rights for blacks and focussed his public attacks on the system of racial segregation and discrimination known as Jim Crow in the South. With eloquent bitterness, he indicted whites for racism. Booker T. Washington took no such public stance and instead directed his efforts toward the internal self-development of blacks in things ranging from personal hygiene to saving, farm management, and the establishment of businesses. The whites he spoke of and to were those whites willing to support such activities, especially those willing to help financially.

The net result was that Washington was often praising whites of good will while Du Bois was attacking whites of ill will. Washington was promoting a kind of vocational education with a heavy moral and self-disciplinary component at Tuskegee Institute, while Du Bois promoted academic education designed to produce militant fighters for their rights against oppressors. However, this historic dichotomy was less sharp at the time than it later became in retrospect, after a new generation of more militant black intellectuals condemned Washington as an Uncle Tom.

At the time, during the early years of the twentieth century, Du Bois was, like Washington, also painfully aware not only of the external dangers from white racists but also of the internal problems of a recently freed people, among whom illiteracy was widespread and experience in the ordinary business of life was still new, uncertain and errant. Du Bois, during this stage of his own development, spoke of "the Great Lack which faces our race in the modern world, Lack of Energy," which he attributed to "indolence" growing out of tropical origins and which had now become a kind of "social heredity."

If white people lost all their racial prejudices overnight, Du Bois said, this would make very little immediate difference in the economic condition of most blacks. While "some few would be promoted, some few would get new places" nevertheless "the mass would remain as they are" until the younger generation began to "try harder" as the race "lost the omnipresent excuse for failure: prejudice." Du Bois' assessment of the black masses at that time was not very different from that of Booker T. Washington, who characterized many of them as sunk into "listless indifference, or shiftlessness, or reckless bravado."

In short, at this particular juncture in history, both Du Bois and Washington saw a great need for the self-development of black Americans. Du Bois would later champion the "talented tenth" of the race who were already prepared for higher education and a more advanced way of life, many of these being people like Du Bois, descended from the antebellum "free persons of color" whose cultural development began while most of their brothers were still in bondage on cotton plantations.

By contrast, Booker T. Washington's lifelong preoccupation would be with those like himself who were "up from slavery" and who needed training in the basics of manual skills, work habits, personal hygiene and moral character. Washington's concern was with "the promotion of progress among the many, and not the special culture of the few."

To some extent the differences between Du Bois and Washington came from their addressing different constituencies living in very different economic and social circumstances, and having correspondingly different priorities. The vocational education that Washington promoted would have been a step backward for Du Bois' constituency. However, Du Bois conceded that vocational education "has accomplishments of which it has a right to be proud" and conversely Washington declared: "I would say to the black boy what I would say to the white boy, Get all the mental development that your time and pocket-book will allow of," though he saw most blacks of his time as needing to acquire practical work skills first.

Even in the present, Booker Washington said, "we need professional men and women" and he looked forward to a time when there would be more successful black "lawyers, Congressmen, and music teachers."

That was not the whole story, however. Washington operated in the Deep South, where he founded Tuskegee Institute in rural Alabama. Du Bois was a Northerner who grew up in Massachusetts and whose following was largely Northern, even when he himself taught at Atlanta University.

Moreover, Washington had an institution to safeguard and promote, using money largely from white philanthropists who were willing to see blacks trained in mechanical skills but some of whom might have had serious reservations about providing them with academic education. Du Bois could be, and was, far more outspoken than Washington on civil rights issues. Indeed, Washington's public posture was one of preoccupation with teaching the basics to his fellow blacks, with little time left to concern himself with legal rights and political issues.

This posture was central to his ability to raise money among many wealthy whites and to exert influence behind the scenes in defense of blacks with federal and state political leaders. In reality, however, when Booker T. Washington's papers were opened after his death, it became clear that privately Washington was not only concerned with civil rights but goaded other blacks into similar concerns and himself secretly financed some of their legal challenges to Jim Crow laws.

In at least one case, even the black plaintiffs themselves did not know why their lawyer accepted such a pittance for his work. He was being paid under the table by Booker T. Washington.

While publicly turning aside questions about political issues during the era of systematic disenfranchising of blacks, Washington privately not only supported efforts to safeguard civil rights but also wrote anonymous newspaper articles protesting the violation of those rights, as did his trusted agents. He also worked behind the scenes to get federal appointments for blacks in Washington and postmaster appointments in Alabama, as well as to get presidents to appoint federal judges who would give blacks a fairer hearing.

What was utterly lacking in Booker T. Washington, however, was the ringing rhetoric of protest, so much beloved of intellectuals, however futile it might be in practice at the time. Washington practiced what militants of a later era would only preach, to advance the interests of blacks "by all means necessary."

Booker T. Washington was, among other things, a master of duplicity and intrigue. But unlike some others who used such talents to line their own pockets while boasting of their concerns for the rights of fellow blacks, he was untouched by any hint of financial scandal and did not even let his fellow blacks know of many of his legal and political efforts in their behalf, for the chances of success in these efforts depended on their being conducted behind the scenes.

In his running of Tuskegee Institute as well, even a critical biographer noted: "Because of its strictness, Tuskegee Institute was almost entirely free of the scandals that racked many other boarding schools." A southern white editor of that era confessed his amazement at how carefully Washington accounted for every dollar that passed through his hands at Tuskegee Institute.

Yet Booker T. Washington was by no means a Sunday school paragon. He was ruthless in the building and maintenance of his power and in the advancement of the causes he believed in. He maintained a network of people around the country who did his bidding in the press, the foundations and in the political back rooms. He headed what was aptly called "the Tuskegee machine," though it was in fact a nationwide operation. He himself was called "the wizard" by those who worked with him. His whole career was, in a sense, a juggling act on a high wire and no one was more aware than he that one misstep could bring everything crashing down.

Washington had a clear sense of his own mission and great confidence in his own abilities. He wrote in his autobiography, *Up from Slavery*: "As for my individual self, it seemed to me to be reasonably certain that I could succeed in political life, but I had a feeling that it would be a rather selfish kind of success— individual success at the cost of failing to do my duty in assisting in laying a foundation for the masses."

He seems to have been a man at peace with himself. As his biographer Louis R. Harlan points out, most photographs of Booker T. Washington show him relaxed, even when others in the picture are stiffly posed. His general bearing was, in Professor Harlan's words, "modest but too dignified to be humble."

Washington neither grinned nor shuffled for white folks, and he was hated by racist bigots in the South. When he had dinner in the White House with President Theodore Roosevelt, there were cries of outrage from across the South, and echoes reverberated for years afterward.

On some occasions, a Pinkerton guard accompanied Washington through redneck territory, and once two black men who had gone to hear him speak were lynched and their bodies hung where the whites thought Booker T. Washington would be sure to see them. He had a tough hand to play and he played it like a master.

Washington and Du Bois were much closer than their public postures would indicate, though Du Bois may not have known how much common ground there was between them. Just as the private Booker T. Washington must be taken into account along with the public image he projected, so it must be noted that W.E.B. Du Bois was, during Washington's lifetime, not yet the far left radical of his later Stalinist years.

Nevertheless the rivalry between the two men— and between their partisans— was both real and sometimes bitter. In part this mirrored a social division within the black community between the freed plantation slaves and their descendants, on the one hand, and the more polished descendants of the "free persons of color" who had been educated for generations. A disproportionate share of the black leadership came from this small elite and continued to do so on past the middle of the twentieth century. Moreover, there were skin color differences between the two groups, of which both were acutely aware, for many of the "free persons of color" became free because they were the offspring of white slave masters and black slave women.

The social snobbishness of this lighter-complexioned elite was as real as the racism of whites— and was sometimes more deeply resented by the black masses, some of whom referred to the N.A.A.C.P. as the National Association for the Advancement of *Certain* People. In a sense, Du Bois and Washington epitomized these differences. Du Bois, with his Ph.D. from Harvard, was aloof and of aristocratic bearing and had little to do socially with the black masses in whose name he spoke. Nor was this a purely personal foible. Washington described other contemporaries as members of the "upper ten" who "very seldom mingle with the masses."

Washington himself had much more of the common touch and mingled easily with other blacks in the cities and backwoods of the South. His talk and his writings were plain and straightforward, lacking the erudition and rhetorical flourishes of Du Bois, but full of tough-minded common sense.

While Du Bois was an intellectual, Washington was shrewd, perhaps the shrewdest of all the black leaders in American history. While Du Bois discussed racial issues on a high moral plane of abstract rights, Washington put his emphasis on developing skills within the black community for a very down-to-earth reason: "In the long run, the world is going to have the best, and any difference in race, religion, or previous history will not long keep the world from what it wants."

The self-interest of whites, rather than any moral commitment on their part to the rights of blacks, was what Washington depended on for the advancement of his people. Although caricatured by some as an Uncle Tom, this complex man was seen very differently by those who actually knew him. It was none other than W.E.B. Du Bois who said of Booker T. Washington: "He had no faith in white people, not the slightest." Washington used their money, however, to advance the causes he believed in and used his influence to get support not only for Tuskegee Institute but even for rival black institutions like Talladega College and Atlanta University, and he served on the board of trustees for Howard and Fisk universities, whose educational missions were very different from his own.

The rivalry between Du Bois and Washington was not based simply on different educational or political approaches, nor even on differences in the social strata from which they came. They held very different amounts of power and influence. Because Booker T. Washington was *the* black leader to many whites with wealth and power, he became the arbiter of the fates of other blacks seeking access to funding for their projects or influence in political circles. Du Bois, for example, left his teaching position at Atlanta University when his opposition to Booker T. Washington made him a financial liability to the institution.

Washington's "Tuskegee machine" was a force to be reckoned with within the black community and a force to be feared and resented by those blacks who were seeking a larger role for themselves. Washington's influence— and money— reached black newspapers across the country and his followers were active, both publicly and behind the scenes, in the North as well as the South.

No one was more keenly aware of the severe limits within which he operated, especially when he operated publicly, than Booker T. Washington. He wrote to Oswald Garrison Villard, one of the founders of the N.A.A.C.P., "there is work to be done which no one placed in my position can do." He realized the time-bound nature of his mission. He said, "we are doing work that is needed to be done in this generation and in this section of our country." He also said: "I have never attempted to set any limit upon the development of our race" and said of this generation of blacks that "their children will be given advantages which the first generation did not possess." He saw his task as being to "lay the foundation" in his own time, not to provide an educational blueprint— or straitjacket— for all time.

What was accomplished by this man and by the movement he led? Tuskegee Institute was of course his most tangible legacy, its early buildings built by the students themselves, using the skills taught to them. The larger legacy— the people who learned such practical lessons as how to take care of their money and their health and how to conduct themselves in public— are things difficult to gauge and impossible to quantify. Neither the internal development stressed by Booker T. Washington nor the quest for civil rights that preoccupied W. E. B. Du Bois has ever been entirely off the agenda of black Americans, though their relative priorities have varied from one era to another and from one organization or movement within a given era.

Ultimately, there was no reason why vocational training and academic education could not both go on, as they both did— indeed, as they both did at Tuskegee Institute, including in classes taught by Booker T. Washington. The needless dissipation of energies in internal strife between the followers of Du Bois and the followers of Washington was an extravagant luxury in an era when blacks could easily have used ten more of each.

Despite today's insatiable demands for "solutions" to racial and other social problems, it would be almost a contradiction in terms to try to "apply" Booker T. Washington directly to our times. He was, consciously and above all else, a man of *his* time. He saw his role quite clearly as preparatory and his work as building a foundation, not providing models for the future. Only the character and strength of the man are a model for today.

AFFIRMATIVE ACTION
AROUND THE WORLD

While controversies rage over "affirmative action" policies in the United States, few Americans seem to notice the existence or relevance of similar policies in other countries around the world. Instead, the arguments pro and con both tend to invoke history and traditions that are distinctively American. Yet group preferences and quotas have existed in other countries with wholly different histories and traditions— and, in some countries, such policies have existed much longer than in the United States.

What can the experiences of these other countries tell us? Are there common patterns, common rationales, common results? Or is the American situation unique?

Ironically, a claim or assumption of national uniqueness is one of the most common patterns found in numerous countries where group preferences and quotas have existed under a variety of names. The special situation of the Maoris in New Zealand, based on the 1840 Treaty of Waitangi, is invoked as passionately in defense of preferential treatment there as the unique position of untouchables in India or of blacks in the United States.

Highly disparate rationales have been used in different societies for programs which share very similar features and often lead to very similar results. Some group preferences have existed for minorities, some for majorities, some for the less fortunate and some for the more fortunate who feel entitled to maintain their existing advantages over other members of the same society. Today, it is programs for the less fortunate which are called affirmative action in the United States or by such other names as "positive discrimination" in Britain and in India, "standardization" in Sri Lanka, "reflecting the federal character of the country" in Nigeria, and "sons of the soil" preferences in Malaysia and Indonesia, as well as in some states in India. Group preferences and quotas have also existed in Israel, China, Australia, Brazil, Fiji, Canada, Pakistan, New Zealand and the Soviet Union and its successor states.[1]

Despite how widespread affirmative action programs have become, even the promoters of such programs have seldom been bold enough to proclaim preferences and quotas to be desirable on principle or as permanent features of society. On the contrary, considerable effort has been made to depict such policies as "temporary," even when in fact these preferences turn out not only to persist but to grow.

Official affirmative action or group preference policies must be distinguished from whatever purely subjective preferences or prejudices may exist among individuals and groups. These subjective feelings may of course influence policies, but the primary focus here is on concrete government policies and their empirical consequences— not on their rationales, hopes, or promises, though these latter considerations will not be wholly ignored. Fundamentally, however, this is a study of what actually happens, rather than a philosophical exploration of issues that have been amply— if not more than amply— explored elsewhere.

LIMITED AND TRANSIENT PREFERENCES

The resurgence of group preferences in societies committed to the equality of individuals before the law has been accompanied by claims not only that these preferences would be temporary, but also that they would be limited, rather than pervasive. That is, these programs would supposedly be limited not only in time but also in scope, with equal treatment policies prevailing outside the limited domain where members of particular groups would be given special help.

In India, for example, a government minister urging lower university admissions standards for untouchables and members of disadvantaged tribes included the proviso that he was recommending "relaxation for admissions and not for passing or grading."[2] Just as he was for limiting the scope of preferential treatment, so others were for limiting its duration. As an advocate of reserving certain numbers of jobs for members of specified groups in India said: "Even the staunchest supporters of reservation acceded that it is a transitory provision."[3] It was the leaders of the untouchables themselves who proposed a ten-year cutoff for reservations, in order to forestall political opposition and social conflict.[4] That was in 1949— and the reservations are still in place today.

Similar reasoning was applied in the United States to both employment and admissions to colleges and universities. Initially, it was proposed that there would be special "outreach" efforts to contact minority individuals with information and encouragement to apply for jobs or college admissions in places where they might not have felt welcome before, but with the proviso that they would not be given special preferences throughout the whole subsequent processes of acceptance and advancement. Much the same rationale appeared in Malaysia— and so did the further extension of preferential treatment which developed despite this rationale:

> Although grading is supposed to be without reference to ethnicity, all grades must be submitted to an evaluation review committee having heavy Malay representation. Individual faculty members report various instances when grades were unilaterally raised, apparently for purposes of "ethnic balance."[5]

Similar policies and results have also been achieved in less blatant ways. During the era of the Soviet Union, professors were pressured to give preferential grading to Central Asian students[6] and what has been called "affirmative grading" has also occurred in the United States, in order to prevent excessive failure rates among minority students admitted under lower academic standards.[7] In India, such practices have been referred to as "grace marks."[8] Similar results can be achieved indirectly by providing ethnic studies courses that give easy grades and attract disproportionately the members of one ethnic group. This too is not peculiar to the United States. There are Maori studies programs in New Zealand and special studies for Malays in Singapore.

In the job market as well, the belief that special concerns for particular groups could be confined to an initial stage proved untenable in practice. Initially, the term "affirmative action" arose in the United States from an executive order by President John F. Kennedy, who called for "affirmative action to ensure that the applicants are employed, and that employees are treated during employment without regard to race, color, creed, or national origin."[9] In short, there were to be no preferences or quotas at all, just a special concern to make sure that those who had been discriminated against in the past would no longer be discriminated against in the future— and that concrete steps should be taken so that all and sundry would be made aware of this.

However, just as academic preferences initially limited in scope continued to expand, so did the concept of affirmative action in the job market. A later executive order by President Lyndon Johnson in 1968 contained the fateful expressions "goals and timetables" and "representation." These were not yet full-blown quotas, for the 1968 guidelines referred to "goals and timetables for the prompt achievement of full and equal employment opportunity." Still later, another executive order in 1970, by President Richard Nixon, spoke of "results-oriented procedures" and, finally, in December 1971, yet another Nixon executive order specified that "goals and timetables" were meant to "increase materially the utilization of minorities and women," with "under-utilization" being spelled out as "having fewer minorities or women in a particular job classification than would reasonably be expected by their availability." Affirmative action was now a numerical concept, whether called "goals" or "quotas."

In a very different society and governmental system halfway around the world— in Pakistan— attempts to confine affirmative action policies within their initial limits proved equally futile.

Here preferential policies began in 1949 as an explicitly "temporary" measure, to be phased out in five to ten years.[10] The principal beneficiaries were to be the very poor Bengalis of East Pakistan who were "under-represented" in business, the professions and the military, while even the administration of East Pakistan was largely in the hands of West Pakistanis.[11] However, the preferential policies continued decades past the initially specified cut-off time by repeated extensions.[12] Even after East Pakistan seceded to become the independent nation of Bangladesh in 1971, the preferential policies in Pakistan had sufficient other political constituencies to continue on after their principal initial intended beneficiaries were gone.

Britain's Lord Scarman expressed a view widely held by those initiating affirmative action in many countries when he said:

> We can and for the present must accept the loading of the law in favour
> of one group at the expense of others, defending it as a temporary
> expedient in the balancing process which has to be undertaken when and
> where there is social and economic inequality.[13]

This confident pronouncement, however, presupposed a degree of control
which has proved illusory in country after country. Moreover, "when and where
there is social and economic inequality" encompasses virtually the entire world
and virtually the entire history of the human race. A "temporary" program to
eliminate a centuries-old condition is almost a contradiction in terms. Equality
of opportunity might be achieved within some feasible span of time, but that
is wholly different from eliminating inequalities of results.

Even an approximate equality of "representation" of different groups in
different occupations, institutions or income levels has been a very rare— or
non-existent— phenomenon, except where such numerical results have
been imposed artificially by quotas. As a massive scholarly study of ethnic
groups around the world put it, when discussing "proportional
representation" of ethnic groups, "few, if any societies have ever
approximated this description."[14] Another international study of multi-
ethnic societies referred to "the universality of ethnic inequality" and pointed
out that these inequalities are multi-dimensional:

> All multi-ethnic societies exhibit a tendency for ethnic groups to
> engage in different occupations, have different levels (and, often, types)
> of education, receive different incomes, and occupy a different place in
> the social hierarchy.[15]

A worldwide study of military forces likewise concluded that "militaries
fall far short of mirroring, even roughly, the multi-ethnic societies" from
which they come.[16] At one time, nearly half the pilots in the Malaysian air
force came from the Chinese minority.[17] In Czarist Russia, 40 percent of the
army's high command came from the German ethnic minority that was only
one percent of the country's population.[18] Similar gross disparities in ethnic
representation in occupations, industries and institutions can be found in
country after country around the world and in century after century.[19] Often
those over-represented in high-level occupations have been minorities with
no power to exclude others, but simply possessing particular skills. Germans,

for example, have predominated among those who created the leading beer companies in the United States, as they created China's famous Tsingtao beer and established breweries in Argentina, Australia, Brazil and other countries. Similarly, Jews have predominated in the manufacturing of clothing in medieval Spain, the Ottoman Empire, Argentina, the United States, and other countries.

In short, the even representation of groups that is taken as a norm is difficult or impossible to find anywhere, while the uneven representation that is regarded as a special deviation to be corrected is pervasive across the most disparate societies. People differ— and have for centuries. It is hard to imagine how they could not differ, given the enormous range of differing historical, cultural, geographic, demographic and other factors shaping the particular skills, habits, and attitudes of different groups. Any "temporary" policy whose duration is defined by the goal of achieving something that has never been achieved before, anywhere in the world, could more fittingly be characterized as eternal.

PREFERRED AND NON-PREFERRED GROUPS

Just as we cannot presuppose continuing control over the scope and duration of preferential policies, so we cannot simply assume what will actually happen to those designated as the preferred group or groups. Neither they nor the non-preferred groups are inert blocks of wood to be moved here and there according to someone else's grand design. Both confront laws and policies as incentives and constraints, not as predestination, and react in their own ways. These reactions include redesignating themselves, altering their own efforts and attitudes toward achievement, and altering their attitudes toward members of other groups.

Designation and Redesignation

One of the reactions of members of non-preferred groups has been to get themselves redesignated as members of the preferred group. This can be done either individually or collectively.

Some individuals of mixed ancestry who have been regarded and self-identified as members of group *A* may choose to redesignate themselves as members of group *B*, when group *B* is entitled to preferential treatment and members of group *A* are not. In the United States, during the Jim Crow era, some light-skinned blacks simply "passed" as white, in order to escape the legal and social disadvantages that went with being designated black. Later, during the era of affirmative action, whites with traces of American Indian or other minority ancestry likewise redesignated themselves, in order to take advantage of preferential policies for disadvantaged groups. These have included blond-haired and blue-eyed individuals with official papers showing some distant ancestor of another race.

The number of individuals identifying themselves as American Indians in the U.S. Census during the affirmative action era rose at a rate exceeding anyone's estimates of the biological growth of this population. Moreover, a breakdown of Census data by age cohort shows that the number of American Indians increased over time *in the same age cohort*— a biological impossibility made possible on paper by redesignations of the same individuals. For example, the number of American Indians who were aged 15–19 in 1960 was just under 50,000. But, twenty years later, when these same individuals would be in the age bracket 35–39 years old, there were more than 80,000 American Indians in that cohort.[20] In other words, more than 30,000 people in the same cohort who had not designated themselves as American Indians in 1960 now did so in 1980, causing more than a 60 percent increase in the number of American Indians in that cohort.

A similar pattern emerged among the Aborigines in Australia. A study in that country found that there was "a 42 percent increase in the size of the Aboriginal population between the 1981 and the 1986 censuses"[21]— virtually a demographic impossibility in five years, except by redesignation of the same individuals with different ethnic labels. As an Australian scholar has noted:

> The dramatic increase in numbers has much to do with record keeping, increasing intermarriage and the growing availability of substantial subsidies to people of Aboriginal descent. . . The definition of 'Aboriginal' includes many persons of predominantly non-Aboriginal descent, who might with equal or greater genetic justification designate themselves as non-Aborigines.[22]

It was much the same story in China where, in the 1990s, more than 10 million Chinese proclaimed their ethnic minority status, in order to gain preferential treatment, such as college admissions. Even China's draconian restrictions on having more than one child did not apply to ethnic minorities as they did to the majority Han Chinese:

> Article 44 states that, "in accordance with legal stipulations," autonomous areas can work out their own family planning measures. As a result, urban minority couples generally may have two children, while urban Han are restricted to one. Rural minorities may have two, three, four or even more children, depending on their ethnicity and location.[23]

An official of China's State Nationality Affairs Committee commented: "Some people would try all means to change their nationality because they wanted to make themselves eligible to enter a university with lower scores or to stand a better chance than their colleagues when it comes to promotion." As in other countries, people with mixed ancestry had the option of choosing how to designate themselves. Some "traced their ancestry back hundreds of years to prove minority blood" and claim the benefits.[24]

Another individual response to preferential policies has been to use someone genuinely of the qualifying ancestry as a "front" for businesses seeking preferential treatment in the awarding of government contracts or other desired benefits. This practice has been so widespread in both Indonesia and Malaysia that it has acquired a name— "Ali-Baba enterprises," where Ali is the indigenous individual who ostensibly owns the business and is legally entitled to government benefits, while Baba is the non-indigenous person (usually Chinese in these countries) who actually controls the enterprise and essentially pays Ali for the use of his name and ancestry.[25] Similar arrangements have been uncovered in the United States and elsewhere. Anti-Semitic policies in Poland during the years between the two World Wars likewise led some Jewish businesses there to operate behind Gentile front men.[26] Decades later, under preferential policies in Kenya, Africans served as fronts for Asian-owned businesses, as they likewise served as fronts for Lebanese-owned businesses in Sierra Leone.[27]

Members of some non-preferred groups can also get themselves redesignated collectively. The Fourteenth Amendment to India's

Constitution, like the Fourteenth Amendment to the Constitution of the United States, provides for equal treatment of individuals but India's Constitution provides explicit exceptions for benefits to the untouchables, disadvantaged tribal groups outside the Hindu caste system and "other backward classes." This last proviso, especially, has created opportunities for many other groups to get themselves collectively designated as being among the "other backward classes." Eventually, this miscellaneous classification provided more individuals with the coveted rights to preferential treatment than were provided to the members of the untouchable and tribal groups for whom the preferences were created. In 1997, organized efforts were also begun to seek preferential treatment for India's 15 million eunuchs,[28] though obviously they were not the descendants of other eunuchs, and so could not inherit historic group disadvantages.

Redesignations of individuals and groups, like the spread of preferences from given groups to other groups, take preferential policies further and further away from the initial rationales on which they were based. No historic sufferings of blacks in the United States can justify preferential benefits to white women or to recently arrived immigrants from Asia or Latin America who happen to be non-white, but whose ancestors obviously never suffered any discrimination in the United States. Similarly, the painful history and continuing oppression of untouchables in India can hardly justify preferential benefits to local majorities in particular states, such as Assam, Maharashtra, and Andhra Pradesh. Yet these local majorities and members of "other backward classes" outnumber the untouchables and are often in a better position to take advantage of the preferences. Thus quotas for government jobs or university admissions have often remained unfilled by untouchables, while this has seldom been the case for members of the "other backward classes."[29]

The spread of benefits from group to group not only dilutes those benefits— especially when more than half the population of the country becomes entitled to them, as in both India and the United States— it can also make the initial beneficiaries worse off after the terms of the competition are altered. For example, in the United States, where hiring and promotions decisions are subject to review by government agencies

investigating discrimination, objective criteria may be used increasingly by
employers for legal self-protection, even if the relevance of these criteria to
the job are questionable. If these criteria are met more often by one of the
preferred groups than by another— if white women have college degrees
more often than black men, for example— then one preferred group may be
no better off, on net balance, than if the preferences did not exist. It is
conceivable that they can be worse off.

Such a situation is not peculiar to the United States. An official report in
India in 1980 noted that the advancement of one preferred group tended to
"push back" another, creating "greater tension between structural neighbors
in this hierarchy than between the top level and the bottom level." That
continued to be so in the 1990s, with violent clashes in several Indian states
being found to be more common among competing poorer groups than
between these groups and the more elite castes.[30] In 2001, a rally was held
in the state of Rajasthan, protesting the inclusion of new groups among the
backward classes and demanding "separate fixed quotas for original
backwards" so that "new entrants" would not be able to reduce the existing
benefits enjoyed by those for whom the preferences were created.[31] Calls
have been made for a "quota within quota" to deal with such situations.[32]

In so far as affirmative action policies are aimed particularly at offsetting
existing economic disadvantages, their rationale is undermined when the
benefits of these policies go disproportionately to those individuals within
the designated groups who are the least disadvantaged— or perhaps are in
more favorable positions than members of the country's general population.

In India's state of Tamil Nadu, for example, the highest of the so-called
"backward classes" legally entitled to preferences, constituting 11 percent of
the total "backward classes" population in that state, received almost half of
all jobs and university admissions set aside for these classes.[33] In Malaysia,
where there are preferences for the indigenous "sons of the soil" majority,
Malay students whose families were in the top 17 percent of the income
distribution received just over half of all scholarships awarded to Malays.[34]
In Sri Lanka, preferential university admissions for people from backward
regions of the country appear likewise to have benefited primarily students
from affluent families in those regions.[35]

This should hardly be surprising, nor is it necessarily a matter of corruption. Preferential access to education or jobs is just one factor in getting the education or the job. Obviously, those people who have more of the other factors required are better able to turn preferential access into actual success. Pre-existing prosperity provides more of those other factors.

Those American minority business owners who participate in the preferential program called business "set-asides" under Section 8(a) of the Small Business Act average a personal net worth that is not only higher than the average net worth of the groups they come from, but also higher than the average personal net worth of Americans in general.[36] A scholarly study of group preferences in India pointed out that preferences that benefit more fortunate members of less fortunate groups "borrow legitimacy from the national commitment to ameliorate the condition of the lowest," while at the same time "they undermine that commitment by broadcasting a picture of unrestrained preference for those who are not distinctly worse off than non-beneficiaries."[37]

Just as specifying the scope and duration of affirmative action policies has proven illusory, so has the designation of the beneficiaries in accordance with the rationales of these policies. Both attempts suffer from assuming far more comprehensive knowledge and control than anyone has been able to exercise, in any of the countries in which preferential programs have been instituted. What has also been over-estimated is the extent to which the attitudes resulting from such programs can be assumed to be beneficial to the groups concerned or to the country at large. These attitudes tend to respond to incentives, rather than to rationales.

Incentives

Both preferred and non-preferred groups have modified their own behavior and attitudes in response to preferential policies and the rationales for such policies. While members of the officially preferred groups who already have the complementary factors needed to take the fullest advantage of preferences can do so, those who lack these factors often feel less incentive to acquire them, now that entitlements are available as substitutes for achievements. The development of job skills, for example, may be de-emphasized. As a leader in a campaign for preferential policies in India's state of Andhra Pradesh put it: "Are we not entitled to jobs just because we are not as qualified?"[38] A Nigerian likewise wrote of "the tyranny of skills."[39] In Malaysia, where group preferences exist for the majority population, "Malay students, who sense that their future is assured, feel less pressure to perform."[40] In the United States, a study of black colleges found that even those of their students who were planning to continue on to postgraduate study showed little concern about needing to be prepared "because they believe that certain rules would simply be set aside for them."[41]

Both preferred and non-preferred groups can slacken their efforts— the former because working to their fullest capacity is unnecessary and the latter because working to their fullest capacity can prove to be futile. After Jamaica gained its independence from British rule, many whites living there no longer bothered to compete for public office because they "felt that the day of the black man had come and questioned why they had to make the effort if the coveted job or the national honor would go to the blacks, despite their qualifications."[42] While affirmative action policies are often thought of, by advocates and critics alike, as a transfer of benefits from one group to another, there can also be net losses of benefits when both groups do less than their best. What might otherwise be a zero-sum game can thus become a negative-sum game.

In some countries, complete physical withdrawal from the country by those in non-preferred groups has occurred in the wake of preferential policies which reduced their prospects. The exodus of Chinese from Malaysia, Indians from Fiji, Russians from Central Asia, Jews from much of prewar Europe, and Huguenots from 17th century France in response to discrimination drained all these countries of much-needed skills and talents. In short, preferential policies represent not simply a transfer of benefits from one group to another, but can also represent a net loss, as both groups respond by contributing less than they could to the society as a whole.

Not all incentives are economic or even tangible. Honors are among the most powerful of incentives in many situations, especially where dangers and death must be faced, and where money is less effective than a sense of honor, as in the military. In less dire circumstances as well, honor and the respect of peers play important roles, not only as rewards for achievements, but also as factors helping to make individual achievements possible in the first place.

The cooperation and collaboration of colleagues can be important in a variety of occupations from scholars to policemen— and that cooperation and collaboration can be compromised by group preferences. For example, minority professors on American campuses have complained that being thought of as "affirmative action" professors[43] by their colleagues has led to less intellectual and research interaction, which in turn reduces the minority faculty's development as scholars.[44] This can be a serious handicap in achieving one's potential. In life and death situations, such as those faced by the police, firefighters, and soldiers, mutual confidence is even more important. Yet black police sergeants promoted in Chicago over white policemen with higher test scores— as a result of a court order— found themselves taunted as "quota sergeants" when they made mistakes.[45]

Intergroup Relations

Even aside from losses to the economy as a whole, because of disincentives created for both preferred and non-preferred groups, there are social losses due to intergroup resentments, which can be even more serious. Nor are these resentments due simply to the transfers of benefits.

When a serious political backlash against affirmative action began in the United States, many in the media were quick to characterize it dismissively as due to "angry white males," resentful of the losses of various benefits to blacks and other minorities— in other words, just an emotional reaction by people irked at losing a few of their many advantages. But this resentment was by no means proportional to intergroup transfers of benefits or it would have been far greater against Asian Americans, who displaced more whites in prestigious universities and in many high-level professions, especially in science and technology. At many of the leading universities in the United States, whites "lost" more places to Asian Americans than to blacks, and yet there was seldom any backlash against Asian Americans. The outstanding academic and other achievements of Asian Americans were widely recognized and widely respected. It was not the intergroup transfer of benefits that was resented, but the basis for those transfers.

Among Americans especially, the idea that some are to be treated as "more equal than others" is galling. It was this feeling in the general population which leaders of the civil rights movement of the 1960s were able to mobilize behind their efforts to destroy the Jim Crow laws of the South, so that a majority of the members in both Houses of Congress from both political parties voted for the landmark Civil Rights Act of 1964 and the Voting Rights Act of 1965. It was this same American resentment of special privilege which responded so strongly to the historic words of the Reverend Martin Luther King, Jr., at the Lincoln Memorial in 1963, that his dream was of a country where people would be judged "not by the color of their skin, but by the content of their character."

It was after the civil rights movement itself began to move away from this concept of equal treatment of all individuals and toward the concept of equalized outcomes for groups, that a backlash against affirmative action set in and grew over the years.

There is yet another sense in which resentments against preferences for other groups are not proportional to the benefits transferred. An observer of preferential policies in India noted the disproportionate resentment of places reserved for "scheduled castes," the official euphemism for untouchables:

> . . . we hear innumerable tales of persons being deprived of appointments in favour of people who ranked lower than they did in the relevant examinations. No doubt this does happen, but if all these people were, in fact, paying the price for appointments to Scheduled Castes, there would be many more SC persons appointed than there actually are. To illustrate: supposing that 300 people qualify for ten posts available. The top nine are appointed on merit but the tenth is reserved, so that the authorities go down the list to find an SC applicant. They find one at 140 and he is appointed. Whereupon all 131 between him and the merit list feel aggrieved. He has not taken 131 posts; he has taken one, yet 131 people believe they have paid the price for it. Moreover, the remaining 159 often also resent the situation, believing that their chances were, somehow, lessened by the existence of SC reservations.[46]

In the United States as well, those who resent group preferences may be some multiple of those who have in fact actually lost anything that they would have had in the absence of these preferences. In the 1978 landmark Supreme Court challenge to affirmative action brought by Allan Bakke, a white student denied admission to a University of California medical school, neither side to the dispute could state with confidence that Bakke would or would not have been admitted in the absence of the affirmative action policies which admitted minority students with lower academic qualifications than his. The admissions process was sufficiently complicated that it was not clear whether some other white or Asian-American students might have been admitted instead of Bakke.

In other words, it was not certain that Bakke had in fact lost anything as a result of affirmative action, and yet his sense of being wronged was sufficient for him to pursue the case all the way up to the highest court in the land. One of the things that prevents affirmative action from being a zero-sum process is that minor transfers of benefits can cause major resentments among far more people than those who have actually lost anything. Moreover, these resentments do not end with political or legal actions.

In India, where preferential policies have a longer history than in the United States, they have also had more bitter consequences. Forty-two people died in riots over places reserved for untouchables in a medical school in the state of Gujarat— just seven places.[47] This was part of a national trend of rising violence against untouchables amid adverse reactions against preferential policies in general.[48] Meanwhile, less than 5 percent of the medical school places reserved for untouchables in Gujarat had actually been filled over a period of years. Studies of university admissions in general, in various parts of India, showed a similar pattern of many places reserved for untouchables going unfilled.[49] Nevertheless, minor transfers of benefits led to major resentments, including resentments erupting repeatedly into lethal violence.

Nowhere has this resentment led to more violence than in India's neighboring nation of Sri Lanka, which has been racked by decades of civil war, in which the non-preferred group— the Tamils— have sought to secede and become an independent nation. It is clear that affirmative action in Sri Lanka has not been a zero-sum process. The material, political, economic, and social havoc created by that country's long civil war has undoubtedly left all segments of the population worse off than they would have been in the absence of group preferences and the reactions to which those preferences led.

TRENDS

Even where there are adequate statistical data on the progress of groups that have been given preferential treatment— and often there are not— it remains a challenge to determine how much of that progress was due to preferential policies, rather than to other factors at work at the same time. Simple before-and-after comparisons will not do, as that would be assuming that nothing else had changed, when in fact the very dynamics of establishing affirmative action programs often reflect changes that were already under way before group preferences began. Seldom is there a stationary situation to which a given "change" is added.

Often it was precisely the rise of newly educated and upwardly mobile groups which led to demands for preferential policies. A study in Bombay, for example, found a "marked advancement of the Maharashtrians occurred prior to the stringent policy measures adopted by the state government" to promote preferential hiring of indigenous Maharashtrians.[50] In part this reflected a prior "enormous growth in school enrollments in Maharashtra" and a "rapid expansion in college enrollment"— also prior to preferences.[51] In Malaysia as well, the number of children attending the government's secondary schools increased by 73 percent in just five years immediately preceding the New Economic Policy which expanded preferences and quotas for Malays.[52] In Sri Lanka likewise, there was a "rapid expansion of educational opportunities in the Sinhalese areas" after independence[53]— and before demands for preferential treatment of the Sinhalese.

A similar growth of an indigenous, newly educated class in Poland, Czechoslovakia, and Lithuania during the years between the two World Wars led to demands for preferential policies in the form of group quotas, in order to relieve them from having to compete on an equal plane with Jews,[54] who were already educated, experienced, and established in the positions to which the newly-educated classes were aspiring. Likewise, in

Nigeria, it was the recent growth of an educated class in the north that led
to demands for preferential policies to relieve them from having to compete
with southern Nigerians, who had predominated in universities and in many
desirable occupations.[55] This same pattern of a rising educated class *prior* to
the preferential policies that they promoted can also be found in Indonesia,
the Quebec province of Canada, and much of sub-Saharan Africa.[56]

In the United States, the proportion of the black population going to
college doubled in the two decades preceding the civil rights revolution of
the 1960s,[57] and this was reflected in the occupational rise of blacks. While
it is an often-cited fact that the proportion of blacks in professional and
other high-level occupations rose substantially in the years following passage
of the Civil Rights Act of 1964, it is an almost totally ignored fact that the
proportion of blacks in such occupations rose even more substantially in the
years *preceding* passage of the Civil Rights Act of 1964.[58]

Dramatic progress was also evident during these same decades in the
lower socioeconomic levels of the American black population. The
percentage of black families with incomes below the official poverty line fell
from 87 percent in 1940 to 47 percent by 1960— all of this before the civil
rights legislation of that decade, much less the affirmative action policies of
the 1970s. Between 1960 and 1970, the poverty rate among black families
dropped an additional 17 percentage points and, after the decade of the
1970s in which affirmative action was established, the poverty rate among
blacks fell one additional percentage point.[59]

This striking difference between the political myth and the economic reality
has many implications. Among them is that what might otherwise be seen as
a remarkable achievement by black Americans is instead seen as an example of
government beneficence and largess— and a reason why affirmative action is
an absolute necessity for black advancement. The effects of this misperception
include white resentments and their questioning why blacks cannot advance
themselves like other groups, when in fact that is what most blacks have done.
Incidentally, it is an equally ignored fact that the incomes of Asian Americans
and Mexican Americans rose substantially— both absolutely and relative to
that of the general population— in the years preceding passage of the Civil
Rights Act of 1964 and its evolution into preferential policies.[60]

Any assessment of preferential policies must take account of pre-existing trends, rather than assume a static world to which "change" was added.

SUMMARY AND IMPLICATIONS

Despite the highly varied rationales for official group preferences and quotas in particular countries around the world, the logic of their incentives and constraints tends to produce similar consequences in very disparate societies. Moreover, both the incentives and the consequences tend to get ignored in political discussions of these policies, which focus on their justifications and presumed benefits, while ignoring actual empirical results. In the United States, mythical results— affirmative action as the basis for the economic rise of blacks, for example— have so completely supplanted facts that few who discuss this policy find it necessary to check historical evidence at all.

For some supporters of affirmative action, it is just a matter of being in favor of helping the less fortunate, with the "details" being left for others to consider and work out. However, even a broad-brush look at what affirmative action programs have actually done in various countries reveals that a failure to achieve their goals may be the least of the problems created by these programs. Poisonous intergroup relations and real dangers to the fabric of society have also been produced by affirmative action in some societies.

THE INFLUENCE OF
GEOGRAPHY

F ew unsubstantiated ideas have done as much social damage—
sometimes tearing whole societies apart— as the assumption that there
is something strange, if not sinister, when racial, ethnic or other groups are
not evenly or randomly distributed in particular endeavors, institutions,
occupations or income levels. However plausible that assumption might
seem when thinking in terms of abstract people in an abstract world, when
it comes to real people in the real world, that assumption is not merely
unsubstantiated but in defiance of mountains of evidence to the contrary in
countries around the world and going back for centuries. Geography alone
is enough to make peoples different, though geography is just one of many
influences that differ from one place to another and therefore from one
people to another.

GEOGRAPHY, ECONOMICS AND CULTURE

The geography of the Mediterranean world is quite different from the
geography of Southeast Asia, not only in terms of such obvious things as soil
and minerals, but also in terms of rivers, mountains, climates, disease
environments, and other factors whose influences expand or limit the
possibilities of different peoples in different ways. The sense of a dependable
abundance— "fish in the water, rice on the land," as a Thai saying has it[1]—
could hardly have been common in the Mediterranean world, where the
barren hills, scanty rainfall, and thin soils made survival a struggle and made
the peoples of the region renowned for their frugality.[2] Moreover, geography
cannot be thought of in two dimensions, as if we were looking down at a
map or globe. While a whole region may be dominated by a particular
culture, as the Middle East and North Africa have been by the Islamic
culture, peoples living in mountainous parts of the same region— in

Armenia or Abyssinia, for example— may preserve a very different religion and culture from that in the lower elevations.

Mountains

Even when Islam became the religion of the Rif mountains of Morocco, this happened centuries after Moroccans in the lowlands had become Muslims.[3] Similarly, the English language prevailed in the Scottish lowlands while Gaelic continued to survive in the highlands for generations, just as the Vlach language survived in the Pindus Mountains of Greece long after Greek prevailed in the lower elevations.[4] Mountains and uplands have in fact isolated peoples culturally and economically, from the Scottish highlands to the highlands of colonial Ceylon, which in both cases maintained their independence for many years after their respective lowlands were conquered and incorporated into another cultural universe. Even mountainous regions nominally under the control of a larger nation or empire have not always and in all places been effectively under such control— the mountains of Montenegro under the Ottoman Empire, the Rif Mountains under Moroccan sultans, and the uplands of India under the Moghal rulers, for example.[5] Isolation has been a key factor in both political autonomy and cultural separatism, as it has been in the enduring poverty of many mountain regions. In the Apennines mountains of southern Italy, 91 out of 123 Lucanian villages had no roads whatsoever in 1860.[6] In parts of the Pindus Mountains of Greece, even in the twentieth century, there were places more accessible to mules and to people on foot than to wheeled vehicles, and one village acquired electricity as late as 1956.[7] In the Rif Mountains of Morocco, snow continued to cut off some communities completely in wintertime, even in the late twentieth century.[8]

The cultural isolation of mountainous communities has been partially relieved by the temporary migrations of its men to lower elevations in search of work, returning with at least a glimpse of another way of life, though the women who remained behind lacked even this.[9] Moreover, few people from other places have come to live in these mountain villages, to present a different viewpoint. Often the great majority of marriages have involved women and men not only from the same mountains but from the same village.[10] Finally, the poverty of many mountain peoples has often led them to utilize their children's labor from an early age, even at the expense of their education,[11] thereby cutting off yet another source of a broader exposure to the outside world.

Another pattern found among mountain people in various parts of the world, at least in recent centuries, has been the production of a wide variety of home-based arts and crafts during the long winter months when time is available. Swiss wood carvings, for example, have had their counterparts halfway around the world in Kashmir, as well as closer to home in Norway.[12] Numerous other products of home-based crafts, from weaving to metalwork, have issued from mountain communities and have been sold in the international markets as items of large value in a small physical size, able to bear the high transportation costs from mountain regions.

The toughness required to survive in many barren and backward mountain regions has produced renowned fighting men in many parts of the world, from the highland Scots[13] to the Gurkhas of India,[14] the Albanians,[15] the Moroccan Rifians,[16] the *Montagnards* of Vietnam,[17] and the Turks[18]— all formidable not only in their own homelands but also in the service of foreign countries. The elite Scottish highland regiments and Gurkha units of the British military forces had as counterparts the Albanians and Rifians who fought in the Ottoman armies, as well as the 50,000 to 60,000 Rifians who fought on the side of Franco during the Spanish civil war of the 1930s.[19] It has been estimated that somewhere in the vicinity of a million Swiss soldiers were killed in other people's wars between the fifteenth and the eighteenth centuries.[20]

The fighting qualities of mountain men have also taken the form of local brigandage and blood feuds in their homelands. Marauders from the highlands have preyed on more prosperous communities in the lowlands for centuries, whether Kurds raiding Armenian villages, Scottish highlanders raiding Scottish lowlanders, or similar activity in Italy, Spain, the Balkans, India, and Tibet.[21] Feuds have also been outlets for the fighting ability of mountain men. The celebrated "Hatfield and McCoy" feud of the American Appalachian region was not only an example of a custom that went back to the parts of Britain from which so many Southerners came,[22] it had its counterparts in similar tribal or clan feuds in the Rif Mountains of

Morocco, in the Balkan mountains of Montenegro, in the mountains of the Caucasus and in the mountains of Taiwan.[23]

The minerals found in some mountains present opportunities for mining and for the development of skills connected with mining. Thus the Germans in the Harz Mountains became renowned as miners, leading to a demand for Germans to work in the mines of other countries, whether in Bohemia, Norway, Spain, the Balkans, or Mexico.[24] However, the very fact that Germans were imported into all these countries suggests that geography presents opportunities which people are not predestined to grasp, for otherwise all the mountains and other sources of mineral deposits in all these other countries would have led to the development of indigenous miners, obviating the necessity to import Germans.

In geographical terms, mountains and highlands in general are important not only as obstacles in themselves, but also as features with both positive and negative effects on other parts of the environment. Rivers and streams flow more steadily because of the snows melting on the mountainsides, whereas their volume of water varies much more widely and more erratically where there are no mountain ranges, as in tropical Africa, where rainfall alone must sustain these waterways— or fail to sustain them. The Sierra Nevada in Spain and the Taurus Mountains in Turkey both supply the water that makes a flourishing irrigated agriculture possible on the plains below,[25] where rainfall alone would not be sufficient. In another sense, however, uplands have a negative effect on rivers, which must plunge more sharply downward, often with rapids and waterfalls, when the streams originate at higher elevations, whether on plateaus, mountains, or foothills. Rivers with steep gradients tend to be less navigable, or not navigable at all.

Mountain ranges also drastically affect rainfall patterns. When moisture-laden air blows across a mountain range, it is not uncommon for the rainfall on the side where the moisture originates to be several times as great as in the "rain shadow" on the other side of the mountain, where the air goes after it has lost most of its moisture while rising over the crest. The net result is that people located on different sides of a range of mountains or foothills may have very different agricultural opportunities. On some western slopes of southern Italy's Apennines Mountains, for example, the annual rainfall reaches 2,000 millimeters while parts of the eastern slopes get as little as 300–500 millimeters.[26] Similarly, in the American Pacific Northwest, precipitation on parts of the west side of the Cascade Mountains averages up to ten times as much as on parts of the Columbia Plateau to the east.[27]

Different sides of a mountain range often have not only different amounts of rainfall but also different slopes. This has had important military implications, where the people on one side have found it easier to climb the gentler slope and then descend upon the other side to invade their neighbors.[28] The locations and shapes of mountain passes have also had other military— and consequently cultural— impacts. The greater ease of Roman soldiers' entry through the mountain passes into Gaul, as compared to the more difficult mountain route into German regions, meant that Roman culture reached Gaul first and only later filtered second-hand into the lands inhabited by Germans.[29]

Coastal Regions

Coastal peoples have also tended to be culturally distinctive. In touch with more of the outside world, they have usually been more knowledgeable and more technologically and socially advanced than interior peoples.[30] As with other geographically-related social patterns, these are not racial but locational. Sometimes the coastal peoples are racially or ethnically different— Germans being particularly represented on the coastal fringes of Russia at one time, for example[31]— but the differences between the interior and the coastal peoples remain, even when they are both of the same racial stock. Thus, in the Middle Ages, the largely Slavic population of the Adriatic port city of Dubrovnik was culturally far more advanced in literature, architecture, and painting, as well as in modern business methods, than the Slavs of the interior hinterlands.[32] In tropical Africa, likewise, the coastal peoples more in touch with outside influences were sufficiently more advanced technologically and organizationally to become enslavers of Africans farther inland.[33] One symptom of the importance of coastal areas as cultural crossroads is that many of the lingua francas of the world have originated in such settings, whether in the Levant, on the Swahili coast of Africa, or in the ports of China and Southeast Asia.[34]

Land, Climate and Waterways

Soil, of course, has profound effects on the kind of agriculture that is possible— and therefore on the kinds of societies that are possible. A pattern of farms that are passed down through the same family for generations is possible in fertile regions, but not in places where the soil is exhausted in a few years and has to be abandoned and a new site found while the first land recovers its fertility. Whole societies may have to be mobile when the land in any given location cannot permanently sustain them. This means that there cannot be cities and all the cultural developments facilitated by cities. Mobile, slash-and-burn agriculture has been common in those parts of tropical Africa and Asia where great cities failed to develop and where the indigenous people long remained vulnerable to conquest or enslavement by peoples from more urbanized societies and larger nation-states elsewhere. In early medieval Europe as well, Slavs in East Central Europe practiced slash-and-burn agriculture, which necessitated very different forms of social organization from those which emerged after the use of the plow enabled them to create sedentary societies.[35] Moreover, just as the nature of agriculture has influenced where urban life is or is not feasible, so the economic and technological advances associated with cities influence agriculture. Thus, in the sixteenth century, the hinterlands of such flourishing cities as Venice, Milan, and Genoa saw great improvements in agricultural methods introduced.[36]

Deserts and steppes, such as those of North Africa, the Middle East, and Central Asia, have often produced societies on the move. These nomads have included some of the great conquerors of all time. Wave after wave of conquerors from Central Asia and the Caucasus have pushed other peoples before them into eastern and southern Europe over the centuries, creating a chain-reaction series of conquests in the Ukrainian, Polish, and Hungarian plains and in the Balkans, as those displaced moved on to displace others.[37] Less dramatic and less extreme have been the seasonal movements in places where sheep, goats, and other animals are herded in different places at different times of the year, rather than exhaust the vegetation in one place. Here there may be permanent dwellings where the women and children stay while the men migrate seasonally with their herds, as in the Balkans, for example.

The significance of particular geographic features— mountains, rivers, climate, soil, etc.— is even greater when these features are viewed in combination. For example, the effect of rainfall on agriculture depends not only on how much rainfall there is but also on the ability of the soil to hold it. Thus a modest amount of rainfall may be sufficient for a flourishing agriculture on the absorbent loess soils of northern China, while rain falling on the limestone soils of the Balkans may disappear rapidly underground. Similarly, the economic value of navigable waterways depends on the lands adjacent to them. Navigable rivers which go through land without the resources for either industry or agriculture— the Amazon for example— are of little economic value,[38] even though navigable waterways in general have been crucial to the economic and cultural development of other regions more fully endowed with other resources. In Russia as well, waterways isolated from the major natural resources of the country, as well as from each other,[39] cannot match the economic role of rivers which flow into one another and into the sea after passing through agriculturally or industrially productive regions. Conversely, harbors that are not as deep, not as wide, nor as well-sheltered as other harbors may nevertheless become busy ports if they represent the only outlets for productive regions in the vicinity, as was the case of Genoa in northwestern Italy or Mombasa in East Africa.[40] Similarly, the port of Dubrovnik on the Dalmatian coast, strategically located for the international trade routes of the Middle Ages, flourished despite a harbor that was not particularly impressive in itself.[41]

Sometimes a variety of favorable geographical features exist in combination within a given region, as in northwestern Europe, and sometimes virtually all are lacking, as in parts of tropical Africa, while still other parts of the world have some of these favorable features but not others. The consequences include not only variations in economic well-being but, more fundamentally, variations in the skills and experience— the human capital— of the people themselves. Given the enormous range of combinations of geographical features, the peoples from different regions of the earth have had highly disparate opportunities to develop particular skills and work experience. International migrations then put these peoples with disparate skills, aptitudes, and outlooks in proximity to one another and in competition with one another in other lands.

While geographical influences may distinguish one cultural universe from another, even another located nearby, the existence of similar geographical influences and similar social patterns in distant regions of the world— marauding and feuds among mountain men, for example— means that such patterns are not "national character" or "racial traits," but are international in scope and geographical in origin. Nor are these patterns necessarily racial characteristics even in the limited sense of characteristics differing from one race to another for non-genetic reasons. Particular cultural universes may be largely coextensive with particular races— the Japanese culture for example— but this is not always or inherently so. In short, geographical influences cut across national borders and racial lines, producing similar effects in different countries and different effects in various regions of the same country or among culturally different members of the same race. This is not to say that there are no national cultural influences. Clearly there are. Language, religion, and political traditions are just some of the cultural values holding together nations composed of peoples subjected to disparate other influences. The point here is simply that a recognition of distinct cultural patterns, whether originating in geography, history, or otherwise, is not the same as a belief in "national character" or "racial traits." These things may overlap or even be congruent in some cases, but they may also be quite separate.

While continents or other regions of the world may not be geographically unique, nor homogeneous within themselves, nevertheless the ensemble of geographical influences operating in one region of the world has differed significantly from the geographical (and other) influences operating elsewhere. These differences are not confined to their original locations but are also imbedded in the cultures of peoples migrating from these different regions of the world.

One of the more geographically fortunate parts of the world, in terms of having the natural resources needed for the development of a modern industrial economy, has been northern and western Europe. Iron ore and coal deposits, the key ingredients of steel manufacturing and the heavy industry dependent on it, are concentrated in the Ruhr valley, in Wales, in Sweden, and in the region so bitterly fought over by France and Germany, Alsace-Lorraine. The broad coastal plains of northern Europe have also provided the peoples of that region with much prime agricultural land and with navigable rivers criss-crossing these lands, knitting large areas together economically and culturally. The fact that Europe has many peninsulas, islands, and numerous harbors gives the continent excellent access to the sea. The Gulf Stream warms Western Europe to give it milder winters than places at similar latitudes in the Western Hemisphere or in Asia. London, for example, is farther north than any place in the 48 contiguous United States, yet it has milder winters than New York City, much less cities in Minnesota or Wisconsin.

Eastern, Central, and Mediterranean Europe do not share all these advantages. The Gulf Stream's influence on the climate of European nations on the Atlantic becomes progressively less in the more distant central and eastern portions of the continent, where rivers are frozen for more days of the year and where winters are longer and more bitterly cold. The natural resources required for modern industry are also less abundant and in many places virtually non-existent in central and eastern Europe. The broad coastal plains of northern Europe have no counterparts in the Balkans, where hills and mountains come down close to the sea and the coastal harbors often have no navigable rivers to link them to the hinterlands. Spain has likewise been lacking in navigable rivers[42] and Sicily lacking in both rivers and rainfall.[43]

These sharp differences in geographical advantages have been reflected not only in great disparities in wealth among the different regions of Europe, but also in similarly large differences in skills, industrial experience, and whole ways of life among the peoples of these regions. Thus, when the peoples of the Mediterranean migrated to the United States or to Australia, for example, they did not bring with them the industrial skills or the whole modern way of life found among German or English immigrants. What they did bring with them was a frugality born of centuries of struggle for survival in the less productive lands and waters of the Mediterranean, and a power of endurance and persistence born of the same circumstances. The ability of the Italian immigrants to endure poor and cramped living conditions and to save out of very low wages, which caused comment among those around them, whether in other European countries or in the Western

Hemisphere or Australia, had both geographical and historical roots. Similar characteristics have marked various other Mediterranean peoples, but the Italians are a particularly interesting group to study because they include not only the Mediterranean people of the south but also people from the industrial world of the Po River valley in the north, whose geographical, economic, and cultural characteristics are much more similar to those found among northern and western Europeans.

The enduring consequences of the different skills and experiences possessed by people from different parts of Europe can be seen in the fact that the average income of immigrants from southern and eastern Europe to the United States in the early twentieth century was equal to what was earned by the bottom 15 percent among immigrants from England, Scotland, Holland, or Norway.[44] Illiteracy was higher among immigrants from southern and eastern Europe.[45] In school, their children tended to lag behind the children of either native-born Americans or the children of immigrants from northern and western Europe,[46] and their I.Q. scores were often very similar to those of American blacks, and were sometimes lower.[47] Nor was all this peculiar to American society. In pre-World War II Australia, immigrants from southern Italy, Dalmatia, Macedonia, and the Greek countryside were typically illiterate and spoke primarily their local dialects rather than the official languages of their respective home countries.[48]

More than three quarters of these southern European immigrants to Australia were from the rugged hills or mountains, the steep coastlines or islands of the region, rather than from the urban areas or plains.[49] Although these remote areas were eventually drawn into the modern world, the skills of their peoples continued to lag behind the skills of peoples in other parts of Europe that were more industrially advanced and this was reflected in their earnings in Australia, as in the United States. As late as the 1970s, the median earnings of immigrants to Australia from Greece, Italy, or Yugoslavia fell below the earnings of immigrants from West Germany or from English-speaking countries.[50] Southern Europeans in Australia remained under-represented in professional and technical occupations[51] and from nearly half among the Italian immigrants to an absolute majority among the Greek and Yugoslavian immigrants were unskilled laborers.[52]

Asia has likewise had sharp cultural divisions, many growing out of its geography. The world's highest mountain range— the Himalayas— separated Asia's two great ancient civilizations, those of China and India, which developed independently of one another to a greater extent than any of the civilizations of Europe or the Middle East. China, in particular, was a world of its own and clearly the most advanced nation on Earth for many centuries. One sign of its preeminence was that Chinese goods were for long in great demand in Europe while Europe had nothing to offer in return except gold and silver. The compass was in use in China's maritime trade decades before it was introduced to Europeans by the Arabs, and books were printed in China centuries before the Gutenberg Bible was printed in Europe. Chinese silks and porcelain were in demand in Asia, Europe, and Africa.[53] While Chinese culture had a major impact on the cultures of Korea and Japan, and an influence felt as far away as Persia and Russia, there were few external cultural influences on China itself from the eighth through the thirteenth centuries.[54] Yet very little of China's culture was spread by migration— certainly nothing to compare with the later massive spread of European culture to the Western Hemisphere, not only by the movement of millions of Europeans but also by the Europeanization of both the indigenous populations of the Western Hemisphere and the millions of descendants of Africans brought to the New World.

The Japanese are a reminder that a meager natural resource base alone is not enough to prevent industrial development, though it may prevent such development from arising spontaneously from within the given society. Japan's industrialization was transplanted from western Europe— notably England and Scotland— and from the United States, as a result of deliberate decisions made by the Japanese government amid a national fervor to catch up with the West. Why this happened in Japan but not in India, Abyssinia, or the Balkans, is a profound question with few answers or even systematic explorations. Many centuries earlier, Japan was likewise very receptive to cultural and technological imports from China, which at that point represented the most advanced culture in the world. In short, geography is a major influence but not a predestination. Otherwise nations like Japan and Switzerland would be among the poorer nations of the world, instead of among the most prosperous.

Even after large numbers of Chinese, Japanese, and Indians migrated to other countries around the world, the cultures they took with them had little or no effect on others outside their own respective groups. To a greater or lesser extent, these migrants from Asia tended to assimilate at least the outward veneer of the Western societies in which they settled, though retaining their own work patterns and discipline which enabled them to rise to prosperity in these countries.

The southwestern part of Asia known as the Middle East has also sent abroad migrants whose cultural endowments reflect the geographical circumstances in which their societies evolved. Lacking both the spontaneous abundance of food found in parts of the tropics and the natural resources for modern industry found in northern Europe, the peoples of the Middle East have historically had to struggle to make a living, whether in the nomadic pattern of the bedouins of the desert or in the irrigated farming of others, or— perhaps most striking of all— in the middleman traders who originated in this region and spread throughout the world. The economically strategic location of the Middle East, for centuries a crossroads of trade between Europe and Asia, fostered the development of many trading ports and many trading peoples,[55] of whom the Jews, the Armenians, and the Lebanese have been particularly prominent, not only in the Middle East itself but also in other countries on every inhabited continent. These kinds of immigrants— middleman minorities— from this part of the world have had patterns of skills and aptitudes strikingly similar to those of the overseas Chinese who originated in similarly demanding regions of southern China, where trade was part of their survival skills in a geographically unpromising region for industry, but which had trading ports.

THE GEOGRAPHY OF AFRICA

In understanding Black Africa, geography is more important than history.
— *Fernand Braudel*[56]

In a strictly geographical sense, all the peoples on the continent of Africa are Africans— from the whites of South Africa to the Arabs of the Mediterranean states— but the term has in practice come to refer primarily to the indigenous peoples of Africa below the Sahara, to black Africans. The basis for this focus is not simply racial but historic, cultural, and geographic as well. As with the British, the Slavs, and others, the influence of geography in Africa has not been simply in its effects primarily on *things*— natural resources or economic prosperity, for example— but on *people*. More specifically, the effect of geography in making cultural interactions more difficult has been particularly striking as between the peoples of sub-Saharan Africa and the outside world, as well as among themselves.

To their north is a desert more vast than the continental United States and to the east, west, and south are the Indian, Atlantic, and Antarctic oceans. Moreover, the smooth coastline of sub-Saharan Africa has offered few harbors which ocean-going ships could enter and in many places the shallow coastal waterways have meant that large ships could not get near the shores. Ironically, for centuries much of the world's international trade was carried in ships that sailed past West Africa on their way between Europe and Asia around the southern tip of the continent. Seldom did they stop. Partly this was a result of wind and ocean currents that made return trips between Europe and sub-Saharan Africa difficult or not economically feasible in the era of wind-driven ships, at least until far greater knowledge of those currents and of alternative routes developed.[57] Relatively little of Africa's trade entered international commerce.[58]

In the era before the modern transportation revolution of railroads, automobiles, and planes— which is to say, throughout most of human history— the geographical barriers surrounding tropical Africa have been formidable, though not absolutely impenetrable. The consequences have been not only economic but cultural. As the eminent French historian Fernand Braudel put it, "external influence filtered only very slowly, drop by drop, into the vast African continent South of the Sahara."[59] The geographic barriers to economic and cultural exchanges within various regions of sub-Saharan Africa have been formidable as well. The most striking of these barriers has been a dearth of navigable rivers or streams, though the land itself also presents difficult terrain in many places in the form of escarpments and rift valleys.

The net effect has been that the peoples of sub-Saharan Africa have historically been insulated not only from the peoples and cultures of the outside world but also from one another. Among the cultural consequences has been a linguistic fragmentation of tropical Africa, which has made African languages one third of all the languages of the world,[60] even though African peoples are only about 10 percent of the world's population. This linguistic fragmentation has been only one aspect of cultural fragmentation in general, including tribalism and many religious differences.

In much of sub-Saharan Africa, a combination of geographic features has had unfavorable— if not devastating— consequences for economic and cultural development, and tragic consequences for the vulnerability of black Africans to outside conquerors.

The Natural Environment

One of the remarkable facts about the African continent is that, despite being much larger than the continent of Europe, its coastline is shorter than the European coastline— indeed, shorter than the coastline of any other continent,[61] even though Africa is second only to Asia in size. This anomaly reflects Africa's lack of the numerous coastal indentations which form natural harbors in Europe, providing places where ships can dock, sheltered from the rough waters of the open seas, thereby enabling European countries to become maritime nations early in their history. In addition to a dearth of harbors, parts of sub-Saharan Africa have shallow coastal waters, so that maritime trade has often had to be conducted by the costly method of having ships anchor off-shore, with their cargoes being unloaded onto smaller vessels which could then make their way to land through these shallow waters.

Africans have generally not been seafaring peoples, except in the Mediterranean, or in parts of East Africa where these geographic constraints have not been as severe. Much of Africa, and especially sub-Saharan Africa, has developed without the benefits of a large maritime trade and the consequent stimulus of economic and cultural interchanges on a large scale with various and disparate peoples. While there has been for centuries some trade between sub-Saharan Africa and Europe, or with the peoples of North Africa and the Middle East, international trade has generally played a relatively smaller part in the total trade of Africa, as compared to other continents, not only because of a dearth of harbors, but also because of a dearth of navigable rivers reaching into the interior of the continent from the sea. River mouths opening into the sea have been blocked by sandbars in some places and in other places the few good harbors have been connected to hinterlands that were not very productive, and so have had little to offer in trade. Thin coastal plains— averaging only 20 miles in width and often backed by steep escarpments— have likewise provided little basis for large-scale international trade, even where other conditions might permit it.[62]

Low and irregular rainfall over many parts of Africa fill rivers and streams to a navigable depth only intermittently[63]— and even when filled, many rivers and streams are navigable only by smaller boats or barges, not ocean-going vessels.[64] Where the volume of water is sufficient for navigation by sizeable vessels, the many rapids and waterfalls of Africa still impede international trade. The Zaire River, for example, is 2,900 miles long and has a volume of water second only to that of the Amazon, but its rapids and waterfalls near the sea prevent ocean-going ships from reaching inland.[65] Thus, the role played by other great rivers of the world in facilitating the development of ports that became great cities, contributing to the economic and cultural development of the surrounding lands and peoples, was denied the Zaire by the intractable facts of geography. Nor is the Zaire unique among Africa's rivers. No river in sub-Saharan Africa reaches from the open sea to deep into the interior.[66] On the Mediterranean coast only the Nile reaches far inland. Significantly, the Nile spawned the most famous of the civilizations developed on the African continent, as well as the two largest cities on the continent, Cairo and Alexandria.

Except for the Nile, Africa's rivers that are even seasonally navigable tend to be concentrated in equatorial West Africa,[67] which has produced larger and more advanced societies than in many other tropical regions of the continent. In short, the peoples of Africa, like the peoples of Europe and Asia, tended to develop urban centers and larger cultural universes around navigable waterways. There have simply been far fewer of them in Africa, which has been and remains the world's least urbanized continent.[68] Among the relatively few things which have had sufficiently concentrated value in a relatively small physical size, so as to be able to repay the high costs of transport from Africa, have historically been gold, ivory, and slaves. All three became major exports. The coast of what is now Nigeria became known as "the slave coast," just as the coast of neighboring Ghana to the west was called "the gold coast" and that west of Ghana was (and still is) called "the ivory coast."

One indicator of differences in access to waterways is that, while more than a third of Europe's land mass consists of islands and peninsulas, only 2 percent of Africa's land mass consists of islands and peninsulas.[69] Such disparities in access to waterways are accentuated when the navigability of these waterways is also taken into account. Even the Niger River— the heart of a great river system in West Africa, draining an area nearly twice the size of Texas[70]— is not navigable everywhere by large vessels, and is not navigable at all in some places because of rapids.[71] At the height of the rainy season, the Niger may become "a 20-mile wide moving lake"[72] but, during the dry season, the average depth of the Niger can in places fall below 4 meters.[73] Despite its serious limitations, the Niger compares favorably with other African rivers with even more serious limitations. The Niger has been characterized as "the easiest to navigate in all of tropical Africa."[74] Navigating the Niger's chief tributary, the Benue River, for example, has been more problematical. Because of seasonal rainfall patterns, the upper Benue has been navigable only two months of the year, leading to hectic and complicated shipping patterns:

> If they let the craft stay up the Benue a day too long, the vessels will be stuck on sandbars for ten months! Yet if through caution or misinformation they withdraw the fleet too soon, much valuable merchandise is left behind and can only be evacuated by land at much greater cost. . . The first boats to go in are the commercial canoes, then follow the larger craft, and finally, when there is sufficient water at Lokoja, the largest power-craft and their barges sail up the river as fast as possible. Towards the end of the short season, the large craft have to come out first because of the fall in the level of the water; the medium-sized craft follow, and the small canoes may continue for some time evacuating small quantities of produce.[75]

Drastic changes in water levels are common in other West African rivers and streams.[76] The Senegal River has been characterized as "precariously navigable"— and only during some months, at that.[77] Like the Niger, the Senegal is not only subject to large seasonal changes in water flow but also contains rocks and rapids.[78] In East Africa, such rivers as the Zambezi are navigable only for relatively short stretches.[79] One reason for the drastic seasonal changes in water levels in African rivers is that tropical Africa is one of the few large regions of the world without a single mountain range to collect snow, whose later melting would supplement rainfall in maintaining the flow of streams and rivers. Rivers in tropical Africa are wholly dependent on rainfall and that rainfall is itself highly undependable, not only from one season to another but also from one year to the next.[80]

The term "navigable" can of course mean many things. In some of the rivers of Angola, for example, it means navigable by boats requiring no more than 8 feet of water,[81] and in parts of West Africa during the dry season, even the Niger will carry barges weighing no more than 8 tons.[82] By contrast, ships weighing 10,000 tons can go hundreds of miles up the Yangtze River in China, and smaller vessels another thousand miles beyond that.[83] Aircraft carriers can go up the Hudson River and dock at a pier in mid-Manhattan. Navigable rivers in Africa seldom mean anything approaching that. Even the Nile was unable to handle the largest vessels in Roman times.[84] Moreover, because so much of tropical Africa consists of high plateaus— almost the entire continent is more than 1,000 feet above sea-level and half the continent is more than 2,500 feet above sea-level[85]— African rivers must plunge greater vertical distances to reach the sea, making them less navigable en route. While the Amazon River falls only about 20 feet during its last 500 miles to the sea,[86] the Zaire River drops about a thousand feet in 250 miles as it approaches the sea.[87] As a geographer has put it, the African continent is "cursed with a mesa form which converts nearly every river into a plunging torrent."[88]

However impenetrable much of the interior of sub-Saharan Africa may have been to large, ocean-going ships, the continent's coastal waters have been plied by smaller boats, which could and did go inland as well, being unloaded and carried around waterfalls. Shipments from ocean-going vessels could also be loaded onto smaller craft for transportation into the interior on rivers. Local water-borne traffic between inland locations was likewise possible by carrying boats and their cargoes around rapids and waterfalls. Sometimes these boats and cargoes were carried from one river to another, thereby expanding the reach of commerce. For example, an overland route requiring 25 days of porterage on land connected the Niger and the Senegal rivers in centuries past.[89] Moreover, even rivers beset with cascades and waterfalls may have navigable stretches that add up to considerable distances— hundreds of miles on the Senegal and more than 1,500 on the Zaire— even though these are not *continuous* distances.[90] Thus the various regions of Africa were not hermetically sealed off from one another or from the outside world, but both the volume and the variety of trade, as well as the distances involved, were nevertheless severely curtailed, in comparison with more geographically fortunate regions of the world, where heavy and bulky cargoes of coal, ores, and grain could be shipped long distances in continuous river and ocean voyages.

A late twentieth-century comparison of the transportation costs of grain in several Asian and African nations found that these transport costs were a higher proportion of the total price paid for grain by consumers in Africa.[91] Moreover, such statistics do not capture the effect of transport costs on grain that was never shipped in the first place, precisely because higher shipping costs would have made it prohibitively expensive. Contemporary transport costs also cannot capture the handicaps created by even higher transport costs in Africa before many of the transportation advances from the rest of the world were introduced in the nineteenth and early twentieth centuries, and before African harbors could be dredged by modern European equipment and Western railroads built.

While it is true, as an historian has said, that "a considerable portion of West Africa" was part of "a hydrographic system that was ultimately connected to the Atlantic,"[92] the limitations of that system are a part of the story that cannot be omitted without serious distortion. Moreover, the distances between the interior hinterlands and the open seas are greater in Africa than in Europe, for example, while the means of covering those distances are much more limited by geography in Africa. In Europe, no part of the continent outside of Russia is more than 500 miles from the sea,[93] but a substantial part of tropical Africa is more than 500 miles from the sea and a portion is more than 1,000 miles from the sea.[94] Only Asia has a larger interior area remote from the sea,[95] though Asia has more navigable rivers connecting its interior with the coast. The geographical positions of African rivers must also be taken into account. Although the Niger River originates just 200 miles from the Atlantic Ocean, it circles far inland before eventually turning back toward the sea, and covers 2,600 miles before actually reaching the ocean.[96] In general, the tenuous connection of the African interior with the sea has been one of the major geographical barriers to the economic, cultural, and political development of the continent south of the Sahara.

Land transportation in large regions of sub-Saharan Africa has also been made more difficult because of the prevalence of the tsetse fly, which has carried a fatal sickness that has affected animals as well as human beings and made the use of pack animals and draft animals impracticable in many places. Denied this aid to land transportation, Africans often carried bundles on their heads in colorful caravans that were reflections of the bleak alternatives left to them without the help of either the waterways or the animal power available to other peoples on other continents. Expensive transportation provided by human beings limited what could be carried, how far it could be carried, and how fast. In addition to the physical limitations, there were narrower limits imposed by economics, as to what items contained enough value in a relatively small space to repay the costs of this expensive method of transport.

The lack of animals' muscle power in tropical Africa has been felt not only in transportation but also in farming. A dearth of draft animals in farming often meant not only a loss of muscle power but also a dearth of fertilizer. The latter has been especially important in those parts of the continent where soils have been very much in need of fertilizer, because their low nutrient content and proneness to erosion meant that their fertility was easily exhausted by cultivation.[97] Rainfall patterns in parts of Africa— long dry spells followed by torrential downpours— increase erosion, since dry, baked soil is more easily washed away.[98] Moreover, these torrential tropical downpours tend to leach the nutrients from the soil in Africa, as in many other tropical regions. Finally, the tropics provide a disease environment in which many more deadly diseases may flourish than in temperate zones, or in mountainous tropical regions that have more temperate climates because of their heights. For example, 90 percent of all deaths from malaria in the world occur in sub-Saharan Africa.[99]

Even a listing of individual geographical disadvantages in Africa may understate the handicap they represent in combination. For example, the problem of poor water transportation, while serious in itself, is still more serious in combination with poor land transportation across much difficult terrain without the aid of pack animals. The highly variable rainfall patterns become more serious in view of where the rain falls. A geographical study of Africa found plenty of water available "where it cannot be used" and a scarcity "where it is most needed."[100]

Not all parts of sub-Saharan Africa have suffered all these disabilities simultaneously. However, the fragile fertility in some regions of tropical Africa has meant that a given territory would not permanently feed people at a given location, and this in turn meant that those people had to move on every few years to find new land that would feed them, while the land they left behind recovered its fertility. Therefore whole societies had to be mobile, foregoing the opportunities to build territorially-based communities with permanent structures, such as other Africans built in more geographically favored parts of the continent, and which were common in Europe, Asia, and the Western Hemisphere.[101]

The provincialism of isolated peoples has not been peculiar to Africa. What has been peculiar to Africa are the geographic barriers to mobility that have pervaded vast areas below the Sahara. Waterways extend the boundaries of cultural interchange, but in much of sub-Saharan Africa they did not extend those cultural boundaries very far. Like other places relatively isolated from broader cultural developments— the Scottish highlands, parts of the Balkans, or the South Sea islands, for example— much of sub-Saharan Africa tended to lag behind the technological, organizational, and economic progress in other parts of the world. A lack of literacy throughout most of sub-Saharan Africa further limited both internal development and the stimulus of contacts with distant times and places via the written word. While similar retardation afflicted particular parts of Europe or Asia, or isolated island communities around the world, in Africa such cultural isolation characterized wide areas and many peoples.

The degree of these cultural handicaps has varied in different parts of the continent, and has changed over time. Railroads, motor transport and airplanes have all added to transportation possibilities, and electronic communication media from cheap radios to television have penetrated cultural isolation, but all this has happened within a recent, minute fraction of human history, long after great cultural differences had developed among peoples with geographically restricted cultures and between them and others with more ample access to wider cultural worlds. Moreover, even in modern times, the sharp changes in altitude of the African landscape continued to make both roads and railroads difficult to build. The rail line from Djibouti to Addis Ababa, for example, rises more than 2,000 feet in its first 60 miles and more than 4,600 feet in its last 180 miles.[102]

Given the multiple and formidable geographical obstacles to its economic and cultural development, Africa's poverty is hardly surprising. This poverty, over much of sub-Saharan Africa, is shown in many ways. Lower incomes per capita are an obvious indicator, though the complexities of international exchange rates make these statistics questionable as measures of relative standards of living. However, when the monetary value of output per capita in Nigeria is less than 2 percent of that in the United States— and in Tanzania less than 1 percent[103]— that clearly cannot all be due to exchange rates. A more meaningful picture of differences in living standards is that average life expectancies are typically more than 70 years in Europe, Australia, the United States, Canada, and Japan, while average life expectancies in sub-Saharan Africa tend to be in the 50s or even the 40s.[104] Moreover, even these life expectancies in Africa have been achieved only with the help of medical and public health measures originating elsewhere in the world.

Within this general picture of lagging economic development in much of Africa, there have been historic and continuing variations in economic development and political organization among the various regions of the continent. One of the more fortunate regions of sub-Saharan Africa, from various perspectives, has been equatorial West Africa— what is today Nigeria, Ghana and their neighboring states. This region has some of the continent's more fertile soil, ample rainfall, and the Niger river system.[105] Here some of the larger African kingdoms arose. However, even in this relatively more favored region of Africa, the states and even empires that arose were often small by world standards. The Oyo empire, in what is today Nigeria, covered an estimated 150,000 square kilometers, which is smaller than the American state of Colorado. The Songhay empire, which included the rich river valleys of the central and western Sudan, was about the size of France, which is to say, smaller than Texas. Yet these were huge states by African standards, since most Africans lived in polities only a fraction as large, with national populations no larger than the populations of cities or even towns in the rest of the world.[106]

In Africa, as in other parts of the world, those peoples who were more fortunate often used their advantages to subjugate others. In West Africa, this subjugation took the form both of conquest and of enslavement of fellow Africans. Across the Sahara, in North Africa, more favorable geographic conditions, including harbors on the Mediterranean, also led to larger and more advanced societies. These too used their advantages to subjugate and enslave sub-Saharan Africans. In East Africa, some of the more geographically favored areas included harbors,[107] such as the large natural harbor on the off-shore island of Zanzibar and such mainland ports as Mombasa and Kilwa. All three became major centers for the trading and shipment of slaves, usually captured from less fortunate inland tribes.[108] Here the enslavers were typically either Arabs or people of mixed Arab and African ancestry and culture, known as Swahilis.[109]

THE GEOGRAPHY OF EASTERN AND WESTERN EUROPE

Among the geographic advantages of Western Europe lacking in Eastern Europe has been ready access to the oceans of the world. While no point in Western Europe is more than 350 kilometers from the sea, there are parts of Eastern Europe more than a 1,000 kilometers from the sea.[110] The warming influence of the Gulf Stream, which moderates the winters in Western

Europe, making them much milder than at corresponding latitudes in Asia or North America, is felt less and less to the east, where the continental climate is more bitterly cold in winter and the rivers are frozen for longer periods of time than the rivers of Western Europe.[111] The Baltic Sea is likewise frozen for months at a time.[112] In the Balkans, the mild, subtropical air of the Mediterranean is blocked off by mountain ranges from reaching much of Eastern and Southeastern Europe, including the hinterlands of the Dalmatian coast. Because of the isolating effect of coastal mountains along the Adriatic shore, winter temperatures inland in Sarajevo may be nearly 50 degrees colder than on the coast, little more than 100 miles away.[113] Many of the rivers of Eastern Europe flow into lakes or inland seas, rather than out into the open waters of the oceans, with their international trade routes, so that the benefits of low-cost access by water to the markets of the world— and the ideas of the world— have historically been far less available in the eastern part of the continent. In the rugged lands of the Balkans, largely lacking navigable rivers and cut off from access to the coast by mountains that come down close to the shore, it has been estimated that in Ottoman times the cost of shipping wheat overland just 100 kilometers exceeded the value of the wheat itself.[114]

The painful economic implications of such high transport costs extended well beyond wheat to commerce and industry in general, and also help explain the cultural insularity which long plagued the region. While Western European nations became the center of trade networks that reached all parts of the world, much of Eastern Europe, and especially the Balkans, remained regions of "self-sufficiency"[115]— which is to say, isolation, backwardness, and poverty. What foreign trade they had was based on supplying raw materials such as wool, grain, and lumber to Western European nations, from whom they bought manufactured goods.[116] Climate and soil are also less favorable in the Balkans, which lacks the more consistent rainfall and more fertile soils of northwestern Europe.[117] The fact that land capable of supporting human life often occurs in isolated patches in mountain valleys has meant that Balkan settlements have often developed in isolation from one another, as well as from the outside world.

For Russia, the colder winter climate of Eastern Europe, compared to Western Europe, means that, although the country has an abundance of rivers, those rivers are not abundantly available for use the year around, nor are the northern seaports, which are likewise frozen a substantial part of the year. Russia's warmer southern ports on the Black Sea have had to connect to the outside world through the narrow straits of the Bosporus and the Dardanelles, controlled by the Turks and by the Byzantines before them. Only after an 1829 treaty were Russian ships allowed through these straits, thus making large-scale grain shipments from Russia economically feasible.[118] The difference that this made is indicated by the fact that Russian grain could then undersell Croatian grain on the Dalmatian coast, since the Russian grain was shipped at low cost by water and the Croatian grain by land,[119] even though the latter was shipped for shorter distances.

While many of the Slavic lands lack the natural resource abundance of Western Europe, Russia's rich deposits of coal, oil and other resources make it one of the most fortunate countries of the world in that regard.[120] However, only relatively recently in its history have Russia's human resources allowed it to realize much of the potential of its natural resources for, as late as the end of the nineteenth century, the vast majority of Russians were still illiterate. As in other regions of the world, physical resources alone have meant little when the complementary human capital was missing.

THE GEOGRAPHY OF THE WESTERN HEMISPHERE

While, in narrowly physical terms, the lands and waters of the Western Hemisphere were the same for the indigenous peoples as they would later be for the transplanted populations from Europe, the complete absence of horses, oxen, cattle, and sheep in the Western Hemisphere before the arrival of the Europeans was momentous in its implications for food supply in general, agriculture in particular, and above all for the size of the cultural universe available to any given Indian tribe, nation, or civilization. Horses and camels made the Silk Road a highway stretching thousands of miles across the Eurasian land mass to connect China with Europe, but nothing comparable was possible in the Western Hemisphere to connect the

Iroquois on the Atlantic seaboard of North America with the Aztecs of Central America. Italians could acquire spaghetti from China but the Iroquois could acquire nothing from the Aztecs, or even be aware of their existence.

Agriculture in the Western Hemisphere was inherently limited to what could be accomplished without animal muscle power to carry or to pull loads or to plow the land, as well as to supply manure to maintain the fertility of farms. Land transport in general was obviously severely limited in the loads and the distances that were possible without animals. Even the navigable waterways were limited in their capacities to move cargo by the absence of pack animals and draft animals to transport these cargoes when they reached land. Indian canoes plied the inland and coastal waterways of the hemisphere long before the white man arrived, but larger vessels with greater cargo capacity would have exceeded the severe physical and economic limits of a land without the kinds of animals needed to make larger cargoes economically viable. Llamas were available as pack animals in limited regions of South America and dogs were used by Eskimos and by some North American plains Indians to pull loads, but these animals did not compare with horses or oxen in what they could transport.

As in much of sub-Saharan Africa, not only were loads and distances limited physically in the Western Hemisphere by an absence of the needed animals, the particular kinds of things that would be economically feasible to trade at considerable distances were even more limited economically to those things whose concentrated value could repay high transport costs, often involving human porters. Tons of grain, for example, could be shipped for hundreds of miles in Europe but not in the Western Hemisphere before the Europeans arrived and brought pack animals and draft animals. Even in those regions of the Western Hemisphere that had networks of waterways comparable to those in Western Europe, limitations on land transport limited cargoes transported by water. Moreover, limitations on the scope and range of trade were also limitations on the scope and range of cultural interchanges.

Specific geographic barriers— the Amazon jungle, the Rocky Mountains, or the vast desert in what is today the southwestern United States— were of course major barriers to large-scale cultural interactions in pre-Columbian times, but the absence of animals for transport was a more general barrier to long-range cultural interactions throughout the Americas. While these barriers were not as severe as the geographic barriers in parts of sub-Saharan Africa, they were more formidable than those in much of Europe and Asia.

The absence of herd animals like sheep and cattle, as well as the absence of load-bearing or load-pulling animals like horses and oxen, had another consequence— an absence of the many diseases carried by such animals and often acquired by human beings living in close proximity with these animals. While, in one sense, the absence of such diseases was of course a benefit, their absence also meant an absence of biological resistance to many potentially devastating diseases such as smallpox. So long as such diseases did not exist in the Western Hemisphere, the Indians' lack of biological resistance to them was of no consequence. But, once people from Europe began arriving with these diseases, the consequences were momentous, not only for those indigenous populations stricken and devastated by these diseases at the time, but also for the historic transfer of North and South America from the indigenous peoples to the European invaders. The most invincible of these invaders proved to be not the Europeans themselves but the invisible carriers of their diseases, whose existence neither they nor the Indians suspected.

The fact that the Eurasian land mass stretches predominantly east and west, while the Western Hemisphere land masses stretch predominantly north and south, means that advances in agriculture and animal husbandry could spread more readily over far more vast distances in the Old World than in the New. Plants and animals are more similar in the same latitudes, while more drastic climate changes accompany north-south movement. Thus rice cultivation could spread across Asia to Europe and ultimately to North America, but bananas could not spread from Central America to Canada. Nor could many of the animals adapted to the tropics survive in the colder climates to the north or south, so that knowledge of how to hunt or domesticate these animals was similarly restricted in how far it would be applicable, even if such knowledge could be transmitted over long distances. Moreover, the northern temperate zone and the southern temperate zone of the Western Hemisphere were too far apart to make any sharing of knowledge between them feasible in pre-Columbian times. In short, climate, like other aspects of geography, limited the size of the cultural universes of the indigenous peoples of the Western Hemisphere.

The geographical environment of the Western Hemisphere itself changed with the European conquest. Vast herds of new animals were transplanted from Europe, along with the invisible transplanting of a whole new disease environment and a whole new technology from Europe. These transplantations changed the lives of the indigenous peoples, as well as allowing the European settlers to bring much of their cultural world to the Americas. Mounted Indian warriors with herds of cattle became a "traditional" way of life on the western plains of the United States, for example, while the gauchos who herded cattle for Spanish landowners on the Argentina pampas were often part or full-blooded Indians as well.

Such physical features of the Western Hemisphere as natural harbors and rivers reaching deep inland from the sea now became far more important economically after the arrival of white invaders and settlers in ships developed in Europe, but better adapted to exploit New World conditions than were the canoes of the Indians. Those parts of the Western Hemisphere most highly developed by the Europeans were not the same as those that had been most highly developed by the indigenous peoples. Whereas the most advanced Indian civilizations developed in Central America and in the Andes Mountains, the most advanced regions developed by Europeans were those regions whose geography was most like that of Western Europe— places with natural harbors and broad coastal plains, criss-crossed by rivers deep enough to carry large ships and, eventually, places with the mineral deposits needed to build an industrial society.

Only in the narrowest physical sense was the geographic setting of the Western Hemisphere the same for the indigenous peoples and for the Europeans. The flora, the fauna, and the disease environments were changed radically, and the natural features of the land and the waters acquired a much wider range of possibilities as a result of this, as well as because of the new technology brought from Europe. Moreover, the technology that the Europeans brought to the Western Hemisphere was not simply the technology of Europe. Because of the geography of the Eurasian land mass, Europeans were able to bring to bear in the Western Hemisphere the cultural features of lands extending far beyond Europe, but incorporated into their civilization. Europeans were able to cross the Atlantic Ocean in the first place because they could steer with rudders invited in China, calculate their position on the open sea through trigonometry invented in Egypt, using numbers created in India. The knowledge they had accumulated from around the world was preserved in letters invented by the Romans and written on paper invented in China. The military power they brought with them increasingly depended on weapons using gunpowder, also invented in Asia. The cultural confrontation in the Western Hemisphere was, in effect, a one-sided struggle between cultures acquired from vast regions of the earth against cultures from much more narrowly circumscribed regions of the New World. Never have the advantages of a wider cultural universe been more dramatically or more devastatingly demonstrated than in the conquests that followed.

EDUCATIONAL

ISSUES

TRAGI-COMIC "EDUCATORS"

American education would be comic if it were not so tragic in its consequences.

Recently I received a letter from a school teacher, asking for an autographed picture for his class because it would "ultemetly" help his students to have me as a "roll model." Atypical? Let us hope so. But a few years ago a study showed the average verbal Scholastic Aptitude Test score for aspiring teachers to be 389 out of a possible 800.

With American school children repeatedly finishing at or near the bottom on international test comparisons, the response of the education establishment has been to seek ever more non-academic adventures to go off on.

Among the latest of these "innovations"— a magic word in the wonderland of educational Newspeak— is called "outcome-based education." Like so many of the catch phrases that come and go, it means nothing like what it seems to mean.

Education based on outcomes might sound to many people like finally creating a bottom line for schools, teachers and administrators to be judged by. Nothing of the sort. It is yet another way of getting away from academic work and indulging in psychological and ideological indoctrination. This is called advancing beyond "rote learning" and teaching school children to "think." Many in the media gullibly repeat such phrases, without the slightest investigation of what concretely they mean in practice.

When concrete specifics leak out, there is often shock, as there currently is in California, where tests are intruding into students' family lives and sexual experiences, among other things. The parents who first protested were predictably labelled "the religious right," but now even some in the educational establishment itself have begun to express concern.

Not long before, parents in Connecticut who objected to film strips of naked couples engaged in sex (both homosexual and heterosexual) being shown in the local junior high school were labelled "fundamentalists" and "right-wing extremists," even though they were in fact affluent Episcopalians.

There are all sorts of prepackaged responses to critics of the public schools, of which this was just one. Recently, I got a first-hand dose of these stereotyped responses when addressing a class of students who are being trained for careers as teachers. They seemed disconcerted by the questions I put to them:

"Suppose you are wrong? How would you know? How would you test for that possibility?"

The very thought that the dogmas they were repeating with such fervor might be open to question or subject to evidence seemed never to have occurred to them. This was a far more ominous sign than their merely being wrong on particular beliefs. How can they teach anybody else to think if they themselves have not reached this elementary level of logic?

By "thinking" too many educators today mean teaching children to reject traditions in favor of their own emotional responses. Objections to such propaganda programs are called objections to letting children think. Anything less than a blank check for indoctrination is called "censorship."

In light of such non-academic activities in our public schools, it can hardly be surprising that American youngsters do so badly on academic tests administered to youngsters around the world. Nor is it surprising that academic work is so readily abandoned for social experiments, ideological crusades and psychological manipulations by educators whose own academic performances have long been shown to be substandard.

It is not uncommon for those few schools with traditional academic programs to have waiting lists of parents who want to get their children admitted. When admission is on a first-come, first-serve basis, it is not uncommon for parents to camp out overnight in hopes of getting their children into institutions that will teach them substance instead of fluff and politically correct propaganda.

Against this background, recent campaigns for a longer school day and a longer school year are farcical. If a lack of time is the problem, why are schools wasting so much time on innumerable non-academic activities? Moreover, there is no amount of additional time that cannot be wasted on similar pursuits.

No small part of the existing problems of the public schools is that the school day is already so long and boring, with so little to challenge the ablest students. Moreover, many average and below-average students who have lost all interest are retained by compulsory attendance laws for years past the point where their presence is accomplishing anything other than providing jobs for educators.

Despite orchestrated hysteria about "the dropout problem," what many apathetic students most need is a cold dose of reality that they can only get out in the workaday world— not in the never-never land of the public schools.

SCIENTISTS NEED
NOT APPLY

It wasn't really news when American high school seniors came in at or near the bottom in recent international math and science tests, but many newspapers gave it headlines. The real story, however, is that three distinguished American scientists, one a Nobel laureate, offered to help design California's new science curriculum last fall— and their offer was rejected.

What this little episode shows is that creating a curriculum in our public schools is not about getting children educated. It is about doing things that teachers like and can handle. The last thing they want is a science curriculum designed by somebody with a Nobel prize.

First of all, the education establishment is not about to give up any part of its turf, much less require its teachers to try to do things that many of them are simply not capable of doing. Anyone familiar with the dismal test scores of students who take education courses knows that it is Utopian to expect such people to turn out students able to stand up to international competition in mathematics and science.

The kinds of people who come out of departments and schools of education need a curriculum focussed on non-academic activities and goals that make them feel good and feel important. Social engineering, indoctrinating students with trendy attitudes and enrolling them in various crusades for environmentalism and "public service" projects fill that bill.

Teaching kids about the square on the hypotenuse is not where it's at, as far as these kinds of teachers are concerned. It is unreasonable, almost cruel, to expect them to play that role. If that role needs to be played— and it definitely does— then we need to get different people teaching in our public schools. Without that, everything else is cosmetics and pouring more money down a bottomless pit.

Where are we to find these new people? They are everywhere. Private schools find them in such abundance that people with solid educations— but often without education courses— can be hired at lower salaries than the public schools pay. Elaborate restrictions on entry to the public schools are necessary to protect existing teachers from their competition.

The National Education Association may make a lot of noise about not wanting "unqualified" people in the classrooms. But this is Newspeak. What they mean by "unqualified" are people who have not jumped through the hoops of the education schools and education departments. Nobel prize-winners are unqualified by this definition.

Our public schools have not failed. They have succeeded incredibly in carrying out their own agenda, wholly at cross-purposes with the goals of those who pay the bills and those who send their children to them to be educated.

Every demand for better results is turned into a demand for more money. Every failure is blamed on parents, television, "society." The greatest success of the educators has been in keeping their own performance off the agenda, the rewards wholly unrelated to classroom performance, and sanctions virtually nil in a tenure system where firing one teacher can cost hundreds of thousands of dollars.

At no point does the education establishment have to put up or shut up. In even the worst of the worst schools, typically in low-income and minority neighborhoods, the teachers unions bitterly oppose letting even a fraction of the students go to private schools with vouchers.

This is not caprice or racism. It is naked self-interest. The whole house of cards could come tumbling down if the failing students from ghetto schools go elsewhere and succeed.

Various studies have already shown that happening. But studies are for scholars and policy wonks. What would be politically devastating would be to have millions of people, all across America, seeing it with their own eyes.

This is only one area where preventing lofty rhetoric from being put to empirical tests is crucial for the education establishment. Federal money plays a key role in this.

This money and the controls that go with it mean that "whole language," "whole math," bilingual education and the rest of the trendy agenda can be mandated from Washington, so that what results they produce will simply not matter.

The survival of the existing system depends on results not mattering.

HIGHER EDUCATION
AND LOW COMEDY

If you liked *Alice in Wonderland*, you will love *The Chronicle of Higher Education*, the trade publication of academia. Just one issue— dated the 13th of October,* for those who are superstitious— contained stories about professors that make you wonder if academics ever grow up.

In that issue, New York University advertised for a faculty member in the performing arts, for what it called "Gendered Performance." The specific duties of the job include "drag, transvestite performance, queer theories." The university "encourages applications from women and members of minority groups." None of the usual stuff about being an "equal opportunity/affirmative action employer," that we have grown so used to that its internal contradictions no longer bother us.

In what literally became a federal case, a professor at the University of Alabama injected his religious views into a physical exercise class that he taught. When the university told him to stop it, he sued. Eventually, he lost the case but gained tenure, so perhaps it was a stand-off.

Had he injected left-wing ideologies into wholly unrelated subjects like biology or English— as happens routinely on many campuses across the country— he would never even have been warned.

Another federal case arose because a professor who cussed out his students in class ignored warnings to stop it and then sued when he was eventually fired. This case went as far as the U. S. Circuit Court of Appeals, where the prof lost.

This does not mean that mere profanity in the classroom is grounds for firing a professor. It was only the fact that the profanity was directed against students that got the professor in trouble. All across the country, and all up and down the academic pecking order from Harvard to Podunk A & M, four-letter words are O.K. in the classroom under the broad umbrella of "academic freedom."

---

* 1993.

340

Professors who go to bed with their students are also covered by "academic freedom," even if they are not covered by anything else. The same issue of *The Chronicle of Higher Education* includes letters from readers responding to an essay by a professor at the University of Massachusetts who says that he has remedied the problem of female students whose virginity was "unnaturally prolonged."

Again, we need have no fear for this professor's job, either for his actions or his subsequent boasts about them. It is very unlikely that his de-flowering of student virgins will add to the congestion of the federal courts.

At Stanford, incidentally, male students can get into all kinds of trouble under a new and vaguely worded "sexual harassment" code, but Stanford professors who go to bed with their students are merely admonished.

Mob rule is also alive and well in academia. The same issue of *The Chronicle of Higher Education* reports on a riot at U.C.L.A. in which students attacked the faculty club. They "broke the club's plate-glass windows, wrecked furniture, and carved graffiti in its walls."

In due course, they were rewarded by the U.C.L.A. administration's promise to add two new professors in Chicano Studies and to exempt ethnic studies programs from any of the cutbacks that might hit such non-relevant subjects as mathematics or economics.

The *Chronicle* also reported on similar events at Berkeley: "Several hundred protesters ran through two campus buildings and pulled fire alarms. No one was arrested."

Note that "protestors" is the politically correct term for rioters, vandals, or storm troopers on campus.

Although these "protestors" are routinely reported as expressing their "rage" or their "anguish," one of the Cornell student leaders may have captured the real spirit more accurately when he said, after various organized acts of vandalism there: "This is very exciting."

One of the reasons we don't hear much about such campus outbursts in the general media, the way we did back in the 1960s, is that they happen too often to be news— and are accepted too supinely to have the drama of conflict.

Experienced academic administrators have also learned how to minimize the number of such episodes by various techniques of pre-emptive surrender.

By staying constantly aware of what is most likely to set off the most volatile elements among the students and faculty, administrators know which way to bend academic policy and whose misconduct or outright crimes are to be overlooked.

This game works only because many outside of academia are not even aware that the game is being played. But, before deciding whether to contribute to dear old Alma Mater, it might be well worthwhile to subscribe to *The Chronicle of Higher Education*. You could end up deciding to donate to medical research instead, or to invest the money in the marketplace, where it will help create jobs.

SUCCESS CONCEALING
FAILURE

Among the many clever and misleading defenses of our failing educational system is the assertion that our universities are among the highest rated in the world and Americans consistently win a disproportionate number of Nobel Prizes. Both these claims are accurate— and irrelevant.

While Americans won the lion's share of Nobel Prizes in 1999, not one of these winners was actually born in the United States. If people born and raised elsewhere choose to come here and use their talents, fine. But do not claim their achievements as some vindication of the American educational system.

On the contrary, the painful question must be faced: Why were a quarter of a billion native-born Americans unable to win a single Nobel Prize in 1999, when a relative handful of naturalized Americans won so many? This is not a vindication but an indictment of our educational system.

The top-rated American universities owe much to the generosity of American donors and the largess of the American government, which enable them to attract top scholars from around the world. It is research, rather than teaching, which determines world rankings, and our well-financed Ph.D.-granting universities are unquestionably among the best at research.

However, when you look at who gets degrees in what, again the picture is very disturbing as regards the track record of the schools and colleges that prepare students to enter these top-rated institutions.

Less than half the Ph.D.s in engineering and mathematics awarded by American universities are received by Americans. Even more revealing, there is a systematic relationship between the difficulty of the subject and the percentage of American doctorates which go to Americans.

In a mushy and undemanding field like education, more than four out of five of the doctorates go to Americans. It is when you start getting into the physical sciences that the proportion drops to barely half and when you get into engineering and math that Americans become a minority among American university Ph.D.s.

Foreign graduate students predominate so heavily in difficult subjects that a common complaint across the country is that undergraduate math courses are being taught by people whose English is hard to understand, quite aside from the difficulty of learning the subject itself.

Yes, our top universities are the cream of the crop. They are so good that people educated in American schools and colleges cannot hold their own with foreign students who go there.

The period during which American public schools have had declining test scores has coincided with the period during which Americans were increasingly displaced by foreigners in the graduate programs of our top universities.

In every field surveyed by the Council of Graduate Schools, the proportion of graduate degrees in the United States going to Americans has declined over a period of two decades, with the worst declines being in the more demanding subjects.

A closer look at those Americans who do still hold their own in difficult fields is also revealing. Nearly 22 percent of all Ph.D.s in engineering received by Americans are received by Asian Americans. Here is the group that is most out of step with the prevailing easy-going education, with its emphasis on "self-esteem" and other mushy fads. Again, this is not a vindication but an indictment of what is being done in our public schools.

Ironically, people who go ballistic when minorities are "under-represented," relative to their percentage of the population, whether among college degree recipients or in various professions, remain strangely silent when the whole American population is under-represented among those receiving postgraduate degrees in science, math and engineering in their own country.

Such under-representation might be understandable if the United States were some Third World country just entering the world of modern science and technology. It is staggering in a country whose people led the world in such things in the recent past. Clearly something has gone very wrong in our educational system.

Our current world leadership in science and technology, like our leadership in Nobel Prizes, owes much to people who never went through the dumbed-down education in American schools and colleges.

Many come from countries which spend far less per pupil than we do but get far better results for their money.

"PUBLIC SERVICE"—
OR DISSERVICE?

According to one of the college guides, students taking English 6 at Amherst "must volunteer" to tutor in a local high school. Orwellian Newspeak has become so common in academia that apparently no one sees the irony in the notion that a student "must volunteer."

Trendy colleges and high schools across the country are requiring "service" to "the community" as ways of earning academic credit or even as a precondition for receiving a diploma. In Washington, "national service" is now in vogue— another "feel good" idea financed with other people's money.

What is truly frightening is the casual ease with which so many people believe that they can define what is and is not a "service" to the society.

Stanford University's law school, for example, sends students and others over to the nearby ghetto in East Palo Alto to fight against the expulsion of hoodlums from the public school system there. It would be hard to imagine a greater disservice to the black community than allowing their children's education to be disrupted, undermined or destroyed by trouble-makers, thugs and young drug dealers who want to remain classified as "students" only so that they can remain on campus and sell crack.

We all know what road is paved with good intentions. Whether students working in a soup kitchen or a homeless shelter or doing any of the other "services" being performed for academic credit are in fact making society better or worse, on net balance, is an open question, not a foregone conclusion.

When weighing the immediate benefits against the promotion of dependency and the enlargement of an army of idle people on the streets, creating more than their share of mischief and crime, the net balance is at least debatable.

But, even if we assume that every "service" performed by students is in fact a service, that still leaves the very large question as to why it should be performed by students.

No doubt rescuing people from burning buildings would be a service, but do we want students to do it— or is this something we want left to professionally-trained fire departments? Even where students have the necessary skills, is there no value to their time in doing what they are in schools and colleges to do— namely to develop their minds in preparation for a lifetime of contributing to society in a wide variety of ways?

Why are parents making financial sacrifices to send their children to colleges and universities, if the time they spend there is of so little value that it can be used to perform the chores of amateur social workers? Does an academic institution have so little dedication to its own mission that it must seek tangential activities to justify its existence?

Much that is done in the name of "service" not only fails to advance the development of thinking skills but positively hinders it by substituting emotionally indelible but superficial experiences.

To call such activities an experience in "real life" is fraudulent, because real life is not pre-arranged for you by academic institutions. Nothing is more misleading than such phony "realism."

Like so much that is done under cover of academic pieties, "service" to others is all too often a means of propagandizing the students themselves with "politically correct" ideologies, getting them to feel sorry for those supposedly neglected or abused by society, and to see handouts and social engineering as the solution to social problems.

It can hardly be coincidental that those pushing hardest for "service" requirements in schools and colleges are so often also those pushing for the "politically correct" agenda of the left in general. This is a cheap way of insinuating their ideologies into inexperienced and vulnerable young minds, without having to make a real case in an open way that could be challenged by others.

Like so much else that is done by those who treat education as the continuation of politics by other means, the lasting damage that is done is not by insinuating a particular ideology, for people's ideologies change over time, regardless of what they were taught. The lasting damage is done to the development of critical thinking.

Learning to think, and to know what you are talking about, is a full-time occupation. Nowhere is this more true than in the formative years. Even naturally bright people can turn out to be nothing more than clever mush heads if the discipline of logic and the analytical dissection of many-sided empirical evidence is slighted for the sake of emotional "experiences."

Defining "service" and assigning it to others may be a big ego trip for some educators, but only to the extent that they are willing to sacrifice or prostitute education itself.

"FORCED TO VOLUNTEER"

The term "liberal" originally referred politically to those who wanted to liberate people— mainly from the oppressive power of government. That is what it still means in various European countries or in Australia and New Zealand. It is the American meaning that is unusual: People who want to increase the power of government, in order to accomplish various social goals.

Typical of what liberalism has come to mean in the United States today is a proposal by California Governor Gray Davis that the state's colleges and universities make "community service" a graduation requirement. His plan immediately won the unconditional support of the state's largest newspaper, the liberal *Los Angeles Times*. There was no sense of irony in its editorial claiming beneficial effects for "students who are forced to volunteer."

Forced to volunteer. That is the Orwellian notion to which contemporary liberalism has sunk.

"What could be wrong," the *L.A. Times* asks, "with teaching students, as the governor puts it, that 'a service ethic. . .[has] lasting value in California?'" A community service requirement "could reap a valuable return in a new generation of civically minded citizens."

Here we get to the heart of the so-called community service idea. Its central purpose is to create a certain set of attitudes in the students. It is compulsory submission to state-sponsored propaganda for the liberals' vision of the world. That is what students must be "forced to volunteer" for.

What is wrong with the idea of a free people, using their own time as they see fit, for those things that matter most to them, instead of being pawns in a propaganda program more in keeping with what happens in totalitarian societies? What is wrong with each individual defining for himself or herself what being civic minded means, instead of having the government define it and impose it?

In a country where more than 90 million people already volunteer for civic projects of their own choosing, why must students be drafted to become "volunteers" for environmentalism or other causes dear to the heart of the *Los Angeles Times* or Governor Davis? The casual arrogance of those who define for other people what is a "community service" is breathtaking.

Environmentalism can— and does— reach extremes where it is a disservice to the community. Programs which subsidize the homeless lifestyle can turn able-bodied men into idle nuisances on streets across America. We need not try to force liberals to believe this. But they have no right to use the educational system to force young people to submit to propaganda for their vision.

The totalitarian mind-set behind the liberal vision shows through in innumerable ways. There are no institutions in America where free speech is more severely restricted than in our politically correct colleges and universities, dominated by liberals.

Students who openly disagree with the left-wing vision that they are being taught in class can find themselves facing lower grades and insults from the professor in front of their classmates and friends. Offend the hyper-sensitivities of any of the sacred cow groups on campus— even inadvertently— and stronger punishments, ranging up to suspension or expulsion, can follow.

On the other hand, if minorities, homosexuals or radical feminists want to shout down speakers they don't like or engage in vandalism or other mob actions to promote their agendas, that's OK.

Campus ideological conformity extends to faculty hiring and even the inviting of outside speakers to give talks on campus. There are scholars of international distinction who would never be offered a faculty appointment in most Ivy League colleges and universities today because they do not march in step ideologically. You can find a four-leaf clover faster than you can find a Republican in most sociology departments or English departments.

If the liberals are teaching any civics lesson with all this, it is that power is what matters— including the power to force people to keep their thoughts to themselves, if those thoughts do not conform to the liberal vision.

Community "volunteer" work is only the latest in a series of uses of schools and colleges to propagandize political correctness, instead of teaching individuals to think for themselves. If liberals do not understand that this is the antithesis of liberation, that makes it all the more urgent for the rest of us to recognize that fact and that danger.

GOODBYE TO SARA
AND BENJAMIN?

Recently a couple of dear friends visited us, bringing with them their six-year-old twins, Sara and Benjamin. These are some of the loveliest children you could meet— not just in appearance, but in their behavior. They are the kinds of kids you can see in Norman Rockwell paintings, but less and less in the real world.

Now Sara and Benjamin are going off to public school and it is painful to imagine what they might be like a year from now. Most people are unaware how much time and effort the public schools— and some private schools— are putting into undermining the values and understanding that children were taught by their parents and re-orienting them toward the avant-garde vision of the world that is fashionable in the educational establishment.

Today's educators believe it is their job to introduce children like Sara and Benjamin to sex when and in whatever manner they see fit, regardless of what the children's parents might think. Raw movies of both heterosexuals and homosexuals in action are shown in elementary schools.

Weaning children away from their parents' influence in general is a high priority in many schools. Children sit in what is called a "magic circle" and talk about all sorts of personal things, with the rule being that they are not to repeat any of these things to anyone outside this magic circle. Sometimes they are explicitly told not to repeat what is said to their parents.

Some handbooks for teachers warn against letting parents know the specifics of what is being done and provide strategies for side-stepping parental questions and concerns. Glowing generalities and high-sounding names like "gifted and talented" programs conceal what are nothing more than brainwashing operations to convert the children from their parents' values to the values preferred by educational gurus.

Right and wrong are among the earliest targets of these programs. "There is no 'right' way or 'right' age to have life experiences," one widely used textbook says. Another textbook tells children that they may listen to their parents "if you are interested in their ideas." But, if there is a difference of opinion, parent and child alike should see the other's point of view "as different, not wrong."

Sara and Benjamin are only six years old and are going into the first grade. Will any of this apply to them? Yes. There is a textbook designed for children ranging from pre-school to the third grade, which tells children about their rights and about asserting those rights to parents. Whenever "things happen you don't like," you have "the right to be angry without being afraid of being punished" it says.

In other words, don't take any guff off mommy and daddy. Who are they? As another textbook says, parents are just "ordinary people with faults and weaknesses and insecurities and problems just like everyone else." In many of the textbooks, movies and other material used in schools, parents are depicted as old-fashioned people who are out of touch and full of hang-ups.

What these smug underminers of parents fail to understand is that the relationship of a child to his or her parents is the most extraordinary relationship anyone is likely to have with another human being. No one else is likely to sacrifice so much for another person's well-being. If the avant-garde ideas taught to children in schools blow up in their faces, it is the parents who will be left to pick up the pieces, not the glib gurus.

Most of the classroom teachers who carry out such educational fashions and fetishes have no idea where they originated or what their underlying purpose is. In reality, many of the techniques and strategies used to break down the child's values, personality and modesty are straight out of totalitarian brainwashing practices from the days of Stalin and Mao.

That is the origin, for example, of the personal journals that children are required to keep in schools all across the United States. These journals are not educational. Gross mistakes in spelling, grammar and usage are ignored, not corrected. These journals are gateways to the psyche and the first step in manipulating little minds.

As our friends departed and went off to enrol their children in the public schools, I could not help wondering if I had seen Sara and Benjamin for the last time. Would they still be the same sweet children after they have been used as guinea pigs by those who claim to be trying to educate them?

CHOOSING A COLLEGE

When a student at New York University committed suicide recently, it was the 6th suicide at that same institution this year. The suicide of someone in the prime of life, and getting an education that promises a bright future, should be much rarer than it is. But NYU is not unique by any means.

Back when I taught at UCLA, one morning on my way to my office I saw an attractive and well-dressed young woman lying quietly in the bushes next to the building, apparently asleep. But the presence of police nearby alerted me to the fact that something was wrong. She had jumped from the roof of the building to her death.

When I taught at Cornell, it averaged a suicide a year.

Selecting a college for a young man or young woman to attend is more than a matter of looking up the rankings and seeing where the chances of admission look good. How the atmosphere of the college matches the personality of the individual can mean far more than anything in the college catalogue or the pretty brochures.

Some young people are not yet ready for coed living arrangements and the pressures and dangers that can lead to. Some are at risk on a campus with widespread drug usage. Some students can get very lonely when they just don't fit in.

Sometimes there is no one to turn to and sometimes the adults they turn to on campus have nothing but psychobabble to offer.

Late adolescence and early adulthood are among the most dangerous times in people's lives, when one foolish decision can destroy everything for which parents and children have invested time and efforts and hopes for years.

Too many know-it-alls in the high schools and colleges urge or warn parents to get out of the picture and let the child decide where to go and what to do. A high school counselor once told me that I would be "kept informed" of the decisions that she and my daughter were making as to which colleges to apply to.

Apparently there are enough sheep-like parents these days to let "experts" take control of their children at a critical juncture in their lives. But these "experts" suffer no consequences if their bright ideas lead some young person into disaster. It is the parents who will be left to pick up the pieces.

Too often parents are pushed to the sideline in the name of the child's need for freedom and autonomy. But what is presented to parents as a need to set their children free as young adults is too often in fact abandoning those children to the control of others. The stakes are too high to let that happen.

From the moment a student sets foot on a college campus, a whole apparatus of indoctrination can go into motion, in the name of "orientation," so as to mold each young mind to politically correct attitudes on everything from sex to "social justice."

Colleges used to say that their job was to teach the student how to think, not what to think. Today, most colleges are in the business of teaching the student what to think or "feel."

Many colleges— even many of the most prestigious— lack any real curriculum, but they seldom lack an ideological agenda. Too often they use students as guinea pigs for fashionable notions about how to live their own lives.

As for education, students can go through many colleges selecting courses cafeteria-style, and graduate in complete ignorance of history, science, economics, and many other subjects, even while clutching a costly diploma with a big name on it.

Students who make more astute choices from the cafeteria of courses can still get a good education at the same colleges where their classmates get mush. But seldom is there any curriculum that ensures a good education, even at prestigious colleges.

Parents need to stay involved in the process of choosing a college. They need to visit college campuses before making application decisions— and remember to take their skepticism with them. They also need to ask blunt questions and not take smooth generalities for an answer.

An indispensable guide to the atmosphere on various college campuses, and the presence or absence of a real curriculum, is a huge book titled *Choosing the Right College*. It is head-and-shoulders above all the other college guides.

Among other things, it tells you which colleges have a real curriculum, rather than a cafeteria of courses, as well as the kind of atmosphere each campus has. The latter is always important and sometimes can even be a matter of life and death.

THE IDIOCY OF "RELEVANCE"

One of the many fashionable idiocies that cause American schools to produce results inferior to those in other countries is the notion that education must be "relevant" to the students— and especially to minority students with a different subculture.

It is absurd to imagine that students can determine in advance what will turn out to be relevant to their progress as adults. Relevance is not something you can predict. It is something you discover after the fact— and after you have left school and are out in the real world.

When I was in high school, I was puzzled when a girl I knew told me that she was studying economics, because I had no idea what that was. It never occurred to me to take economics, so it was certainly not something that seemed relevant to me at the time.

Had someone told me then that I would someday spend more than 30 years as an economist at a think tank, I wouldn't have known what they were talking about, because I had no idea what a think tank was either.

When students are going through medical school, they may not see the relevance of all the things they are taught there. But someday they may have a patient at death's door, whose life may depend on how well the doctor remembers something he was taught in medical school— and whose relevance may not have been all that clear to him at the time.

People who have already been out in the real world, practicing for years whatever their particular specialty might be, have some basis for determining which things are relevant enough to go into a curriculum to teach those who follow. The idea that students can determine relevance in advance is one of the many counterproductive notions to come out of the 1960s.

The fetish of "relevance" has been particularly destructive in the education of minority students at all levels. If the students do not see immediately how what they are studying applies to their lives in the ghetto, then it is supposed to be irrelevant.

How are these students ever going to get out of the poverty of the ghetto unless they learn to function in ways that are more economically productive? Even if they spend all their lives in the ghetto, if they are to spend them in such roles as doctors or engineers, then they are going to have to study things that are not peculiar ("relevant") to the ghetto.

Worst of all, those teachers who teach minority students things like math and science, whose relevance the students do not see, may encounter resistance and resentment, while those teachers who pander to minority students by turning their courses into rap sessions and ethnic navel-gazing exercises capture their interest and allegiance.

Some educators embrace relevance out of expediency, rather than conviction or confusion. It is the path of least resistance, though that path seldom leads upward. By the time minority students get out into the real world and discover the uselessness of what they were taught in "relevant" courses, it is too late for them— but they are no longer the teachers' responsibility.

Even as a graduate student in economics, I did not see the relevance of a little article by Friedrich Hayek, titled "The Use of Knowledge in Society," that was assigned reading in Milton Friedman's course at the University of Chicago. A few years later, however, I was beginning my own teaching career and had to teach a course on the Soviet economy— about which I knew nothing.

As I read through many studies of the Soviet economy in preparation for teaching my course, and was puzzled by all the strange and counterproductive economic practices in the Soviet Union, it then began to dawn on me that what Hayek had said applied to these otherwise inexplicable Soviet actions. For the first time, years later, I saw the relevance of what he had written.

Fast forward another 15 years. I was now writing a book that would be a landmark in my career. It was titled *Knowledge and Decisions*— a 400-page book building on what Hayek had said in a little essay.

Just a few years ago, I was stopped on the streets of San Francisco by a young black man who shook my hand and told me that reading *Knowledge and Decisions* had changed his life. He had seen the relevance of these ideas— at a younger age than I had.

JULIAN STANLEY AND BRIGHT CHILDREN

Bright children and their parents have lost a much-needed friend with the death of Professor Julian Stanley of Johns Hopkins University. For decades he not only researched and ran programs for intellectually gifted students, he became their leading advocate in books and articles.

His efforts were very much needed. Unusually bright children are too often treated like stepchildren by the American educational system.

While all sorts of special classes and special schools are created for various categories of students, there is resistance and even hostility to the idea of creating special classes or schools for intellectually gifted students.

Not only are such elite public schools as New York's Stuyvesant High School and the Bronx High School of Science rare, they are under political pressure to admit students on other bases besides pure academic achievement. So is San Francisco's Lowell High School, where ethnic "balance" affects admissions decisions.

While it is well known that the average American student does poorly on international tests, what is not so well known is that gifted American students lag particularly far behind their foreign counterparts.

Professor Julian Stanley pointed out that the performance level of gifted American students "is well below both the level of their own potential and the achievement levels of previous U.S. generations." In other words, our brightest kids have been going downhill even faster than our average kids.

Part of the reason is undoubtedly the general dumbing down of American education since the 1960s but what has also been happening since the 1960s has been a preoccupation with the "self-esteem" of mediocre students and a general hostility to anything that might be construed as intellectual elitism.

Even classes in so-called "gifted and talented" programs are too often just more of the same level of work as other students do, or trendy projects, but not work at a greater intellectual depth.

Sometimes, as Professor Stanley has pointed out, it is just busy work, in order to keep bright students from being bored and restless when classes are being taught at a pace far too slow for very intelligent youngsters.

It is not at all uncommon for the brightest students to become problem students in their boredom and frustration, to develop negative attitudes towards education and society— and to fail to develop their inborn talents.

Julian Stanley did not just criticize existing practices. He created special programs for unusually bright high school students on weekends and during the summer at Johns Hopkins University. The success of these programs has inspired similar programs at Purdue University and elsewhere.

Such programs have not only produced academic benefits, the gifted students in such programs have expressed an almost pathetic gratitude for finally being in a setting where they are comfortable with their peers and are viewed positively by their teachers.

In regular public school classrooms, these gifted students have been too often resented by their classmates and their teachers alike. Some teachers have seemed glad to be able to catch them in occasional mistakes.

Given the low academic records of most public school teachers, it is hard to imagine their being enthusiastic about kids so obviously brighter than they were— and often brighter than they are. No small part of the gross neglect of gifted students in our public schools is the old story of the dog in the manger.

Julian Stanley made a unique contribution to the development of gifted children, both directly through his program at Johns Hopkins and indirectly through his research and advocacy. Fortunately, he is survived by collaborators in these efforts, such as Professors Camilla Persson Benbow and David Lubinski of Vanderbilt University.

The effort must go on, both to stop the great waste of gifted students, whose talents are much needed in the larger society, and for the humane purpose of relieving the frustration and alienation of youngsters whose only crime is being born with more intellectual potential than most of those around them.

ANTI-"ELITISM" IN EDUCATION

It caused twinges of nostalgia when I read about Stuyvesant High School's classes of 1947 and 1948 holding a joint 50th year reunion. I went to New York's Stuyvesant High School but, by 1948, I had dropped out and was getting my education from the school of hard knocks.

The most startling part of the story was that Stuyvesant High School now has an Olympic-sized swimming pool. No way could the old and battered school that I went to have such a thing. This was a new and palatial Stuyvesant, at a new location overlooking the Hudson River. The school I went to overlooked the tenements on the lower east side.

Stuyvesant is and was something very unusual in American public schools— a high school that you had to pass a test to get into. Back in my day, only about a third of those who took the test got in. And our junior high school in upper Manhattan limited how many would even be allowed to go take the test.

The Bronx High School of Science used the same test as Stuyvesant, while Brooklyn Tech used an even tougher one. While such schools have always been rare outside of New York, and have come under increasing political pressure to be more "open," even within the city, they provided both the poor and the society with golden opportunities. You could come from the poorest family in town and yet receive a high-quality education that would enable you to go anywhere and compete with the graduates of Exeter or Andover.

The envy-laded concept of "elitism" has been thrown at these and other high-quality schools across the country, and political pressures have been put on them to admit more students without such high academic skills. Seldom do the people who push such notions stop to think that you cannot let everyone go to Stuyvesant without its ceasing to be the kind of school that makes them want to go there.

You cannot teach everyone at the same pace, unless that pace is slowed down to accommodate the lowest common denominator. There are kids who can handle calculus in the tenth grade— and others who struggle with it in college.

Ironically, many so-called minority "leaders" have led the charge to get top-level public schools to admit students on some basis other than academic achievement. Yet no one needs such schools more than poor and disadvantaged children who want to rise to higher levels in the economy and the society.

There may not be a high percentage of minority students who are currently able to take advantage of outstanding high schools. But part of the reason is that the elementary schools in many minority communities have deteriorated so much since the days when I went to P.S. 5 in Harlem. Kids in P.S. 5 in the 1940s had test scores equal to those of white kids in the immigrant neighborhoods on the lower east side.

One revealing statistic is that more black boys went to Stuyvesant in 1938 than in 1983— even though the black population of New York was much smaller in 1938. Moreover, those black kids who did not want to make the long trip from Harlem down to Stuyvesant had some decent high schools available to them closer to home.

In Washington, D. C., the similarly old and battered Dunbar High School has likewise been replaced by a modern building. But the new Dunbar is not even in the same league with the old school that once housed the finest black high school in the nation. Back in the 1930s, Dunbar's all-black student body had test scores above the national average, while going to a rundown school with overcrowded classes.

The old Dunbar turned out the first black general, the first black federal judge, the first black cabinet member, . . . and on and on. More than one-fourth of the Dunbar graduates who later graduated from Amherst College during the period from 1892 to 1954 graduated Phi Beta Kappa. Of the few high-level black military officers in World War II, more than two dozen with ranks of major to brigadier general were Dunbar graduates.

You might think that black political leaders would move heaven and earth to preserve a school like this. But you would be wrong. The Marion Barry generation of "leaders" in Washington have promoted the same class-warfare envy found in the larger society and denounce the very memory of this "elitist" school, whose quality was destroyed overnight back in the 1950s, by turning it into a neighborhood school.

May Stuyvesant and other high schools like it escape the sad fate of Dunbar.

THE OLD NEIGHBORHOOD

Recently I got together with a guy who grew up in my old neighborhood in Harlem, around 145th St. and St. Nicholas Avenue. As we talked about the old days, the world that we discussed seemed like something from another planet, compared to today.

There have been many good changes but, on net balance, it is doubtful whether kids growing up in our old neighborhood today have as much chance of rising out of poverty as we did.

That is not because poverty is worse today. It is not. My friend remembers times when his father would see that the children were fed but would go to bed without eating dinner himself. There were other times when his father would walk to work in downtown Manhattan— several miles away— rather than spend the nickel it took to ride the subway in those days.

Things were not quite that grim for me, but my family was by no means middle class. None of the adults had gotten as far as the seventh grade. Down South, before we moved to New York, most of the places where we lived did not come with frills like electricity or hot running water.

Some people have said that my rising from such a background was unique. But it was not. Many people from that same neighborhood went on to have professional careers and I am by no means either the best known or the most financially successful of them.

Harry Belafonte came out of the same building where my old school-mate lived. One of the guys from the neighborhood was listed in one of the business magazines as having a net worth of more than $200 million today.

If anyone had told me then that one of the guys on our block was going to grow up to be a multi-millionaire, I would have wondered what he was drinking.

Not everybody made it. One of my old buddies was found shot dead some years ago, in what looked like a drug deal gone bad. But many people from that neighborhood went on to become doctors, lawyers, and academics— at least one of whom became a dean and another a college president.

My old school-mate retired as a psychiatrist and was living overseas, with servants, until recently deciding to return home. But home now is not Harlem. He lives out in the California wine country.

Why are the kids in that neighborhood today not as likely to have such careers— especially after all the civil rights "victories" and all the billions of dollars worth of programs to get people out of poverty?

What government programs gave was transient and superficial. What they destroyed was more fundamental.

My old school-mate recalls a teacher seeing him eating his brown bag lunch in our school lunchroom. A forerunner of a later generation of busybodies, she rushed him over to the line where people were buying their lunches and gave some sign to the cashier so that he would not have to pay.

Bewildered at the swift chain of events, he sat down to eat and then realized what had happened. He had been given charity! He gagged on the food and then went to the toilet to spit it out. He went hungry that day because his brown bag lunch had been thrown out. He had his pride— and that pride would do more for him in the long run than any free lunches.

His father also had his pride. He tore to shreds a questionnaire that the school had sent home to find out about their students' living conditions. Today, even middle-class parents with Ph.D.s tamely go along with this kind of meddling. Moreover, people like his father have been made superfluous by the welfare state— and made to look like chumps if they pass it up.

What the school we went to gave us was more precious than gold. It was an education. That was what schools did in those days.

We didn't get mystical talk about the rain forests and nobody gave us condoms or chirped about "diversity." And nobody would tolerate our speaking anything in school but the king's English.

After finishing junior high school, my friend was able to pass the test to get into the Bronx High School of Science, where the average IQ was 135, and yours truly passed the same test to get into Stuyvesant High School, another selective public school that today's community "leaders" denounce as "elitist."

The rest is history. But it is a history that today's young blacks are unlikely to hear— and are less likely to repeat.

WASTING MINDS

Menlo-Atherton High School in an affluent California community is considered to be very good academically, at least by current standards, in an era of dumbed-down education. Yet its problems are all too typical of what is wrong with American education today.

A gushing account of the free breakfast program and other giveaways to lower-income students who attend this high school recently appeared in the *San Francisco Chronicle*, while the *Wall Street Journal* presented a sympathetic account of the school's attempt to teach science to students of very disparate abilities in the same classroom.

Even more revealing, the villains in this story— as seen by both the educators and by the reporter for the *Wall Street Journal*— are those parents who want their children to get the best education they can, instead of being used as guinea pigs for social and educational experiments.

Creating a science class that included students of very different levels of ability and motivation was one of these experiments. These disparities were especially great in this particular school, since its students come from both highly-educated, high-income families in Silicon Valley and low-income Hispanic and other minority families from the wrong side of the local freeway. Moreover, they were fed into the high school from their respective neighborhood schools with very different standards.

The science class turned out to be a disaster. While the principal admired the good intentions behind it, he also admitted "it was almost impossible to pull off in real life. The disparity was too great." Yet the science teacher blamed the ending of this experiment on affluent parents who "really didn't give it a chance" and the principal spoke of the "heat" he got from such parents, who "thought their kids were being held back by the other kids, that their children's chances for MIT or Stanford were being hampered."

This was seen as a public relations problem, rather than as a perfectly legitimate complaint from parents who took their responsibilities for their children's education seriously— more seriously than the "educators" who tried to be social workers or world savers.

In a school where 40 percent of the children are Hispanic and 38 percent are white, sharp income and cultural divisions translate into racial or ethnic divisions plainly visible to the naked eye. This also arouses the ideological juices and emotional expressions of resentment, both inside and outside the school.

Stanford University's school of education is reluctant to send its graduates to teach at Menlo-Atherton High School because the latter doesn't make enough effort to overcome "inequalities" and uses politically incorrect "tracking" by ability "to keep affluent kids protected from the other kids."

In other words, a school that takes in fifteen-year-olds from radically different backgrounds is supposed to come up with some miracle that can make them all equal in ability, despite fifteen years of prior inequality in education and upbringing. Somehow, there are always magic solutions out there, just waiting to be found, like eggs at an Easter egg hunt.

Make-believe equality at the high school level fools nobody, least of all the kids. White kids at Menlo-Atherton refer to the non-honors courses as "ghetto courses," while a black kid who enrolled in honors courses had his friends demand to know why he was taking "that white-boy course."

If you are serious about education, then you need to start a lot earlier than fifteen years old to give each child a decent shot at life in the real world, as distinguished from make-believe equality while in school. Ability grouping or "tracking"— so hated by the ideological egalitarians— is one of the best ways of doing that.

If you were a black kid in a Harlem school back in the 1940s, and you had both the desire and the ability to get a first-rate education, it was there for you in the top-ability class. The kids who were not interested in education, or who preferred to spend their time fighting or clowning around, were in other classes and did not hold back the ones who were ready to learn.

Our egalitarian dogmas prevent that today, destroying low-income and minority youngsters' opportunities for real equality. A mind is indeed a terrible thing to waste, especially when it is the only avenue to a better life.

DO FACTS MATTER?

Recently a young black man sent a thoughtful e-mail to me. Among his kind comments was an expression of sympathy for the racism that he thought blacks of my generation must have experienced in going through college.

In reality, it is his generation of blacks who have encountered more racial hostility on campus than mine. But his was an understandable mistake, given how little attention is paid to accuracy in history and how often history is used as just a propaganda tool in current controversies.

My college and early postgraduate education took place during the 1950s— that decade before the political left brought its light into the supposed darkness of the world. During the decade of the 1950s I attended four academic institutions— a year and a half at a black institution, Howard University, three years at Harvard, where I graduated, nine months at Columbia, where I received a master's degree, and a summer at New York University.

I cannot recall a single racist word or deed at any of these institutions. The closest thing to a racist remark was made about a student from England who was referred to as "nasty, British and short." It was I who made that remark.

My first encounter with racism on campus came toward the end of my four years of teaching at Cornell in the 1960s— and it erupted after black students were admitted under lower standards than white students and were permitted to engage in disruptions that would have gotten anyone else suspended or expelled. I was not the target of any of these racist incidents, which were directed against black students. I received a standing ovation in the last class I taught at Cornell.

One of the black students at Cornell moved in with my wife and me for a while, because she was afraid of both the black militants and those whites who were increasingly bitter about both the trouble that the militants were causing and the way the administration was catering to them. This backlash was not peculiar to Cornell, but developed on many campuses and became so widely known over the years that it acquired a name— "the new racism."

In the late 1980s, for example, a dean at Middlebury College reported that— for the first time in her 19 years at that institution— she was getting requests from white students not to be housed with black roommates. People who had taught at Berkeley for similar periods of time likewise reported that they were seeing racist graffiti and hate mail for the first time. More than two-thirds of graduating seniors at Stanford said that racial tensions had increased during their years on campus.

All this is the direct opposite of what you might be led to believe by the politically correct history or theory of race in America. The endlessly repeated mantra of "diversity" implies that such things as group quotas and group identity programs improve race relations. Quotas are often thought to be necessary, in order to create a "critical mass" of black students on campus, so that they can feel sufficiently comfortable socially to do their best academic work.

That there are various opinions on such things is not surprising. What ought to be surprising— indeed, shocking— is that these social dogmas have been repeated for decades, with no serious effort to test whether or not they are true.

When elite liberal institutions like Stanford, Berkeley and the Ivy League colleges have been scenes of racial apartheid and racial tensions on campus, have more conservative institutions that have resisted quotas and preferences been better or worse in these respects? My impression has been that they have been better. But the real problem is that we must rely on impressions because all the vast research money and time that have gone into racial issues have still not even addressed this key question that goes to the heart of the dogmas pervading academia today.

Over a period of more than three decades, during the first half of the 20th century, 34 students from all-black Dunbar High School in Washington were admitted to Amherst College. Of these, about three-fourths graduated and more than one-fourth of these graduates were Phi Beta Kappa. But there were never more than a handful of black students at Amherst during that era— nothing like a "critical mass."

Is this evidence conclusive? No. But it is evidence— and the political left avoids evidence like the plague.

DEEP TROUBLE FROM
SHALLOW PEOPLE

A recent news story told of an Asian-American girl applying to Wesleyan University with test scores in the 1400s and a Dominican girl applying to the same institution with test scores in the 900s. A member of the admissions committee recommended against admitting the Asian-American girl and in favor of admitting the Dominican girl.

Why? The Dominican girl had more handicaps to overcome. Besides, the admissions committee member, added, "I am willing to take a chance on her."

Actually, he is taking no chance whatever. He will not lose one dime if this girl fails miserably. The people who will lose will be the people who have contributed their money to Wesleyan University, in order to promote education, and instead have their contributions used to make some admissions committee member feel like a little tin god.

The Dominican girl herself will also lose if she goes in unprepared and fails, when she could have gotten some additional preparation first and then applied to a less demanding college, where she would have a better chance of success. Above all, American society loses when such feel-good self-indulgences undermine the connection between performance and reward, reducing incentives for high-ability, low-ability, and average students alike.

Unfortunately, this admissions committee member is by no means unique. All across the country, at both elite institutions and non-elite institutions, admissions committee members act as if they have some deep insight which enables them to judge individuals' inner motivations, rather than their actual record— and to pick out those who will become "leaders," as that undefined term is conceived in the psychobabble of the day.

This would be incredible arrogance, even if admissions committees were composed of higher-caliber people than they usually are. Given the kinds of third-raters who too often find their way onto admissions committees, even at elite colleges, it is a tragic farce. After all, someone who has graduated from Harvard or M.I.T. with top honors is likely to have a lot better career options than becoming a staffer on an admissions committee at Harvard or M.I.T.

The mystery is not why shallow people do shallow things. The mystery is why we put so much arbitrary power in the hands of shallow people— especially when that power would be dangerous in anybody's hands. College admissions committees are just one example.

Social workers have gotten gestapo-like powers to snatch people's children from their homes on the basis of unsubstantiated charges that have never even been heard in a court of law. They can deny an orphan a decent home because the family that wants to adopt does not fit their arbitrary notions and unproven theories. Minority children have especially been denied homes with white families who want them and instead have been consigned to a life of drifting from one foster home to another for years on end.

Our public schools are the most massive examples of arbitrary power put into the hands of shallow people. While social work and college admissions committees usually fail to attract people of high intelligence, the public schools positively repel many such people by requiring them to sit through years of unbelievably stupid education courses, as a precondition for a permanent career.

Students' whole futures depend on getting a decent education, but their teachers may prefer using them as guinea pigs for the latest fads, such as psychological manipulation, social engineering and proselytizing for politically correct causes. If— heaven help us— the child is very bright and is bored to death by the drivel presented by shallow teachers, the answer may well be to drug the student with Ritalin, rather than let him or her become restless.

The time is long overdue for us all to recognize that there are tasks and roles beyond the capacity of even the most intelligent people— and that only the least intelligent are likely to take on those impossible roles. It has been known for centuries that fools rush in where angels fear to tread.

There is no need to abolish college admissions committees, social workers or teachers. But their roles need to be kept within much narrower and more defined bounds. Above all, what they do must be subjected to some test other than what makes them feel good or what sounds good to their like-minded colleagues. Otherwise, we are putting the inmates in charge of the asylum.

"GOOD" TEACHERS

The next time someone receives an award as an outstanding teacher, take a close look at the reasons given for selecting that particular person. Seldom is it because his or her students did higher quality work in math or spoke better English or in fact had any tangible accomplishments that were better than those of other students of teachers who did not get an award.

A "good" teacher is not defined as a teacher whose students learn more. A "good" teacher is someone who exemplifies the prevailing dogmas of the educational establishment. The general public probably thinks of good teachers as people like Marva Collins or Jaime Escalante, whose minority students met and exceeded national standards. But such bottom line criteria have long since disappeared from most public schools.

If your criterion for judging teachers is how much their students learn, then you can end up with a wholly different list of who are the best teachers. Some of the most unimpressive-looking teachers have consistently turned out students who know their subject far better than the students of teachers who cut a more dashing figure in the classroom and receive more lavish praise from their students or attention from the media.

My own teaching career began at Douglass College, a small women's college in New Jersey, replacing a retiring professor of economics, who was so revered that I made it a point never to say that I was "replacing" him, which would have been considered sacrilege. But it turned out that his worshipful students were a mass of confusion when it came to economics.

It was much the same story at my next teaching post, Howard University in Washington. One of the men in our department was so popular with students that the big problem every semester was to find a room big enough to hold all the students who wanted to enroll in his classes. Meanwhile, another economist in that department was so unpopular that the very mention of his name caused students to roll their eyes or even have an outburst of hostility.

Yet when I compared the grades that students in my upper level economics class were making, I discovered that none of the students who had taken introductory economics under Mr. Popularity had gotten as high as a *B* in my class, while virtually all the students who had studied under Mr. Pariah were doing at least *B* work. "By their fruits ye shall know them."

My own experience as an undergraduate student at Harvard was completely consistent with what I later learned as a teacher. One of my teachers— Professor Arthur Smithies— was a highly respected scholar but was widely regarded as a terrible teacher. Yet what he taught me has stayed with me for more than 40 years and his class determined the course of my future career.

Nobody observing Professor Smithies in class was likely to be impressed by his performance. He sort of drifted into the room, almost as if he had arrived there by accident. During talks— lectures would be too strong a word— he often paused to look out the window and seemingly became fascinated by the traffic in Harvard Square.

But Smithies not only taught us particular things. He got us to think— often by questioning us in a way that forced us to follow out the logic of what we were saying to its ultimate conclusion. Often some policy that sounded wonderful, if you looked only at the immediate results, would turn out to be counterproductive if you followed your own logic beyond stage one.

In later years, I would realize that many disastrous policies had been created by thinking no further than stage one. Getting students to think systematically beyond stage one was a lifetime contribution to their understanding.

Another lifetime contribution was a reading list that introduced us to the writings of top-notch minds. It takes one to know one and Smithies had a top-notch mind himself. One of the articles on that reading list— by Professor George Stigler of Columbia University— was so impressive that I went to graduate school at Columbia expressly to study under him. After discovering, upon arrival, that Stigler had just left for the University of Chicago, I decided to go to the University of Chicago the next year and study under him there.

Arthur Smithies would never get a teaching award by the standards of the education establishment today. But he rates a top award by a much older standard: By their fruits ye shall know them.

BEHIND "PUBLISH
OR PERISH"

"**P**ublish or Perish: A Well-Liked Professor is Bumped by Rutgers."
That was the headline in the *New York Times*.
Perhaps the most surprising thing about the story was that anyone was
surprised— or even considered it news. The story was all too familiar. Professor
Richard L. Barr had won three awards for his teaching during his six years at
Rutgers University and was then told that his contract would not be renewed.

This has happened so often, on so many campuses across the country,
that many in academia regard teaching awards as the kiss of death. Two of
my college roommates went into teaching and each won teaching awards,
one at Harvard and the other at M.I.T. Each was then told that his contract
would not be renewed.

A quarter of a century ago, a colleague who had the same experience at
Brandeis University referred to the teaching award as "travel money."

From time to time, college and university presidents announce that they
are going to restore the balance between teaching and research by giving
more emphasis to teaching. This too is usually treated in the media as if it
were news. What would be news would be if it happened. Few professors are
prepared to jeopardize their careers by depending on such statements— and
those who do usually end up paying the price for their naiveté.

Although things have been going this way for some decades now, colleges
and universities were not always like this from time immemorial. How did
they get this way and what can be done about it?

They got this way, in large part, because of the vast sums of money made
available for research by federal and state governments. Unlike other social
problems whose solutions are said to require more "funding," this is a
problem that can be dealt with by budget-cutting.

Medical, scientific and engineering research produce many benefits for
the larger society. But English professors writing far-out drivel produce
benefits only for English professors trying to publish to keep from

perishing. It is hard to imagine how the world would be any worse off, on net balance, if the entire output of the sociology profession over the past 50 years had never been published.

Unfortunately, colleges and universities have become bloated with research money, spawning all sorts of expensive boondoggles and layers of bureaucracy to oversee the boondoggles. To keep all this going, academic institutions have to have the kind of professors who can keep the research money flowing in. Thus means have become ends in themselves— and have sacrificed the original ends of education.

One of the few legitimate points made in defense of publishing requirements is that it is very difficult to make valid assessments of teaching quality. Popularity is not profundity, so there must be some other way to determine whether a professor has "the right stuff." Subjecting his thinking to quality control by others in his profession via the publishing route makes more sense than depending on whether he wows the sophomores three mornings a week. Every campus has its flashy mush heads on the faculty.

However, you do not need a constant stream of articles and books tumbling off the press on the heels of one another, in order to tell whether you have someone with a serious mind or just a clever talker. The argument against Professor Barr at Rutgers— at least what appeared in the news story— was not that he hadn't published anything or that its quality was low, but that his collection of publications was "not so thick as the usual packet for tenure."

If publication is going to be a numbers game, then we need to recognize that Charles Darwin, Adam Smith, and Sir Isaac Newton would never have gotten tenure because they didn't grind it out as fast as an ambitious assistant professor at an Ivy League university. There is no inherent reason why tenure decisions have to be made the same way for all individuals in all fields and in all institutions. Indeed, there is no inherent reason to have tenure in the first place.

The "academic freedom" argument for tenure gets more and more threadbare as more and more scholars work in think tanks where there is no tenure. The research coming out of these think tanks is at least as independent as that coming out of universities operating under the stultifying conformity of political correctness.

Can academia kick its research addiction cold turkey? Only if those who supply the money learn to "just say no."

GLIMPSES OF ACADEME

The *Chronicle of Higher Education* recently gave us its annual glimpse into the minds of college professors. Perhaps the most salient item, for parents preparing to send their children off to college, was the professors' response to the statement, "The faculty are rewarded for good teaching." Only 13 percent agreed with that statement. There was no "gender gap"; it was 13 percent for both male and female professors.

The professors surveyed were not just from big-name research universities. Research has become the golden idol across most of the academic spectrum. On many campuses, bringing in research money is a precondition for getting tenure. It is not just research but research money that talks, especially to the academic administration, which gets its cut as "overhead" reimbursement.

Although fewer professors declared that their own primary interest was in research, as compared to teaching, they also know which side their bread is buttered on, so most have published in academic journals more than once and 16 percent have published 20 or more times in such journals, not counting their books and monographs.

The *Chronicle of Higher Education*'s survey did not get into the quality or relevance of what is published, but editors of leading scholarly journals in various fields have said that much of the research that is done is a waste of time. However, the money received to finance time-wasting research is just as valuable to a college or university as money received to find a cure for fatal diseases.

About two-thirds of all professors spend no more than 12 hours per week in the classroom. This includes 35 percent who spend no more than 9 hours per week in the classroom. A roughly comparable amount of time is spent preparing for classes, but these two activities put together add up to what most people would consider to be a part-time job.

Not all the other time is spent in research. There are also committee meetings and work for clients, for those who are consultants. About 40 percent of the women and 48 percent of the men worked as paid consultants. Then there are off-campus meetings at various watering holes under the general heading of "professional activities."

A recent supplement to the *Chronicle of Higher Education* listed conventions, symposia and conferences for academics for the coming year. This supplement was about the size of a tabloid newspaper, but with much smaller type, so that most of its 40 pages had 5 columns of listings of these academic get-togethers.

Most were in places like the Caribbean or Hawaii and the hotels were typically Hiltons, Sheratons or Hyatt Regents. I did not notice any meetings being held in Gary, Indiana, or Newark, New Jersey, nor any meetings in the Motel 6 chain.

As for the quality of students the colleges are getting these days, only 24 percent of professors agreed with the statement, "Faculty feel that most students are well-prepared academically" and only 12 percent agreed that most of the students are "very bright."

These professors were by no means all old-timers, nostalgic for a different world. Fewer than 10 percent of these faculty members received their highest degree before the 1960s. Most received their highest degree within the past 20 years. In other words, the professors consider the students ill-prepared even by the more lax standards of recent times.

The least surprising finding from this survey is that liberalism reigns supreme in academe. Three-quarters of the professors are for a "national health care plan" to "cover everybody's medical costs." However, a statement that the undergraduate curriculum should be based on Western civilization gets only a 53 percent agreement.

Only 28 percent thought it essential or very important to teach students the classic works of Western civilization, while 80 percent thought that colleges should encourage students to get involved in "community service" activities and nearly a third thought that this should be a requirement for graduation.

In other words, Plato and Shakespeare should be optional, but such things as working in a homeless shelter should be pushed or compelled.

Perhaps the most encouraging statistic is that 31 percent of these professors are considering early retirement. On the other hand, it is by no means clear that their replacements will be any better.

BIOGRAPHICAL
SKETCHES

CAROLINA IN
THE MORNING

Henry was about to become a father again— if he lived that long. He probably knew he was dying, though he may not have known exactly what he was dying of. Black people in the South did not always go to doctors when they were sick, back in 1929. In any case, when Willie became pregnant, Henry went to his Aunt Molly to ask if she would take the baby to raise. There were four children to take care of already and there was no way that Willie could take care of a new baby, all by herself, while trying to earn a living without Henry.

Aunt Molly was the logical person to turn to. Her own children were grown and she had recently tried to adopt a baby boy, but the baby's mother had changed her mind and returned after a few months to take him back. It was an experience that may have left a lasting mark on Aunt Molly. But she was willing to try again. Willie's new baby turned out also to be a boy— and Henry was dead before he was born.

Willie had little choice but to go through with the arrangements that Henry had made with his aunt. Feeding four children and herself on a maid's wages turned out to be very hard, even after she gave the baby to Aunt Molly to raise as her own. Still, Willie managed somehow to visit the little boy regularly, even though Aunt Molly lived 15 miles away. These visits had to be carefully managed, as if Willie were visiting Aunt Molly, so that the boy— "little Buddy," she called him— would never suspect that he was adopted, much less that Willie was his mother. This was in fact managed so well that he grew up to adulthood with no memory of the woman who came by unobtrusively in his early years, supposedly to visit with the adults.

Willie could see that her son had a better material life than she could give him. He wore better clothes than her other children and had toys that she could not buy them. He was also loved, and perhaps even spoiled, in his new family. Aunt Molly's youngest child was a 20-year-old girl named Birdie, who was especially fond of him. Still, Willie sometimes returned home in tears after a visit and spoke wistfully of someday being able to go get little Buddy and bring him back. But it was not to be. Willie died in childbirth a few years later.

Aunt Molly was very possessive of the boy, perhaps in reaction to having had the other little boy taken away from her after she had become attached to him. Whatever the reason, when she eventually moved away from North Carolina to New York, some relatives said that she did it to put distance between the boy and those who knew the family secret that he was adopted. Though there were in fact other, more compelling reasons to move to New York, it is significant that those who knew her could believe that she would do it to preserve her secret. In any event, she severed all links between the boy and his past. His brothers and a sister in North Carolina all knew of his existence, but he did not know of theirs, and they heard about him as he grew up in New York only through the family grapevine.

His original family continued to refer to the boy as Buddy, but he never heard that name as he grew up, for his new family renamed him in infancy. Birdie prevailed upon Aunt Molly to name him after her boyfriend, Thomas Hancock. Aunt Molly's legal name was Mamie Sowell.

My earliest memories were of Mama and Daddy, and Birdie and Ruth. Daddy was my favorite— and I was his. He was a construction worker, a short man, and an elder in the church until I came along. One of the scenes that came down in family legend was his standing up in front of the congregation, with me in his arms and a baby bottle in his pocket, explaining that he now had new duties to take the place of those he was resigning in the church.

Daddy had a certain gruffness about him but was usually good-natured with people and was extremely patient with me. However, he became angry whenever he thought anyone was not treating me right.

He would fuss with Mama if he found out that she had spanked me while he was at work. (I was, of course, the usual source of this information). Once he almost got into a fight with a man on the street, who inadvertently frightened me by pointing his walking stick in my general direction, while trying to give another man directions. Mama was more enigmatic, with changeable moods. A woman with very little education— she wrote her name with painful slowness— she was nevertheless shrewd and even manipulative, but she was also emotional and subject to an unpredictable sentimentality which sometimes brought her to tears over small things.

Birdie and I were very close in those early years, and remained so on into my teens. She taught me to read before I was four years old. We read stories in the comics together, so some of the first words I learned to spell were words like "pow" and "splash." Birdie also read to me some of the usual children's stories. One story that I found sad at the time, but remembered the rest of my life, was about a dog with a bone who saw his reflection in a stream and thought that the dog he saw had a bigger bone than he did. He opened his mouth to try to get the other dog's bone— and of course lost his own when it dropped into the water. There would be many occasions in life to remember that story.

Birdie gave me most of the mothering I received in these early years, with Mama being more concerned with teaching me practical things and maintaining discipline. But Mama also put some of her practical responsibilities on Birdie or others. One summer, when I was playing outside barefoot, as Southern kids did then, I stepped on some jagged glass and suffered a bad gash on the bottom of my feet. As I came running up the long back stairs, crying and yelling and trailing a stream of blood, Mama came out on the back porch, took one look at the scene and seemed to turn sick. She said, "Oh, Gosh!" and went back inside to lie down on the sofa, sending Birdie out to take care of me. Birdie soon had me calmed down and comforted, and my foot bandaged up.

Ruth was a few years older than Birdie and was a more reserved person, with an occasional enigmatic smile and a more worldly air about her. But she was softer and warmer than her more sophisticated exterior would suggest. However, to me Ruth was always an adult, while Birdie and I sometimes played rough-house together, as if we were both kids.

A fifth person who entered my life so early that I was unaware of a time when I did not know him was Birdie's new boyfriend, Lacy. He was a debonair young man with a gift for words and a way of jauntily tilting his head as he strode along. In later years, after he and Birdie were married, he would recall that the first time he saw me, I was swinging on the front gate, with my diapers very much in need of changing.

Lacy was to become a major influence in my formative years, especially after Daddy and Mama broke up and we moved to New York. Though it would be many years later before I would understand Lacy's background, he had himself been adopted and had not always been treated well. He not only took a special interest in me, but was also quick to speak up if he thought I was being unfairly punished or even unfairly criticized. Over the years, he many times charmed Mama out of punishing me.

A more remote figure was Mama's oldest child, Herman, who was married and lived in the country on his own farm. Herman was a dignified, even stuffy, individual. He also owned a car, which to us was a sign of prosperity well beyond our reach. He was not a fan of mine nor I of his. We seldom saw each other, however, and showed no sign of suffering from each other's absence. Herman's wife, Iola, was an attractive woman with a certain genteel quality, and she had several children from an earlier marriage. One of them, Gladys, was about three years older than me. One Sunday, when I fell asleep in church, Gladys picked me up and held me on her lap. When I woke up, I was outraged at the indignity of having a mere girl holding me like a baby. I tore loose from Gladys' embrace and punched her. Apparently this shocked even Herman's low expectations of me.

By this time, Birdie was in her mid-twenties, Ruth was around thirty, and Herman was in his early forties. This meant that Mama was already elderly when I was a small child— more like my grandmother than my mother. My grandmother was in fact her sister. They were part of the first generation of our family born after slavery.

The first house I remember our living in was a wooden house at 1121 East Hill Street in Charlotte, North Carolina. It was near the bottom of a tall hill on an unpaved street, like most of the streets in the black neighborhoods. Daddy put a paved walkway in our yard and made a little window in the kitchen door in the back. Both were marks of distinction in which we took pride.

Like most of the houses in the area, ours had no such frills as electricity, central heating, or hot running water. There was a living room, a kitchen and two bedrooms. In the kitchen there was a wood-burning stove, with the brand name "Perfection" on it. They said it was the first word I spelled. The toilet was a little shed on the back porch. To take a bath, you heated water on the kitchen stove and poured it into a big metal portable tub. For heat in the winter, we had the stove, a fireplace in the living room, and a kerosene heater. For light at night, we had kerosene lamps.

It never occurred to me that we were living in poverty, and in fact these were some of the happiest times of my life. We had everything that people around us had, except for a few who had electricity and one lady who had a telephone. Once I tagged along with Ruth when she went to her job as a maid in the home of some white people. When I saw two faucets in their kitchen, I was baffled and said:

"They sure must drink a lot of water around here."

When Ruth showed me that there was hot water coming out of one of the faucets, I thought it was the most amazing thing.

We grew flowers in our front yard, but there was no back yard, just an alley way. On the side of the house, however, there was a space fenced in, where we kept chickens. I can still remember the shock of seeing a chicken's head chopped off and watching the headless body running frantically around the yard, until it collapsed in the convulsions of death. But all that was forgotten when it reappeared hours later at dinner, completely transformed into beautiful and delicious pieces of Southern fried chicken.

Here and there I encountered white people— usually grocers, peddlers, or occasionally policemen. But white people were almost hypothetical to me as a small child. They were one of the things that grown-ups talked about, but they had no significant role in my daily life. That remained largely true until after we left Charlotte, when I was almost nine years old, and moved to New York. Then it came as a shock to me to be told that most of the people in the United States were white. Most of the people I had seen were black, everywhere I went. In reading the Sunday comics, I was not bothered by the fact that the characters were almost always white, but I could not understand why some of these characters had yellow hair. I had never seen anybody with yellow hair, and doubted that there were any such people.

The only books I remember seeing in our home during those early years in North Carolina were the Bible and books of the children's stories from which Birdie read to me. Daddy read the newspaper and the grown-ups sometimes talked about things that were happening in the world. There was a war going on between the Ethiopians and the Italians, and I knew that we were on the side of the Ethiopians, though I am not sure that I knew why or what color either of them were. However, I did know that there was a young black boxer coming along and that we were all very proud of him— as a man, as well as a fighter. Some said that he was going to be a champion someday. His name was Joe Louis.

One news story that got Mama emotionally involved was the kidnapping of the Lindbergh baby. For reasons unknown, she became convinced that the convicted kidnapper, Bruno Richard Hauptmann, was innocent. She cried when he was executed. Some time later, after we had moved and Daddy and Mama had split up, we got a big white dog, who was given the name Bruno— even though it was a female dog. Later, Bruno had pups.

Daddy did not stop seeing me after he and Mama broke up. He came back regularly and once took me to where he was now living. He asked me if I wanted to come and live with him and I said "yes," but nothing came of it. A couple of years later, he and Mama reunited for a while, but it was not to last. I have no idea what their differences were.

Whenever I think of Daddy, I think of the joy of riding on his shoulders as a child. In fact, whenever I see a child riding on his father's shoulders, I still think of him. He was a good man, but it would be many years later before I would fully realize how good.

When Birdie and Lacy were courting, they often sat in the swing out on the front porch in the evenings. It was very romantic— just the three of us. They often let me sit in the swing beside them. I was fond of Lacy and looked up to him, but somewhere I had heard that he would take Birdie away, so I had mixed feelings, and I think they let me sit with them for reassurance.

Birdie and Lacy were high-spirited young people and even drank, despite Mama's disapproval. From them I acquired an early taste for beer.

One day, while Mama was away, I asked them for some beer. In order to discourage me, they said that I could have some only if I also drank some whiskey— which they knew I didn't like. However, I took them up on it and quickly downed some whiskey and then claimed my beer. This combination was pretty potent stuff for a five-year-old, so I became woozy and they became alarmed, fearing a scene when Mama returned. They had me lie down and I slept it off before she came back home. But I don't recall having any more taste for any form of alcohol for many years and, even in adulthood, I never became a really enthusiastic drinker.

Bruno's pups were growing and I became very fond of them, as I was of Bruno. One day, however, I was puzzled as she began walking away from the pups when they wanted to nurse from her. She was of course starting to wean them, but I had no idea what she was doing. To me, it seemed like a mean way to treat the little puppies, who looked so pitiful as they ran after her, yelping and trying vainly to keep up, with their short legs scrambling.

Finally, I pounced on Bruno and held her, so that the pups could catch up and get some milk. Fortunately, the grown-ups saw what was happening and explained to me one of the lessons of life, that pups must be weaned for their own good. That experience was also one that came back to me many times later, in my adult years.

Beginning about the age of four or five, my world began to contract painfully. The first loss was when Daddy and Mama separated, for though he came back to see me, it wasn't the same as having him there all the time. Then Lacy went north to New York City, to look for work and a better life. Once he had a foothold, he sent for Birdie and they were married in 1934 in New York. They returned in 1935 but, after a few months, they went back to New York again, for good. A year later, Ruth followed in their footsteps. By the time I was six, only Mama and I were left and we lived in a smaller place. To make matters worse, I came down with mumps and whooping cough, so that I couldn't go to school until I was seven. None of the kids my age were around any more on school days, so it was a lonely time.

There was a pretty little girl in our new neighborhood. She used to walk by our house around sunset and pat me on the back as she passed by, saying, "Hi, Tom."

I was tongue-tied and flustered, but Mama told me that just meant that the little girl liked me. Since I liked her too, I decided to show her in the same way. One day I turned and enthusiastically pounded her on the back as she passed. She collapsed like a house of cards, got up crying and ran home. She never spoke to me again and I was heart-broken. It was not the last time I was baffled by the opposite sex, nor perhaps they by me.

Another unsettling episode of this period was the only time that Ruth ever spanked me. I cannot recall what it was for, but it had something to do with her being up on a ladder. I cannot believe that I would have tried to pull the ladder out from under her, but it is hard to imagine Ruth's spanking me for anything less. At the time, however, I was highly indignant.

We moved again before I began school in September 1937. There was a house at 1212 East Brown Street, owned by some of our more prosperous relatives by marriage. It had acquired a reputation as a place where Sowells died, shortly after moving in. They were usually of advanced years when they decided to settle down there to retire, so it is not all that surprising that they died there. However, in a place and time where superstition was a force to be reckoned with, not many Sowells wanted to move into that house, which was considered haunted. But we were too poor to be able to afford superstition, so that was where we went.

It wasn't a bad house and it even had electricity. I remember listening to Bing Crosby on the radio there. The backyard was large enough for us to grow a considerable amount of vegetables, and there was a large tree that gave us apples. Someone planted a cotton plant, apparently for my benefit, so that a Southern boy should not grow up without knowing what cotton looked like. I remember Ruth's living there for a while and Daddy's living there for a while.

Bruno got into the habit of going off by herself on long excursions by a stream in the area. We would watch from the house until she disappeared around a bend. She would usually return much later. But one day she didn't return at all. To me, it was as if someone had died. It was part of a melancholy time, when I seemed to be losing a whole happier world of earlier years.

There was a knock on our door one day, but when Mama went to answer it, there was no one to be seen. Later, we learned that one of the young Sowell women had decided to brave the haunted house (after much teasing) and come to visit us. However, after she knocked on the door and saw Mama's silhouette coming down the hall— looking just like the silhouette of her dead Aunt Alma— she fled fast enough to be out of sight by the time the door was opened.

We enjoyed many a laugh recounting this incident to others, and it had a lasting effect in making me consider all superstition ridiculous.

A white fruit-and-vegetable peddler came by the neighborhood regularly in his horse-drawn wagon. One day he had his little girl— about my age— riding beside him. She decided to get down off the wagon and come join me where I was playing in the yard alone, while her father made his rounds on the street. We hit it off wonderfully, had a great time playing together, and waved happy good-byes when the time came for her to leave. But when I turned to Mama to enthuse about my new playmate, I found her unsmiling and even grim.

"You've just taken your first step toward the gallows," she said.

From then on, whenever the girl and her father came around, there was always some excuse why I was not available to play with her.

Another chapter of my life opened when I finally entered school in September 1937, a year older than the other kids in my class because of my year out with illness. Mama did not take me to school herself, but instead paid one of the older girls in the neighborhood to take me with her. Mama often tended to avoid confronting situations where she would feel awkward and out of place.

I went along quietly enough with the girl— until we were out of sight. Then I told her in no uncertain terms that there was no way I was going to have some girl bring me to school. She conscientiously insisted, but when I discovered that words were not enough, I resorted to throwing rocks— and arrived at school in splendid isolation.

It was an attractive little building and I was fortunate enough to have a pleasant teacher. My memories of the first grade include nothing that I learned. I already knew how to read and count before going to school. My only memories are of fights, being spanked by the teacher, having crushes on a couple of girls and the long walk to and from school.

The next year, in the second grade, I encountered one of those mindless educational routines, which happened to work to my advantage in this case. During the reading period, a child would be asked to read aloud until he or she made a mistake, after which the book would then be passed on to the next child. (There was no such thing as issuing a book to each child). Because I had already been reading for some years, I could go straight through one of these books without making a mistake— and when I did so, I was simply handed the next book in the series and told to continue. Within a couple of weeks, I had done all the reading for the term.

One day, when the rest of the kids were acting up, the teacher said in a pique that this was a silly bunch for me to be stuck with, and arranged to have me promoted immediately into the third grade— only a few weeks after the beginning of the term. Suddenly I was with kids my own age.

One of these kids was a boy named Henry, whom I knew from the days when we lived on East Hill Street. Henry and I looked so much alike that Mama had once mistakenly called to him to come to dinner. He was also the toughest kid in the class, which came in very handy. Apparently I had rubbed one of the other boys in class the wrong way and he decided to beat me up— but he jumped on Henry by mistake. It was not a mistake that anyone wanted to repeat, so I had relatively little fighting to contend with in the third grade.

Academically, there were some difficulties at first, partly because I lacked everything that I was supposed to have learned in the second grade. For example, I had to learn division in the third grade without having stayed in the second grade long enough to learn addition and subtraction. However, I was soon at or near the top of the class. It was a nice feeling, but of course I had no inkling as to what it might mean for my future.

Somewhere in 1938 or 1939, Mama and I— there were now just the two of us— moved again, this time to 1123 East Hill Street. It was next door to the house we had lived in several years earlier. We were now living at the end of the street, so we had neither a backyard nor a side yard. We no longer had electricity— and now I missed it, especially when some of the other kids talked about hearing a new radio program called "The Lone Ranger."

Like most of the other houses in the neighborhood, ours did not have a paved walkway like the one Daddy had built next door. Seeing that walkway was just one of the painful reminders of happier times, when Daddy, Birdie, Lacy, and Ruth were all part of my world.

To make matters worse, the family living next door was awful and their children were brats. When one of them started a fight with me one day, I beat him up. This brought his parents over to our house, making threats against Mama and me. Fortunately, it wasn't long before we moved to New York. For all I know, that may be what prompted the move. In any event, there had been talk before about our going to New York, and now we did it. We left before the school year was out, on Mother's Day, 1939.

My last day in Charlotte was spent at Herman's house, while Mama went off somewhere to make the last-minute arrangements. Herman was now living in town, not far from us, in a bigger and nicer home. I wasn't happy with the idea of going to spend the day at Herman's, and he probably wasn't overjoyed at my being there, but it went better than either of us might have expected. Eventually, Mama returned and we headed for the train that would take us to a new life.

MEMORIES

In some ways, my life was much like that of many other blacks growing up in New York during the 1930s and 1940s. In other ways, it was quite different. It was still more different from the lives of blacks growing up in urban ghettoes during a later era. My life has been an even more radical contrast with the lives of many other black intellectuals, activists and political "leaders" and "spokesmen."

Perhaps most important, I grew up with no fear of whites, either physically or intellectually. Had I remained in the South, such fear might have become necessary for survival in adulthood, assuming that I would have survived. But fear is all too often the enemy of rational thought. Many blacks during the 1960s (and later) were inordinately impressed with strident loudmouths whose chief claim to fame was that they "stood up to the white man."

As someone who first decked a white guy at age twelve, and who last did it at age thirty five, I was never really impressed by such credentials— and certainly did not regard them as a substitute for knowing what you were talking about.

With all the vicissitudes of my life, and the long years of living close to despair, nevertheless in retrospect I can see that I was lucky in many ways— not only in escaping permanent harm in many dicey situations, but also in more general ways, both genetically and environmentally. It was clear from meeting my brothers and my sister in adulthood that much of my ability was simply inherited. This was true not only of the general level of ability but also of the particular type of ability— namely analytical reasoning of the sort found in mathematics, science, chess and economics— as distinguished from the kind of ability required in poetry or politics, where my achievements have been virtually non-existent.

My brother Charles, though valedictorian of his high school class, never had an opportunity to go on to college. Yet he trained himself in electronics sufficiently well to build his own ham radio transmitter and his own stereo systems. Later, after some small formal training in electronics, he became sufficiently knowledgeable about electronic mail-sorting equipment to be made a supervisor in that department in the Washington post office and to be sent around the country by the postal authorities to advise local post offices on the installation and operation of the new system.

Of Charles' two sons, one became a mathematics teacher and the other received a Ph.D. in mathematical economics at Princeton.

One of Mary Frances' teenage granddaughters was tested for a program for mathematically precocious children at Johns Hopkins University and also received a summer scholarship, while in high school, for a special program in computer science at Brandeis University. My brother Lonnie became an engineer whose research advanced the development of both rocket and aircraft engines. His sons went on to become engineers as well.

My own children have tested consistently higher for mathematical ability than for verbal ability. My son was on his high school chess team that competed for a national championship and he graduated from college with a degree in statistics, with a specialty in computer science.

Mathematics was always my best subject throughout my school years. Unfortunately, a whole decade away from math eroded my skills and denied me the foundation needed to develop much further in this field, so environment obviously had its influence as well. Nevertheless, when I was a graduate student at the University of Chicago, Milton Friedman said to me: "Although you don't have that much mathematics, you have a mathematical kind of mind."

I didn't learn chess until I was in my thirties, which is much too late to develop your full potential. I could beat other duffers who played an occasional game at lunchtime, but not many tournament players. Checkers was a different story because I played checkers as a child. When I first met my brother Lonnie, when we were both young men, we spent the evening playing checkers— each being astonished whenever the other won a game. At that time, I usually had only victories and draws. Judging from his reactions, apparently his experience was similar.

Some remarkable similarities in personality traits also showed up as between me and my siblings, even though we were raised in separate households hundreds of miles apart. The most common characteristic was that most of us were loners. This was brought home to me when I passed through Washington on my way out to California in 1969. We stopped at the home of Charles' former wife, and waited there for him to come over and join us. Meanwhile, my son went outside to play with kids in the neighborhood. When Charles arrived, I said:

"Let me take you outside to meet my son."

"I've already met him," Charles said. "We've had a long conversation."

"How did you know who he was?" I asked.

Charles smiled indulgently.

"Tommy," he said, "when I see a dozen kids, all doing the same thing, and in the midst of them is one kid who is doing something entirely different, I don't have to guess which one is our mother's grandson."

Charles himself was a prime example of a similar pattern of marching to his own drummer. During one of the ghetto riots of the 1960s, Charles was out in the midst of the rioters, asking them such questions as: "After you burn down this man's store, where are you going to shop?"

It never occurred to Charles that a riot is not the place for a Socratic dialogue. Apparently there is no gene for politic behavior in our family.

Although marching to your own drummer has its down side, both personally and professionally, it also made me no stranger to controversy, decades before my controversies became public. Without already being pre-hardened against vilification, my research and writings on racial issues would not have been possible.

Although the environment in which I grew up was very deficient in the kinds of things measured by sociologists and economists, it nevertheless provided some of the key ingredients for advancement. I was, for much of my formative period, an only child in contact with four adults who took an interest in me, even if they were not all under the same roof all the time. Contrast that with being one of several children being raised by a single woman— or, worse yet, a teenage girl. The amount of adult time per child was many times greater in my case.

Although none of these adults had much education, and certainly no knowledge as to what was good or bad education, Birdie and Lacy cared enough about my development to see to it that I met another boy who could be a guide to me. Meeting Eddie Mapp was another remarkable— and crucial— piece of good fortune.

The luck of passing through particular places at particular times was also on my side. Some of my happiest times were spent in the South, though I was very fortunate to leave before I would have fallen irretrievably far behind in the inferior schools provided for Southern blacks— and before I would have had to confront the corrosive racism faced by black adults. In New York, I passed through the public schools at a time when they were better than they had been for the European immigrant children of a generation earlier and far better than they would be for black children of a later era.

Once, when my niece in New York was lamenting that she had not done more with her educational opportunities, she said:

"I went to the same school you went to, Uncle Tommy."

"No," I said. "You went to the same *building* I went to, but it was no longer the same school."

The family in which she was raised was also no longer the same family that it was when I was growing up. Her parents were no longer a carefree young married couple, with time and money to spare, and an upbeat outlook on the new world of New York. They were now care-worn parents, preoccupied with trying to cope with multiple hardships, punctuated by tragedy. Although my niece came ultimately to live in the same apartment in which I had grown up a decade before her, the life in that apartment was now even more bitter than that which had sent me out into the world at seventeen.

My early struggle to make a new life for myself under precarious economic conditions put me in daily contact with people who were neither well-educated nor particularly genteel, but who had practical wisdom far beyond what I had— and I knew it. It gave me a lasting respect for the common sense of ordinary people, a factor routinely ignored by the intellectuals among whom I would later make my career. This was a blind spot in much of their social analysis which I did not have to contend with.

With all that I went through, it now seems in retrospect almost as if someone had decided that there should be a man with all the outward indications of disadvantage, who nevertheless had the key inner advantages needed to advance.

The timing of that advance was also fortuitous. My academic career began two years before the Civil Rights Act of 1964 and I received tenure a year before federal "goals and timetables" were mandated under affirmative action policies. The books that made the key differences in my career— *Say's Law*, whose manuscript was crucial to my receiving tenure at U.C.L.A. and *Knowledge and Decisions*, which brought an offer of appointment as Senior Fellow at the Hoover Institution— were both books on non-racial themes. Altogether, these facts spared me the hang-ups afflicting many other black intellectuals, who were haunted by the idea that they owed their careers to affirmative action or to the fact that writings on race had become fashionable. I knew that I could write for a whole decade without writing a single book or article on race— because, in fact, I had done that during the 1960s.

Timing was on my side in another way. I happened to come along right after the worst of the old discrimination was no longer there to impede me and just before racial quotas made the achievements of blacks look suspect. That kind of luck cannot be planned.

Crucial pieces of good fortune like these would have made it ridiculous for me to have offered other blacks the kind of advice which the media so often accused me of offering— to follow in my footsteps and pull themselves up by their bootstraps. The addiction of the intelligentsia to catchwords like "bootstraps" has made it all but impossible to have even a rational discussion of many issues. As for following in my footsteps, many of the paths I took had since been destroyed by misguided social policy, so that the same quality of education was no longer available to most ghetto youngsters, though there was never a time in history when education was more important.

Most of my writings on public policy issues in general, and on racial issues in particular, were directed toward the public or toward policy-makers, and tried to show where one policy would be better than another. These writings were not advice directed toward less fortunate people as to how they could cope with their misfortunes. I am not Dear Abby. My hope was obviously that better policies would reduce those misfortunes. Nevertheless, clever media interviewers insisted on asking me such questions as:

"But what do you say to the welfare mother or to the ghetto youth?"

I cannot imagine what would have led anybody to think that I was writing handbooks for welfare mothers or ghetto youths, or that either would be reading them, if I were. Even worse were suggestions that I thought that too many benefits were being given to minorities, whether by the government or by other institutions. Yet, from the very beginning, I have argued that many of these "benefits" were not in fact beneficial, except to a relative handful of middle-class people who ran the programs or who were otherwise in some special advantageous position. Whether or not I was correct in my analysis or conclusions, that was the issue raised— and the issue evaded by red herrings about "bootstraps" and the like.

By and large, my books on racial controversies attracted more media attention and had larger sales than my books on economics, politics, or the history of ideas. However, the books on racial issues were not written as an intellectual outlet, but because there were things I thought needed saying and I knew that other people were reluctant to say them. More than one colleague has suggested to me that I would be better off to stop writing about race and to return to the things in which I did my best professional work— books on economics like *Knowledge and Decisions* or books on ideas like *A Conflict of Visions* and *The Quest for Cosmic Justice.*

What, if anything, will endure from what I have written is of course something that I will never know. Nor is what I have said and done enhanced or reduced by my personal life, however fashionable amateur psychology has become. What has been done stands or falls on its own merits or applicability.

The whole point of looking back on my life, aside from the pleasure of sharing reminiscences, is to hope that others will find something useful for their own lives. Justice Oliver Wendell Holmes said it best:

> If I could think that I had sent a spark to those who come after I should be ready to say Goodbye.

RANDOM

THOUGHTS

R andom thoughts on the passing scene:
Someone said that human beings are the only creatures that blush—
and the only ones that need to.

Ad for a ski resort: "If swimming is so healthful, why are whales so fat?"

One of the sad signs of our times is that we have demonized those who produce, subsidized those who refuse to produce, and canonized those who complain.

Let's face it, most of us are not half as smart as we may sometimes think we are— and for intellectuals, not one-tenth as smart.

There is no greater indictment of judges than the fact that honest people are afraid to go into court, while criminals swagger out its revolving doors.

Few skills are so well rewarded as the ability to convince parasites that they are victims.

Someone said that Congress would take 30 days to make instant coffee.

Politics is the art of making your selfish desires seem like the national interest.

Many of those in the so-called "helping professions" are helping people to be irresponsible and dependent on others.

People who cannot be bothered to learn both sides of the issues should not bother to vote.

The old adage about giving a man a fish versus teaching him how to fish has been updated by a reader: Give a man a fish and he will ask for tartar sauce and French fries! Moreover, some politician who wants his vote will declare all these things to be among his "basic rights."

There are people who can neither find happiness in their own lives nor permit those around them to be happy. The best you can do is get such people out of your life.

War makes me respect soldiers and despise politicians.

What is called an educated person is often someone who has had a dangerously superficial exposure to a wide spectrum of subjects.

If navel-gazing, hand-wringing or self-dramatization helped with racial issues, we would have achieved Utopia long ago.

Government bailouts are like potato chips: You can't stop with just one.

University students rioting against tuition increases on both sides of the Atlantic are painful signs of the degeneracy of our times. The idea that taxpayers owe it to you to pay for what you want suggests that much of today's education fails to instill reality, and instead panders to a self-centered sense of entitlement to what other people have earned.

If the battle for civilization comes down to the wimps versus the barbarians, the barbarians are going to win.

We pay our public officials too much for what they are and too little for what we want them to be.

When you want to help people, you tell them the truth. When you want to help yourself, you tell them what they want to hear.

I am going to stop procrastinating— one of these days.

Thanksgiving may be our most old-fashioned holiday. Gratitude itself seems out of date at a time when so many people feel "entitled" to whatever they get— and indignant that they didn't get more.

The problems growing out of short cuts and abbreviations have probably wasted far more time than these short cuts and abbreviations will ever save.

If it were possible to enforce a ban on lying, a ghastly silence would fall over the city of Washington.

When this column predicted that a discredited study would continue to be cited by gun control advocates, I had no idea that it would happen the next week in the 9th Circuit Court of Appeals.

California students in Monroe High School and Cleveland High School were surprised to learn that their schools were named for presidents. One girl at Cleveland High School said: "I thought it was named for that city in Canada."

Ideology is fairy tales for adults.

"Funding" is one of the big phony words of our times— used by people too squeamish to say "money" but not too proud to take it, usually from the taxpayers.

It is important that young children be able to rely on their parents completely— and equally important that grown children not be able to.

Have you ever seen some painting, writing, or clothing that you thought looked awful? Some music that you thought sounded terrible? You are free to say so only when these are products of Western civilization. Say that about something from some other culture and you are considered a terrible person, if not a racist.

Envy plus rhetoric equals "social justice."

The one thing that no policy will ever change is the past.

People who are trying to prove something usually don't prove anything, except what jerks they are.

All human beings are so fallible and flawed that to exempt any category of people from criticism is not a blessing but a curse. The intelligentsia have inflicted that curse on blacks.

I can understand that some people like to drive slowly. What I cannot understand is why they get in the fast lane to do it.

Subtlety counts. If Mona Lisa had broken into a big toothy grin, she would have been forgotten long ago.

People who pride themselves on their "complexity" and deride others for being "simplistic" should realize that the truth is often not very complicated. What gets complicated is evading the truth.

The national debt is the ghost of Christmas past.

There should be a special contempt for those who sit in safety and comfort, second-guessing at their leisure the split-second decisions that policemen had to make at the risk of their own lives.

Being slick is the way to gain little things and lose big things.

Historians of the future will have a hard time figuring out how so many organized groups of strident jackasses succeeded in leading us around by the nose and morally intimidating the majority into silence.

No matter how disastrously some policy has turned out, anyone who criticizes it can expect to hear: "But what would you replace it with?" When you put out a fire, what do you replace it with?

Those who want to take our money and gain power over us have discovered the magic formula: Get us envious or angry at others and we will surrender, in installments, not only our money but our freedom. The most successful dictators of the 20th century— Hitler, Lenin, Stalin, Mao— all used this formula, and now class warfare politicians here are doing the same.

There is something obscene about people holding protest rallies in order to try to keep getting money that someone else worked for.

The biggest disappointment is disappointment with yourself.

People who are very aware that they have more knowledge than the average person are often very unaware that they do not have one-tenth of the knowledge of all of the average persons put together.

I hate to think that someday Americans will be looking at the radioactive ruins of their cities and saying that this happened because their leaders were afraid of the word "unilateral."

My favorite New Year's resolution was to stop trying to reason with unreasonable people. This has reduced both my correspondence and my blood pressure.

No matter how much people on the left talk about compassion, they have no compassion for the taxpayers.

People who send me letters or e-mails containing belligerent personal attacks probably have no idea how reassuring their messages are, for they show that critics seldom have any rational arguments to offer.

Sometimes life seems like Italian opera music— beautiful but heart-breaking.

While it is true that you learn with age, the down side is that what you learn is often what a damn fool you were before.

If you talk to yourself, at least carry a cell phone, so that people won't think you are crazy.

Judges should ask themselves: Are we turning the law into a trap for honest people and a bonanza for charlatans?

Why is there so much hand-wringing about how to keep track of violent sex offenders after they have been released from prison? If it is so dangerous to release them, then why are they being released, when laws can be rewritten to keep them behind bars?

Both the Sicilian mafia and the criminal tongs in China began as movements to defend the oppressed, so perhaps we should not be so painfully surprised that venerable American civil rights organizations have begun to degenerate into extortion rackets.

A reader writes: "I want to live in the country I grew up in. Where is it?"

Too often what are called "educated" people are simply people who have been sheltered from reality for years in ivy-covered buildings. Those whose whole careers have been spent in ivy-covered buildings, insulated by tenure, can remain adolescents on into their golden retirement years.

Some ideas sound so plausible that they can fail nine times in a row and still be believed the tenth time. Other ideas sound so implausible that they can succeed nine times in a row and still not be believed the tenth time. Government controls in the economy are among the first kinds of ideas and the operations of a free market are among the second kind.

It is amazing how many people seem to think that the government exists to turn their prejudices into laws.

Among the sad signs of our times are the twisted metal "sculptures" put in front of public buildings at the taxpayers' expense— obviously never intended to please the public, and in fact constituting a thumbing of the artist's nose at the public.

"Tell all" autobiographies sometimes tell more than all.

Much of what are called "social problems" consists of the fact that intellectuals have theories that do not fit the real world. From this they conclude that it is the real world which is wrong and needs changing.

Thank heaven human beings are born with an ability to laugh at absurdity. Otherwise, we might go stark raving mad from all the absurd things we encounter in life.

A recently reprinted memoir by Frederick Douglass has footnotes explaining what words like "arraigned," "curried" and "exculpate" meant, and explaining who Job was. In other words, this man who was born a slave and never went to school educated himself to the point where his words now have to be explained to today's expensively under-educated generation.

Egalitarians create the most dangerous inequality of all— inequality of power. Allowing politicians to determine what all other human beings will be allowed to earn is one of the most reckless gambles imaginable.

Great Predictions Department: "I do not mind saying I think they are taking a gamble." That was what Red Sox owner Harry Frazee said after selling Babe Ruth to the Yankees.

A magician was asked what had happened to the lady he used to saw in half in his act. "Oh, she's retired," he said. "Now she lives in Chicago— and Denver."

The people I feel sorry for are those who do 90 percent of what it takes to succeed.

Trust is one of those things that is much easier to maintain than it is to repair.

It is self-destructive for any society to create a situation where a baby who is born into the world today automatically has pre-existing grievances against another baby born at the same time, because of what their ancestors did centuries ago. It is hard enough to solve our own problems, without trying to solve our ancestors' problems.

Have you ever heard a single hard fact to back up all the sweeping claims for the benefits of "diversity"?

We seem to be getting closer and closer to a situation where nobody is responsible for what they did but we are all responsible for what somebody else did.

The people I feel sorry for are those who insist on continuing to do what they have always done but want the results to be different from what they have always been.

Alaska is much larger than France and Germany— combined. Yet its population is less than one-tenth that of New York City. Keep that in mind the next time you hear some environmentalist hysteria about the danger of "spoiling" Alaska by drilling for oil in an area smaller than Dulles Airport.

Bad credit affects many things, including your chances of getting a job that requires responsibility. On the other hand, if your credit is too good, you get inundated with junk mail.

I am so old that I can remember when other people's achievements were considered to be an inspiration, rather than a grievance.

Considering that we all enter the world the same way and leave in the same condition, we spend an awful lot of time in between trying to show that we are so different from other people.

A careful definition of words would destroy half the agenda of the political left and scrutinizing evidence would destroy the other half.

How anyone can argue in favor of being non-judgmental is beyond me. To say that being non-judgmental is better than being judgmental is itself a judgment, and therefore a violation of the principle.

As a rule of thumb, Congressional legislation that is bipartisan is usually twice as bad as legislation that is partisan.

How many other species' members kill each other to the same extent as human beings?

Nolan Ryan's baseball career was so long that he struck out seven guys whose fathers he had also struck out. (Barry Bonds and Bobby Bonds, for example.)

If people had been as mealy-mouthed in centuries past as they are today, Ivan the Terrible might have been called Ivan the Inappropriate.

When my sister's children were teenagers, she told them that, if they got into trouble and ended up in jail, to remember that they had a right to make one phone call. She added: "Don't waste that call phoning me." We will never know whether they would have followed her advice, since none of them was ever in jail.

Sign on a monument to people who served in the military: "All gave some. Some gave all."

SOURCES

SOURCES

SOCIAL ISSUES:

The essay "'Dead Ball' versus 'Lively Ball'" was written for this book and was not previously published.

ECONOMICS:

"One-Stage Thinking," "The Economics of Crime" and "The Economics of Discrimination" are from my book *Applied Economics*.

"Income Distribution" is from my *Intellectuals and Society*.

"Saving Lives," "Minimum Wage Laws" and "The Role of Economics" are all from my *Basic Economics: A Common Sense Guide to the Economy*.

POLITICAL ISSUES:

"The Pattern of the Anointed" is from my *The Vision of the Anointed: Self-Congratulation as A Basis for Social Policy*.

"*On Liberty* Reconsidered" is from my *On Classical Economics*.

"Marx the Man" is from my *Marxism: Philosophy and Economics*.

LEGAL ISSUES:

"Judicial Activism and Judicial Restraint" is from my *Intellectuals and Society*.

RACE AND ETHNICITY:

"Affirmative Action Around the World" is from my book of the same title.

"The Influence of Geography" is excerpted from my *Migrations and Cultures* and from my *Conquests and Cultures*.

NOTES

One-Stage Thinking

1. Michael Wines, "Caps on Prices Only Deepen Zimbabweans' Misery," *New York Times*, August 2, 2007, pp. A1, A8.

Saving Lives

1. "Catastrophes," *The Economist*, March 20, 2004, p. 116.

The Economics of Crime

1. James Q. Wilson and Joan Petersilia, editors, *Crime* (San Francisco: ICS Press, 1995), p. 492.
2. Ibid., p. 43.
3. "Why We Are, As We Are," *The Economist*, December 20, 2008, p. 128.
4. Richard J. Herrnstein and Charles Murray, *The Bell Curve* (New York: Simon & Schuster, 1996), pp. 242–243.
5. Joyce Lee Malcolm, *Guns and Violence: The English Experience* (Cambridge, Massachusetts: Harvard University Press, 2002), p. 165.
6. David Fraser, *A Land Fit for Criminals: An Insider's View of Crime, Punishment and Justice in England and Wales* (Sussex: Book Guild Publishing, 2006), pp. 82, 279, 294, 295, 297.
7. Gary Kleck, *Point Blank: Guns and Violence in America* (New Brunswick, NJ: Aldine Transaction, 2009), p. 140.
8. Ibid., p. 136.
9. James Q. Wilson and Richard J. Herrnstein, *Crime and Human Nature* (New York: Simon & Schuster, 1985), p. 409.
10. Charles E. Silberman, *Criminal Violence, Criminal Justice* (New York: Random House, 1978), p. 4.

11. Peter Saunders and Nicole Billante, "Does Prison Work?" *Policy*, Vol. 18, No. 4 (Summer 2002–03), pp. 6, 7; David Fraser, *A Land Fit for Criminals*, p. 97.

12. Adam Liptak, "World Spurns Bail for Profit, But It's a Pillar of U.S. Justice," *New York Times*, January 29, 2008, pp. A1, A16.

13. Peter Hitchens, *The Abolition of Britain* (San Francisco: Encounter Books, 2000), p. 32.

14. Joyce Lee Malcolm, *Guns and Violence*, p. 225.

15. Ibid., pp. 164–166, 168; Peter Hitchens, *A Brief History of Crime: The Decline of Order, Justice and Liberty in England* (London: Atlantic Books, 2003), p. 151.

16. Michael Brick, "'80s Plot to Hit Giuliani? Mob Experts Doubt It," *New York Times*, October 26, 2007, p. B2.

The Economics of Discrimination

1. Harold J. Laski, *The American Democracy* (New York: Viking Press, 1948), p. 480; George J. Stigler, *Memoirs of an Unregulated Economist* (New York: Basic Books, 1988), p. 31.

2. Ezra Mendelsohn, *The Jews of East Central Europe Between the World Wars* (Bloomington: Indiana University Press, 1983), pp. 23, 27.

3. Bernard E. Anderson, *Negro Employment in Public Utilities* (Philadelphia: Industrial Research Unit, Wharton School of Finance and Commerce, University of Pennsylvania, 1970), pp. 73, 80.

4. Ibid., p. 150.

5. Jerry Bowles, "Diversity to Work," *BusinessWeek*, April 16, 2007, pp. 70–75 (special section).

6. Brian Lapping, *Apartheid: A History* (London: Grafton, 1986), p. 164.

7. Merle Lipton, *Capitalism and Apartheid: South Africa, 1910–84* (Aldershot, Hants, England: Gower, 1985), p. 152.

8. Walter E. Williams, *South Africa's War against Capitalism* (New York: Praeger, 1989), p. 78.

9. Jonathan I. Israel, *European Jewry in the Age of Mercantilism, 1550–1750*, second edition (Oxford: Clarendon Press, 1989), pp. 87–93.

10. Louis Wirth, *The Ghetto* (Chicago: The University of Chicago Press, 1964), p. 229.

"Income Distribution"

1. "Class and the American Dream," *New York Times*, May 30, 2005, p. A14.

2. Evan Thomas and Daniel Gross, "Taxing the Super Rich," *Newsweek*, July 23, 2007, p. 38.

3. Eugene Robinson, "Tattered Dream; Who'll Tackle the Issue of Upward Mobility?"*Washington Post*, November 23, 2007, p. A39.

4. Janet Hook, "Democrats Pursue Risky Raising-Taxes Strategy," *Los Angeles Times*, November 1, 2007.

5. Andrew Hacker, *Money: Who Has How Much and Why* (New York: Scribner, 1997), p. 10.

6. E.J. Dionne, "Overtaxed Rich Is A Fairy Tale of Supply Side," *Investor's Business Daily*, July 29, 2010, p. A11.

7. See, for example, David Wessel, "As Rich-Poor Gap Widens in the U.S., Class Mobility Stalls," *Wall Street Journal*, May 13, 2005, pp. A1 ff.

8. "Movin' On Up," *Wall Street Journal*, November 13, 2007, p. A24.

9. David Cay Johnston, "Richest Are Leaving Even the Rich Far Behind," *New York Times*, June 5, 2005, section 1, pp. 1 ff.

10. U.S. Department of the Treasury, "Income Mobility in the U.S. from 1996 to 2005," November 13, 2007, p. 12.

11. Tom Herman, "There's Rich, and There's the 'Fortunate 400,'" *Wall Street Journal*, March 5, 2008, p. D1.

12. "The 400 Individual Income Tax Returns Reporting the Highest Adjusted Gross Incomes Each Year, 1992–2000," *Statistics of Income Bulletin*, U.S. Department of the Treasury, Spring 2003, Publication 1136 (Revised 6–03).

13. W. Michael Cox & Richard Alm, "By Our Own Bootstraps: Economic Opportunity & the Dynamics of Income Distribution," *Annual Report*, 1995, Federal Reserve Bank of Dallas, p. 8.

14. Peter Saunders, "Poor Statistics: Getting the Facts Right About Poverty in Australia," *Issue Analysis* No. 23, Centre for Independent Studies (Australia), April 3, 2002, p. 5; David Green, *Poverty and Benefit Dependency* (Wellington: New Zealand Business Roundtable, 2001), pp. 32, 33; Jason Clemens & Joel Emes, "Time Reveals the Truth about Low Income," *Fraser Forum*, September 2001, pp. 24–26.

15. U.S. Department of Labor, Bureau of Labor Statistics, *Characteristics of Minimum Wage Workers: 2005* (Washington: Department of Labor, Bureau of Labor Statistics, 2006), p. 1 and Table 1.

16. U.S. Department of the Treasury, "Income Mobility in the U.S. from 1996 to 2005," November 13, 2007, p. 2.

17. Computed from Carmen DeNavas-Walt, et al., "Income, Poverty, and Health Insurance Coverage in the United States: 2005," *Current Population Reports*, P60–231 (Washington: U.S. Bureau of the Census, 2006), p. 4.

18. See, for example, "The Rich Get Richer, and So Do the Old," *Washington Post*, National Weekly Edition, September 7, 1998, p. 34.

19. Computed from *Economic Report of the President* (Washington: U.S. Government Printing Office, 2009), p. 321; Ibid, 2008 edition, p. 263.

20. Herman P. Miller, *Income Distribution in the United States* (Washington: U.S. Government Printing Office, 1966), p. 7.

21. Rose M. Kreider and Diana B. Elliott, "America's Family and Living Arrangements: 2007," *Current Population Reports*, P20–561 (Washington: U.S. Bureau of the Census, September 2009), p. 5.

22. Robert Rector and Rea S. Hederman, *Income Inequality: How Census Data Misrepresent Income Distribution* (Washington: The Heritage Foundation, 1999), p. 11.

23. Data on numbers of heads of household working in high-income and low-income households in 2000 are from Table HINC–06 from the *Current Population Survey*, downloaded from the Bureau of the Census web site.

24. Alan Reynolds, *Income and Wealth* (Westport, CT: Greenwood Press, 2006), p. 28.

25. Michael Harrington, *The Other America: Poverty in the United States* (New York: Penguin Books, 1981), pp. xiii, 1, 12, 16, 17.

26. Alan Reynolds, *Income and Wealth*, p. 67.

27. Andrew Hacker, *Money*, p. 31.

28. Steve DiMeglio, "With Golf Needing a Boost, Its Leading Man Returns," *USA Today*, February 25, 2009, pp. A1 ff.

Minimum Wage Laws

1. U.S. Department of Labor, Bureau of Labor Statistics, *Characteristics of Minimum Wage Workers: 2004*, (Washington: Department of Labor, Bureau of Labor Statistics, 2005), p. 1 and Table 1.

2. "Economic and Financial Indicators," *The Economist*, March 15, 2003, p. 100.

3. "Hong Kong's Jobless Rate Falls," *Wall Street Journal*, January 16, 1991, p. C16.

4. The Economist Intelligence Unit, *Country Commerce: Hong Kong 2002*, December 2002, p. 45.

5. Philip Segal, "Hong Kong Solutions," *Far Eastern Economic Review*, March 20, 2003, p. 13.

6. "World Watch," *Wall Street Journal*, June 18, 2003, p. A14.

7. Gary Becker and Guity Nashat Becker, *The Economics of Life* (New York: McGraw-Hill, 1997), p. 39.

8. Erin Lett and Judith Banister, "Labor Costs of Manufacturing Employees in China: An Update to 2003–04," *Monthly Labor Review*, November 2006, p. 41.

9. Jason Clemens, et al., *Measuring Labour Markets in Canada and the United States: 2003 Edition* (Vancouver, Canada: The Fraser Institute, 2003).

10. U.S. Department of Labor, Bureau of Labor Statistics, *Characteristics of Minimum Wage Workers: 2004*, p. 1 and Table 1.

11. "Bad Law, Worse Timing," *Wall Street Journal*, July 25, 2008, p. A14.

12. Scott Adams and David Neumark, "A Decade of Living Wages: What Have We Learned?" *California Economic Policy*, July 2005, pp. 1–23.

13. See, for example, Donald Deere, Kevin M. Murphy, and Finis Welch, "Employment and the 1990–1991 Minimum-Wage Hike," *The American Economic Review*, May 1995, pp. 232–237.

14. ACIL Economics and Policy, Pty. Ltd, *What Future for New Zealand's Minimum Wage Law?* (Wellington: New Zealand Business Roundtable, 1994), pp. 32–34.

15. David Neumark and William Wascher, "Minimum Wages and Employment: A Review of Evidence From the New Minimum Wage Research," National Bureau of Economic Research, Working Paper 12663, November 2006, p. 123.

16. "Unions v Jobs," *The Economist*, May 28, 2005, p. 49.

17. "No Way To Start Out in Life," *The Economist*, July 18, 2009, p. 53.

18. Donald Deere, Kevin M. Murphy, and Finis Welch, "Employment and the 1990–1991 Minimum-Wage Hike," *The American Economic Review*, May 1995, pp. 232–237.

19. "Pelosi's Tuna Surprise," *Wall Street Journal*, January 16, 2007, p. A20.

20. David Neumark, Wendy Cunningham, Lucas Siga, "The Effects of the Minimum Wage in Brazil on the Distribution of Family Incomes, 1996–2001," *Journal of Development Economics*, Vol. 80 (2006), pp. 157–158.

21. "Long-Term Unemployment," *The Economist*, June 23, 2007, p. 105.

22. Walter Williams, *Youth and Minority Unemployment* (Stanford: Hoover Institution Press, 1977); ACIL Economics and Policy, Pty. Ltd, *What Future for New Zealand's Minimum Wage Law?*, pp. xvi, xvii, 23, 24, 33–35, 45.

23. "A Divided Self: A Survey of France," *The Economist*, November 16, 2002, p. 11.

24. Holman W. Jenkins, Jr., "Shall We Eat Our Young?" *Wall Street Journal*, January 19, 2005, p. A13.

25. Nelson D. Schwartz, "Young, Down and Out in Europe," *New York Times*, January 1, 2010, pp. B1, B4.

26. Jennifer Buckingham, *State of the Nation* (St. Leonards, NSW: Centre For Independent Studies, 2004), p. 110.

27. Des Moore, "Who is the Fairest of Them All?" *Policy* (Australia), Spring 2007, p. 8.

28. Walter Williams, *Youth and Minority Unemployment*; Charles H. Young and Helen R. Y. Reid, *The Japanese Canadians* (Toronto: The University of Toronto Press, 1938), pp. 49–50.

29. David E. Bernstein, *Only One Place of Redress* (Durham: Duke University Press, 2001), p. 103.

30. Edward C. Banfield, *The Unheavenly City* (Boston: Little, Brown, 1970), p. 98.

31. Walter Williams, *Youth and Minority Unemployment*, p. 14.

32. "Left Behind," *The Economist*, August 22, 2009, p. 26.

The Role of Economics

1. Thomas S. Kuhn, *The Structure of Scientific Revolutions*, second edition (Chicago: University of Chicago Press, 1970), p. 17.

2. Jacob Viner, *The Long View and the Short* (Glencoe, IL: Free Press, 1958), p. 79.

3. Karl Marx, "Wage Labour and Capital," section V, Karl Marx and Frederick Engels, *Selected Works* (Moscow: Foreign Languages Publishing House, 1955), Vol. I, p. 99; Karl Marx, *Capital: A Critique of Political Economy* (Chicago: Charles H. Kerr & Co., 1909), Vol. III, pp. 310–311.

4. Adam Smith, *The Wealth of Nations* (New York: Modern Library, 1937) p. 423.

5. Karl Marx and Frederick Engels, *Selected Correspondence 1846–1895*, translated by Dona Torr (New York: International Publishers, 1942), p. 476.

6. Joseph A. Schumpeter, "Science and Ideology," *American Economic Review*, March 1949, p. 352.

7. Ibid., p. 353.

8. Ibid., p. 355.

9. Ibid., p. 346.

10. Ibid., p. 358.

11. J.A. Schumpeter, *History of Economic Analysis* (New York: Oxford University Press, 1954), p. 43.

12. Joseph A. Schumpeter, "Science and Ideology," *American Economic Review*, March 1949, p. 359.

13. John Maynard Keynes, *The General Theory of Employment Interest and Money* (New York: Harcourt, Brace and Company, 1936), p. 383.

14. George J. Stigler, *Essays in the History of Economics* (Chicago: University of Chicago Press, 1965), p. 21.

The Pattern of the Anointed

1. Joseph A. Schumpeter, Review of Keynes's General Theory, *Journal of the American Statistical Association*, December 1936, p. 795.

2. "Public Welfare Program— Message from the President of the United States (H. Doc. No. 325)," *Congressional Record— House*, February 1, 1962, p. 1405.

3. Ibid., p. 1406.

4. Ibid., p. 1405.

5. "Relief is No Solution," *New York Times*, February 2, 1962, p. 28.

6. *Congressional Quarterly*, February 2, 1962, p. 140.

7. Marjorie Hunter, "Johnson Signs Bill to Fight Poverty; Pledges New Era," *New York Times*, August 21, 1964, p. 1.

8.   Ibid.

9.   "Excerpts from President Lyndon B. Johnson's Address to the Nation on Civil Disorders, July 27, 1967," *Report of the National Advisory Commission on Civil Disorders*, March 1, 1968, p. 297; "Transcript of Johnson's TV Address on the Riots," *New York Times*, July 28, 1967, p. A11.

10. *Report of the National Advisory Commission on Civil Disorders*, March 1, 1968, p. 91.

11. Robert B. Semple, Jr., "Dr. King Scores Poverty Budget," *New York Times*, December 16, 1966, p. A33; Robert B. Semple, Jr., "2 More Score U. S. on Help for Poor," *New York Times*, December 7, 1966, p. A32.

12. See, for example, Daniel Patrick Moynihan, *Maximum Feasible Misunderstanding: Community Action in the War on Poverty* (New York: The Free Press, 1969), pp. xxvi–xxvii.

13. Charles Mohr, "'Viva Goldwater' Greets Senator," *New York Times*, February 16, 1964, p. 47.

14. "Goldwater Sees Johnson Retreat," *New York Times*, January 19, 1964, p. 49.

15. James T. Patterson, *America's Struggle Against Poverty: 1900–1980* (Cambridge, Mass.: Harvard University Press, 1981), pp. 145, 146, 149, 152.

16. Henry Hazlitt, "The War on Poverty," *Newsweek*, April 6, 1964, p. 74.

17. Charles Murray, *Losing Ground: American Social Policy, 1950–1960* (New York: Basic Books, Inc., 1984), p. 57.

18. Ibid., p. 64.

19. James T. Patterson, *America's Struggle Against Poverty*, p. 132.

20. Ibid., pp. 64–65.

21. U. S. Bureau of the Census, *Current Population Reports*, Series P–60–185 (Washington: U.S. Government Printing Office, 1993), p. ix. The poverty rate as a percentage of the total population was not yet as high as in 1964 but the absolute number of people in poverty was. This rise in the absolute number of people in poverty began in the late 1970s. U. S. Bureau of the Census, *Current Population Reports*, Series P–23, No. 173 (Washington: U. S. Government Printing Office, 1991), p. 18.

22. Charles Murray, *Losing Ground*, pp. 49, 67.

23. James T. Patterson, *America's Struggle Against Poverty*, p. 170.

24. Ibid., pp. 164–165.

25. Ibid., p. 164.
26. See, for example, Daniel Patrick Moynihan, *Maximum Feasible Misunderstanding*, pp. liii, 150, 156.
27. Hodding Carter III, "'Disarmament' Spells Defeat in War on Poverty," *Wall Street Journal*, August 11, 1983, p. 21.
28. "How Great Was the Great Society?" *The Great Society: A Twenty Year Critique* (Austin, TX: The Lyndon Baines Johnson Library, 1986), p. 125.
29. Hodding Carter III, "'Disarmament' Spells Defeat in War on Poverty," *Wall Street Journal*, August 11, 1983, p. 21.
30. Harry J. Middleton, "Welcome," *The Great Society*, p. 1.
31. Mrs. Lyndon B. Johnson, "Welcome," Ibid., p. 2.
32. Lucia Mount, "U. S. War on Poverty: No Sweeping Victory, But Some Battles May Have Been Won," *Christian Science Monitor*, September 19, 1984, pp. 3–4.
33. United States Senate, Ninetieth Congress, first session, *Hearings Before the Subcommittee on Employment, Manpower, and Poverty of the Committee on Labor and Public Welfare*, Part 7 (Washington: U. S. Government Printing Office, 1967), pp. 2170–2171.
34. Aida Tores, Jacqueline Darroch Forrest, and Susan Eisman, "Family Planning Services in the United States, 1978–79," *Family Planning Perspectives*, Volume 13, No. 3 (May/June 1981), pp. 139, 141.
35. Patricia Schiller, "Sex Education That Makes Sense," *NEA Journal*, February 1968, p. 19.
36. Theodore Ooms, *Teenage Pregnancy in a Family Context* (Philadelphia: Temple University Press, 1981), p. 26.
37. Alan Guttmacher Institute, *Informing Social Change* (New York: The Alan Guttmacher Institute, 1980), p. 7.
38. Cheryl D. Hayes, editor, *Risking the Future: Adolescent Sexuality, Pregnancy, and Childbearing* (Washington: National Academy Press, 1987), p. 160.
39. Theodore Ooms, *Teenage Pregnancy in a Family Context*, pp. 39–40.
40. H. S. Hoyman, "Should We Teach About Birth Control in High School Sex Education?" *Education Digest*, February 1969, p. 22.
41. United States Senate, Eighty-Ninth Congress, second session, *Family Planning Program: Hearing Before the Subcommittee on Employment,*

Manpower and Poverty of the Committee on Labor and Public Welfare
(Washington: U. S. Government Printing Office, 1966), p. 84.

42. Joanne Zazzaro, "Critics or No Critics, Most Americans Still Firmly Support Sex
     Education in Schools," *American School Board Journal*, September 1969, p. 31.

43. Robert P. Hildrup, "Why Sex Education Belongs in the Schools," *PTA
     Magazine*, February 1974, p. 13.

44. Jacqueline Kasun, *The War Against Population* (San Francisco: Ignatius Press,
     1988), p. 144.

45. *Today's VD Control Problem: Joint Statement by American Public Health
     Association, American Social Health Association, American Venereal Disease
     Association, Association of State and Territorial Health Officers in Co-operation
     with the American Medical Association*, February 1966, p. 20.

46. Lester A. Kirkendall, "Sex Education: A Reappraisal," *The Humanist*, Spring
     1965, p. 82.

47. "Three's a Crowd," *New York Times*, March 17, 1972, p. 40.

48. Fred M. Hechinger, "Introduction," *Sex Education and the Schools*, edited by
     Virginia Hilu (New York: Harper & Row, 1967), p. xiv.

49. John Kobler, "Sex Invades the Schoolhouse," *The Saturday Evening Post*, June 29,
     1968, p. 26.

50. Jacqueline Kasun, *The War Against Population*, pp. 142, 144.

51. Cheryl D. Hayes, editor, *Risking the Future*, p. 66.

52. Ibid., p. 58.

53. Alan Guttmacher Institute, *Informing Social Change*, p. 30.

54. Hearings before the Select Committee on Population, Ninety-Fifth Congress,
     second session, *Fertility and Contraception in America: Adolescent and Pre-
     Adolescent Pregnancy*, (Washington: U. S. Government Printing Office, 1978),
     Vol. II, p. 253.

55. Ibid., p. 625.

56. Les Picker, "Human Sexuality Education Implications for Biology Teaching,"
     The American Biology Teacher, Vol. 46, No. 2 (February 1984), p. 92.

57. Hearings before the Select Committee on Population, Ninety-Fifth Congress,
     second session, *Fertility and Contraception in America: Adolescent and Pre-
     Adolescent Pregnancy*, Vol. II, p. 1.

58. Paul A. Reichelt and Harriet H. Werley, "Contraception, Abortion and Venereal Disease: Teenagers' Knowledge and the Effect of Education," *Family Planning Perspectives*, March/April 1975, p. 83.

59. Ibid., p. 88.

60. Peter Scales, "The New Opposition to Sex Education: A Powerful Threat to a Democratic Society," *The Journal of School Health*, April 1981, p. 303.

61. *Fertility and Contraception in the United States: Report Prepared by the Select Committee on Population* (Washington: U. S. Government Printing Office, 1978), p. 5.

62. Sylvia S. Hacker, "It Isn't Sex Education Unless. . ." *The Journal of School Health*, April 1981, p. 208.

63. See, for example, Thomas Sowell, *Inside American Education: The Decline, The Deception, The Dogmas* (New York: Free Press, 1992), Chapter 3.

64. Suzanne Fields, "'War' Pits Parents vs. Public Policy," *Chicago Sun-Times*, October 17, 1992, p. 19.

65. Ibid.

66. See, for example, Thomas Sowell, *Inside American Education*, pp. 51–53, 255.

67. On the denigration of parents within the classroom, see Ibid., pp. 48–53.

68. James Hottois and Neal A. Milner, *The Sex Education Controversy: A Study of Politics, Education, and Morality* (Lexington, Mass: D. C. Heath and Co., 1975), p. 6.

69. Judge David L. Bazelon, "The Imperative to Punish," *The Atlantic Monthly*, July 1960, p. 41.

70. U. S. Bureau of the Census, *Historical Statistics of the United States: Colonial Times to 1970* (Washington: U.S. Government Printing Office, 1975), p. 414.

71. Ibid.

72. Judge David L. Bazelon, "The Imperative to Punish," *The Atlantic Monthly*, July 1960, p. 41.

73. Ibid., p. 42.

74. Ibid., p. 43.

75. Ibid.

76. Ibid.

77. Ibid.

78. Ibid.

79. Ibid., p. 47.

80. William J. Brennan, "Foreword," David L. Bazelon, *Questioning Authority: Justice and Criminal Law* (New York: Alfred A. Knopf, 1988), pp. ix–xii.

81. Ibid., pp. xi, xii.

82. William O. Douglas, *The Court Years: The Autobiography of William O. Douglas* (New York: Random House, 1980), p. 84.

83. Ramsey Clark, *Crime in America: Observations on Its Nature, Causes, Prevention and Control* (New York: Simon & Schuster, 1970), p. 220.

84. Ibid., p. 202.

85. Tom Wicker, "Introduction," Ibid., pp. 11, 14.

86. "Pick of the Paperbacks," *Saturday Review*, November 27, 1971, p. 48.

87. Robert Shnayerson, "Force and the Law," *Time*, November 30, 1970, pp. 83–84.

88. Herbert Packer, "Causes of Crime," *New Republic*, November 7, 1970, pp. 28–30.

89. "The Liberals' Friend," *Times Literary Supplement*, November 26, 1971, p. 1467.

90. See, for example, Macklin Fleming, *The Price of Perfect Justice* (New York: Basic Books, 1974), Chapter 9.

91. James Q. Wilson, *Thinking About Crime* (New York: Basic Books, 1975), p. 173; Ernest van den Haag, *Punishing Criminals: Concerning a Very Old and Painful Question* (New York: Basic Books, 1975), p. 158; U. S. Department of Justice, *The Case for More Incarceration*, 1992, NCJ–139583 (Washington: U. S. Department of Justice, 1992), pp. 1–5.

92. Judge David L. Bazelon, "The Imperative to Punish," *The Atlantic Monthly*, July 1960, p. 42.

93. Ibid., p. 46.

94. Max Frankel, "Johnson Derides Urban Reform Foes," *New York Times*, June 26, 1967, p. 45.

95. Thomas A. Johnson, "Muskie, in Jersey, Calls Wallace 'The Man We've Got to Defeat,'" *New York Times*, October 24, 1968, p. 42.

96. Fred P. Graham, "Dissenters Bitter: Four View Limitation on Confessions as Aid to Criminals," *New York Times*, June 17, 1966, pp. 1 ff.

97. Sidney E. Zion, "Attack on Court Heard by Warren," *New York Times*, September 10, 1965, pp. 1 ff.

98. James Q. Wilson and Richard J. Herrnstein, *Crime and Human Nature* (New York: Simon & Schuster, 1985), p. 409.

99. Charles E. Silberman, *Criminal Violence, Criminal Justice* (New York: Random House, 1978), p. 4.

100. U. S. Bureau of the Census, *Historical Statistics of the United States: Colonial Times to 1970*, p. 415.

101. Federal Bureau of Investigation, *Crime in the United States, 1991: Uniform Crime Reports, 1991* (Washington: U. S. Government Printing Office, 1992), p. 280.

102. "No Shackles on the Law," *New York Times*, August 15, 1966, p. 26.

103. "There are striking examples of 'crime waves' which turned out to be nothing more than statistical reporting waves." Yale Kamisar, "Public Safety v. Individual Liberties: Some 'Facts' and 'Theories'," *The Journal of Criminal Law, Criminology and Police Science*, Vol. 63 (1962), p. 187. "They have made loud noises about the 'disastrous' and 'catastrophic' prices we are paying to effectuate constitutional liberties, but they have yet to furnish convincing evidence that the price is even substantial." Ibid, p. 193.

104. James Q. Wilson, *Thinking About Crime*, p. 75.

105. Michael Stern, "Menninger Discounts Criminality in Nation," *New York Times*, October 30, 1968, p. 49.

106. Charles E. Silberman, *Criminal Violence, Criminal Justice*, p. 261.

107. James Q. Wilson and Richard J. Herrnstein, *Crime and Human Nature*, pp. 424–425.

108. Ibid., p. 429.

109. U. S. Bureau of the Census, *Historical Statistics of the United States: Colonial Times to 1970*, p. 414.

110. James Q. Wilson, *Thinking About Crime*, p. 17.

111. Federal Bureau of Investigation, *Crime in the United States, 1991: Uniform Crime Reports, 1991*, p. 13.

112. *Newsweek* called Silberman's book "one of the most thorough and provocative studies ever made of crime in America." Jerold K. Footlick, "White Fear, Black Crime," *Newsweek*, October 23, 1978, p. 134. Similar praise appeared in *The New Yorker, The New York Review of Books*, and other bastions of the anointed. See Naomi Bliven, "Crime and Punishment," *The New Yorker*, March 26, 1979, pp. 131–134; Graham Hughes, "American Terror," *New York Review of Books*, January 25, 1979, pp. 3–4; "As American as Jesse James,"

Time, November 6, 1978, pp. 76, 78; Peter Gardner, Review, *Psychology Today*, January 1979, p. 99.

113. Fred P. Graham, "Warren Says All Share Crime Onus," *New York Times*, August 2, 1968, pp. 1, 13.

114. Chief Justice Earl Warren, *The Memoirs of Earl Warren* (Garden City, N.Y.: Doubleday & Co., Inc., 1977), p. 317.

"On Liberty" Reconsidered

1. John Stuart Mill, "On Liberty," *Essays on Politics and Society*, edited by J. M. Robson (Toronto: University of Toronto Press, 1977), p. 228.

2. Ibid., p. 228n.

3. Ibid., p. 240.

4. Ibid., p. 219.

5. Ibid., p. 272.

6. Ibid., pp. 222–223.

7. Ibid., p. 217.

8. Ibid., p. 220.

9. Ibid.

10. Ibid., p. 241.

11. Ibid., p. 223.

12. Ibid., p. 270.

13. Ibid., p. 262.

14. Ibid., p. 267.

15. John Stuart Mill, "De Tocqueville on Democracy in America [I]," Ibid., p. 86.

16. John Stuart Mill, "Civilization," Ibid., p. 128.

17. John Stuart Mill, "On Liberty," Ibid., p. 269.

18. John Stuart Mill, "Civilization," Ibid., p. 139.

19. John Stuart Mill, "Civilization," Ibid., p. 121.

20. John Stuart Mill, "De Tocqueville on Democracy in America [I]," Ibid., p. 86.

21. John Stuart Mill, "On Liberty," Ibid., p. 222.

22. John Stuart Mill, Letter to Alexander Bain, August 6, 1859, *Collected Works of John Stuart Mill*, Vol. XV: *The Later Letters of John Stuart Mill*, edited by

Francis E. Mineka and Dwight N. Lindley (Toronto: University of Toronto Press, 1972), p. 631.

23. F. A. Hayek, *John Stuart Mill and Harriet Taylor: Their Correspondence and Subsequent Marriage* (Chicago: University of Chicago Press, 1951), p. 191.

24. Ibid., p. 92.

Marx the Man

1. David McLellan, *Karl Marx: His Life and Thought* (New York: Harper & Row, 1973), p. 15n. Baron von Westphalen did not live next door, however, as sometimes stated.

2. Robert Payne, *Marx: A Biography* (New York: Simon & Schuster, 1968), p. 21.

3. Ibid., p. 20.

4. Karl Marx, *The Letters of Karl Marx*, translated by Saul K. Padover (Englewood Cliffs: Prentice-Hall, Inc., 1979), p. 171. See also Robert Payne, *Marx*, pp. 316, 345.

5. David McLellan, *Karl Marx*, p. 15.

6. Ibid., p. 17.

7. Ibid, p. 33.

8. Karl Marx, *The Letters of Karl Marx*, translated by Saul K. Padover, pp. 490–511, *passim*.

9. David McLellan, *Karl Marx*, p. 22.

10. Robert Payne, *Marx*, pp. 59–74, *passim*.

11. Ibid., p. 62.

12. Ibid., p. 63.

13. David McLellan, *Karl Marx*, pp. 32–33.

14. Ibid., p. 31.

15. Ibid., p. 34.

16. Robert Payne, *Marx*, p. 77.

17. Ibid., p. 79.

18. David McLellan, *Karl Marx*, p. 40.

19. Ibid., p. 53.

20. Ibid.

21. Ibid., p. 59. Franz Mehring, *Karl Marx: The Story of His Life* (London: George Allen & Unwin Ltd., 1966), p. 51.
22. David McLellan, *Karl Marx*, pp. 51–53.
23. Ibid., p. 55.
24. Robert Payne, *Marx*, p. 85.
25. Ibid., p. 88.
26. Saul K. Padover, *Karl Marx: An Intimate Biography* (New York: New American Library, 1978), p. 76.
27. Robert Payne, *Marx*, p. 117; Saul K. Padover, *Karl Marx*, p. 89.
28. Saul K. Padover, *Karl Marx*, p. 89.
29. Gustav Mayer, *Friedrich Engels: A Biography* (New York: Alfred A. Knopf, Inc., 1936), p. 4.
30. Saul K. Padover, *Karl Marx*, p. 94.
31. Gustav Mayer, *Friedrich Engels*, p. 9.
32. David McLellan, *Engels* (Glasgow: Fontana/Collins, 1977), p. 16.
33. K. Marx and F. Engels, *The Holy Family* (Moscow: Foreign Languages Publishing House, 1956), p. 16.
34. Faith Evans, translator, *The Daughters of Karl Marx* (New York: Harcourt Brace Jovanovich, 1970), p. 281n. See also David McLellan, *Karl Marx*, pp. 285–286.
35. Robert Payne, *Marx*, p. 160.
36. Ibid., p. 161.
37. Saul K. Padover, *Karl Marx*, p. 115.
38. Karl Marx and Frederick Engels, *Collected Works* (New York: International Publishers, 1982), Volume 38, p. 143.
39. Robert Payne, *Marx*, p. 183.
40. David McLellan, *Engels*, p. 19.
41. Ibid., p. 66.
42. Karl Marx and Frederick Engels, *Collected Works*, Volume 38, p. 153.
43. Ibid.
44. Ibid., p. 115.
45. David McLellan, *Karl Marx*, pp. 222–223.
46. Robert Payne, *Marx*, p. 338.
47. Saul K. Padover, *Karl Marx*, p. 132.
48. Karl Marx and Frederick Engels, *Collected Works*, Volume 38, p. 30.

49. David McLellan, *Engels*, p. 17.

50. Ibid., p. 20.

51. Karl Marx and Friedrich Engels, *Selected Letters*, edited by Fritz J. Raddatz (Boston: Little, Brown & Company, 1980), p. 23.

52. See David McLellan, *Karl Marx*, pp. 264, 357n.

53. Ibid., p. 264.

54. Saul K. Padover, *Karl Marx*, p. 182.

55. Ibid., p. 184.

56. Ibid., p. 264. Marx himself confessed to Engels that "I live too expensively for my circumstances." Karl Marx and Friedrich Engels, *Selected Letters*, edited by Fritz J. Raddatz, p. 112.

57. See Boris Nicolaievsky and Otto Maenchen-Helfen, *Karl Marx: Man and Fighter* (Philadelphia: J. B. Lippincott Company, 1936), p. 239; Robert Payne, *Marx*, pp. 349–350.

58. See, for example, Karl Marx and Frederick Engels, *Collected Works*, Volume 38, p. 227; Volume 39, p. 85.

59. Robert Payne, *Marx*, p. 266.

60. Ibid., pp. 537–538.

61. Ibid., p. 534.

62. Karl Marx and Friedrich Engels, *Selected Letters*, edited by Fritz J. Raddatz, p. 95.

63. Ibid., p. 27.

64. Karl Marx and Frederick Engels, *Collected Works*, Volume 38, p. 323.

65. Karl Marx and Friedrich Engels, *Selected Letters*, edited by Fritz J. Raddatz, p. 108.

66. Ibid., p. 44.

67. Ibid., p. 68.

68. Ibid., p. 66.

69. Ibid., p. 81.

70. Ibid., p. 82.

71. Robert Payne, *Marx*, p. 71.

72. Ibid., p. 72.

73. As is done by Dagobert D. Runes, "Introduction," Karl Marx, *A World Without Jews* (New York: Philosophical Library, 1960), p. xi.

74. K. Marx and F. Engels, *The Holy Family*, pp. 117–121, 127–133, 143–159.

75. Ibid., p. 148.

76. Karl Marx and Frederick Engels, *Letters to Americans* (New York: International Publishers, 1953), pp. 65–66.

77. See Karl Marx, *Letters of Karl Marx*, translated by Saul K. Padover, pp. 197, 214–216.

78. Karl Marx and Frederick Engels, *Collected Works*, Volume 38, p. 372.

79. See, for example, Robert Payne, *Marx*, p. 426; Saul K. Padover, *Karl Marx*, pp. 216–221.

80. There is not one reference to Marx in all of Mill's voluminous writings, nor in his voluminous correspondence.

81. Franz Mehring, *Karl Marx*, p. 323.

82. Robert Payne, *Marx*, p. 366.

83. Ibid., p. 369.

84. Ibid.

85. Ibid., pp. 369, 372.

86. Ibid., p. 373.

87. Karl Marx and Frederick Engels, *Selected Correspondence*, translated by Dona Torr (New York: International Publishers, 1942), p. 330.

88. David McLellan, *Karl Marx*, p. 422.

89. Ibid.

90. Karl Marx and Friedrich Engels, *Selected Letters*, edited by Fritz J. Raddatz, p. 9.

91. David McLellan, *Karl Marx*, p. 353.

92. Robert Payne, *Marx*, p. 426.

93. Ibid., p. 327.

94. Ibid., p. 355.

95. Saul K. Padover, *Karl Marx*, p. 271.

96. Ibid., pp. 270–271.

97. Karl Marx and Friedrich Engels, *Selected Letters*, edited by Fritz J. Raddatz, p. 52.

98. Ibid., p. 81.

99. Ibid., p. 98.

100. Saul K. Padover, *Karl Marx*, p. 277.

101. See, for example, Frederick Engels, Paul and Laura Lafargue, *Correspondence* (Moscow: Foreign Languages Publishing House, 1959), Volume I, pp. 49, 50, 51, 52, 54, 55, 57, 60, 62, 68, 104, 110, 119, 131, 133, 136, 174, 185, 214, 245,

255, 257, 295, 309, 316, 345, 367. There are two additional volumes of their correspondence, for others to explore.

102. Robert Payne, *Marx*, pp. 522–531.

103. Boris Nicolaievsky and Otto Maenchen-Helfen, *Karl Marx*, pp. 243–245.

104. Karl Marx, *Letters of Karl Marx*, translated by Saul K. Padover, p. 414.

105. Robert Payne, *Marx*, p. 295.

106. Maximilien Rubel and Margaret Manale, *Marx Without Myth: A Chronological Study of His Life and Work* (New York: Harper & Row Publishers, 1975), p. 14.

107. Robert Payne, *Marx*, p. 321.

108. Ibid., p. 143.

109. Ibid., pp. 155–156.

110. Karl Marx and Friedrich Engels, *Selected Letters*, edited by Fritz J. Raddatz, p. 106.

111. Karl Marx, *The Letters of Karl Marx*, translated by Saul K. Padover, pp. 163–166.

112. Karl Marx and Friedrich Engels, *The German Ideology* (New York: International Publishers, 1947), pp. 100–101; K. Marx and F. Engels, *The Holy Family*, pp. 78–80, 144.

113. Karl Marx and Frederick Engels, *Collected Works*, Volume 6, p. 350.

114. Ibid., p. 354.

115. Robert Payne, *Marx*, p. 192.

116. Graeme Duncan, *Marx and Mill* (Cambridge: Cambridge University Press, 1973), p. ix.

117. Karl Marx and Frederick Engels, *Selected Correspondence*, translated by Dona Torr, pp. 48–52.

118. Ibid.

119. Frederick Engels, "Speech at the Graveside of Karl Marx," Karl Marx and Frederick Engels, *Selected Works*, Volume II (Moscow: Foreign Languages Publishing House, 1955), p. 167.

120. Ibid., pp. 168–169.

121. Ibid., p. 169.

122. Franz Mehring, *Karl Marx*, p. xii.

Judicial Activism and Judicial Restraint

1.   *Dred Scott v. Sandford*, 60 U.S. 393 (1857), at 407.
2.   Ibid., at 562, 572–576.
3.   *Wickard v. Filburn*, 317 U.S. 111 (1942), at 114.
4.   Ibid., at 118.
5.   Ibid., at 128.
6.   *United Steelworkers of America v. Weber*, 443 U.S. 193 (1979), at 201, 202.
7.   Ibid., at 222.
8.   Oliver Wendell Holmes, *Collected Legal Papers* (New York: Peter Smith, 1952), p. 307.
9.   *Adkins v. Children's Hospital*, 261 U.S. 525 (1923), at 570.
10. *Day-Brite Lighting, Inc. v. Missouri*, 342 U.S. 421 (1952), at 423.
11. *Griswold v. Connecticut*, 381 U.S. 479 (1965), at 484.
12. Michael Kinsley, "Viewpoint: Rightist Judicial Activism Rescinds a Popular Mandate," *Wall Street Journal*, February 20, 1986, p. 25.
13. Linda Greenhouse, "Justices Step In as Federalism's Referee," *New York Times*, April 28, 1995, pp. A1 ff.
14. Ruth Colker and James J. Brudney, "Dissing Congress," *Michigan Law Review*, October 2001, p. 100.
15. "Federalism and Guns in School," *Washington Post*, April 28, 1995, p. A26.
16. Joan Biskupic, "Top Court Ruling on Guns Slams Brakes on Congress," *Chicago Sun-Times*, April 28, 1995, p. 28.
17. Linda Greenhouse, "Farewell to the Old Order in the Court," *New York Times*, July 2, 1995, section 4, pp. 1 ff.
18. Cass R. Sunstein, "Tilting the Scales Rightward," *New York Times*, April 26, 2001, p. A23.
19. Cass R. Sunstein, "A Hand in the Matter?" *Legal Affairs*, March-April 2003, pp. 26–30.
20. Jeffrey Rosen, "Hyperactive: How the Right Learned to Love Judicial Activism," *New Republic*, January 31, 2000, p. 20.
21. Adam Cohen, "What Chief Justice Roberts Forgot in His First Term: Judicial Modesty," *New York Times*, July 9, 2006, section 4, p. 11.
22. "The Vote on Judge Sotomayor," *New York Times*, August 3, 2009, p. A18.

23. Cass R. Sunstein, "Tilting the Scales Rightward," *New York Times*, April 26, 2001, p. A23.

24. "Inside Politics," CNN Transcripts, July 11, 2005.

25. See, for example, Anthony Lewis, "A Man Born to Act, Not to Muse," *New York Times Magazine*, June 30, 1968, pp. 9 ff.

26. Jack N. Rakove, "Mr. Meese, Meet Mr. Madison," *Atlantic Monthly*, December 1986, p. 78.

27. Antonin Scalia, *A Matter of Interpretation: Federal Courts and the Law* (Princeton: Princeton University Press, 1997), pp. 17, 45.

28. William Blackstone, *Commentaries on the Laws of England* (New York: Oceana Publications, 1966), Vol. 1, p. 59.

29. Oliver Wendell Holmes, *Collected Legal Papers*, p. 204.

30. Ibid., p. 207.

31. Mark DeWolfe Howe, editor, *Holmes-Pollock Letters: The Correspondence of Mr. Justice Holmes and Sir Frederick Pollock, 1874–1932* (Cambridge, Massachusetts: Harvard University Press, 1942), Vol. 1, p. 90.

32. *Northern Securities Company v. United States*, 193 U.S. 197 (1904), at 401.

33. Robert H. Bork, *Tradition and Morality in Constitutional Law* (Washington: American Enterprise Institute, 1984), p. 7.

34. Jack N. Rakove, "Mr. Meese, Meet Mr. Madison," *Atlantic Monthly*, December 1986, p. 81.

35. Ibid., pp. 81, 82.

36. Ibid., p. 84.

37. Ronald Dworkin, *A Matter of Principle* (Cambridge, Massachusetts: Harvard University Press, 1985), pp. 40, 43, 44.

38. Ibid., p. 42.

39. Jack N. Rakove, "Mr. Meese, Meet Mr. Madison," *Atlantic Monthly*, December 1986, p. 78.

40. Stephen Macedo, *The New Right v. The Constitution* (Washington: Cato Institute, 1986), p. 10.

41. Ronald Dworkin, *A Matter of Principle*, p. 318.

42. Ibid., p. 331.

43. "The High Court Loses Restraint," *New York Times*, April 29, 1995, section 1, p. 22.

44. Mark DeWolfe Howe, editor, *Holmes-Laski Letters: The Correspondence of Mr. Justice Holmes and Harold J. Laski 1916–1935* (Cambridge, Massachusetts: Harvard University Press, 1953), Volume I, p. 752.
45. *Abrams v. United States*, 250 U.S. 616 (1919), at 629.
46. Mark DeWolfe Howe, editor, *Holmes-Laski Letters*, Volume I, p. 389.
47. Mark DeWolfe Howe, editor, *Holmes-Laski Letters*, Volume II, p. 913.

Affirmative Action Around the World

1. See, for example, Rita Jalali and Seymour Martin Lipset, "Racial and Ethnic Conflicts: A Global Perspective," *Political Science Quarterly*, Vol. 107, No. 4 (Winter 1992–1993), p. 603; Robert Klitgaard, *Elitism and Meritocracy in Developing Countries* (Baltimore: Johns Hopkins University Press, 1986), pp. 25, 45; Terry Martin, *The Affirmative Action Empire: Nations and Nationalism in the Soviet Union, 1923–1939* (Ithaca: Cornell University Press, 2001); Dorothy J. Solinger, "Minority Nationalities in China's Yunnan Province: Assimilation, Power, and Policy in a Socialist State," *World Politics*, Vol. 30, No. 1 (October 1977), pp. 1–23; Miriam Jordan, "Quotas for Blacks in Brazil Cause Hubbub," *Wall Street Journal*, December 27, 2001, p. A6; Priscilla Qolisaya Pauamau, "A Post-colonial Reading of Affirmative Action in Education in Fiji," *Race, Ethnicity and Education*, Vol. 4, No. 2 (2001), pp. 109–123; Matthew Hoddie, "Preferential Policies and the Blurring of Ethnic Boundaries: The Case of Aboriginal Australians in the 1980s," *Political Studies*, Vol. 50 (2002), pp. 293–312; Mohammed Waseem, "Affirmative Action Policies in Pakistan," *Ethnic Studies Report* (Sri Lanka), Vol. XV, No. 2 (July 1997), pp. 223–244; "New Zealand: Landmark Decisions," *The Economist*, November 20, 1993, p. 93; Rainer Knopff, "The Statistical Protection of Minorities: Affirmative Action in Canada," *Minorities & the Canadian State*, edited by Neil Nevitte & Allan Kornberg (Cincinnati: Mosaic Press, 1985), pp. 87–106.
2. A. K. Vakil, *Reservation Policy and Scheduled Castes in India* (New Delhi: Ashish Publishing House, 1985), p. 127.
3. Sham Satish Chandra Misra, *Preferential Treatment in Public Employment and Equality of Opportunity* (Lucknow: Eastern Book Company, 1979), p. 83.

4. Shri Prakash, "Reservations Policy for Other Backward Classes: Problems and Perspectives," *The Politics of Backwardness: Reservation Policy in India* (New Delhi: Konark Publishers, Pvt. Ltd., 1997), pp. 44–45.

5. Gordon P. Means, "Ethnic Preference Policies in Malaysia," *Ethnic Preference and Public Policy in Developing States*, edited by Neil Nevitte and Charles H. Kennedy (Boulder: Lynne Reinner Publishers, Inc., 1986), p. 108.

6. Nancy Lubin, *Labour and Nationality in Soviet Central Asia: An Uneasy Compromise* (Princeton: Princeton University Press, 1984), p. 162.

7. David Riesman, *On Higher Education: The Academic Enterprise in an Age of Rising Student Consumerism* (San Francisco: Jossey-Bass Publishers, 1980), pp. 80–81. See also Thomas Sowell, *Black Education: Myths and Tragedies* (New York: David McKay, 1972), pp. 131–132, 140.

8. Editorial, "Reservations and the OBCs," *The Hindu* (India), April 4, 2000.

9. Executive Order No. 10,925.

10. Charles H. Kennedy, "Policies of Redistributional Preference in Pakistan," *Ethnic Preference and Public Policy in Developing States*, edited by Neil Nevitte and Charles H. Kennedy, p. 69.

11. Donald L. Horowitz, *Ethnic Groups in Conflict* (Berkeley: University of California Press, 1985), p. 242.

12. Mohammed Waseem, "Affirmative Action Policies in Pakistan," *Ethnic Studies Report* (Sri Lanka), Vol. XV, No. 2 (July 1997), pp. 226, 228–229.

13. Quoted in Alan Little and Diana Robbins, *'Loading the Law'* (London: Commission for Racial Equality, 1982), p. 6.

14. Donald L. Horowitz, *Ethnic Groups in Conflict*, p. 677.

15. Myron Weiner, "The Pursuit of Ethnic Inequalities Through Preferential Policies: A Comparative Public Policy Perspective," *From Independence to Statehood: Managing Ethnic Conflict in Five African and Asian States*, edited by Robert B. Goldmann and A. Jeyaratnam Wilson (London: Frances Pinter, 1984), p. 64.

16. Cynthia H. Enloe, *Police, Military and Ethnicity: Foundations of State Power* (New Brunswick: Transaction Books, 1980), p. 143.

17. Ibid., p. 75.

18. Ingeborg Fleischauer, "The Germans' Role in Tsarist Russia: A Reappraisal," *The Soviet Germans* (New York: St. Martin's Press, 1986), edited by Edith Rogovin Frankel, pp. 17–18.

19. Numerous, documented examples can be found in just two books of mine: *Conquests and Cultures* (New York: Basic Books, 1998), pp. 43, 124, 125, 168, 221–222; *Migrations and Cultures* (New York: Basic Books, 1996), pp. 4, 17, 30, 31, 118, 121, 122–123, 126, 130, 135, 152, 154, 157, 158, 162, 164, 167, 176, 177, 179, 182, 193, 196, 201, 211, 212, 213, 215, 224, 226, 251, 258, 264, 265, 275, 277, 278, 289, 290, 297, 298, 300, 305, 306, 310, 313, 314, 318, 320, 323–324, 337, 342, 345, 353–355, 356, 358, 363, 366, 372–373. Extending the search for intergroup statistical disparities to the writings of others would of course increase the number of examples exponentially.

20. Bernard Grofman and Michael Migalski, "The Return of the Native: The Supply Elasticity of the American Indian Population 1960–1980," *Public Choice*, Vol. 57 (1988), p. 86.

21. Matthew Hoddie, "Preferential Policies and the Blurring of Ethnic Boundaries: The Case of Aboriginal Australians in the 1980s," *Political Studies*, Vol. 50 (2002), p. 299.

22. Wolfgang Kasper, *Building Prosperity: Australia's Future as a Global Player* (St. Leonard's, NSW: The Centre for Independent Studies, 2002), p. 45.

23. Barry Sautman, "Ethnic Law and Minority Rights in China: Progress and Constraints," *Law & Policy*, Vol. 21, No. 3 (July 3, 1999), p. 294.

24. "Chinese Rush to Reclaim Minority Status," *Agence France Presse*, May 17, 1993.

25. See, for example, "Indians: In the Red," *The Economist*, February 25, 1989, pp. 25–26; Bob Zelnick, *Backfire: A Reporter Looks at Affirmative Action* (Washington, D.C.: Regnery Publishing Inc., 1996), pp. 301–303.

26. Celia S. Heller, *On the Edge of Destruction: Jews of Poland Between the Two World Wars* (New York: Columbia University Press, 1987), p. 102.

27. Maria S. Muller, "The National Policy of Kenyanisation: Its Impact on a Town in Kenya," *Canadian Journal of African Studies*, Vol. 15, No. 2 (1981), p. 298; H. L. van der Laan, *The Lebanese Traders in Sierra Leone* (The Hague: Mouton & Co., 1975), pp. 141, 171.

28. "Indian Eunuchs Demand Government Job Quotas," *Agence France Presse*, October 22, 1997. See also David Orr, "Eunuchs Test Their Political Potency,"

The Times (London), February 17, 2000, downloaded from the Internet: http://www.the-times.co.uk/pages/tim/2000/02/17/timfgnasi01001.html?1123027.

29. Marc Galanter, *Competing Equalities: Law and the Backward Classes in India* (Berkeley: University of California Press, 1984), p. 64.

30. Human Rights Watch, *Broken People: Caste Violence Against India's "Untouchables"* (New York: Human Rights Watch, 1999), p. 39.

31. "Rajasthan's 'Original Backwards' Rally for Justice," *The Hindu*, May 28, 2001. (on-line)

32. "India: Mayawati Expels Three Leaders," *The Hindu*, July 22, 2001. (on-line)

33. Marc Galanter, *Competing Equalities*, p. 469.

34. Ozay Mehmet, "An Empirical Evaluation of Government Scholarship Policy in Malaysia," *Higher Education* (The Netherlands), April 1985, p. 202.

35. Chandra Richard de Silva, "Sinhala-Tamil Relations in Sri Lanka: The University Admissions Issue— The First Phase, 1971–1977," *From Independence to Statehood*, edited by Robert B. Goldmann and A. Jeyaratnam Wilson, p. 133.

36. Rep. David Dreir, "'Disadvantaged' Contractors' Unfair Advantage," *Wall Street Journal*, February 21, 1989, p. A18.

37. Marc Galanter, *Competing Equalities*, p. 552.

38. Myron Weiner, *Sons of the Soil: Migration and Ethnic Conflict in India* (Princeton: Princeton University Press, 1978), p. 250.

39. John A. A. Ayoade, "Ethnic Management of the 1979 Nigerian Constitution," *Canadian Review of Studies in Nationalism*, Spring 1987, p. 127.

40. Donald L. Horowitz, *Ethnic Groups in Conflict*, p. 670.

41. Daniel C. Thompson, *Private Black Colleges at the Crossroads*, (Westport, Connecticut: Greenwood Press, 1973), p. 88.

42. Carol S. Holzbery, *Minorities and Power in a Black Society: The Jewish Community of Jamaica* (Lanham, Maryland: The North-South Publishing Co., Inc., 1987), p. 420.

43. See, for example, William Moore, Jr., and Lonnie H. Wagstaff, *Black Educators in White Colleges* (San Francisco: Jossey-Bass Publishing Co., 1974), pp. 130–131, 198.

44. Ibid., pp. 130–131, 198.

45. Bob Zelnick, *Backfire*, p. 113.

46. Lelah Dushkin, "Backward Class Benefits and Social Class in India, 1920–1970," *Economic and Political Weekly*, April 7, 1979, p. 666. Although the example is hypothetical, it is not out of line with what has actually occurred: "Although 18% of the places in each of the two services were reserved for Scheduled Castes, there was just one successful SC candidate, who had scored 105th on the examination." Marc Galanter, *Competing Equalities*, p. 425.

47. Barbara R. Joshi, "Whose Law, Whose Order: 'Untouchables,' Social Violence and the State in India," *Asian Survey*, July 1982, pp. 680, 682.

48. A. K. Vakil, *Reservation Policy and Scheduled Castes in India*, p. 67; Ghagat Ram Goyal, *Educating Harijans* (Gurgaon, Haryana: The Academic Press, 1981), p. 21.

49. Suma Chitnis, "Positive Discrimination in India with Reference to Education," *From Independence to Statehood*, edited by Robert B. Goldmann and A. Jeyaratnam Wilson, p. 37; Padma Ramkrishna Velaskar, "Inequality in Higher Education: A Study of Scheduled Caste Students in Medical Colleges of Bombay," Ph.D. Dissertation, Tata Institute of Social Sciences, Bombay, 1986, pp. 234, 236.

50. Myron Weiner and Mary Fainsod Katzenstein, *India's Preferential Policies: Migrants, The Middle Classes, and Ethnic Equality* (Chicago: University of Chicago Press, 1981), p. 54.

51. Ibid., pp. 54, 55.

52. Harold Crouch, *Government and Society in Malaysia* (Ithaca: Cornell University Press, 1996), p. 186.

53. K. M. de Silva, *Sri Lanka: Ethnic Conflict, Management and Resolution* (Kandy, Sri Lanka: International Centre for Ethnic Studies, 1996), p. 21.

54. Celia Heller, *On the Edge of Destruction*, pp. 16, 17, 107, 123–128; Ezra Mendelsohn, *The Jews of East Central Europe Between the World Wars* (Bloomington: Indiana University Press, 1983), pp. 99, 105, 167, 232, 236–237.

55. Larry Diamond, "Class, Ethnicity, and the Democratic State: Nigeria, 1950–1966," *Comparative Studies in Social History*, July 1983, pp. 462, 473.

56. Donald L. Horowitz, *Ethnic Groups in Conflict*, pp. 221–226; Myron Weiner and Mary Fainsod Katzenstein, *India's Preferential Policies*, pp. 4–5, 132; Myron Weiner, "The Pursuit of Ethnic Equality Through Preferential

Policies: A Comparative Public Policy Perspective," *From Independence to Statehood*, edited by Robert B. Goldmann and A. Jeyaratnam Wilson, p. 78; K. M. de Silva, "University Admissions and Ethnic Tensions in Sri Lanka," Ibid., pp. 125–126; Donald V. Smiley, "French-English Relations in Canada and Consociational Democracy," *Ethnic Conflict in the Western World*, edited by Milton J. Esman (Ithaca: Cornell University Press, 1977), pp. 186–188.

57. U.S. Bureau of the Census, *Historical Statistics of the United States: Colonial Times to 1970* (Washington: Government Printing Office, 1975), p. 380.

58. Daniel P. Moynihan, "Employment, Income, and the Ordeal of the Negro Family," *Daedalus*, Fall 1965, p. 752.

59. Stephan Thernstrom and Abigail Thernstrom, *America in Black and White: One Nation, Indivisible* (New York: Simon & Schuster, 1997), p. 232.

60. Ibid., p. 50.

The Influence of Geography

1. James A. Haetner, "Market Gardening in Thailand: The Origins of an Ethnic Chinese Monopoly," *The Chinese in Southeast Asia*, edited by Linda Y. C. Lim and L. A. Peter Gosling (Singapore: Maruzen Asia, 1983), Vol. I, *Ethnicity and Economic Activity*, p. 40.

2. Fernand Braudel, *The Mediterranean and the Mediterranean World in the Age of Philip II*, translated by Sian Reynolds (New York: Harper & Row, 1972), Volume I, pp. 238, 241–243. See also John R. Lampe, "Imperial Borderlands or Capitalist Periphery? Redefining Balkan Backwardness, 1520–1914," *The Origins of Backwardness in Eastern Europe: Economics and Politics from the Middle Ages until the Early Twentieth Century*, edited by Daniel Chirot (Berkeley: University of California Press, 1989), p. 180.

3. J. R. McNeill, *The Mountains of the Mediterranean World: An Environmental History* (Cambridge: Cambridge University Press, 1992), p. 47.

4. Ibid., p. 29.

5. Ibid., p. 206; William H. McNeill, *The Age of Gunpowder Empires: 1450–1800* (Washington: The American Historical Association, 1989), p. 38.

6. J. R. McNeill, *The Mountains of the Mediterranean World*, p. 143.

7. Ibid., pp. 27, 54.

8. Ibid., p. 46.

9. See, for example, Ibid., p. 110.

10. Ibid., pp. 142–143.

11. Ibid., pp. 116–117, 139.

12. Ellen Churchill Semple, *Influences of Geographic Environment* (New York: Henry Holt and Co., 1911), pp. 578–579.

13. William S. Brockington, "Scottish Military Emigrants in the Early Modern Era," *Proceedings of the South Carolina Historical Association* (1991), pp. 95–101.

14. Byron Farwell, *The Gurkhas* (New York: W. W. Norton, 1984).

15. Fernand Braudel, *The Mediterranean and the Mediterranean World in the Age of Philip II*, translated by Sian Reynolds, Vol. I, pp. 48–49.

16. J. R. McNeill, *The Mountains of the Mediterranean World*, pp. 205–206.

17. Gary Snyder, "Beyond Cathay: The Hill Tribes of China," *Mountain People*, edited by Michael Tobias (Norman: University of Oklahoma Press, 1986), pp. 150–151.

18. N. J. G. Pounds, *An Historical Geography of Europe: 1500–1840* (Cambridge: Cambridge University Press, 1988), p. 102.

19. J. R. McNeill, *The Mountains of the Mediterranean World*, pp. 119, 213.

20. N. J. G. Pounds, *An Historical Geography of Europe: 1500–1840*, p. 102.

21. Ellen Churchill Semple, *Influences of Geographic Environment*, pp. 586–588.

22. David Hackett Fischer, *Albion's Seed: Four British Folkways in America* (New York: Oxford University Press, 1989), p. 767.

23. J. R. McNeill, *The Mountains of the Mediterranean World*, pp. 48, 205, 206; Ellen Churchill Semple, *Influences of Geographic Environment*, pp. 592, 599.

24. See, for example, William H. McNeill, *The Age of Gunpowder Empires: 1450–1800*, p. 4; Jean W. Sedlar, *East Central Europe in the Middle Ages, 1000–1500* (Seattle: University of Washington Press, 1994), pp. 115, 126, 131; Victor Wolfgang von Hagen, *The Germanic People in America*, (Norman: University of Oklahoma Press, 1976), pp. 75–76.

25. J. R. McNeill, *The Mountains of the Mediterranean World*, pp. 20, 35, 41.

26. Ibid., p. 31.

27. H. J. de Blij and Peter O. Muller, *Physical Geography of the Global Environment* (New York: John Wiley & Sons, Inc., 1993), pp. 132–133.

28. Ellen Churchill Semple, *Influences of Geographic Environment*, pp. 542–543.

29. Ibid., pp. 532–533.

30. Ibid., Chapter VIII.

31. Ibid., p. 272.

32. Peter F. Sugar, *Southeastern Europe under Ottoman Rule, 1354–1804* (Seattle: University of Washington Press, 1993), pp. 178–183; Jean W. Sedlar, *East Central Europe in the Middle Ages, 1000–1500*, pp. 454–457.

33. Francois Renault, "The Structures of the Slave Trade in Central Africa in the 19th Century," *The Economics of the Indian Ocean Slave Trade in the Nineteenth Century*, edited by William Gervase Clarence-Smith (London: Frank Cass & Co., Ltd., 1989), pp. 148–149; James S. Coleman, *Nigeria: Background to Nationalism* (Berkeley: University of California Press, 1971), p. 65.

34. Ellen Churchill Semple, *Influences of Geographic Environment*, p. 276.

35. Jean W. Sedlar, *East Central Europe in the Middle Ages, 1000–1500*, p. 84.

36. Fernand Braudel, *The Mediterranean and the Mediterranean World in the Age of Philip II*, translated by Sian Reynolds, Vol. I, p. 84.

37. Jean W. Sedlar, *East Central Europe in the Middle Ages, 1000–1500*, pp. 3–13.

38. The Amazon, for example, is by far the world's greatest river but the soils in its region have been characterized as "startlingly poor" and it has led to no great cities being established along its banks. See Jonathan B. Tourtellot, "The Amazon: Sailing a Jungle Sea," *Great Rivers of the World*, edited by Margaret Sedeen (Washington: National Geographic Society, 1984), p. 302.

39. William L. Blackwell, *The Industrialization of Russia: A Historical Perspective*, third edition (Arlington Heights, Illinois: Harland Davidson, 1994), p. 2.

40. Ellen Churchill Semple, *Influences of Geographic Environment*, pp. 263, 283.

41. Josip Roglic, "The Geographical Setting of Medieval Dubrovnik," *Geographical Essays on Eastern Europe*, edited by Norman J. G. Pounds (Bloomington: Indiana University Press, 1961), p. 147.

42. James Vicens Vives, *An Economic History of Spain* (Princeton: Princeton University Press, 1969), p. 365.

43. Constance Cronin, *The Sting of Change: Sicilians in Sicily and Australia* (Chicago: University of Chicago Press, 1970), p. 35.

44. U. S. Commission on Civil Rights, *The Economic Status of Americans of Southern and Eastern European Ancestry* (Washington: U. S. Commission on Civil Rights, 1986), p. 15. It also took the immigrants from southern and

eastern Europe, and from Ireland and the French-speaking regions of Canada, more years to reach the average income of native-born Americans. Barry R. Chiswick, "The Economic Progress of Immigrants: Some Apparently Universal Patterns," *The Gateway: U. S. Immigration Issues and Policies* (Washington: The American Enterprise Institute, 1982), p. 147.

45. Stanley Lieberson, *Ethnic Patterns in American Cities* (New York: Free Press of Glencoe, 1963), p. 72.

46. See, for example, Peter Fox, *The Poles in America* (New York: Arno Press, 1970), p. 96; Leonard P. Ayres, *Laggards in Our Schools: A Study of Retardation and Elimination in City School Systems* (New York: Russell Sage Foundation, 1909), pp. 107–108; *Reports of the Immigration Commission*, 61st Congress, 3rd Session, Vol. I: *The Children of Immigrants in Schools* (Washington: U.S. Government Printing Office, 1911), pp. 48–49, 89, 90.

47. Thomas Sowell, "Race and I.Q. Reconsidered," *Essays and Data on American Ethnic Groups*, edited by Thomas Sowell (Washington: The Urban Institute, 1978), p. 207.

48. Charles A. Price, *Southern Europeans in Australia* (Canberra: Australian National University, 1979), p. 58.

49. Ibid., p. 24. See also pp. 16, 17n.

50. Helen Ware, *A Profile of the Italian Community in Australia* (Melbourne: Australian Institute of Multicultural Affairs, 1981), p. 68.

51. Ibid., p. 47.

52. Ibid., p. 63.

53. John K. Fairbank, Edwin O. Reischauer, and Albert M. Craig, *East Asia: Tradition and Transformation* (Boston: Houghton-Mifflin, 1989), pp. 133, 135.

54. Ibid., pp. 143, 174.

55. Ellen Churchill Semple, *Influences of Geographic Environment*, pp. 266–271.

56. Fernand Braudel, *A History of Civilizations*, translated by Richard Mayne (New York: The Penguin Group, 1994), p. 120.

57. John Thornton, *Africa and Africans in the Making of the Atlantic World, 1400–1680* (Cambridge: Cambridge University Press, 1995), pp. 15–16.

58. Janet L. Abu-Lughod, *Before European Hegemony: The World System A. D. 1250–1350* (New York: Oxford University Press, 1989), p. 36.

59. Fernand Braudel, *A History of Civilizations*, translated by Richard Mayne, p. 124. Likewise, a geographer said: "Enlightenment filtering in here was sadly dimmed as it spread." Ellen Churchill Semple, *Influences of Geographic Environment*, p. 392.

60. H. J. de Blij and Peter O. Muller, *Geography: Regions and Concepts* (New York: John Wiley & Sons, Inc., 1992), p. 394.

61. Jocelyn Murray, editor, *Cultural Atlas of Africa* (New York: Facts on File Publications, 1981), p. 10.

62. William A. Hance, *The Geography of Modern Africa* (New York: Columbia University Press, 1964), p. 4.

63. Margaret Sedeen, editor, *Great Rivers of the World*, p. 24. See also P. T. Bauer, *West African Trade: A Study of Competition, Oligopoly and Monopoly in a Changing Economy* (Cambridge: Cambridge University Press, 1954), p. 14.

64. Edward A. Alpers, *Ivory and Slaves: Changing Pattern of International Trade in East Central Africa to the Later Nineteenth Century* (Berkeley: University of California Press, 1975), p. 5.

65. Margaret Sedeen, editor, *Great Rivers of the World*, pp. 69–70; Daniel R. Headrick, *The Tools of Empire: Technology and European Imperialism in the Nineteenth Century* (New York: Oxford University Press, 1981), p. 196.

66. See, for example, the map of Africa's navigable rivers in L. Dudley Stamp, *Africa: A Study in Tropical Development* (New York: John Wiley & Sons, 1964), p. 182.

67. J. F. Ade Ajayi and Michael Crowder, editors, *Historical Atlas of Africa* (Essex: Longman Group Ltd., 1985), map facing Section 1.

68. Jocelyn Murray, editor, *Cultural Atlas of Africa*, p. 73.

69. Roy E. H. Mellor and E. Alistair Smith, *Europe: A Geographical Survey of the Continent* (New York: Columbia University Press, 1979), p. 3.

70. Georg Gerster, "River of Sorrow, River of Hope," *National Geographic*, Vol. 148, No. 2 (August 1975), p. 162.

71. R. J. Harrison Church, *West Africa: A Study of the Environment and of Man's Use of It* (London: Longman Group, Ltd., 1974), pp. 16–18.

72. Georg Gerster, "River of Sorrow, River of Hope," *National Geographic*, Vol. 148, No. 2 (August 1975), p. 154.

73. J. M. Pritchard, *Landform and Landscape in Africa* (London: Edward Arnold, Ltd., 1979), p. 46.

74. Daniel R. Headrick, *The Tools of Empire*, p. 74.

75. F. J. Pedler, *Economic Geography of West Africa* (London: Longman, Green and Co., 1955), p. 118.

76. See, for example, J. M. Pritchard, *Landform and Landscape in Africa*, pp. 46–47.

77. Virginia Thompson and Richard Adloff, *French West Africa* (Stanford: Stanford University Press, 1957), p. 292.

78. Ibid., p. 21.

79. William A. Hance, *The Geography of Modern Africa*, p. 33.

80. Kathleen Baker, "The Changing Geography of West Africa," *The Changing Geography of Africa and the Middle East*, edited by Graham P. Chapman and Kathleen M. Baker (London: Routledge, 1992), p. 105.

81. Ibid., p. 499.

82. Virginia Thompson and Richard Adloff, *French West Africa*, p. 305.

83. Edwin O. Reischauer and John K. Fairbank, *A History of East Asian Civilization* (Boston: Houghton Mifflin, 1960), Volume I, pp. 20–21.

84. Ellen Churchill Semple, *Influences of Geographic Environment*, p. 260.

85. H. J. de Blij and Peter O. Muller, *Geography: Regions and Concepts*, p. 399. See also J. M. Pritchard, *Landform and Landscape in Africa*, p. 14.

86. H. J. de Blij and Peter O. Muller, *Physical Geography of the Global Environment*, p. 399.

87. J. M. Pritchard, *Landform and Landscape in Africa*, p. 7.

88. Ellen Churchill Semple, *Influences of Geographic Environment*, p. 341.

89. John Thornton, *Africa and Africans in the Making of the Atlantic World, 1400–1680*, p. 18.

90. Lewis H. Gann and Peter Duignan, *Africa and the World: An Introduction to the History of Sub-Saharan Africa from Antiquity to 1840* (San Francisco: Chandler Publishing Company, 1972), pp. 24, 26.

91. Eric Thorbecke, "Causes of African Development Stagnation; Policy Diagnosis and Policy Recommendations for a Long-Term Development Strategy," *Whither African Economies?*, edited by Jean-Claude Berthélemy (Paris: Organisation for Economic Co-operation and Development), p. 122.

92. John Thornton, *Africa and Africans in the Making of the Atlantic World, 1400–1680*, p. 19.

93. Ray H. Whitbeck and Olive J. Thomas, *The Geographic Factor: Its Role in Life and Civilization* (Port Washington, N.Y.: Kennikat Press, 1970), p. 167.

94. L. Dudley Stamp, *Africa*, p. 5.

95. William A. Hance, *The Geography of Modern Africa*, p. 4.

96. Georg Gerster, "River of Sorrow, River of Hope," *National Geographic*, Vol. 148, No. 2 (August 1975), p. 162.

97. J. F. Ade Ajayi and Michael Crowder, editors, *Historical Atlas of Africa*, Section 2.

98. Jocelyn Murray, editor, *Cultural Atlas of Africa*, p. 13.

99. Jeffrey Sachs, "Nature, Nurture and Growth," *The Economist*, June 14, 1997, pp. 19, 22.

100. William A. Hance, *The Geography of Modern Africa*, p. 15.

101. Elizabeth Colson, "African Society at the Time of the Scramble," *Colonialism in Africa 1870–1960*, Volume I: *The History and Politics of Colonialism 1870–1914*, edited by L.H. Gann and Peter Duignan (Cambridge: Cambridge University Press, 1981), p. 41.

102. William A. Hance, *The Geography of Modern Africa*, pp. 4–5.

103. Computed from *The World Almanac and Book of Facts: 1992* (New York: Pharos Book, 1991), pp. 789, 806, 815. Some of the problems with official Tanzanian statistics are discussed in Alexander H. Sarris, "Experiences and Lessons from Research in Tanzania," *Whither African Economies?*, edited by Jean-Claude Berthélemy, pp. 99–110.

104. H. J. de Blij and Peter O. Muller, *Geography*, pp. 589–592.

105. J. F. Ade Ajayi and Michael Crowder, editors, *Historical Atlas of Africa*, Section 1.

106. John Thornton, *Africa and Africans in the Making of the Atlantic World, 1400–1680*, pp. 104–105.

107. Edward A. Alpers, *Ivory and Slaves*, pp. 2–4.

108. See, for example, A. Sheriff, "Localisation and Social Composition of the East African Slave Trade, 1858–1873," *The Economics of the Indian Ocean Slave Trade in the Nineteenth Century*, edited by William Gervase Clarence-Smith, pp. 133–134, 142, 144; Francois Renault, "The Structures of the Slave Trade in Central Africa in the 19th Century," Ibid., pp. 146–165; Edward A. Alpers, *Ivory and Slaves*, p. 242.

109. Francois Renault, "The Structures of the Slave Trade in Central Africa in the 19th Century," *The Economics of the Indian Ocean Slave Trade in the Nineteenth Century*, edited by William Gervase Clarence-Smith, p. 148; Edward A. Alpers, *Ivory and Slaves*, pp. 191–193.

110. Michel Mollat du Jourdin, *Europe and the Sea* (Oxford: Blackwell Publishers, Ltd., 1993), p. 4; Roy E. H. Mellor and E. Alistair Smith, *Europe: A Geographical Survey of the Continent*, p. 4.

111. Ibid., pp. 14–17. See also N. J. G. Pounds, *An Historical Geography of Europe, 1800–1914* (Cambridge: Cambridge University Press, 1985), p. 444.

112. Charles Kindleberger, *World Economic Primacy: 1500 to 1990* (Oxford: Oxford University Press, 1996), p. 91.

113. George W. Hoffman, "Changes in the Agricultural Geography of Yugoslavia," *Geographical Essays on Eastern Europe*, edited by Norman J. G. Pounds, p. 114.

114. John R. Lampe, "Imperial Borderlands or Capitalist Periphery? Redefining Balkan Backwardness, 1520–1914," *The Origins of Backwardness in Eastern Europe*, edited by Daniel Chirot, p. 184.

115. N. J. G. Pounds, *An Historical Geography of Europe: 1800–1914*, p. 488.

116. Ibid., p. 15.

117. Joseph R. Lampe, "Imperial Borderlands or Capitalist Periphery? Redefining Balkan Backwardness, 1520–1914," *The Origins of Backwardness in Eastern Europe*, edited by Daniel Chirot, p. 180.

118. Peter Gunst, "Agrarian Systems of Central and Eastern Europe," Ibid., p. 72.

119. Robert A. Kann and Zdenek V. David, *The Peoples of the Eastern Habsburg Lands, 1526–1918* (Seattle: University of Washington Press, 1984), p. 270.

120. See, for example, David E. McClave, "Physical Environment and Population," *Soviet Union: A Country Study*, second edition, edited by Raymond E. Zickel (Washington: U. S. Government Printing Office, 1991), p. 112.

A complete listing of my writings can be found on my website (www.tsowell.com)

INDEX